SCHOOL COUNSELING PRINCIPLES

ETHICS AND LAW

THIRD EDITION

CAROLYN STONE, ED.D.

AMERICAN
SCHOOL
COUNSELOR
ASSOCIATION

The American School Counselor Association (ASCA)
supports school counselors' efforts to help students focus on
academic, personal/social and career development so they
achieve success in school and are prepared to lead fulfilling lives
as responsible members of society. ASCA, which is the school
counseling division of the American Counseling Association,
provides professional development, publications and other
resources, research and advocacy to professional school
counselors around the globe. For more information, visit
www.schoolcounselor.org.

Copyright 2013 by the American School Counselor Association.

1101 King St., Suite 625, Alexandria, VA 22314
(703) 683-ASCA, (800) 306-4722, fax: (703) 683-1619
www.schoolcounselor.org

ISBN 978-1-929289-41-7

Dedication

School counselors and counselor educators work tirelessly to deliver ethical and legal school counseling programs. Over the years, thousands of you have informed and inspired me, and I dedicate this book to you.

Acknowledgements

I would like to thank Darlene Ferranti, Sarah Beth Glicksteen, Kelly Anne Kozlowski and Tracy Steele for their help with survey development. Thank you to the professionals who lent their voices to the *In a Position to Know* sections, which wrap up each chapter: Leslie Anderson, Bob Bardwell, Katrina Beddes, Chloe Benjamin, Christy Clapper, Mary Ann Dyal, Ken Elliott, Karen Gannon Griffith, Mary Hermann, Alexia Huart, Paul Meyers, Doug Morrissey, Theodore Remley, Marilyn Rengert, Russell Sabella, Rebecca Schumacher, Eric Sparks, Bob Tyra, Robert Weiss and Rhonda Williams. Onie Thomas, Doug Stone and Tara Blaylock, thank you for your help with research and editing. I would like to thank Kathleen Rakestraw, the editor of so many ASCA publications, for her support in getting this book to press.

Preface

Welcome to "School Counseling Principles: Ethics and Law." As all school counselors can attest, the profession offers many unique, interesting and often formidable legal and ethical challenges and responsibilities, primarily because we are working with minors in a school setting. School counselors live and work in an increasingly litigious society and are called to a high ethical standard. Professionals who work with minors are sensitive to the fact that issues for counselors who work with adults are far different. Each day school counselors have to consider the legal and ethical ramifications of their work in fostering academic, personal and social growth with students, while being faithful to their obligations to parents, administrators and the community.

This book is written for practicing school counselors and candidates for the profession. It is intended to raise awareness of legal and ethical issues and reduce the risk of unethical or unlawful behavior that might result in legal complications for school counselors. Although avoiding legal liability is a common thread throughout the book, the larger purpose is to enhance our obligations and responsibilities to students. School counselors are rarely at the center of a lawsuit but daily are called on to act in the best interest of students and their families. Creating sensitivity to legal and ethical issues will heighten our awareness and help us examine the implications of our professional behavior for students.

Throughout this book we will examine the legal and ethical complications involved in working with minors in school settings primarily through the use of case studies. Case studies help school counselors reflect on possible consequences before they actually have to deal with real-student situations, so that when in the throes of a dilemma, school counselors can ethically and legally justify their courses of action. The case studies represent a wide range of circumstances and situations. They were developed from actual situations that American School Counselor Association members posed to the ASCA Ethics Committee and from ethical dilemmas the author encountered when practicing as an elementary school counselor, high school counselor and director of school counseling. The more than 100 cases presented here will help the reader connect the reality of school counseling to critical federal and state statutes, ASCA's Ethical Standards for School Counselors (American School Counselor Association, 2010), the American Counseling Association's Code of Ethics and Standards of Practice (American Counseling Association, 2005), case law and school board policies that shape work with minors in schools.

The Organization of This Book

The chapter titled "Introduction to Legal and Ethical Issues" gives an overview of challenges and dilemmas school counselors face on a daily basis when working with minors in a school setting. As leaders and advocates, school counselors must choose the best path to support and assist students, and the ethical dilemmas and legal interpretations can at times make this feel overwhelming. This chapter presents key principles that are integral to ethical and legal understanding.

The remaining 13 chapters follow a template that will help you understand the concepts presented and will maximize effectiveness of the case-study format as a learning tool. Each chapter follows a similar outline:

- Objectives
- Ethical Standards Addressed in This Chapter
- Introduction
- Getting Started: What Would You Do?
- Working Through Case Studies
  Points to Consider
- In a Position to Know: A School Counselor Speaks
- Making Connections
- Key Terms

Here is a brief description of these organizational items.

OBJECTIVES

The objectives section contains the intended learning outcomes the reader will take from each chapter. As an example, listed below are the book's overarching goals:

- Examine the legal and ethical obligations of the school counseling profession through application of case studies.
- Raise awareness about and implications of professional behavior and professional actions.
- Examine case law, court decisions and legislation that have an impact on practice.
- Become familiar with legal and ethical terminology.
- Apply legal and ethical professional reasoning to concrete examples.
- Create sensitivity as to the difficulties and complexities of working with minors in a school setting.
- Increase tolerance for ambiguity.
- Lower the risk of legal liability in terms of professional practice.

ETHICAL STANDARDS ADDRESSED IN THIS CHAPTER

Each chapter highlights the most salient codes that address the ethical dilemmas presented. The American School Counselor Association's Ethical Standards for School Counselors (ASCA, 2010) and the American Counseling Association's Code of Ethics and Standards of Practice (ACA, 2005) provide direction to school counselors for answering the cases by applying the ethical codes. Discussion will also include reference to ethical codes, interpretations and practices formulated and promulgated by other professional organizations. However, the emphasis is on how to apply the ASCA and ACA codes to the resolution of cases.

INTRODUCTION

This section gives a brief overview of salient points that will be discussed in the chapter and sets the stage for learning.

GETTING STARTED: WHAT WOULD YOU DO?

This section presents an ethical dilemma to be answered at the end of the chapter by a practicing school counselor educator, administrator or community member who has a special interest, understanding or experience. The intent is to generate interest and excitement for the material you are about to read and to have you develop your own resolution to the case before seeing how a colleague chooses to answer it.

WORKING THROUGH CASE STUDIES

The case studies are the heart of each chapter. In five or more case studies, this section presents common daily dilemmas school counselors face, as well as a few obscure legal and ethical pitfalls. We will also look at some cases whose answer can be found in the law. We will consider the Constitution, statutes, regulatory law and case law. We will talk about some cases where school counselors have been found negligent under civil liability. Some of the cases presented will have both a legal and an ethical dilemma. The cases in the upcoming chapters are designed to challenge you and make you uncomfortable as you wrestle with problems that defy easy answers.

Points to Consider
Following each case presented, this section gathers court cases and legislation that affect the answer and allows you to apply some of the principles of ethics or law in context. It does not offer a black-and-white, right-or-wrong, concrete answer.

IN A POSITION TO KNOW: A SCHOOL COUNSELOR SPEAKS

This section provides you with a response from a practicing school counselor or someone who is in a position to know and understand how to approach the case in "Getting Started: What Would You Do?" School counselors, counselor educators, administrators or community members respond to the case based on their own personal and professional experience.

MAKING CONNECTIONS

These questions give you an opportunity to extend your learning as you consider five to eight questions posed to help you apply what you learned in the chapter.

KEY TERMS

This section identifies the key terms and phrases used in the chapter, giving you a chance to review your understanding and reflect on what you learned.

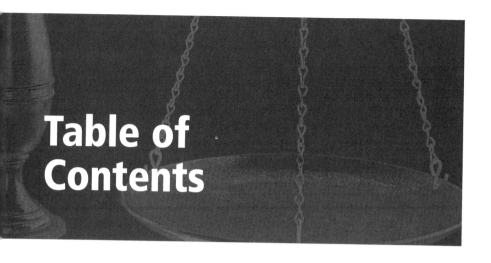

Table of Contents

CHAPTER 4: FAMILY EDUCATIONAL RIGHTS AND PRIVACY ACT

CHAPTER 5: NEGLIGENCE

CHAPTER 6: OBLIGATIONS TO THE COURT

CHAPTER 9: SEXUALLY ACTIVE STUDENTS

CHAPTER 10: LESBIAN, GAY, BISEXUAL, TRANSGENDER AND QUESTIONING STUDENTS

CHAPTER 11: SEXUAL HARASSMENT

CHAPTER 1

Introduction to Legal and Ethical Issues

IN THIS CHAPTER

Objectives

By the time you have completed this chapter, you should be able to:

- Define the difference between laws and ethics.
- Apply the ethics of the school counseling profession.
- Describe 13 of the most complicating factors of working with minors in schools.
- Understand the courts' stance toward parental rights to guiding their children.

Introduction

A working knowledge of the ethical standards and codes of the school counseling profession enables us to develop an understanding of the norms, customs and practices of the ethical school counselor. An understanding of laws, elements of negligence and principles established by courts informs us as to the implications and consequences of our work with minors in school settings. An ability to reason ethically and to understand tenets of laws governing the school counselor's work affords us a greater comfort level with the ambiguous and situational dilemmas that are part of our profession. We hope this book will guide school counselors toward strategies for handling the ethical and legal dilemmas that are part of a school counselor's daily life.

It is not the intent of this book to provide you with the "answers" but to equip you with a working knowledge of certain principles of law and standards of ethical practice that you can apply to your everyday work. By raising awareness, professional school counselors reduce their risk of backlash and develop a tolerance for ambiguity. Simple dogmatic solutions are seldom in the best interest of students, whose personal histories, developmental stages, family situations and problem-solving abilities are as complex as their conflicts. School counselors who consider the complications of their work with minors in schools appreciate the need to consider each ethical or legal dilemma in context.

Law and Ethics

The concepts we call law and ethics are ambiguous and contextual by nature. Law and ethics seldom provide us with black-and-white answers, nor should they. As frustrating as it may be for school counselors caught in a conundrum, there is always room for interpretation in each situation.

The U.S. Constitution, federal and state statutes, and regulatory and case laws are based on precedence or common law. Common law is judge-made law. This type of law is based on legal precedents developed over hundreds of years. Common law also has been referred to as the "body of general rules prescribing social conduct" (Alexander & Alexander, 2011, p. 4). Because common law is not written by elected politicians but by judges, it can be referred to as "unwritten" law. The purpose of law is to codify a value or set of values. Law is the minimum standard society will tolerate. However, in our legal system, laws and their interpretation differ from one geographic location to another (Alexander & Alexander, 2011). Common law often contrasts with civil law systems, which require all laws to be written down in a code. Judges look for prior cases that have similar law and facts to the case at hand – precedents – and render a judgment consistent with prior case law (Alexander & Alexander, 2011; Duhaime's Online Legal Dictionary, 2012).

Ethics are agreed-upon values, norms, customs and mores that have withstood the test of time (Fischer & Sorenson, 1996). Ethical codes and behavior are the result of values within a profession or organization and bind those who, by membership, ascribe to them. Our focus is on applied professional ethics, which is a combination of ethical principles and rules, ranging from the more basic guiding norms of the profession to rules of professional etiquette, that guide the conduct of school counselors in their professional interactions with others (Jacob, Decker & Hartshorne, 2010). An ethical dilemma is not a clear-cut breach of the law but a complex situation from which positive or negative consequences can result, even when the problem is handled optimally. The nature of an ethical dilemma is that there is more than one right answer, thus the term "ethical dilemma." An ethical decision-making model empowers school counselors to make the best choices as they become more comfortable with ethical and legal ambiguity (Remley & Herlihy, 2009).

Cases presented throughout this book have both legal and ethical origins, specifically as regarding the ethics of professionalism and confidentiality. Professionalism is the internal motivation to perform at the level of practice representing the ideals of the profession (Remley & Herlihy, 2009). Confidentiality issues can have both legal and ethical implications. For example, a state statute may require confidentiality but cite exceptions that render the issue an ethical one. Conflicts between the law and ethics are not uncommon, as we will see in several court cases presented in this book. In such cases, the law takes priority for school counselors. Remember, every decision a school counselor makes hinges on the context of a situation and deserves examination from multiple perspectives.

It is essential to keep in mind that school counselors do not practice in a protective bubble. Even our most well-founded and researched interventions can have unintended consequences (W. Bridges Esq., personal communication, Jan. 17, 2000). A thorough knowledge of the laws, ethical codes, school board policies and prevailing community standards arms the school counselor with tools to make difficult decisions. This book endeavors to help school counselors not only accept risk but also to be willing to take steps to reduce risk.

The Complications of Working With Minors in a School Setting

The legal and ethical complications of any human-service profession are daunting; working with minors in a setting designed for academics only adds to the complexity. On any given day, a school counselor may navigate such charged, delicate subjects as abortion, harassment or suicide. In addition, the school counselor's influence extends well beyond the student to include parents/guardians, teachers, administrators, the school district and the community. Throw in legal and ethical complications, and when all these elements converge, school counseling can feel like walking a tightrope in a hurricane.

It might help to remember the acronym COMPLICATIONS as it applies to the difficulties school counselors face. The acronym will remind you of the following 13 factors that bear on your work in the legally and ethically complicated setting of schools, working with minors.

    Counselor's values
    Obligations beyond the student
    Minors' developmental and chronological levels
    Privacy rights of minors
    Legal status of minors

In *loco parentis*
Community and institutional standards
Academic instruction
Trusting relationship
Informed consent
Opacity of laws and ethical codes
Number of student-clients
Standard of care

COUNSELOR'S VALUES

We are our values; we cannot simply leave them at the schoolhouse door. Almost all individuals harbor biases against groups of people who they consider to be different from them. Such prejudices (racism, sexism, homophobism, ageism, ableism, etc.) are sometimes grouped together and referred to as "isms." Some people maintain isms as a conscious part of their value system, choosing to believe certain groups of people or behaviors are inferior; other people may have biases of which they are completely unaware. Isms sabotage objectivity and inhibit a school counselor's ability to work productively with all students. As advocates for all students, it is essential that school counselors examine their isms and seek to temper them so as not to unconsciously or consciously oppress students who may already be marginalized.

Ethical school counselors examine their biases and seek to eradicate or soften them, "through consultation, professional development opportunities, continuing education, exposure to others, introspection and deliberate self-examination. Mitigating isms is a critical component of the personal growth that school counselors must seek as they position themselves to provide unconditional positive regard for all students" (S.B. Glicksteen, personal communication, Sept. 20, 2012).

Promoting a student's autonomy and independence is one of the moral principles of the school counseling profession (Kitchener, 1984). Imposing one's own values rooted in religion or culture disregards the moral principle of autonomy. For example, if a school counselor is vehemently opposed to abortion, it is appropriate to recognize this as a personal bias and work to soften this bias so as to be able to affirm students who are pregnant and approach you to discuss abortion. Referring a student to avoid harming that student may be an appropriate ethical response in a few select cases, but this should be the exception rather than the rule.

In a 2012 survey of ASCA members by Stone and Glicksteen, 81 percent of respondents strongly agreed or agreed with the statement: "Referring to another professional to avoid harming a student may be an appropriate ethical response in a few select cases, but this should be the exception rather than the rule" (Stone & Glicksteen, 2012b).

School counselors must work to soften biases so students are not systematically referred to other school counselors to accommodate a litany of biases. School counselors cannot pick and choose their clients so if school counselors believe abortion, homosexuality, sex out of wedlock, etc. are wrong then they have to ask themselves if they are going to be leaving out large pockets of their charges. If your isms involve a person's identity, such as sexual identity, then a referral may well read to students as a rejection of who they are as a person, quite different from a rejection of a temporary situation such as a student's pregnancy. Certain school settings, grade levels or perhaps even the school counseling profession may not be the right choice for those who will be unable to work with different segments of the student population because their values will too often conflict with students' needs for support. For any professional career, people have to be honest and self-examine their suitability to that career, and this is never truer than the profession of school counseling as this work involves supporting vulnerable, minor clients.

In a 2012 survey of ASCA members by Stone and Glicksteen, 63 percent of respondents strongly agreed or agreed with the statement: "If a school counselor/school counseling candidate is generally unwilling to work with students who request help with same-sex relationships then the school counseling profession is not an appropriate choice for this person" (Stone & Glicksteen, 2012b).

In the case of *Grossman v. South Shore Public School District* (2007), the 7th U.S. Circuit Court of Appeals barred Grossman, a Wisconsin school counselor from going forward with her Title VII religious discrimination claim against a school district citing that the district had a legitimate concern. This district did not renew the school counselor's contract because of concerns that the school counselor's promotion of prayer and abstinence was antagonistic to officials' efforts to prevent additional pregnancies and contends the firing was not because of Grossman's Christian values. Grossman failed to show that school district officials were reacting to her religious beliefs, rather than to her advocacy of prayer and abstinence, when they decided to cancel her contract. This community had a high teen-pregnancy rate, and the school counselor discarded school pamphlets teaching condom use. Grossman then ordered literature advocating abstinence. On two occasions, she prayed with distressed students. The superintendent allegedly informed Grossman that her prayer violated separation of church and state rules and that her promotion of abstinence was thwarting school officials' efforts to prevent additional pregnancies. The district chose not to renew her contract.

OBLIGATIONS BEYOND THE STUDENT

The ASCA Ethical Standards for School Counselors (2010) dictate that school counselors owe students loyalty and a trusting relationship. Students are a school counselor's primary clients; however, because school counselors are part of an educational community their loyalty and obligation extend to parents/guardians, teachers, administrators, the school district and the community. The ASCA Ethical Standards direct school counselors to respect parents' and/or guardians' rights and responsibilities for their children and advise a school counselor to make "reasonable efforts to honor the wishes of parents and guardians concerning information that he/she may share regarding the counselee" (p. 4). ASCA (Standard D. 1) includes references to school counselors' responsibilities to other school professionals such as faculty, staff and administrators, specifying that the school counselors "inform appropriate officials, in accordance with school policy, of conditions that may be potentially disruptive or damaging to the school's mission, personnel and property while honoring the confidentiality between the student and the school counselor" (p. 5). In attempting to weigh our legal and ethical obligations, it is helpful to clearly identify those we consider to be "clients." It is important for school counselors to clarify that their consultation is on behalf of students (Iyers & Baxter-MacGregor, 2010).

School counselors respect students' confidences and balance minors' rights with parents' and/or guardians' rights. Knowing when to invoke confidentiality at the exclusion of a parent's right to know is a daily struggle. Conflicts arise with regard to information shared in counseling sessions because, historically, parents or legal guardians control the legal rights of their children, while the ethical codes extend confidentiality to all clients (ASCA, 2010; Iyers & Baxter-MacGregor, 2010).

Our courts are continually vesting parents/guardians with legal rights to guide their children (*Bellotti v. Baird* (1979); *H.L. v. Matheson* (1981); *Miller v. Mitchell* (2010)). In *H.L. v. Matheson*, the U.S. Supreme Court said "constitutional interpretation has consistently recognized that the parents' and/or guardians' claim to authority in their own household to direct the rearing of their children is basic in the structure of our society." The Supreme Court emphasized that there are three reasons parents/guardians are the guiding voices in their children's lives:

- The peculiar vulnerability of minors to make life-altering decisions;
- A minor's inability to make informed, competent decisions, particularly under emotional stress; and
- The concept that parents/guardians are the guiding voice in their child's life.

In *Quilloin v. Walcott* (1978), the court expanded on this theme, "We have recognized on numerous occasions that the relationship between parent and child is constitutionally protected. The U.S. Supreme Court granted a stepfather the right to adopt a child born out of wedlock as the biological father had never made any attempts to be in the child's life. The courts allowed it was in the best interest of the child to remain with the family he/she knew (*Quilloin v. Walcott*, 434 U.S. 246 (1978)).

In *Wisconsin v. Yoder*, the U.S. Supreme Court found that mandating Amish children to remain in school past the eighth grade was against parents' fundamental right to freedom of religion. The Amish church found that higher education is not necessary for their simple way of life and may hinder their salvation (*Wisconsin v. Yoder*, 406 U.S. 205, 231-233 [**1172] (1972)).

In *Meyer v. Nebraska* (1923), at issue was a Nebraska law restricting foreign-language education. In the course of the case, the court said, "It is cardinal with us that the custody, care and nurture of the child reside first in the parents/guardians, whose primary function and freedom include preparation for obligations the state can neither supply nor hinder." We have recognized that parents/guardians have an important "guiding role" to play in their children's upbringing, which presumptively includes counseling them on important decisions (Bellotti II, supra, at 633-639).

In addition to the extensive legal privileges of parents/guardians, school counselors owe parents/guardians an ethical obligation. Occasionally, parents/guardians express the obligation or right to know the contents of the school counselor's session with their child. In a survey by Stone (2013a), 17.9 percent of school counselor respondents reported that in the last three years they have had parents/guardians ask about the contents of their counseling sessions. This low percentage is indicative of school counselors largely being able to respect the confidentiality of the counseling relationship. Corey, Corey and Callanan (2010) noted the school counselor's ethical obligation: "If parents or guardians of minors request information about the progress of the counseling, the counselor is expected to provide some feedback" (p. 190). This implies that specific information does not necessarily have to be revealed; yet some general feedback may be expected. In a survey by Stone (2013a), 23 percent of respondents said if pressured from a child's parent to breach confidences they would. As comprehensive as the law may appear, noted discretion can and should be used when inquisitive parents/guardians seek information disclosed in counseling sessions (Iyers & Baxter MacGregor, 2010).

Professional school counselors seek to build collaborative relationships with parents/guardians. In doing so, they help parents/guardians better understand the role of the school counseling program and the ethical issues involved (privacy, confidentiality and privileged communication) that are crucial in creating effective counseling relationships with students. Building these collaborative relationships may require implementing activities to educate parents/guardians such as brief discussions or programs at parent meetings. Creating collaborative relationships with parents/guardians may help to increase their sense of trust in the school counselors they will notify the school counselors when they need to be informed (Huss, Bryant & Mulet, 2008).

Welfel (2012) indicated that positions validating minors' rights have increased since a 1967 Supreme Court ruling concluded that equal protection under the law granted by the 14th Amendment and the Bill of Rights, as a whole, was not solely for adults. In an extensive search of state statutes by Stone (2012a) following a 1996 conclusion drawn by Fischer and Sorenson (1996) it can be stated with confidence that state laws typically do not address questions related to school counselors' keeping information from parents/guardians and that school counselors should use their professional judgment regarding when, how much and what information to share with parents/guardians, remembering that if parents/guardians insist on specifics and we are not able to dissuade them through generalities, they probably have a right to know in most states. State statutes are unique, and it is always best practice to determine if students have protection in law for their confidences.

Parents' and/or guardians' desires, expectations and wishes regarding their children's welfare can be varied and diffused, complicating our work. The courts and laws of the United States give legal latitude to parents/guardians regarding the care and upbringing of their children. The legal and ethical ramifications of this concept take on greater importance in those situations in which school counselors have to weigh minors' privacy rights with parents' and/or guardians' Supreme Court-given right to be the pre-eminent voice in their children's lives (Stone & Zirkel, 2010).

MINORS' DEVELOPMENTAL AND CHRONOLOGICAL LEVELS

Minors' competency and developmental levels cannot be attached neatly to a chronological age. Not all seventh-graders, for example, will behave the same way in the same situation. These middle school students may present themselves developmentally as mature 13 year olds one day only to surprise us the next day with behavior typical of 9 year olds. A developmental approach, while more complex than a chronological approach, is based on characteristics and abilities of the students involved and the nature of their discussion with their school counselors. Based on developmental theories (e.g., Piaget), most school counselors would assume there is a stage at which the developing young person could better understand complex concepts (Koocher, 2008). Research indicates that school counselors implicitly endorse such a developmentally based approach when faced with the dilemma of whether or not to breach confidentiality (Stone & Glicksteen, 2012b; Moyer, Sullivan & Growcock, 2012).

To highlight these differences, consider the juvenile justice system. In February 2012, a 17-year-old high school student fatally shot three students and wounded two others at his school. This student, on the day of a shooting, wore a T-shirt with the word "killer" and admitted to the shooting. A psychiatric evaluation determined this student to be competent enough to understand the case against him and therefore would be charged as an adult (Associated Press, 2012). As an adult he could face life in prison whereas if the case had gone to juvenile court the maximum possible penalty would have been jail until he turned 21 (Associated Press, 2012). Only three years younger, a 14-year-old ninth-grader, at a middle school for seventh through ninth grades, intentionally and fatally shot a classmate in February 2010. A psychiatric analysis found the student had the emotional make-up of an 8 year old and was acutely suicidal (Lawson, 2012). While both the 17- and 14-year old students should chronologically be in the same developmental level (i.e. Piaget's formal operational stage) the difference between them is their cognitive functioning; the 14 year old may be categorized in Piaget's concrete operational stage for 7-11 years (Newman & Newman, 2012) as he was evaluated to be developmentally an 8 year old. School counselors' sensitivity to the unique and holistic picture of each student is an important consideration when dealing with developmental and chronological complications of working with minors in schools.

PRIVACY RIGHTS OF MINORS

Overall, although minor clients have an ethical right to privacy and confidentiality in the counseling relationship, the privacy rights of minors legally belong to their parents or guardians (Remley & Herlihy, 2009). The issue of students' privacy rights is a frequent topic of professional discussion because there are no easy answers to the questions typically raised by school counselors who are concerned about students' ethical rights and parents' and/or guardians' legal rights. These conflicting legal and ethical obligations can create dilemmas for school counselors. Although, ethically, minor clients have a right to confidentiality, federal law does not protect school counselors who seek to keep information from the students' parents/guardians. In most states, school counselors who protect student confidentiality must negotiate with parents/guardians on ethical grounds as opposed to standing on legal grounds. Our guidance for this is found in two federal statutes, the Family Educational Rights and Privacy Act (FERPA, 1974) and the Health Insurance Portability and Accountability Act (HIPAA, 1996). Exceptions may exist in some states that specifically protect student privacy, so school counselors must make themselves aware of their state statutes.

Further, the parents/guardians of minors have a legal right, except for limited exceptions, to control the professional services provided to their children and to be involved in planning those services (ASCA, 2010; Health Insurance Portability and Accountability Act [HIPAA], 1996). Generally speaking, if parents/guardians refuse the school counselor's individual counseling support for their child, we comply unless our administration has reason to ask us to go forward.

A parent request to cease services sometimes comes after the parent has been reported for child abuse or is otherwise angry with the school counselor. Parents/guardians do not have the right to keep us from checking on the welfare of their child, and we are especially vigilant in child abuse cases where parents/guardians want us out of the picture. However, our care usually comes in the form of teacher collaboration and other strategies that adhere to parental requests.

> In a 2012 survey of ASCA members by Stone, 46 percent of respondents answered yes to the question: "Has this ever happened to you? A family who you reported for child abuse figured out you were the reporter and now demands you no longer counsel their child."
>
> The overwhelming majority of respondents confirmed they would discontinue counseling at the family's request but seek to get teachers and others in the building to closely watch the child. Only 6 percent of the respondents would continue counseling (Stone, 2012c).

The parent, not the student, makes critical decisions about disclosure of personal information. Parents/guardians have the final word on who has access to certain details of their child's medical conditions, such as HIV-positive status. Unless an entity is exempt from FERPA, such as a private school not receiving federal funds, the parent, not the student, gives permission to release education records.

LEGAL STATUS OF MINORS

The legal status of minors is difficult to define. For example, the age at which a student can drive, marry and be held to legal contracts differs among states. Typically, 18 is considered the legal age of majority, unless otherwise designated. Minors, therefore, can legally be defined as those persons under the age of 18. The 26th Amendment (1971) to the U.S. Constitution established the right of 18-year-old citizens to vote and by extension has influenced the generally accepted age at which minors are extended other adult rights. For example, 18 is cited in FERPA as the age at which students as well as their parents can have the rights to records (1974).

All minors share the legal characteristic that they are unable to make decisions on their own behalf. Minors are "a group of individuals with few responsibilities, many restrictions and a complex legal status that maintains a dependency on adults for privilege and access to resources" (Sanger & Willemsen, 1992). The legal concept of the age of majority has implications for minor clients' rights to make choices about entering into counseling as well as their rights to privacy and confidentiality. The

Supreme Court has upheld parents' and/or guardians' legal right to make critical decisions about their children (*Bellotti v. Baird* (1979)). Because counseling is considered to be a contractual relationship, minors are not afforded the opportunity to legally agree to counseling on their own (Remley & Herlihy, 2009). There are some exceptions as given in most states' statutes allowing minors younger than 18 to receive counseling or medical services without parental consent.

Additionally, most states have laws allowing minors to be declared "legally emancipated" from their parents/guardians, and a few states allow for minors to be deemed a mature minor and capable of understanding the ramifications of counseling (Koocher, 2008). However, in a secondary school setting when a student turns 18, this student is not yet completely emancipated if he or she is still a dependent as defined under the federal income tax code. For example, even though adult students are now considered eligible to access their own education records under FERPA, the parents/guardians also still have access to their children's education records.

The lack of congruency among laws regarding minors adds to the difficulties of working with minors, because we are unable to rely on clearly stated principles of legal policy to guide us. Scott (2001) states, "The legal regulation of children is extremely complex. Much of the complexity can be traced ultimately to a single source – defining the boundary between childhood and adulthood. Thus, the question, 'What is a child?' is readily answered by policy makers, but the answer to the question, 'When does childhood end?' is different in different policy contexts. This variation makes it very difficult to discern a coherent image of legal childhood. Youths who are in elementary school may be deemed adults for purposes of assigning criminal responsibility and punishment, while seniors in high school cannot vote, and most college students are legally prohibited from drinking" (pp. 562-563).

IN LOCO PARENTIS

Another complication of working with minors in a school setting is the interpretation of the common-law doctrine "*in loco parentis*," which at times allows school personnel to act in place of the parent. Common-law thinking on this issue has prevailed for many years. The Wisconsin Supreme Court recognized that educators must be able to address the diversity of expectations placed upon them and have sufficient control over the decorum and climate of the school to ensure learning can take place (*Burpee v. Burton* (1878)).

"Inherent in this thinking is the necessity that educators, by virtue of their positions, have the authority to govern school in a reasonable and humane manner. General education and control of pupils who attend public schools are in the hands of school boards, superintendents, principals, teachers and [school counselors]. This control extends to health, proper surroundings, necessary discipline, promotion of morality and other wholesome influences, while parental authority is temporarily superseded" (*Richardson v. Braham* (1933)). Educators have an ethical obligation to promote harmony in the school while simultaneously advancing and protecting students' interests.

Though "*in loco parentis*" translated to English means "in place of the parent," the courts never intended that school authorities, teachers or school counselors would fully stand in place of the parent in relationship to their children (Alexander & Alexander, 2012). The courts have recognized that although children's legal status is not identical to that of adults, they nonetheless are entitled to constitutional protection. Students also have an obligation to follow the laws and school rules, assume responsibilities and follow the commands of school authorities (Imber & Van Geel, 2009). Current thinking suggests it may be more appropriate to view the school as an extension of the state rather than as a substitute parent (Imber & Van Geel, 2009).

Constitutional law that bears on the interests of students and protects their First- and Fourth-Amendment rights also reiterates the importance of *in loco parentis* in protecting children and charges school personnel with the responsibility to protect the rights of the child when the child is in their care, control and protection in the school environment. The Supreme Court, in *Bethel School District No. 403 v. Fraser* (1986), also reminded us of our obligation to protect children "from exposure to sexually explicit, indecent or lewd speech." The school counselor owes a special duty to exercise reasonable care to protect a student from harm and intervene if necessary (Stone, 2001). *In loco parentis* is also explored in the Negligence Chapter and Obligations to the Courts Chapter.

COMMUNITY AND INSTITUTIONAL STANDARDS

As difficult as it may be to accept, ethics are situational. Your ethical behavior is determined in large part by your school's location. This challenges the idea of the school counselor as advocate and purveyor of justice. However, the prevailing community and institutional standards dictate to a large degree what school counselors can do and remain ethical.

For school counselors it can seem counterintuitive that the support we give students should depend on the community's values. We fight against the notion of treating students differently based on their ZIP code. As much as it might bother us, we have to know and be respectful of the wishes of the community in which we work. In some communities, the school counselor has the freedom to direct a student to a health clinic for contraceptives. In September 2012, the New York City Department of Education made the morning-after pill available to high school girls at 13 public schools. Girls as young as 14 will be able to get the Plan B emergency contraception without parental consent as part of a pilot program. Parents/guardians can opt their daughters out of the program. New York City schools already distribute free condoms to students (Dell'Antonia, 2012). This is an example of community standards at work. In many schools, school counselors would not even suggest students visit a local clinic for contraceptives as this would dramatically cross the line of community or institutional standards. This does not mean, however, that we sit idly by and accept the status quo; rather, we work responsibly to change standards that stratify students' opportunities.

Court cases have demonstrated that community standards can be an issue contributing to the outcome of a case. In *Grossman v. South Shore School District* (2007), the school counselor, alleging religious discrimination, worked in a district where there were 838 churches within 40 miles (Andrews and Beard Education Law Report, 2008). In finding in favor of the school district's right to fire her, the court said it was not her religious beliefs as her views on contraceptives were shared by the Christian school administrators who did not renew her contract. Rather, the court cited, it was her approach to the problem that was cause for concern (*Grossman v. South Shore School District* (2007)).

School counselors can learn about the internal and external community standards by questioning, listening and observing. Are you in an ultra-conservative part of the world, a bastion of liberalism, a middle-class suburb or an urban setting? Ask other educators, especially your fellow school counselors, about hypothetical and real cases and what the prevailing standard would be for handling sensitive, value-laden cases. School counselors have to understand what threads comprise the community's fabric to discern how to behave ethically in a particular environment.

It is important to have a feel for the local level of tolerance for school involvement in value-laden issues. Understand the prevailing written and unwritten standards of the community, school district and individual work site, and behave consistently within the parameters of those standards while working responsibly to change the ones detrimental to students. School counselors behave as change agents when community and institutional standards of behavior limit students' opportunities, at which point our ethical standards and codes give us a directive to act responsibly to try and change policies and practices impeding student success (ASCA, 2010).

ACADEMIC INSTRUCTION

The setting in which school counselors work defines the student/school counselor relationship. Parents send their children to school for academic instruction, not individual counseling. When the school counselor enters the equation in personal counseling, there is the possibility of tension between parents' rights to be the guiding force in their children's lives and children's rights to privacy. The definition of a counseling session is more complex because we are not in a formal counseling setting as are our colleagues in private or agency practice, school counselors interact with students virtually everywhere from the bus loading zone to the privacy of their offices. Does the law recognize these interactions as counseling sessions? "No [court] cases give us authoritative guidance on this matter" (Fischer & Sorenson, 1996, p. 18).

TRUSTING RELATIONSHIP

Trust is an essential component in the development of helping relationships. School counselors regard the promise of confidentiality to be essential for the development of client trust. Most individuals seeking counseling services, by the nature of the relationship, assume that what they divulge in counseling will be kept in confidence by their counselor, with limited exceptions (Kampf , 2009). This is most likely true for children and adolescents as well as adults. Managing confidentiality when counseling minors, however, is more complex than when counseling adults, because school counselors must balance their ethical and legal responsibilities to students, parents/guardians and the school system (ASCA, 2010; Doll, 2011; Huss, Bryant and Mulet, 2008; Moyer, Sullivan & Growcock, 2012). This complex balancing act is one reason the topic of maintaining the confidences and trust of student clients is raised in virtually every discussion of ethical and legal issues in school counseling.

The school counselor must provide a safe and secure environment in which trust can be established and maintained. Without the assurance of confidentiality, many students would not seek help or would censor what they tell the school counselor. Therefore, confidentiality is the foundation for meaningful and honest dialogue (Iyer & Baxter-MacGregor, 2010). School counselors must keep confidential information related to counseling services unless disclosure is in the best interest of students or is required by law (Fischer & Sorenson, 1996; Isaacs & Stone, 1999; Iyer & Baxter-MacGregor, 2010; Lazovsky, 2008; Moyer, Sullivan & Growcock, 2012; Remley & Herlihy, 2009).

INFORMED CONSENT

Informed consent is both a legal and ethical principle requiring school counselors to inform students about the purposes, goals, techniques and rules of procedure under which students may receive counseling (ASCA, 2010). The ASCA Ethical Standards for School Counselors (2010) tell us that at the beginning of the counseling session, the professional school counselor must tell students in terms the students can understand about the limits of their confidentiality so students can decide if they want to participate in the counseling session.

School counselors work diligently to respect students' confidences except when there is serious and foreseeable harm for the student or others. One way to effectively approach the ethics of informed consent is to view it as an on-going process rather than trying to cover every possible consideration in the first meeting. In addition, tailoring informed consent practices to a student's developmental level is critical. It is good practice to discuss examples in which the school counselor may need to disclose confidential information to the student's parents/guardians or to school personnel.

When feasible, obtaining parental permission for individual counseling that will extend beyond one or two sessions is considered best practice in the school counseling profession. Some school districts have policies or procedures requiring school counselors to obtain parents' and/or guardians' permission before counseling students. However, just as the mathematics teacher can do his or her job, the school counselor can work with students individually in absence of a state or federal law or school board policy forbidding this. It is best practice, however, to seek not only the assent of students but also of their parents/guardians (Welfel, 2012).

OPACITY OF LAWS AND ETHICAL CODES

The multifaceted nature of working with minors in schools makes it difficult to develop law, ethical codes, written school board policies or procedures covering all the potential situations school counselors might face. For example, laws addressing malpractice, negligence and student privacy rights are complex (Primary & Secondary Education, 2012; Russo, 2010). Laws often are defined case by case. Federal courts in each state can interpret the same law in different ways, and the interpretation will remain unresolved until a higher court can hear the matter, if ever. Although there is some legal guidance to be found in education law, state department regulations and local school board policy, school counselors often must practice in the absence of clear-cut guidelines.

NUMBER OF STUDENT-CLIENTS

The very nature of our role as school counselors affects our legal and ethical obligations. As leaders, advocates and change agents, we are charged with reaching every student, but the multiplicity of our role and the obligations we have to so many stakeholders considerably reduce the amount of supervision we can give to each student, the extent to which we can document what we have done and the effort we can undertake to see to each and every child's individual needs.

Although ASCA (n.d.) recommends a 250-to-1 ratio of students-to-school-counselors, the national average is actually 471-to-1 (2010–2011 school year). The demands placed on school counselors, including career and academic advising, paperwork and individual counseling, increase the importance of school counselor assignment in order to deliver services via the most effective, efficient and equitable means possible (Akos, Schuldt & Walendin, 2009).

Caseloads do not spell the difference between a school counselor who behaves professionally, ethically and legally and one who does not; however, caseloads influence the thoroughness school counselors can devote to each case.

STANDARD OF CARE

Standard of care is defined as what the reasonably competent professional would do under similar circumstances. Remley and Herlihy (2009) argued that the best way for school counselors to defend their ethical decision-making is to act as a reasonable school counselor would in a similar situation. Although helpful, the idea of "reasonable school counselor" potentially is subject to many interpretations, especially when it comes to breaching confidentiality with students and negligence. Negligence cases are founded on the assumption that the standard of care was not met. If you find yourself in legal hot water, your attorney will want to demonstrate that you behaved as any other person in your profession would have. The following criteria are just a few types of information your legal counsel will gather to show you behaved within the standard of care for your profession:

- Laws
- Ethical codes
- School board policy
- Case law
- Expert witnesses
- Length of career
- Professional development such as in-service training, professional conference attendance, books and publications read

Standard of care is explained more fully in the Obligations to the Courts Chapter.

Ethical Codes

All professional counselors are required to abide by the ethical standards of their particular professional organization. In the case of school counselors, this adherence is to the American School Counselor Association Ethical Standards for School Counselors (2010). Ethical standards are established as a guideline to use and refer to in situations that create dilemmas or situations in which choices have good but contradictory reasons to take conflicting and incompatible courses of action (Kitchener and Anderson, 2010).

The ASCA Ethical Standards for School Counselors (2010) are an attempt by the profession to standardize professional practice for the purpose of protecting students, parents/guardians and school counselors. The Ethical Standards are a guide to help us meet the needs of individual situations but seldom are appropriate for rote application, as it is the context of a dilemma that determines appropriate action. Only the school counselor, in consultation with other professionals, can determine how to apply an ASCA Ethical Standard to further a student's best interest. Codes are guides or frameworks requiring professional judgment in context to make each standard meaningful; they are not intended to provide answers but are meant to guide.

ASCA ETHICAL STANDARDS FOR SCHOOL COUNSELORS

At a glance, here are the basic concepts found in the ASCA Ethical Standards for School Counselors (2010):

Standard A.1 discusses the responsibilities to students. Under this standard are enumerated obligations of respect toward students and their values, encouragement of students and knowledge of appropriate laws and policies regarding students.

Standard A.2 explores the issue of confidentiality and its limits. Although school counselors try to maintain confidentiality at all costs, there may be times when it must be breached, as in cases of potential suicide or risk of harm to another person. This standard also discusses the school counselor's responsibility in legal matters where confidentiality is breached as a result of a court order. Finally, school counselors must also balance the need to maintain confidentiality with their students against the right of parents to be involved in all aspects of their children's lives.

Standard A.3 concerns counseling plans and implementation of a school counseling program that is comprehensive and supports students' choices for a wide variety of postsecondary education options.

Standard A.4 is about dual relationships. Under this standard, school counselors have the responsibility to remove themselves from dual relationship situations or proceed with extreme caution when such a relationship is unavoidable. This standard also addresses school counselors' dual relationships with other school personnel that might harm the school counselor/student relationship.

Standard A.5 addresses appropriate referral of students and parents to outside professionals and guides school counselors in the proper referral process.

Standard A.6 deals with group work. This standard guides the school counseling professional who works with students in groups and defines the selection, notification of parents (if necessary) and expectations of confidentiality for students in this setting.

Standard A.7 discusses the school counselor's responsibilities when students are a danger to themselves or others. These situations almost always require a breach of confidentiality, and this standard helps school counselors seek to maintain the highest level of trust and confidence possible with the student in spite of the breach.

Standard A.8 covers the issues of records, both educational and sole-possession records, and gives the school counselors guidance about disposition of sole-possession records.

Standard A.9 deals with the use of assessment instruments and the school counselor's role in their administration, interpretation and use.

Standard A.10 is concerned with the appropriate use of technology.

Standard A.11 concerns the unique responsibilities school counselors have to students involved in peer-to-peer programs.

Standard B.1 requires school counselors to respect the inherent rights and responsibilities of parents for their children and endeavors to establish, as appropriate, a collaborative relationship with parents to facilitate the counselee's maximum development. School counselors must be sensitive to cultural and social diversity among families and recognize that all parents, custodial and noncustodial, are vested with certain rights and responsibilities for the welfare of their children by virtue of their role and according to law.

Standard B.2 instructs school counselors to (1) inform parents of the school counselor's role with emphasis on the confidential nature of the counseling relationship between school counselor and counselee; (2) provide parents with accurate, comprehensive and relevant information in an objective and caring manner as is appropriate and consistent with ethical responsibilities to the counselee; and (3) make reasonable efforts to honor the wishes of parents and guardians concerning information the school counselor may share regarding the counselee.

Standards B through G are, respectively, responsibilities to parents/guardians, responsibilities to colleagues and professional associates, responsibilities to the school and community, responsibilities to self, responsibilities to the profession and maintenance of standards. This last section discusses procedures to rectify situations with individuals or groups who are in conflict with the ethical standards.

The standards demonstrate the scope and depth of the role of school counselor to school personnel, parents/guardians and students. School counselors can find a great deal of information about professional behavior by carefully reading the standards. Furthermore, professionals in schools can use the standards to improve effectiveness, avoid ethical problems and escape legal entanglements.

The ASCA Ethical Standards guide school counselors in their ethical responsibility to students and parents/guardians but do not attempt to provide complete answers. Ethics are situational and must be considered in context of institutional and community standards, school board policy and individual circumstances. Ultimately, the school counselor has the responsibility to determine the appropriate response for students who put their trust in the security of the counseling relationship (Stone & Isaacs, 2002a).

Ethical Decision Making

Even more so than laws, ethical codes and standards are open to interpretation. Different professionals may implement varying courses of action in the same situation; there seldom is one right answer to a complex ethical dilemma. However, if you follow a systematic model, you can be assured that you will be able to provide a professional explanation for the course of action you chose. Van Hoose and Paradise (1979) suggest that a counselor "is probably acting in an ethically responsible way concerning a client if (1) he or she has maintained personal and professional honesty, coupled with (2) the best interests of the client, (3) without malice or personal gain, and (4) can justify his or her actions as the best judgment of what should be done based upon the current state of the profession" (p. 58). Following this model will help ensure that all four of these conditions have been met.

FIVE MORAL PRINCIPLES

School counselors also look to moral principles to develop sound ethical decision-making skills. Moral principles can be defined as beliefs or assumptions that are shared or agreed upon by professionals and guide their ethical reasoning (Remley & Herlihy, 2009). This is the foundation upon which the codes of ethics are based. Kitchener's (1984) five moral principles can serve as a guide to ethical decision-making:

- Autonomy refers to promoting students' ability to choose their own direction. The school counselor makes every effort to foster maximum self-determination on the part of students.

- Beneficence refers to promoting good for others. Ideally, counseling contributes to the growth and development of the student, and whatever school counselors do should be judged against this criterion.

- Nonmaleficence means avoiding doing harm, which includes refraining from actions that risk hurting students.

- Justice, or fairness, refers to providing equal treatment to all people. This standard implies that anyone, regardless of age, sex, race, ethnicity, disability, socioeconomic status, cultural background, religion or sexual orientation, is entitled to equal treatment.

- Loyalty, or fidelity, refers to staying connected with your students and being available to them to the extent possible. School counselors often carry heavy caseloads, and loyalty takes on a different dimension in the school setting than at an agency. Loyalty for the school counselor does not necessarily mean 50-minute sessions once a week with students. Staying loyal may include connecting with students by encouraging them to stop by before and after school, visiting them at the bus-loading zone or briefly visiting their classrooms.

School counselors are confronted daily with ethical dilemmas requiring them to skillfully, and usually quickly, decide on an appropriate course of action. Results of a survey asking public school counselors in Virginia to indicate their most common and most challenging ethical dilemmas indicated that student confidentiality of personal disclosures (67 percent), confidentiality of student records (36 percent), acting on information of danger to self or others (33 percent), parental rights (22 percent) and dual relationships with faculty (20 percent) were the five most prevalent areas in which school counselors experienced ethical dilemmas (Bodenhorn, 2006).

Because of the complicated and multifaceted work associated with minors, an ethical decision-making model for school counselors must give special consideration to allow for the fact that our work setting is not intended primarily for individual therapy but for academic instruction.

ACA PRACTITIONER'S GUIDE TO ETHICAL DECISION MAKING

The American Counseling Association has developed A Practitioner's Guide to Ethical Decision Making (Forest-Miller & Davis, 1996 as cited by ACA, 2012). The model presents a framework for sound ethical decision-making and incorporates the work of Van Hoose and Paradise (1979), Kitchener (1984), Stadler (1986), Haas and Malouf (1989), Forester-Miller and Rubenstein (1992), and Sileo and Kopala (1993). The practical, sequential seven-step model has served counselors in all settings. Following the seven steps in this model, a counselor would:

- Identify the problem.
- Apply the American Counseling Association's Code of Ethics and Standards of Practice (2005).
- Determine the nature and dimensions of the dilemma.
- Generate potential courses of action.
- Considering the potential consequences of all options, choose a course of action.
- Evaluate the selected course of action.
- Implement the course of action

THE STEPS MODEL FOR SCHOOL SETTINGS

Stone (2001) furthered the ACA model by addressing the unique circumstances for school counselors in the school setting. STEPS, an acronym for Solutions To Ethical Problems in Schools (2001), adapts the seven steps in the ACA model and extends the conceptual and contextual applications. A nine-step model, STEPS addresses the emotional influences of a problem and considers chronological and developmental appropriateness as well as parental rights.

STEPS helps school counselors negotiate the nuances of ethical dilemmas arising within an environment significantly different from those found in agency, community, private or hospital counseling settings. Counseling is another matter altogether when you primarily serve minors mandated by law to be in attendance in an environment designed for academic instruction and not for counseling.

Following are the nine steps in the STEPS model. Although the model is presented sequentially here, it seldom will occur sequentially in the field when you are tackling an ethical problem.

1. Define the Problem Emotionally and Intellectually
- How do your emotions define this problem (your initial reaction)?
- What does your heart tell you should happen in this case? File this initial reaction away for later reference.
- How does your intellect define the problem unemotionally, objectively?

■ What are the facts? Separate the hearsay, but remember rumors often inform.

It is important to acknowledge our first reaction to the problem. When a student in need comes through the door crying and in pain, our initial reaction generally is, "What can I do to help this student?" Our emotional reaction and supportive instincts are important because they help us protect our students' confidences. Because we care about our students, we don't want to discard the emotional reaction but use it to guide us along with a healthy combination of reason and judgment.

In defining the problem, school counselors are careful not to act on emotion without considering the other ethical decision-making steps. Make the necessary effort to gather the facts while weeding out innuendoes, rumors, hearsay and hypotheses. Remember, however, that in school settings we cannot rule out hearsay or rumors, as they are often a source for school counselors to discover the truth about situations involving their students.

2. Apply the ASCA and ACA Ethical Codes and the Law
Ask yourself whether your code of ethics or the law offers a possible solution to the problem. Ethical dilemmas are often complex, and we will not usually find a definitive answer in the codes or laws. The very nature of an ethical dilemma means there is more than one acceptable answer; so we must apply good judgment by proceeding with all steps of the ethical decision-making model and paying careful attention to steps six and eight, which emphasize seeking consultation supervision.

3. Consider the Student's Chronological and Developmental Levels
How does the student's developmental level affect the dilemma, and how you will approach it? This step is critical, yet it has been left out of decision-making models. A child's age, and the ability to show that he or she can make informed decisions, matters. Also, school counselors must remember that the younger and more immature the child, the greater our responsibility to the parents or guardians.

4. Consider the Setting, Parental Rights and Minors' Rights
You must consider the rights of parents/guardians to be the guiding voice in their children's lives, especially in value-laden decisions. You must also honor parents' and/or guardians' rights to be informed and involved when their children are in harm's way. Clear and imminent danger can take many forms.

Furthermore, you must consider the dilemma in the context of the school setting. Ethical dilemmas in a school take on a different meaning from ethical issues in other contexts. Students come to school for academic instruction, and when students enter into the personal or emotional arena school counselors should consider that this will carry obligations to other educators and to parents/guardians.

5. Apply the Moral Principles

Consider the basic moral principles of autonomy, beneficence, nonmaleficence, justice and loyalty (Kitchener, 1984) and apply them to the situation. It may help to prioritize these principles and think through ways in which they can support a resolution. Decide which principles apply, and determine which principle takes priority for you in this case. In theory, each principle is of equal value, which means it is your challenge to determine the priorities when two or more of them conflict. Review the relevant professional literature to ensure that you are using the most current professional thinking in reaching a decision.

6. Determine Your Potential Courses of Action and Their Consequences

Brainstorm as many possible solutions as possible. Be creative. If possible, enlist the assistance of at least one colleague to help you generate options. Consider possible and probable courses of action, write down the options and discuss them with a colleague if you can. Examine the consequences of various decisions. Ponder the implications of each course of action for the student, for others who might be affected and for you. List the good and bad consequences of each decision.

7. Evaluate the Selected Action

Considering the information you have gathered and the priorities you have set, evaluate each option and assess the potential consequences for all the parties involved. Eliminate the options that clearly do not give desired results or cause even more problematic consequences. Then decide which combination of options best fits the situation and addresses the priorities you have identified.

Review the selected course of action to see if it presents any new ethical considerations. Stadler (1986) suggests applying three simple tests to ensure the decision is appropriate. In applying the test of justice, assess your own sense of fairness by determining if you would treat others in this situation the same way. For the test of publicity, ask yourself if you would want your behavior reported in the press, and if so, can you defend your behavior? The test of universality asks you to assess whether you could recommend the same course of action to another counselor in the same situation (Forest-Miller & Davis, 1996 as cited by ACA, 2012).

If the course of action you have selected seems to present new ethical issues, then you'll need to go back to the beginning and re-evaluate each step. Perhaps you have chosen the wrong option or identified the problem incorrectly (Forest-Miller & Davis, 1996 as cited by ACA, 2012).

If you can answer in the affirmative to each of the questions suggested by Stadler (1986) – thus passing the tests of justice, publicity and universality – and you are satisfied you have selected an appropriate course of action, then you are ready to move on to implementation (Forest-Miller & Davis, 1996 as cited by ACA, 2012).

8. Consult
Discuss your case with an experienced fellow professional, preferably a supervisor, to help you illuminate the issues. As your colleague reviews the information with you, he or she may see other relevant issues, offer a new perspective or identify aspects of the dilemma you are not viewing objectively. Consult your state or national professional associations to see if they can help.

When caught in an ethical dilemma it is sometimes difficult to see all the issues clearly. School counselors must often do their ethical problem solving on the run; it is not always feasible for school counselors to close their office doors, sit with paper and pencil and follow the ethical decision-making model. Consultation is one step that you should never skip (Stone, 2001).

In fact, consulting is such a critical part of ethical behavior that you should routinely and confidentially consult with a network of professionals when difficult situations arise. School counselors need to be constant consumers of legal and ethical information by seeking the counsel of colleagues, administrators, supervisors and school attorneys. When you routinely consult with other professionals, you will find the complexity of the legal and ethical world less daunting. More importantly, consultation can help school counselors provide increased safety and security for students.

9. Implement the Course of Action
Go forward with your decision after you have considered the previous steps. Regardless of your decision there will be risk, but you will have made the best decision based on the advice and information you had at

the time. School counselors cannot practice risk free, but we can reduce our risk and raise our support for students by using ethical reasoning.

You may find taking the final step in the ethical model disconcerting. In a real-life ethical dilemma the final step never will be easy, but by strengthening your confidence through continuous professional development you will find it easier to carry out your plans. After implementing your course of action, it is good practice to follow up on the situation to assess whether your actions had the anticipated effect.

When following the STEPS to ethical decision-making, school counselors should keep up-to-date with ethical codes and state and federal laws; maintain a network of colleagues with whom to consult; educate parents/guardians and other stakeholders of school counselors' responsibilities when faced with issues such as student confidentiality; and establish, in advance, procedures and alternatives for responding to delicate situations. Such efforts will provide a foundation from which to respond and help to eliminate the stresses school counselors face as they walk the tightrope of legal and ethical dilemmas.

Ethics and laws are not clear-cut when dealing with issues of confidentiality. School counselors have the ethical obligation to respect the privacy of minor clients and maintain confidentiality. This obligation is often in conflict with laws related to minors because parents/guardians have the right to know and to decide what is in their children's best interest. School counselors must also take into consideration codes of ethics, applicable statutes and policies of their local education agencies and their individual schools (Mitchell, Disque & Robertson, 2002).

Making Connections

1. Discuss your opinion of the premise that a thorough knowledge of the laws, ethical codes, school board policies and prevailing community standards better prepares school counselors to make tough decisions.

2. Why is the school counselor's job so much more difficult legally and ethically than that of fellow counselors in agency and private settings?

3. Discuss how you as a school counselor have the ethical imperative to promote the autonomy of your minor students.

4. Discuss each of the points that the courts stress as reasons children should be guided by their parents/guardians:

- The peculiar vulnerability of minors to make life-altering decisions
- A minor's inability to make informed, competent decisions, particularly under emotional stress
- The concept that parents/guardians are the guiding voice in their child's life

5. Why is it impossible to develop laws, ethical codes, written school board policies or procedures that cover all the potential situations school counselors might face? How should we proceed, in light of the fact that we cannot always find guidance in laws, codes or policies for all the situations we face?

Key Terms

Autonomy
Beneficence
Case law
Chronological levels
Civil law
Common law
Community standards
Consequences
Counselors' values
Developmental levels
Dogmatic solutions
Ethics
Expert witnesses
Federal statutes
Informed consent
Institutional standards
Isms
Justice

Laws
Legal status
Loyalty
Moral principles
Nonmaleficence
Opacity of law
Personal bias
Potential courses of action
Precedents
Prejudice
Privacy rights
School board policy
Standard of care
State statutes
STEPS
Tolerance for ambiguity
Vested with rights

Professionalism

IN THIS CHAPTER

Objectives

By the time you have completed this chapter, you should be able to:
Define professionalism.

- Discuss how professionalism is demonstrated in behavior, attitudes and beliefs.
- Identify standard of care and the behavior of the reasonably competent professional.
- Apply your ethical standards of behavior.
- Discuss how personal behavior affects professional standing, and determine when your personal behavior has crossed the line of professionalism.
- Reflect on your group membership and the additional responsibilities school counselors carry to be inclusive with all faculty and staff.
- Define professional competence, and discuss how it should influence your behavior.
- Identify the difference between defamation and qualified privilege.
- Discuss dual relationships, professional distance and how to protect students from possible harm that can result from dual relationships.

Ethical Standards Addressed in This Chapter

Professionalism means knowing your professional associations' codes and adhering to them. The ASCA Ethical Standards for School Counselors most germane to this chapter are the following:

- Professional school counselors avoid dual relationships that might impair their objectivity and increase the risk of harm to the student (e.g., counseling one's family members or the children of close friends or associates). If a dual relationship is unavoidable, the school counselor is responsible for taking action to eliminate or reduce the potential for harm to the student through use of safeguards, which might include informed consent, consultation, supervision and documentation. (A.4.a)
- Professional school counselors avoid dual relationships with school personnel that might infringe on the integrity of the school counselor/student relationship. (A.4.d)

- Professional school counselors establish and maintain professional relationships with faculty, staff and administration to facilitate an optimum school counseling program. (C.1.a)
- Professional school counselors treat colleagues with professional respect, courtesy and fairness. (C.1.b)
- Professional school counselors are aware of and utilize related professionals, organizations and other resources to whom the student may be referred. (C.1.d)
- Professional school counselors provide professional personnel with accurate, objective, concise and meaningful data necessary to adequately evaluate, counsel and assist the student. (C.2.b)
- Professional school counselors advocate that administrators hire only qualified, appropriately trained and competent individuals for professional school counseling positions. (D.1.f)
- Professional school counselors monitor emotional and physical health and practice wellness to ensure optimal effectiveness. Seek physical or mental health referrals when needed to ensure competence at all times. (E.1.b)
- Professional school counselors conduct themselves in such a manner as to advance individual ethical practice and the profession. (F.1.b)
- Professional school counselors do not use their professional position to recruit or gain clients, consultees for their private practice or to seek and receive unjustified personal gains, unfair advantage, inappropriate relationships or unearned goods or services. (F.1.g)
- Professional school counselors provide support, consultation and mentoring to novice professionals. (F.2.b)

The full text of the ASCA Ethical Standards for School Counselors is available at *www.schoolcounselor.org*.

Introduction

Professionalism is not easily defined; however, there are some core characteristics distinguishing the professions from other occupations (Remley & Herlihy, 2009). Professionals have special skills and competence in the application of knowledge, and their behavior is guided by a code of ethics (Froeschle & Crews, 2010; Wilczenski & Cook, 2011). This chapter enlarges on some of the core characteristics of the school counseling profession and the behavior, attitude, beliefs and philosophy of school counseling that shape professionalism.

The school counseling profession has the ASCA Ethical Standards for School Counselors (ASCA, 2010). All school counselors have the responsibility to understand the ethical standards and to apply them to their work with peers, teachers, staff members, administrators, parents and students at their schools. These principles clarify the ethical responsibilities of the entire school counseling profession, whether or not the school counselor is an ASCA member. The ethical code requires adherence to local, state and federal laws and school board policies; when there is conflict, the law supersedes. At all times school counselors work diligently to be both ethical and legal.

School counselors develop their principles of professional behavior through membership in organizations, reading and research and attendance at professional opportunities, such as conferences, regional meetings, district in-services, networking with peers and training sessions. Lambie, Ieva, Mullen and Hayes (2011) found that greater ethical and legal knowledge led to more sound ethical decision-making. Being aware of the latest research, techniques and knowledge will help school counselors protect their professionalism, remain current and serve students' needs.

Unprofessional behavior is usually handled through school districts' due-process procedures, the courts, principals' annual evaluations of school counselors or other local procedures. Rarely are ethical violations brought to the ASCA Board of Directors. However, ASCA has developed a means to revoke membership for violation of the association's ethical standards. Further, ASCA's Board of Directors can also revoke membership for "any other reason deemed...to be in the best interests of ASCA" (ASCA, 2009a, p. 3).

The process of membership revocation is straightforward. Individuals must submit in writing, along with the support of other ASCA members, a request to expel a member. The member in question has a right to remediate the situation within a specified period of time and the right to respond to the charges in person, including the option of questioning witnesses. The ASCA Board of Directors must approve revocation of membership by a two-thirds majority, and the decision is considered final.

This chapter will wrestle with the meaning of school counselors' professional conduct and how personal conduct can affect one's professional standing with fellow faculty members and the larger school community. At the heart of a number of case studies is the collaborative role of the school counselor with other educators, boundary issues with students, and legal and ethical communication. It is not possible to address all the pitfalls and complications that can threaten professionalism, but this chapter will address many of the guiding principles of professional behavior essential for effective school counseling.

Getting Started: What Would You Do?

The following case is answered at the end of this chapter by practicing school counselors. Before you read their responses, formulate in your own mind how you would approach this ethical dilemma.

GIFT TAKING

Dear School Counselor:

You are cordially invited to an all-expense-paid trip to Central University. Accommodations will be at a bed-and-breakfast. Activities will include golfing at a country club, a trip to the racetrack, and you will receive $50 for gambling on the horses. The purpose of the trip is to familiarize you with our university to enable you to speak with first-hand knowledge about the fine programs we have to offer your students.

Sincerely,
Your College Admissions Representative

Is it unethical to receive perks with more than a token monetary value? For elementary and middle school counselors, consider a parallel situation. Can you accept gifts from parents whom you know want to influence you to gain advantage for their child, such as placement with certain teachers?

Working through Case Studies

PROFESSIONAL COMMUNICATION: QUALIFIED PRIVILEGE

Greg was not promoted to ninth grade because he did "nothing," according to his eighth-grade teacher. His parents argue that he should be promoted because his failure to do work was the result of his disability (he has been diagnosed as mildly ADHD). Greg's parents, the principal, his teacher and you hold a joint conference. During the course of the conference, you explain to Greg's parents that he is "lazy and interested only in his social life." Greg's parents bring suit against you for defamation. How will the court rule?

Points to Consider

"A qualified privilege protects the teacher or school official when statements are made in good faith and without malice." Under this definition, it is clear that the communication must be made in good faith, without intent to harm, upon reasonable grounds, and it must be made with regard to assisting or protecting the interests of "either of the parties involved in performing a duty to society. The school official's or employee's communication is qualified privileged if it is prompted by a duty owed to either the public or third party and is made in good faith and without malice" (Alexander & Alexander, 2011, p. 688-689).

Legally, administrators and other educators may say unpleasant things about students but only when it is necessary to fulfill their obligations to educate and care for students while the student is in their charge (*in loco parentis*). Legally, a school counselor may say that a student is "lazy" and failed because the student did not complete work; however, ethically "lazy" is not the best choice of words. The school counselor's words were legally tolerable since this was, in the school counselor's opinion, a true statement based on her observations. When this school counselor was named in a larger court case involving the retention issue, the case for defamation against the school counselor was thrown out with due speed because, as educators, school counselors have qualified privilege, or the right to say things about students that are not flattering but necessary to fulfill their duties. School counselors may have to make unflattering statements but do so only in the context of the situation at hand (Imber & Van Geel, 2004; Alexander & Alexander, 2011) and ever mindful of their ethical obligations. Using terms like "lazy" can serve only to make parents and students defensive and angry.

Collaboration with parents cannot proceed effectively in a climate of hostility and defensiveness. Using "lazy" to describe the student might have been accurate, but it might also have been construed as mean-spirited. School counselors' word choices can be powerful, positive or negative motivating factors. Failure to recognize the power of words in conveying difficult information diminishes opportunities for growth and moves people away from rather than toward good resolutions. When conveying difficult information, school counselors should choose their words judiciously in an effort to maintain optimal communication with parents and students.

PROFESSIONAL COMMUNICATION: SENSITIVE INFORMATION

You are aware that Robert has been sexually abused. During a child study meeting in which exceptional student education is being considered for Robert, you become convinced that it is in Robert's best interest if you reveal to the child study team that he was a victim of sexual abuse. His parents, who did not attend the child study team meeting, find out about this revelation and sue you and the school district. Were you legal? Were you ethical?

Points to Consider

Substantial interest is the key consideration in this case. In the case of *N.C. v. Bedford Central School District* (2004), social worker Reulbach and school counselor Mackie were at the center of a lawsuit that helped define and refine the limits of our substantial interest.

N.C., the parents of the abused child, A.J., had a strong interest in keeping their child's abuse private. His parents feared, because of the nature of the offense, disclosure to his peers or other members of the community might cause A.J. more trauma. However, Reulbach and Mackie, in their respective responsibilities as social worker and school counselor, have a substantial interest in revealing relevant details about events, which likely affect the student's emotional well-being. All of the communications cited by the parents occurred during the course of the child study team evaluation, which was conducted at the parents' request. The communications took place only between the educators so they could adequately determine the student's need for exceptional student education.

The parents were upset because Reulbach was the only school district employee they had informed about the abuse. When Reulbach told Mackie, the parents said he relayed incorrect information about A.J.'s sexual-abuse history. However, the court said the facts provided no basis to infer that Reulbach and Mackie were engaging in "gossip" rather than professional communication. No communications had occurred outside of a professional setting, outside of the scope of the psychological and emotional evaluation of the student or among individuals without a significant interest in communicating about the student's sexual-abuse history. Therefore, the court found that the defendants' interest in professional communication for the student's benefit outweighed the student's and the parents' rights to confidentiality (*N.C. v. Bedford Central School District* (2004)).

We may often find it necessary to share information among other professionals in the same school or, as in this case, in the same school district. If the information about this child's sexual abuse had not occurred during professional discussions intended to help A.J., then the court might have ruled differently. We are cautioned to reveal such private and potentially prejudicial information in a formal setting and with parent permission if at all possible or only to educators who have the "need to know" and to be able to defend our actions as necessary to the student's well-being.

The social worker was legal. Was she ethical? Law and ethics can conflict, and when there is conflict the law takes priority. The law is the minimum standard of care, and ethics are aspirational. School counselors must always be legal but school counselors do not leave their ethical obligations behind just because they have managed to be legal. Holding ourselves to a high standard of ethics is sometimes tough when the law conflicts with our ethics. This social worker could have remained ethical by encouraging the parents to tell the school counselor about their son's abuse, reminding them that the school counselor is a professional and will respect confidentiality. If the parents explicitly asked that the social worker not reveal the sexual abuse then the onus would be on the social worker to try and convince the parents to engage other professionals.

PROFESSIONAL COMMUNICATION: DEFAMATION

At a faculty social gathering some colleagues are engaged in a heated debate about teenage pregnancy. You reveal that one of your students, Randall, has impregnated two girls, refused to accept responsibility and "he seems quite proud of his accomplishment." Your comments reach Randall. He and his mother seek legal counsel about whether or not you have committed slander (defamation that is orally conveyed). Have you committed slander?

Points to Consider

"A communication is defamatory if it tends so to harm the reputation of another as to lower him in the estimation of the community or to deter third persons from associating or dealing with him" (Alexander & Alexander, 2011, p. 685). In defamation, "the plaintiff is not required to prove actual injury or out-of-pocket monetary loss but rather must merely show that the words were of such kind as to impair his or her reputation or standing in the community or to cause personal anguish, suffering or humiliation. The plaintiff need not prove that he or she suffered special harm or direct loss" (Alexander & Alexander, 2011, p. 685).

Gossiping about a student's behavior at a social gathering is not protected by qualified privilege or substantial interest and may fall under defamation. Information should not be conveyed to other teachers or administrators unless the motive and purpose is to assist and enhance the student's educational opportunities. Transmittal should be made in the proper channels and to persons assigned the responsibility for the relevant educational function. Gossip or careless talk among teachers which is not calculated to help the student may be shown to be malicious and not protected by the cloak of qualified privilege" (Alexander & Alexander, 2011, p. 707-708).

Qualified privilege is defined by the setting and circumstances in which we discuss a student, not by our job titles. It is unprofessional to mishandle information we have obtained in the course of doing our work. Social settings are the time to be especially discreet about sensitive, confidential information. School counselors only reveal sensitive information with great reluctance and care to make certain the recipients have a "need to know" and are in a position to benefit the student if they have the information we share (ASCA, 2010).

COLLABORATION: GROUP MEMBERSHIP

You are trying to develop a place for yourself in a deeply divided faculty. Three faculty members control much of the group dynamics, deciding who will be accepted into the "in group" and who will be ostracized. The "in" group has a great deal of fun together and take care of each other. However, a few teachers are treated as outcasts and appear to spend some lonely hours at the school. It is not apparent to you why some are accepted and others are not; it just appears that the leaders decide who will be included, and everyone goes along. You have been chosen to be included, and you love having the warmth and camaraderie of a large portion of the faculty. However, the fun you are having is tempered by the nagging voice that good people are being ignored. You have made a few suggestions about including the others without much response. You feel you are not being true to yourself by participating in a group that hurts others through social isolation. You view your behavior as weakness in not standing on your principles; yet, you fear being pushed out. How can you deal with this ethical dilemma?

Points to Consider

Group membership can be difficult, yet success as a group member is critical for school counselors to develop a place as collaborators and team builders. Collaborative skills are a building block for the development of leadership skills (Bowers, 2005; Bryan & Griffin, 2010). Relationships with fellow teachers and other critical stakeholders pave the way for an effective school counseling program. The title "school counselor" adds the additional responsibility to be inclusive of all faculty to the fullest extent possible.

A school counselor should reflect on the implications of having or not having membership in this group. A few questions to consider are:

- In an effort to fit in and not be ostracized, do you try to match the behavior of others even though it is against your better judgment and your own feeling of self-respect?
- Have you grown past peer pressure and the need to be accepted at the expense of your own inner voice?
- Can you preserve your place with this group and still reach out to the ostracized faculty members?
- Do you believe your self-respect is your primary consideration in this situation?
- Can you fight through your own inhibitions and fears and learn how to be a better group member?
- Do you have the ability to survey a person's situation and decide how best to support that person?
- Do you challenge yourself to step out of your comfort zone?
- Do you expend more energy on trying to find the good in people than you do trying to point out their flaws?

This case can only be answered by each individual professional in the context of his or her situation. There are no hard and fast rules of behavior that say a school counselor must abandon new friends. However, there is professional fallout when the school counselor is viewed as marginalizing part of the faculty. Guidance in ethical codes and a history of practice imply that school counselors adhere to a higher standard of professionalism in interactions with fellow professionals. School counselors should aspire to the standard of demonstrating strong interpersonal skills and the ability to successfully move within and among the different "camps" that can be found in schools (Clark & Horton-Parker, 2002). School counselors want to be bridge builders, helping all members of the school community find emotional safety (Hernández & Seem, 2004; Schaefer & Bambrick, 2005; Bowers, 2005). Additionally, when school counselors show warmth toward the ostracized group they strengthen their relationships with not only that person but gain respect from quite a few of the "in" group even if not the three bullies. School counselors invest in their relationships to yield results to advantage their students (Stillman, 2011).

COLLABORATION: ADMINISTRATORS

Occasionally, the principal shares sensitive information with you. Last summer, he told you that he interviewed a recent graduate and hoped to hire her for a school counseling position. However, any surplus school counselors had to be placed prior to hiring the new graduate. He explained that he was temporarily dropping the position out of the budget so he wouldn't have to hire a particular surplussed school counselor who was considered weak. He explained that he would pick up the new school counselor by reinstating the position after the surplus school counselor was placed at another school. At the 12-day count, the position is reinstated, and the new school counselor is hired. The teacher's union is filing a grievance and asks what you know about the entire situation. What should you do in this situation? Are you bound by your ethical standards to keep this confidential? Must you tell the union what you know?

Points to Consider

The school counselor could explain to the union representative that it is a regular occurrence in the school counselor's relationship with the principal that sensitive information is discussed with the understanding that it will be kept confidential. This situation is no different than other conversations in which the principal's confidence has been respected. If more information is demanded the school counselor should seek legal counsel.

Privity is involved in this case. Privity is defined as having an interest in a transaction, contract or legal action to which one is not a party (Stone, 2005b). In this instance, the surplussed school counselor believes she has privity to the relationship with the principal and other school counselor's discussion since it involved her job and contract. There is no privity here. The school counselor does not have a legal obligation to tell the union the details of her conversations with the principal. However, if the school counselor is a union member, he or she may have agreed to cooperate with union investigations as a condition of membership.

COLLABORATION: TEACHERS

You have, over the course of time, learned a great deal about different teachers' classroom management effectiveness. You believe certain students assigned to one particular teacher are suffering academically and emotionally because this teacher has chronic behavior problems. School administration seems to be unaware of her ineffectiveness with many students. What is your role in this situation?

Points to Consider

The school counselor cannot afford to come across as an informant or align too closely with anyone's "camp." The school atmosphere is not unlike the United Nations, and in cases where potentially divisive situations arise the school counselor is advised to remain like Switzerland: neutral and nonjudgmental. Like a good ambassador, the school counselor's job is to develop relationships with administrators and teachers, listening to the concerns of each and helping warring factions arrive at compromises. Having a solid, professional relationship with the principal benefits the students, teachers and support personnel (Cromarty & Richards, 2009). Regarding the above case in which a teacher's conduct may be a concern, the school counselor's role is not to spy and report to the principal but to glean as much information from different sources as possible, assess the problem and share potential solutions with the principal without compromising confidentiality of sources or damaging the teacher's reputation (ASCA, 2010).

The key to success in difficult situations such as the one described here is to genuinely respect and support teachers with their difficult jobs. Think of teachers in terms of being trusted allies helping you advantage students. Study the faculty to determine who is functioning high on the personal-social consciousness continuum, and use their talents to help you advantage students. Avoiding a "them" and "us" mentality will pay off for your students. Support teachers and the instructional program as it pays in huge dividends for students.

Also essential is to make the effort to build trust between the school counselor and principal, firmly establishing respect of confidences (Dahir, Burnham, Stone & Cobb, 2010). It will be helpful for the school counselor to know how information will be used, to feel secure that it will be used to help the teacher make strides toward a better academic and social environment. If the school counselor is uncertain the principal will deal deftly with a delicate situation, he or she may have to develop another plan. Identifying allies early on, such as the assistant principal or someone else who will use compassion and a nonjudgmental approach to problem solving, will help during the throes of a dilemma. Remember, the best mentality for a school counselor to have is to think like an ambassador, and be neutral to the greatest extent possible.

COLLABORATION: FELLOW SCHOOL COUNSELORS

Greg is a school counselor serving the eighth-graders in a 7-12 school counseling department. Certification authorizes him to counsel elementary and middle school students, grades K-8. During his five years at the school he has earned a wonderful reputation, especially among the students. During your second year, about a dozen ninth-graders who were former students came back to him after they reported feeling dismissed by their high school counselor. This practice has continued for four years. Now he has too many students coming back to see him, and it is becoming stressful. Although he encourages these students to seek help from their own school counselors or from outside agencies, they are reluctant and continue to see him. Is he behaving ethically? What should he do?

Points to Consider

Supporting former students is admirable, but the school counselor in this scenario has unwittingly set up an unmanageable workload, and everyone suffers. The school counselor has enabled students to rely on him too much and in the process may have alienated the rest of the school counseling staff and compromised his well-being by taking on too much. The professional school counselor is obligated to be aware of her or his limitations (ASCA, 2010, E.1), hence the need to work within one's certification and caseload. Although this school counselor may be an intuitive school counselor for preteens, older teenagers bring with them a different set of developmental issues – issues the school counselor is not certified to address and may not be qualified to handle.

It is important to discontinue taking on former students and to find a way to ease out of a relationship with those who have been receiving counseling. Set time limits so these students are gradually able to make the transition. Tell the students, "I can only meet with you two more times, but I can set up an appointment for you with Mrs. Jones, who is terrific with people your age. With your permission I can sit down with Mrs. Jones and brief her about some of the things we've been talking about the past couple of years so she can have a sense of who you are." If the students balk then offer them the option of seeing someone in an outside agency. The primary objective is to ease the transition to their own counselor.

The school counselor should inform the other school counselor about the extra students and ask the other school counselor for help in finding a solution. It might be prudent not to mention the names of the students who have been seeking your help but to stay general and to focus on an overall strategy for managing the cases. By fostering cooperation with the school counselor whose students have been seeking your help, you may be able to avoid fissures in your relationship with your colleague.

School counselors must practice within the parameters of their certificate (ASCA, 2010). If school counselors are accused of wrongdoing, negligence or incompetence, legal counsel will have a difficult time defending them if they are practicing outside their certification, especially when the school district did not hire them to be out of field and did not sanction their out-of-field practice.

PROFESSIONAL BEHAVIOR: COMPETENCE AND PERFORMANCE

A colleague, Randolph, seems well-meaning, is good with students but indifferent to the paperwork involved in his job. Randolph's happy-go-lucky attitude is attractive to the students, but his lack of attention to detail has meant that several of his students have almost missed graduation due to his failure in academic advising. Randolph's inability to maintain solid recordkeeping is bound to catch up with him and cause a problem that can't be fixed. You are not his boss nor do you have any authority over him, but as his colleague do you have an ethical or legal obligation to do anything more to help Randolph or his students? Can the school district fire Randolph? Must the school district offer remediation for Randolph before firing him?

Points to Consider

In the case of *Carroll v. Rondout Valley Central School District* (1999), the school district in Ulster County, N.Y., fired a tenured school counselor of 19 years. The dismissal was a result of the school counselor's failure to maintain required records, to arrange required remedial assistance for students who failed the Regents Competency Test, to schedule students for required courses and for falsifying records. School counselors have an ethical and sometimes a legal duty to maintain records on behalf of their students. The following are recommendations for school counselors to enhance their recordkeeping abilities.

1. Keep records.
Students, parents and administrators routinely rely on the school counselor to stay current on students' academic progress. The ethical codes for school counselors state that school counselors "maintain and secure records necessary for rendering professional services to the student as required by laws, regulations, institutional procedures and confidentiality guidelines" (ASCA, 2010, A.8.a).

2. Set up redundancy systems.
With the computer capability available in most schools today, a redundancy system is likely already in place. Get to know the technical expert in your building, and ask him or her to help you create and maintain a sys-

tem that is fail-safe for students. This type of collaboration with colleagues can be powerful for students, freeing up your time to attend to other counseling responsibilities and giving you and the other school counselors ample warning should a red flag occur.

3. Involve the students.
While it is your obligation to maintain good records, it is also a good counseling and learning opportunity for students. Professional ethics for school counselors mandate that they help students to "move toward self-direction and self-development" (ASCA, 2010, Preamble). By partnering with students and giving them the chance to chart their own progress, school counselors can become an empowering force for young people.

4. Consult often with other school counselors and teachers.
When in doubt it is always best practice to consult with another professional. School counselors who choose to act alone have the greatest chance of landing in legal trouble.

5. If possible, set aside time specifically for record keeping.
Having a set time is so hard for school counselors; so much pulls at their time. The goal is to maximize time spent with students while minimizing time spent in documenting interaction. School counselors benefit by having clear, organized counseling notes, in that they have peace of mind should they be asked to provide documentation. Ideally, the school counselor would set aside a specific time each day to record important contacts and information regarding interventions provided but realistically grabbing a few minutes following each interaction might be all that can be accomplished in a typical day. It is true that unexpected events occur consistently in the work of a school counselor, but having time scheduled for documentation encourages the routine use of this practice (Wehrman, Williams, Field & Schroeder, 2010).

Are school counselors responsible for their colleagues and their successes or failures as school counselors? To a certain degree they are. ASCA gives guidance in the ethical standards as to how colleagues have to hold each other accountable for ethical behavior. The ASCA Ethical Standards state, "The school counselor should consult confidentially with a professional colleague to discuss the nature of a complaint to see if the professional colleague views the situation as an ethical violation. When feasible, the school counselor should directly approach the colleague whose behavior is in question to discuss the complaint and seek resolution" (American School Counselor Association, 2010, G.1). Professionals work hard to portray the fraternity of education and to support each other to be competent school counselors. We are not entirely responsible for our fellow school counselors, but it is ethical to exhaust our options in trying to help colleagues.

PROFESSIONAL BEHAVIOR: SCHOOL DISTRICT POLICIES

You believe the school district's policy for calculating grade-point averages is unfair. If a student fails a course but subsequently retakes the course and passes, the original F is permanently removed from the student's record and is never factored into the final grade-point average. This practice has affected rank in class and has given students who failed and retook a course a better class rank than students who passed the course the first time with less stellar grades. To get this policy reviewed and possibly changed, you have tried to go through the correct channels in the district, but no one seems to be listening. You resort to writing a letter to the editor of the local newspaper criticizing the policy, hoping public opinion will bring needed change. Does writing a letter to the editor constitute a legal or ethical concern?

Points to Consider

It is legal for educators to write a letter to the editor critical of a school district's practice or policy if it is a matter of public importance. The Supreme Court supported educators' right to voice their opinions in the public forum of newspaper editorials in *Pickering v. Board of Education* (1968). Marvin Pickering was dismissed for writing and sending a letter to the editor that was critical of the superintendent and the Illinois Board of Education. The board said it could dismiss Pickering under Illinois statute because the letter was detrimental to the efficient operation and administration of the district's schools. The Supreme Court ruled in Pickering's favor because it said the statements in the letter were neither false nor recklessly made and that educators exercising their freedom of speech on issues of public importance is not basis for dismissal from public employment (Imber & Van Geel, 2004; Alexander & Alexander, 2011). The test has been applied to protect Pickering as well as a teacher who complained to her principal about racist hiring policies (*Givhan v. Western Line Consol. School District* (1979)) and a police dispatcher who expressed a negative opinion about the president to co-workers while on the job (*Rankin v. McPherson* (1987)). In *Connick v. Myers* (1983) the test did not protect an attorney who was fired for circulating a questionnaire about personnel matters, which either posed questions not of public concern (e.g., the department's transfer policy) or was sufficiently disruptive to office morale to justify a disciplinary response (Ludington, n.d.).

In most school districts, newspaper editorials are not considered an appropriate way for educators to voice their concerns about the district. In cases of public importance they are probably legal, but are they ethical? Educators work extremely hard and are sometimes judged harshly by public opinion and the media. When a fellow educator criticizes the school district in a public forum, it can be disheartening or embarrassing to many in the district. It is best practice to work within the boundaries of professional behavior to change policy and procedures (ASCA, 2010). An alternative method might be to send an e-mail to district-level administrators and continue to make the case internally. Taking the case to the press is subject to public misinterpretation, and your colleagues and supervisors may view you with suspicion.

The school counselor who is an advocate will want to raise awareness of barriers that adversely stratify students' opportunities. However, knowing how to negotiate the political landscape is also critically important. Frustration with ridiculous policies is understandable, but failure to understand the political climate and act in inappropriate ways to advocate is just as damaging as not advocating at all (Stone & Zirkel, 2010). Acting in an adversarial manner will almost certainly minimize the school counselor's effectiveness in all future dealings with certain school district officials. School counselors should use finesse and diplomacy to navigate the political landscape and to determine the least disruptive way to get what students need. Learn the rules so you know how to break them properly (author unknown), politically astutely and ethically.

In the case study above, the school district is not doing anything illegal or unethical. School districts are allowed to establish a pupil progression plan, and it may include a forgiveness policy whereby a student can retake a course and be held accountable only for the passing grade or higher grade. Professional behavior requires a school counselor to abide by the district policy while advocating appropriately for change.

Not since *Pickering* has a court case on First-Amendment rights received so much attention as the recent court case, *Garcetti v. Ceballos* (2006). In this case, the Supreme Court held that "when public employees make statements pursuant to their official duties, the employees are not speaking as citizens for First Amendment purposes, and the Constitution does not insulate their communications from employer discipline." *Garcetti* is an important case for school counselors to know as it limits First Amendment protection. The facts in brief are that Ceballos, a deputy district attorney in the Los Angeles County District Attorney's Office, determined a sheriff misrepresented facts in an affidavit used to obtain a search warrant. In a memorandum to his superiors, Ceballos recommended the case should be dismissed. The sheriff's department criticized Ceballos for his handling of the situation, and the district attorney sided with the sheriff and allowed the case to proceed. Ceballos asserts that following these events he was retaliated against by being transferred and denied a promotion. Ceballos filed suit alleging that the district attorney had violated his First- and 14th-Amendment rights. The case was heard by the Supreme Court, which sided with the district attorney, ruling that a government employer can discipline an employee for job-related speech without offending the First Amendment. "In so holding, the Court carefully distinguished its prior employee-speech cases, leaving fundamentally intact the doctrine established by *Pickering v. Board of Education of Township High School District*" (Ludington, n.d., p.1).

The Supreme Court emphasized that it found in favor of the district attorney because Ceballos wrote the memorandum pursuant to his duties and not as a citizen, which was the case for Pickering, so the effect of the Ceballos case may be less significant than at first glance. At this point, the clearest message of the Ceballos decision is that employees who want to complain or express controversial opinions related to their job duties should do so as citizens. Government agencies are well-advised to heed Justice Kennedy and implement speech protections for their employees, providing a safe forum for employees to express their concerns internally before going public (Ludington, n.d.).

PROFESSIONAL BEHAVIOR: FALSIFYING RECORDS

You are a school counselor who works diligently on behalf of students. Your students have greater challenges than most students in your school system of 19 high schools, including a higher retention rate and very few four-year university admissions. Your school's practice when a student retakes and passes a previously failed course is to change an F grade to the new grade; therefore, many F's are permanently deleted from student transcripts. This is not a district practice or policy, but it has worked for your students and been silently blessed by the administration of your school. Your school's practice has resulted in more students being given an opportunity to graduate and/or attend a four-year university. Are there any legal or ethical concerns with the school's practice?

Points to Consider

School counselors are system change agents, but advocacy must be ethical. In the high-stress world of college admissions, where a university acceptance brings political capital to a high school and increased social status for parents and students, school counselors can feel the pressure to get students into Ivy League schools and provide the high school with more bragging rights. Sometimes, school counselors follow the unwritten rules and practices that have gone on before them in an effort to help a student secure a college admission or help an athlete comply with NCAA eligibility. Cases involving the manipulation of records have played out in administrative hearings, state professional practice commission hearings and courts of law. Following are four cases that resulted in school counselors being fined, losing professional credentials, having their jobs taken away and ending up in court accounting for irregularities in transcripts

> "In the Matter of New Jersey Department of Education... on this 16th day of June 2011, Judith Meller's Teacher of Elementary School Certificate of Eligibility and her Student Personnel Services certificate are hereby revoked effective immediately. It is so ordered."
> – Robert R. Higgins, Secretary, State Board of Examiners

Falsifying college transcripts: Longtime school counselor Judith Meller, who worked at Fort Lee, N.J., High School, was investigated for changing grades on transcripts sent to colleges. Dozens of college applicants had their grades boosted without their knowledge. The school district's website bragged about the success their students had in admissions into prestigious colleges: "The graduating class of 2007 surpassed our wildest expectations with the acceptance of students to five Ivies and 35 of the top 50 top-tier colleges in the nation." Indications were that part of the motivation to change grades was not just to help the students but also to enhance the school's reputation. The district found six altered transcripts for current seniors. Meller lost her job and her certificate to practice as a school counselor (Applebome, 2009).

Grade change practice not sanctioned by the school board: Jolyon Raymond, Kory Kumasaka and Acie Dubose were accused of altering 200 grades during the 2002–2003 school at Franklin High School in Seattle, Wash. All three of the school counselors had glowing reputations and support from the internal and external community. Their advocacy was widely respected among all the students of the school, especially the senior class. Allegations arose when dozens of grades were changed that helped 55 students meet the necessary 2.0 grade-point average for graduation, but the changes were not properly documented or supported by written district policy. The school counselors were placed on leave during the investigation (Komo Staff & News Services, 2003). Students started a petition to reinstate the school counselors, and teachers and parents voiced their support. "If they did anything, it's because they care too much," said Lucy Gaskill-Gaddis, former chairwoman of Franklin's site council (Bhatt, Vinh & Shaw, 2003, p1). Teacher Nan Johnson explains that the reason six of her former students graduated from high school is that Raymond persuaded them to enroll in night classes and not give up. She said, "These three cared." The testimonials in support of these three school counselors were stellar. Following the investigation, all of the school counselors were allowed to return to the school (Roberts, 2003). Investigators found the practice of grade-changing did not occur in isolation; in fact, hundreds of grades had been changed for students in 10 Seattle public high schools in recent years. Investigators deemed that the school and district shared the blame as the practice of substituting F's for subsequent passing grades was well-known and part of the culture of the school.

Personal gain from falsifying records: Sanzone was a high school counselor in the school his daughter attended. As part of his job, he was able to access course grades and could make grade changes when necessary. His daughter was in the running for valedictorian of her class, which allowed her access to many scholarships and would considerably soften the burden of financing her education. A transfer student became part of the same class as Sanzone's daughter. Sanzone was in charge of inputting the transfer student's grades into the school's computer system. Sanzone intentionally lowered several of the transfer student's grades, which lowered the student's overall cumulative average and class rank. He then raised some of his daughter's grades, securing his child's place as the valedictorian. Sanzone resigned from his position a year later and paid a civil penalty of $2,000 (Massachusetts State Ethics Commission, 1997).

National Collegiate Athletic Association eligibility: In August 2012, a Memphis City Schools high school counselor resigned after admitting to creating a fraudulent transcript for an athlete at the school. The user account for Wooddale High School counselor Valerie Starks-Sykes showed she made substantial grade changes for a student, Javon Robinson, who went on to be an Auburn running back (Solomon, 2012). One week after the school district acknowledged the manipulation of his transcript, the NCAA ruled Robinson ineligible to play. Although it appeared to investigators that several school counselors and possibly other adults outside the school counseling department were involved, Starks-Sykes chose to resign instead of taking the suspension the school district recommended (Veazey, 2012). Starks-Sykes admitted to making the changes, saying she was certain someone had asked her to make the changes but refused to name anyone else who was involved.

Most if not all of the school counselors involved in these cases were well-meaning, hard-working advocates who cared about making better lives for their students. It may be tempting to manipulate transcripts in favor of students, even when written policy does not support your actions. However, school counselors who seek to advocate for students should do so by advocating for changes to written policies. In the absence of supportive policies, falsifying records or using discretion in changing records can lead to negative consequences for students (e.g., the disqualification of the Auburn football player) and also discipline for school counselors, including forced resignation, firing and losing certification. Adhering to district policies can be especially difficult in situations where school counselors face pressure from others in the school, including administrators and supervisors, to alter grades or transcripts. School counselors, however, must heed these cases as a warning; pressure from others will not lead to legal or political protection for their jobs. Falsifying records for any reason follows the tenet "the end does not justify the means."

PROFESSIONAL BEHAVIOR: PREVAILING COMMUNITY STANDARDS

You are new to the community, and you have just accepted your first school counseling position. Prior to becoming a school counselor, you were a teacher in four other school districts. You continue to be surprised by this school's approach to working with sexually active students. The general approach to anything involving a students' sexuality is a hands-off approach. In your previous school, the nurse was able to give out contraceptives and the morning-after pill. You are afraid to even give out the phone number for Planned Parenthood, as this is interpreted by community and school members as involving yourself too much in family values. You are perplexed how the school counselors can know that students are engaged in dangerous behavior and not give them access to contraceptives that could protect them. You have a student who has asked you for help, and you are considering giving her the phone number to Planned Parenthood. You are well aware this action would be an affront to the community, but you intend to put your students' welfare above your own. Are you behaving ethically? Are there aspects of being a school counselor that you are not considering?

Points to Consider

Ethics are situational. School counselors avoid the temptation to impose their own values on students, parents and the community. Community and institutional standards can differ significantly from school to school and community to community. It is difficult to accept that professional behavior varies according to the prevailing standards of the community, but our ethical imperative is to be aware and respectful of the school community's standards. It is acceptable behavior for school counselors in certain schools and communities to refer pregnant students to Planned Parenthood; yet in many other communities, this action would be considered a serious breach of ethics and infringing on family values and parents' rights to be the guiding voice in their children's lives.

School counselors acknowledge the prevailing standards of the community in which they are working and respectfully adhere to those standards. However, adherence does not mean we unconditionally accept all community standards. If we believe a practice, policy or law of a particular school or community is detrimental to students, it is our ethical obligation to work in a responsible manner to try to influence a change so students are advantaged. The professional school counselor supports and protects the educational program against any infringement not in students' best interest (ASCA, 2010, D.1). School counselors are politically minded and work adroitly with internal and external stakeholders, such as families, parents, guardians, administrators and teachers, when change is needed. School counselors have an ethical responsibility to ask tough questions in a respectful way and to encourage fellow educators to evaluate their stance on controversial topics.

PROFESSIONAL BEHAVIOR:
PREVAILING INSTITUTIONAL STANDARDS

You had no idea when you signed on to be the school counselor at Rhinehart Elementary School that staff still meted out corporal punishment. You thought this practice had long ago disappeared from America's schools. You are in your 30s, and you never attended a school that administered corporal punishment. You are shocked at the prevalence, and you are coming apart at the seams, but quitting or transferring is not an option. What do you do?

Points to Consider

The ASCA position statement on corporal punishment (2007a) advocates for the abolishment of corporal punishment in schools. "Professional school counselors believe corporal punishment teaches children violence is an acceptable way to resolve differences. In many states, children are the only individuals who officially may be punished, under law, by physical force. Corporal punishment seriously compromises self-esteem and contradicts the fundamental right of all children to be free from bodily pain and injury" (ASCA, 2007a, p. 13).

ASCA further challenges school counselors to advocate: "The professional school counselor acts as a resource person to school personnel for the implementation of effective intervention strategies that facilitate positive individual development" (ASCA, 2007a, p. 13). "It is school counselors' professional responsibility to advocate for public and legislative bodies to abolish corporal punishment in schools. Professional school counselors encourage public recognition of the consequences of corporal punishment, disseminate research on alternatives to corporal punishment and encourage legislation prohibiting continued use of corporal punishment in states where such use exists" (ASCA, 2007a, p. 13).

Other educators have weighed in on the controversy also: "The National Association of School Psychologists (NASP) opposes the use of corporal punishment in schools and supports removal of legal sanctions for its use. Further, NASP resolves to educate the public about the effects of corporal punishment and to provide alternatives to its use and will encourage research and the dissemination of information about corporal punishment effects and alternatives" (National Association of School Psychologists, 2006, p. 1).

This school counselor may have to eventually leave this school if change does not happen; otherwise the school counselor may risk burnout or physical maladies from stress. "Coming apart at the seams" is not something to ignore. The school counselor should share with administration how he or she is feeling and ask permission to put more positive behavior plans in place. The school counselor can advocate for change by providing research, helping to establish a schoolwide behavior management program, working individually or in small groups with offenders on school success skills. The school counselor might want to bring in speakers to talk about positive ways of controlling classroom behavior to name a few proactive approaches.

The school counselor could research the incidence of domestic violence and child abuse in her school's community and compare this research with other parts of the United States. These data might show how this school's children live with and witness too much physical violence, and educators should not be one more source of it. By engaging others in conversation about how child-abuse victims and domestic-violence witnesses more frequently grow up themselves to be abusers, and other conversations about the cycle of abuse, then perhaps some support for corporal punishment might wane. Initiate conversations around this topic for thoughtful examination (Stone, 2008).

PROFESSIONAL AND PERSONAL BEHAVIOR

You are a school counselor in a conservative small town. You are fulfilling a lifelong dream of writing a book. The book turns out to be highly controversial. The book recounts sexually explicit details about acts women should perform in relationships that are often considered demeaning to women. You believe the book was misinterpreted; you intended for it to give women the upper hand in relationships with men. Should you be fired for writing a book that is sexually explicit? If you are fired has the school district violated your freedom of speech?

Points to Consider

In September 2012, Brian Craig, a school counselor and former girls' basketball coach at Rich Central High School, received a letter from the school district stating it "had received concerns from members of the school district community regarding the publication of his book." The letter added that an investigation found Craig had violated the district's policies and procedures (*Chicago Tribune*, 2012). The school board terminated Craig citing his book, "It's Her Fault," when unanimously voting to fire him (*Chicago Tribune*, 2012). Board president Betty Owens said, "Mr. Craig's conduct in this matter fell far short of our expectations and evoked outrage for me, members of this board and many others in this district who have come to expect the highest level of professionalism and sound judgment from the people they entrust with their children each day." Craig filed suit in federal court charging he was terminated in violation of his First-Amendment rights. He contends that the publication of the book was not part of his official duties and should not have been used to fire him. He also noted the book was of public interest, meant to give women a road map to having the upper hand in relationships with men (Harris-Williams, 2012). In February 2013, an Illinois federal district court ruled school district officials did not violate Craig's First Amendment free speech or his 14th Amendment liberty interest rights when they dismissed him from his employment based on a "self-help" book he published on relationships. The court concluded that although the school counselor was speaking as a private citizen, he was not speaking on a matter of public concern. As a result, the court dismissed his First Amendment free speech claim (National School Boards Association, 2013. The court also rejected Craig's claim that the dismissal violated his 14th Amendment liberty interest in reputation. The court stated that "[b]y failing to plead any publication on the part of defendants, plaintiff has not stated a claim for deprivation of his liberty interest without due process." (*Craig v. Rich Township High School District*, No. 12-7581 (N.D. Ill. Feb. 19, 2013).

Tiffany Webb was a 37-year-old school counselor at Murry Bergtraum High School for Business Careers in New York City when she was fired for online pictures characterized as racy. Webb pursued a modeling career in her late teens to early 20s before joining the teaching profession. She was dismissed from her school counseling position after pictures of her in skimpy lingerie appeared online. Webb's 12-year career as an educator came to an end after a student showed the principal, Andrea Lewis, the pictures. Lewis terminated Webb stating that the students could no longer view her as a role model due to the improper photos. Webb's case was overseen by the chancellor's committee, which voted 2-to-1 against her. Her tenure was retracted, and she was dismissed for "conduct unbecoming" of a New York Department of Education employee (Edelman, 2012, p.1). The opposing chancellor later stated that Webb was an excellent school counselor, and her past should have never dictated her future.

Nevertheless, Webb is now working in New Jersey with a changed name. Webb is suing to return to her position in Brooklyn with back pay and punitive damages. Her claim is wrongful termination, sex discrimination and First-Amendment rights violation.

Webb may very well win or receive a settlement in her court case. However, if Craig's case is an example of outcomes in these kind of cases then the court may simply dismiss the case stating that their Amendment rights were not violated. Even though both cases were widely published, only one case made a solid outcome available – *Craig v. Rich Township High School District* (2013).

Enter into a debate with other professionals about these two cases. Should Craig have been fired? Should Webb have been fired? Did either school district overstep its boundaries in your opinion? Did the school board members exercise their role appropriately by removing Craig and Webb, whose behavior was seen by some members of the school community as damaging their ability to be a positive role model?

PROFESSIONAL BOUNDARIES: ROLE, TIME AND PLACE

Cedric seeks you out for counseling whenever something is on his mind. You try to show him loyalty by never turning him away. Additionally, you check on him when a week or two goes by, and he has not made a visit to your office. You consider these exchanges with Cedric important as his chaotic family life makes him especially vulnerable. He has never known his dad. His mother is an infrequent presence due to drug abuse, and his grandmother, who is the most constant member of his family, is frail and physically limited. Cedric is a talented wrestler and seems to find a healthy escape in the sport, but no one in his family has ever seen him wrestle. You have decided you will go to his next match, which is 170 miles away to be held at 7 p.m. on a Saturday night. You do not plan to drive him either way. You are simply going to go alone, watch his match and return home alone. Are there any ethical considerations in this case?

Points to Consider

Roughly 50 percent of school counselor workshop participants have taken the position that they will go to the wrestling match when posed with the choice. They are perplexed when asked to debate their position with the opposing side because they are unable to identify why it should be an issue. These well-meaning school counselors want to support their student. The opposing side has no problem identifying why they consider going to the match problematic. The answers run the gamut from the humorous, "The price of gas is too high," to the pragmatic, "I need time off," to the sober, "I am afraid this student will think I have a romantic interest in him." Once the situation is modified to include the school counselor taking Cedric out to dinner after the match and giving him a ride home, almost 100 percent of participants will say "no" to this arrangement.

A boundary crossing is a departure from the verbal and physical distances normally maintained in a counseling interaction. Respecting the boundaries between school counselor and student is a hallmark of the school counseling profession. Once minor professional distance is breached it becomes easier to soften, blur and then violate a boundary.

Counselors of every stripe have long recognized the need to turn the highly charged atmosphere of the counseling dyad into a safe space for the counselee's intimate explorations. The counseling profession developed boundary lines out of the effort to take advantage of the benefits while minimizing the risks of the emotional dynamics of the dyad. Appropriate boundaries have been carefully crafted and built as a protection of the student, who is turning to the school counselor for help, to keep violations such as emotional dependency or the most egregious violation, sexual abuse, from ever being perpetrated.

Secure boundaries of time and place give the counseling frame structure, security and predictability. Boundary violations often begin in three basic areas: role, time and place.

Role: School counselors are working with minors who are still developmentally immature, mandated to be in school settings and are susceptible to becoming too attached to the school counselor or to misinterpret the school counselor's attention as something other than advocacy. In this complex role, there is also the danger of counter-transference, which is when a school counselor projects his or her own unresolved needs and conflicts onto the student. School counselors are careful not to blur the scope of their school counseling role with broader roles, such as being a student's friend, surrogate parent, outside school support or always-on-call counselor. Without question the school counselor's role is that of advocate and supporter, but there is a line that needs to be respected. As much as this student needs a positive adult to take an interest in him, there is concern and sometimes a danger when developmentally immature students start distorting in their own mind why their school counselor is moving far outside the scope and boundaries of the normal school counselor/student relationship.

Cedric's life has been compromised with disrupted attachments. It appears he lacks a protective and loving caregiver, and except for his grandmother, who is limited in what she can do, he is missing the safety and security that comes from a protective, attentive parent. He needs support, warmth and positive regard. Going to an away game, alone, and setting up an opportunity for a meal after the match seems like a gift to give this student, but there are ways to be just as supportive without confusing the role of school counselor with that of caregiver. The school counselor could send Cedric a note of support the Friday before the game and follow up on Monday to ask about how it went. The whole team could be recognized for its efforts on the Monday morning announcements. Other efforts might include accessing resources such as the Big Brother Big Sisters program, finding an agency that gives rides for the medically challenged so his grandmother might be able to attend a home game and/or finding a mentor for Cedric.

The school counselor's role is also defined by what he or she can reasonably do for other students who need support just as much as Cedric. School counselors try to provide within reason what each child needs and not cast a blanket that everyone has to be treated the same when clearly some students have greater needs. Yet, this differentiation of support does not mean school counselors violate boundaries that have long been established for the protection of the school counselor and the student. Making such an effort on Cedric's behalf is quite beyond the boundaries when contrasted with what we are able to do for other students equally as needy as Cedric.

Time: Cedric is allowed to pop in at will to see the school counselor. This flexibility isn't unusual because of the nature of schools and the school counselor's role. It is not that school counselors want to rigidly say, "I cannot see you without an appointment" and turn students away; however, to regularly support or encourage overly fluid arrangements can feed unhealthy school counselor/student relationships. The issue of counseling outside normal working hours is so important to the profession that when a school counselor is going to work with a student beyond the work day hours, there should be at the very least an informal consideration of the necessity and risks and efforts to find an alternative structure so boundaries can be maintained.

Place: A long drive to a match, a dinner and then a ride home between Cedric and his school counselor is not a benign event. Boundary violations do not necessarily arise from bad character. When school counselors do not recognize boundary crossings, innocent acts merely intended to be supportive can spiral downward to boundary violations such as countertransference or worse. Egregious boundary violations are usually preceded by relatively minor boundary excursions.

School counselors are continuously balancing the complex work of trying to show loyalty and support with developmentally immature students. This work is fraught with shades of gray and requires a hyper-vigilance on the school counselor's part to avoid boundary crossings. Any deviation from standard practice should cause school counselors to reflect on their rationale for the action. Finding other ways to support Cedric is safer for him and the school counselor's professional longevity.

PROFESSIONAL BOUNDARIES: DUAL RELATIONSHIPS

You love being a school counselor, especially for a select group of students you describe as bright, engaging and accomplished. This group receives most of your time and attention. You attend select students' piano recitals, tennis tournaments and soccer games. You treat these students as your adult friends, encouraging them to call you by your first name, giving them your home phone number and your home e-mail address. You go out of your way to be extraordinarily responsive to their parents, and you encourage their praise, gifts, invitations and personal favors. One parent who is an attorney helped you with your house closing without charging you. Are you behaving ethically and legally?

Points to Consider

School counselors have an ethical imperative to maintain a professional distance from students and parents. Professional distance is the appropriate familiarity and closeness a school counselor engages in with students and their family members. When professional distance is violated, then dual relationships occur (ASCA, 2010, A.4).

Dual relationships involve personal gains. While professional school counselors work diligently to make certain they do not even give the appearance of gaining any unfair advantages through their work, unethical school counselors cross boundaries for personal gain, a disturbing ethical violation. Examples of personal gain might include using the relationship to boost one's ego, sense of self-worth or self-importance or image with select parents. For others, the gain might be the need to nourish the belief that the school counselor is the only one in the school who is a student-centered advocate.

School counselors must continually examine their actions and ask the question, "Whose needs are being met by my behaviors?" If the answer is "only a select few students in my charge" or "I am feeding my own personal needs by my behavior," then the school counselor is in the throes of a serious ethical violation.

School counselors, more than any other group of educators, have a responsibility to ensure the emotional safety of minor students. It is a strongly recognized and respected tenet in the profession that school counselors should avoid dual relationships since they have the potential for harm to the students and the profession. The power differential between the school counselor and student makes it impossible for students to give equal consent to the extraprofessional relationship. It is considered exploiting the relationship when a school counselor crosses the boundaries and tries to establish friendships with students (Remley & Herlihy, 2009). Violating professional distance with students suggests a school counselor is engaged in a dual relationship.

Dual relationships, which are addressed in Code A.4. of ASCA's Ethical Standards for School Counselors (2010), evolve in many ways. To avoid such interpersonal conflicts, the school counselor must maintain professional distance with students and parents.

Accepting an invitation to attend a special event may simply be a show of support for a student who needs to know someone cares. However, when you also exhibit behaviors such as singling out a few on whom to lavish attention, you have breached professional distance. Professional distance or appropriate familiarity with clients and their family members will help avoid dual relationships that violate trust in the counseling relationship.

Currying favor with students or their parents or establishing yourself as the hero for students is unethical. It's not necessary to be part of the "in" crowd as a school counselor, nor is it advisable to accept in-kind services from family members of your students. While school counselors may convince themselves they are performing good deeds, the truth is no one benefits from the school counselor showing favoritism, especially the students who have been excluded from selective acts of altruism. Sometimes a school counselor will feel the need to massage policies, ignore school practice and hound administrators and teachers to make certain selected students get all the benefits.

Heroism can be intoxicating, especially for the school counselor who craves attention and celebrity. The parents of the chosen few may even act like fans, creating a loyal, vocal support system. But such backing never comes without a price. Inevitably the school counselor who campaigns for allies will be indebted to these parents at the expense of others. What happens, for example, when the parent who provided free legal services asks the school counselor to pull strings for his son, the one just suspended from school for drug use?

A compromised school counselor loses her or his effectiveness. No one loses more from a lack of professional clarity than the neglected children. All students should receive our services, not just the select few.

PROFESSIONAL BOUNDARIES: THE COMMUNITY

You have lived in the same small, tight-knit community your entire life, and you know nearly every person in the town through religious affiliation and the fact that your father was a popular coach who always had a houseful of people. You worry that you will never feel comfortable working with students on a personal or emotional level, as you will probably know too much about their parents and family history. Do you have reason for concern?

Points to Consider

School counselors should avoid dual relationships with students if at all possible, but in some instances it is impossible. When a school counselor works in a small community where social circles are tight-knit, dual relationships may be unavoidable. The school counselor is responsible for taking action to eliminate or reduce the potential for harm. Such safeguards might include informed consent, consultation, supervision and documentation (ASCA, 2010). Dual relationships also involve a differentiation in power, with the student seeking services from the school counselor having less power and all the possible negative ramifications that can occur with power differentials.

The best practice is for the school counselor to be vigilant about recognizing when she or he is engaged in a dual relationship and being prepared with steps to minimize negative implications. The personal relationships this school counselor has with many of the families and their children will sometimes require that the prudent professional refer students to others with a more objective eye. For example, if a friend's child asks you for help with her or his schedule, and you are treating this child the way you would any other, then you have minimized any negative impact on this student or others. If the same child seeks your help during a relationship crisis with her mother (your close friend), then you will need more objectivity than you are able to deliver in this situation. Referring students to another school counselor, if possible, may be the most ethical response.

Some safeguards against dual relationships can be established in advance. For instance, a school counselor may want to stay clear of the teacher's lounge, where students and their families are often discussed. When it comes to dual relationships, school counselors must exercise caution and handle each situation on a case-by-case basis.

In a Position to Know: School Counselors Speak

The case presented at the beginning of the chapter is revisited here and answered by practicing school counselors. Read their opinions carefully to see what you can learn. Compare their answers with your approach.

GIFT TAKING

Dear School Counselor:
You are cordially invited to an all-expense-paid trip to Central University. Accommodations will be in a bed-and-breakfast. Activities will include golfing at a country club, a trip to the racetrack, and you will receive $50 for gambling on the horses. The purpose of the trip is to familiarize you with our university to enable you to speak with first-hand knowledge about the fine programs we have to offer your students.

Sincerely,
Your College Admissions Representative

Responses from School Counselors

This hypothetical case took an all-too-real twist when *The New York Times* ran the article "Wooing of Guidance Counselors is Raising Profiles and Eyebrows" (Winter, 2004). Shift your focus from the hypothetical case study to the responses of ASCA members who addressed the issues raised in this newspaper article. The article talked about school counselors receiving expensive perks such as trips to Vail, hockey tickets, nights at luxury hotels, spa treatments and other presents with monetary value in return for favorable or preferential treatment toward their universities. In the words of Mr. Davolt, a Denver College admissions representative who has been playing host to high school counselors, "It makes a huge difference as to how they're going to convey our university" (Winter, 2004). Although the writer interviewed only one school counselor at a private school, the article read as if lavish trips were the norm.

The ASCA membership debated whether the article was intended to make school counselors look as if they were committing ethical violations, or if the intent was to criticize practices of college admissions personnel. *The New York Times* is one of the most respected newspapers in the world; therefore, when it states that school counselors are willing partners in accepting perks designed to influence their college-advising role, school counselors' ethics are being called into question. Whether *The New York Times* intended to place the focus on admissions representatives or on school counselors, the situations described require cooperative agreement between them.

Consider the rules and regulations about limits in campaign contributions: "We question a politician who receives gifts and then votes for a law favorable to the gift giver," said Doug Morrissey, former president of the New York State School Counselor Association (D. Morrissey, personal communication, Oct. 14, 2004). If elected officials receive money in exchange for awarding certain companies lucrative contracts to build roads, we place them behind bars for racketeering.

Are there any standards applicable to the school counseling profession that parallel those governing campaign contributions? Isn't it true that the overwhelming majority of school counselors would take these trips, learn about the schools' offerings, place the information in their memory banks and use it only in appropriate and fair manners? School counselors will do what is best for students; the only advantage the college can expect is that as a result of the visit to the campus and meetings with the college representatives, the school counselor will know more about the school.

Previously, the college might have been simply a name in the college admissions guide.

However, there is the concern of perception. Since it is the nature of school counselors to provide students with trustworthy, objective advice, should we worry about the perception of others who may question the influence gifts will have? *The New York Times* stated, "First and fore-most...guidance counselors are supposed to do just what their title implies: provide students with trustworthy, objective advice. By that logic, accepting gifts from the very universities they are paid to assess poses a conflict of interest that undermines the covenant between counselors and students" (Winter, 2004).

Bob Bardwell, a school counselor at Monson High School, Monson, Mass., wrote in a personal communication (March 14, 2013), "This sce-nario is certainly a slippery slope. My guess is that most every high school counselor has benefited in some way (free meal, article of clothing, recep-tion, trinket) from a college trying to market its program. While some may view these activities as selling the institution, others view these opportunities as a way to get to know the school better and thus better assist students in their college search and decision process. Those who choose to take this perspective feel there is no perceived conflict of inter-est. The problem with the given scenario is the extent of the gift. It would be one thing to simply invite the school counselors to the Central University, feeding them and putting them up overnight, but to include golfing and money for gambling is excessive. In the past I have been offered Broadway tickets and tickets to professional sporting events, which I have declined because I considered them excessive. For a school counselor to visit a college, eat a meal, take a tour and leave with a col-lege T-shirt – all while knowing that he or she will not give that college an advantage when working with students – that is a different story."

It is unethical to receive perks more than a token monetary value especial-ly if the college is overtly trying to influence the school counselor. To ban school counselors (legally or ethically) from participating in such events to better get to know the institution, which in turn will likely help students, would be problematic. The key is to find a compromise in which the col-lege gets its name and opportunities for students known to school coun-selors, for the school counselors to receive some incentive for their time and willingness to participate and for school counselors to be careful not to cross a line as to unethically steer a student to a college that is not a good fit.

Steve Schneider, former ASCA secondary vice president and current high school counselor, wrote in a personal communication (March 13, 2013), "The ASCA Ethical Standards for School Counselors state, 'The professional school counselor collaborates with agencies, organizations and individuals in the community in the best interest of students and without regard to personal reward or remuneration.' Our ethical standards serve two important functions for our profession. First, to provide a basis for self-reflection on what motivates our practice and secondly to assure others where our motivation lies. Living by ethical standards requires honest reflection about why we do what we do. Reflecting on the following questions could provide some direction. Do a lot of the students from my school attend this school, making it important for me to know more about it? Visiting schools to learn about programs is a good practice, especially local schools that pull large numbers of graduates. If this college or university has little to no draw from your school and is hoping you can help recruit students, the motive behind the visit is suspect. Would I visit this school without the offer of the extra gifts? If the answer is no, then the visit is clearly self-serving and unethical. There is a distinction between receiving a notepad as a token of thanks for your time and the extravagant gifts in this example."

Marilyn Rengert, state leader in Oregon, wrote in a personal communication (March 14, 2013), "To me it seems clear that if school counselors truly serve each and every student, it would be unethical to accept anything more than a token gift. We have a professional commitment to provide information, opportunities and to help remove barriers to learning, so each and every student can succeed. Once we begin accepting expense-paid trips, expensive gifts, etc., we enter into a political arena with lobbyists (whether they are parents or wealthy universities). Because school counselors are pivotal staff in a school and must maintain transparent relationships with all stakeholders, it is critical that our actions be transparent as well."

Making Connections

1. You are a school counselor who has a solid reputation as an effective professional. Your live-in boyfriend parties hard on weekends, and along with a group of friends, you usually end up consuming large quantities of alcohol. Several times the police have come when the neighbors have complained about cars and loud music. Lately, the parties have been getting longer and wilder. Does your behavior pose an ethical question? Answer

the case by discussing how your behavior is affected by "standard of care" or the behavior expected of the reasonably competent professional.

2. Your principal occasionally asks questions about the content of your counseling sessions. You worry about this principal's trustworthiness with information, as you have heard her repeat information others have told her, embellishing the information to make herself look important. What do you do when the principal asks you for information? How would you use your ethical codes and qualified privilege to help you in this situation without alienating your principal?

3. Currently grant money for career programs is plentiful, and your school is submitting a proposal. However, the equipment and expertise required to be in place at the time of grant submission are currently non-existent. Administration tells you not to worry, that if your school receives the grant it will quickly gather the equipment needed and send you for training to acquire the needed expertise. Are there ethical violations here?

4. School climate is especially glum at your school. Your principal asks you if you will try to help her with the situation by conducting small focus groups with all grade levels to try to determine the causes. You are certain you will find that many faculty members are discontented with the principal, as faculty members constantly exchange complaints that the principal is inconsistent, shows favoritism and micromanages. Do you agree to hold the focus groups? If you do agree, what must you consider in advance before conducting the focus groups? What are the pitfalls and the possible advantages of agreeing to help in this manner? What parameters must you set with the principal in advance? Discuss how confidentiality and informed consent should play a role in this ethical dilemma.

5. Your principal wants you to conduct focus groups to evaluate a disciplinary policy that is drawing much fire from faculty as too permissive. Defend one of these two statements:

- A school counselor is an appropriate person to lead a focus group of this nature.
- A school counselor should always try to avoid running a focus group of this type.

6. You are concerned about a policy that your school district has established for reporting students who express suicidal ideation. The policy requires that a three-part form be completed, with one part going in the

educational record, one part going to the district level and one part staying in the school counselor's office. You think the policy is an invasion of students' confidentiality and that it eliminates school counselor judgment. Discuss how you will address this situation. Whom would you involve? Who can help you advocate for a change?

7. One of your students, 11-year-old Erin, lost a parent to cancer two months ago. Throughout her parent's illness you tried to help Erin, but her grades continued to slip, and she lost her enthusiasm for playing soccer. You have a good relationship with Erin, and you continue to see her as often as you can. The last conversation you had with her surviving parent turned flirtatious, and you accepted a date. Are you involved in an ethical dilemma? Whose needs are being met?

Key Terms

Corporal punishment
Defamation
Dual relationships
Ethical standards
Falsifying student records
Maintaining student records
Monitoring your competence
Planned Parenthood

Prevailing community standards
Privity
Professional communication
Professional distance
Professionalism
Qualified privilege
Self-direction
Slander

CHAPTER 3

Cyberspace

IN THIS CHAPTER

Objectives

By the time you have completed this chapter, you should be able to:

- Discuss the influence technology has on the school counseling profession.
- Identify the different aspects of the ASCA National Model related to the use of technology in school counseling.
- Understand safety precautions that students, school counselors and parents/guardians can take while interacting on social media websites.
- Reflect on the consequences of unprofessional behavior on websites.
- Discuss policies and regulations regarding the use of technological devices in schools and the appropriate response taken in the case of a breach of those policies.

Ethical Standards Addressed in This Chapter

Professionalism means knowing your professional associations' codes and adhering to them. The ASCA Ethical Standards for School Counselors most relevant to this chapter are the following:

A.10. TECHNOLOGY
Professional school counselors:

a. Promote the benefits of and clarify the limitations of various appropriate technological applications. Professional school counselors promote technological applications (1) that are appropriate for students' individual needs, (2) that students understand how to use and (3) for which follow-up counseling assistance is provided.

b. Advocate for equal access to technology for all students, especially those historically underserved.

c. Take appropriate and reasonable measures for maintaining confidentiality of student information and education records stored or transmitted through the use of computers, facsimile machines, telephones, voicemail, answering machines and other electronic or computer technology.

d. Understand the intent of FERPA and its impact on sharing electronic student records.

e. Consider the extent to which cyberbullying is interfering with students' educational process and base school counseling curriculum and intervention programming for this pervasive and potentially dangerous problem on research-based and best practices.

The full text of the ASCA Ethical Standards for School Counselors is available at *www.schoolcounselor.org*.

Introduction

Technology has influenced the school counseling profession, including fundamentally altering the way school counselors interact with students, school personnel, parents/guardians and school counseling supervisors. School counselors are using technology in their school counseling programs and are often comfortable with technology. In a survey by Steele, Ferranti & Stone (2013), 78 percent of the ASCA member respondents agreed or strongly agreed that they like to experiment with new technologies. Only 1 percent strongly disagreed. When asked if they were confident using technology in their professional practice, 74 percent agreed, and no one strongly disagreed.

School counselors can now disseminate new knowledge and best practices through their institutions' available technology mechanisms for the purpose of interacting and communicating with their students, families, co-workers and other stakeholders.

The prevalence of educators using technology was the focus of a study from Gray, Thomas, Lewis (2010): 96 percent of educators use educational technology for word processing, 61 percent for spreadsheets and graphing programs, 80 percent to manage student records, 63 percent to deliver presentations and 94 percent for Internet searches of resources and information. A March 2013 survey of ASCA members showed similar results (Steele, Ferranti & Stone, 2013). Respondents rated 11 devices or applications as to frequency of use within their professional tasks: never, rarely, occasionally, moderate amount, great deal. The percentages for the two highest-use ratings show a sizable number of ASCA members are using technology in their work:

Device or Application	Percentage who gave the highest ratings of "moderate use" or "a great deal of use"
Computer	99 percent
Internet	97 percent
Microsoft Office (Word, Excel, PowerPoint)	97 percent
Student information system	90 percent
Document sharing, e.g. Google Docs	37 percent
School counseling department website	37 percent
iPad or other mobile device	36 percent
School counseling software application	20 percent
School counseling department blog, Twitter, Facebook or other social media	11 percent
Instant messaging	9 percent
Video conferencing program, e.g. Skype	5 percent

The simple Internet application called e-mail has significantly changed the way school counselors communicate with parent/guardians, students, families, teachers and administrators. E-mail is now a necessary part of school counselors' approach to implementing their program. In the Steele, Ferranti & Stone (2013) survey 99 percent of the respondents said they have a school district e-mail account, and 96 percent can access the school district e-mail remotely. School counselors are even able to access student data remotely (71 percent).

School counselors are wired even during off hours. According to this same survey 53 percent of respondents check their e-mail regularly outside of work hours, 25 percent check it occasionally, and only 22 percent check it rarely or not at all. Forty-four percent of respondents have their work e-mail connected to an iPad, personal phone or other personal mobile device.

This same survey demonstrated that e-mail is used as a way to communicate with students and/or families for academic planning (37 percent), college counseling (29 percent) and career counseling (25 percent). E-mail is also used to offer resources such as scholarship/program opportunities (41 percent). A sizable percentage of the work school counselors do with families, students and other staff members is through e-mail, especially with other school staff.

How often do you use e-mail to communicate with	students and/or families	other school staff (e.g. teachers, administrators)
Schedule meetings	62 percent	94 percent
Discussing concerns regarding students' academic progress	47 percent	77 percent
Discussing social and emotional concerns	28 percent	56 percent
Sharing school or counseling department bulletins or information	51 percent	70 percent
Sending surveys and other feedback solicitations regarding your school counseling program	18 percent	33 percent

(Steele, Ferranti & Stone, 2013)

Face-to-face interaction is still the primary means of communicating with all stakeholders, but e-mail trumps phone calls as a means for school counselors to communicate with other educators (Steele, Ferranti & Stone, 2013).

Means of Communication	**Students and Families** Within the time you spend communicating with students and families, what percentage do you use each of the following means of communication: Respondents spending half or more than half their time in this mode of communication.	**School Staff** Within the time you spend communicating with school staff, what percentage do you use each of the following means of communication: Respondents spending half or more than half their time in this mode of communication.
Face-to-face	67 percent	59 percent
Phone	29 percent	16 percent
E-mail	21 percent	49 percent
Video conferencing	1 percent	1 percent
Instant messaging	1 percent	2 percent
Texting	1 percent	3 percent

One of the advantages of using technology within the school counseling practice is the access it affords as a common platform for communication and dissemination of information. Technology is viewed as an essential component of life for students in today's schools. Integrating and using technological advancements show the school counselor is keeping up and trying to stay engaged with students and parents/guardians (Hayden Poynton & Sabella, 2010).

Approximately 39 states offer some type of online public school courses to resident students. Some states offer full online high school diploma programs, while others offer a limited number of virtual courses (Littlefield, n.d.). For example, Florida Virtual School (FLVS) is a public school that is free to any Florida resident and is completely online. FLVS offers 120 courses, from geometry to AP art history. FLVS has eight school counselors, who each take a portion of the state. Its website is full of interesting webinars the school counselors provide for the students from step-by-step instructions for completing the Free Application for Federal Student Aid to self-harm topics.

As more and more states and private enterprises are offering alternatives to traditional brick-and-mortar instruction, more school counselors will become part of what Tracy Steele, school counselor, Stanford Online High School, describes as a valid, much-needed alternative for some students. Steele explains that students come to online high schools for many different reasons. Some students need choices in their curriculum, an unorthodox schedule, credit recovery, rigorous coursework they cannot find at their local school or relief from the social pressures of a traditional high school. Steele says students have come to their school because "they have exhausted the curriculum at their local school and are looking for opportunities to engage in rigorous coursework. Other students come to the Stanford Online High School for a collegiate schedule that is more flexible, allowing them an opportunity to both engage in challenging coursework while also pursue significant activities such as professional acting or competitive athletics. These students deserve to have access to a school counselor who can provide support and guidance in the many ways that school counselors do at traditional brick-and-mortar schools" (Steele, personal communication, April 2013).

ASCA NATIONAL MODEL AND TECHNOLOGY

It is more efficient and effective to implement the ASCA National Model through the use of technology. The four components of a comprehensive school counseling program are: foundation, management, accountability and delivery. The delivery component is 80 percent or more of the ASCA National Model and is significantly aided by the use of technology (ASCA, 2012).

Direct Student Services

Within the delivery component of the ASCA National Model are direct and indirect services. Direct services are in-person interactions between school counselors and students and include: core curriculum, individual student planning and responsive services (ASCA, 2012). The language of the ASCA National Model says "in person," but it is really about "person to person" rather than "in-person" since methods of school counseling delivery can include synchronous and asynchronous online delivery where one is not physically co-located with the student.

Core curriculum: School counseling core curriculum is structured lessons built around competencies for students' developmental level. The core curriculum is delivered throughout the school's overall curriculum and is systematically presented by school counselors in collaboration with other professional educators in K-12 classroom and group activities (ASCA, 2012).

School counselors are using technology more than ever to deliver their core curriculum.

When asked how often, if at all, they deliver or perform school counseling curriculum such as structured lessons, events or activities (e.g. classroom curriculum, career fair) in an online setting ASCA members responded as follows:

A great deal: . . . . .7 percent
A moderate amount: . . . . .11 percent
Occasionally: . . . . .11 percent
Rarely: . . . . .13 percent
Never: . . . . .59 percent

Individual student planning: Individual student planning is a systemic, ongoing set of activities to help students in setting and reaching goals for their future plans. The college and career piece of the ASCA National Model is just one area where school counselors are aided by technology in individual student planning. For school counselors to adequately equip students with valuable information about college and career readiness they must access the same technology resources as students and parents (Hayden, Poynton & Sabella, 2010).

Throughout the years educators have found additional ways to use computers to promote career development and exploration like computer-assisted career guidance systems (Bobek, Robbins, Gore, Harris-Bowlsbey, Lapan, Dahir & Jepsen, 2005).

According to the Steele, Ferranti & Stone (2013) survey, technology is now used at least occasionally for online remote delivery of individual student planning by 28 percent of the ASCA members responding.

How often, if at all, do you deliver or perform advisement to help students establish personal goals and future plans using technology:

A great deal: . . . . .6 percent
A moderate amount: . . . . .9 percent
Occasionally: . . . . .13 percent
Rarely: . . . . .20 percent
Never: . . . . .53 percent

(Steele, Ferranti & Stone, 2013)

Responsive services: Responsive services are activities designed to meet students' immediate needs and concerns. Responsive services include individual or small-group counseling or crisis response (ASCA National Model).

According to this same survey (Steele, Ferranti & Stone, 2013), technology is now used at least occasionally for online remote delivery of responsive services by 26 percent of the ASCA members responding.

How often, if at all, do you deliver or perform group counseling, referrals, psycho-education, peer helping, consultation with other stakeholders (including parents, educators) using technology:

A great deal: . . . . .7 percent
A moderate amount: . . . . .7 percent
Occasionally: . . . . .12 percent
Rarely: . . . . .19 percent
Never: . . . . .55 percent

Indirect Student Services

Indirect services are provided on behalf of students as a result of school counselors' interactions with others. These services are delivered through strategies such as referrals, consultation and collaboration. ASCA member respondents indicated how frequently they used an online or remote setting for system support.

How often, if at all, do you use technology for system support (includes professional development, consultation, collaboration, program management, operations):

A great deal: . . . . .9 percent
A moderate amount: . . . . .15 percent
Occasionally: . . . . .25 percent
Rarely: . . . . .18 percent
Never: . . . . .33 percent

(Steele, Ferranti & Stone, 2013)

In addition to technology contributing to the delivery component of the ASCA National Model, data use under the management component happens more efficiently with technology. A school counselor has access to computer programs to manage and analyze student data. Curriculum, small-group and closing-the-gap action plans are all positively affected by technology (ASCA, 2012; Hayden, Poynton & Sabella, 2010).

Finding their technological voice helps school counselors with the closing-the-gap action plans of the ASCA National Model to demonstrate the discrepancies between those students who are advantaged and those students who are being left out of the success equation. Technology increases effective advocacy by helping school counselors connect students to challenging coursework, safety nets and opportunities.

In the accountability component, technology helps school counselors demonstrate the effectiveness of the school counseling program in measurable terms. School counselors analyze school and school counseling program data to determine how students are different as a result of the school counseling program. School counselors use that data to show the impact of the school counseling program on student achievement, attendance and behavior. The data are then used to guide future action and improve future results for all students. It is easy to see how school counselors can incorporate technology to improve this process (ASCA, 2012; Hayden, Poynton & Sabella, 2010).

School districts are equipped to maintain student information in database systems, unleashing the power of simple and complex data analyses to identify and track student outcomes. Districts and school counselors with data access can cross-tabulate data to look at more than one factor at a time. For example, data on the students with the highest number of discipline referrals can be cross-tabulated with factors such as grades and attendance to discover factors for intervention and measure outcomes.

ASCA POSITION STATEMENT ON TECHNOLOGY

ASCA has issued a position statement regarding "The Professional School Counselor and Student Safety and the Use of Technology" (ASCA, 2012). The position seeks to support professional school counselors in encouraging students to take full advantage of technological resources. The collaboration of school counselors, educators, parents and law enforcement officials is necessary to ensure students' protection and aid in disclosing possible risks of Internet use. Risks constantly increase as more students access and use the Internet. Hence, students must be taught to excel in an industrialized world where high-paying jobs and business growth are dependent on technology (ASCA, 2012). The ability to navigate technological devices determines how students survive and excel globally. As early as the postsecondary level, students must be able to use technology and be aware of their "digital foot print," which allows them to be vulnerable to privacy invasion and may even jeopardize their safety (ASCA, 2012). Other behavioral, safety and privacy risks students may face due to technology are:

- online addictions
- invasion of privacy and disclosure of personal information
- inappropriate online communications
- easy access to inappropriate media
- cheating and copyright infringement
- cyberbullying/harassment
- sexual predators (ASCA, 2012)

Professional school counselors can be part of the collaborative team that helps educate parents/guardians and students about the dangers of the Internet. Parents/guardians and school personnel can collaborate with school counselors to advise students of the appropriate use of technology that will advance academic achievement and personal social achievement. Some actions professional school counselors can take to promote the safe use of technology are:

- collaborate on the development of school policies
- respond to online incidents affecting conditions for learning

- assist the community in detecting at-risk behavior
- address digital citizenship: technology literacy, privacy, reputation and social awareness

Professional school counselors engage in professional development to improve and maintain digital literacy, which, coupled with expertise in human development, allows them to provide educators and families with guidelines for the appropriate use of technology by students (ASCA, 2012).

Professional school counselors must always consider actions that are in students' best interest when using and advising students about technology. Technology has many advantages for students in today's society, such as providing opportunities for growth, learning, exploration, communication, networking and collaboration (ASCA, 2012). However, students are especially vulnerable to the benefits and risks of technology. Therefore, school counselors, school personnel and parents/guardians can collaborate to promote Internet safety.

Getting Started: What Would You Do?

The following two cases are answered at the end of this chapter by practicing school counselors. Before you read their responses, formulate in your own mind how you would approach this ethical dilemma.

CONFIDENTIALITY IN A VIRTUAL HIGH SCHOOL

You are the department head at your state's first virtual high school. The administration is looking to you for suggestions regarding procedures the school counseling department will use for the section of the server where all educators are to keep notes on every student. The notes section is to record summaries of e-mails, phone calls, text messages and face-to-face interactions. The principal explains that it is not optional. Every faculty and administrative staff member must use this section so collaboration can happen to optimize each student's education. This means it will be visible to all educators at the school. You are uneasy about the fact that school counselors' notes will be there for all educators to see. You are thinking of suggesting school counselors be allowed to record only codes such as A for academic, P for personal, S for social or E for emotional or, if that is not acceptable, then something vague and generic. Yet, even these approaches might be a breach of confidentiality. What will you advocate for when you meet with the principal?

ONLINE COUNSELING AND SUICIDAL IDEATION

Seth, one of your students in your online high school, lost his mother a year ago. As is typical in an online school, Seth lives hours away from you and the school. Immediately after his mother's death he goes into a tailspin academically. He gets back on track only to begin slipping again this semester. Of tremendous concern to you is the fact that his teachers and friends report he has expressed the desire to stop living. These conversations can be found in the students' chat room groups, which were forwarded to you by a concerned friend. The situation is critical, but Seth's father feels his son is being overly dramatic and does not believe Seth would ever harm himself. Then, in a panicked call, Seth describes a rough fight with his father, mumbling how he could use his father's gun or pills and end it all. You keep Seth on the phone while you try to get his father on another line, but Seth informs you his father's cell phone is ringing right next to him as his father forgot to take it with him. He says he must go, and hangs up the phone with you abruptly. What do you do?

Working Through Cases

PERSONAL LIFE AND ELECTRONIC PICTURES

You are celebrating a friend's bachelorette party, and cameras are taking it all in. You end up drinking too much, and pictures surface on Facebook, where it looks like your hand is on the crotch of the male dancer hired for the occasion. In your words, you truly look "awful, drunk and vulgar." To your horror, someone who has had it in for you forwarded the picture to your principal, who is considering taking action against you. Can you be disciplined or terminated for your behavior?

Points to Consider

In the past, school counselors found it easy to separate their personal and professional lives, but now, with the emergence of electronic media, the lines are easily blurred. Standard of care, the benchmark defining what the reasonable, competent educator would do, is a high standard for school counselors specifically and educators in general (see the Professionalism Chapter for more information on standard of care). Through technology, some educators have been caught irreparably denting their standard of care in moments of lapsed judgment. Many educators have been terminated or reprimanded because of personal messages displayed on their social networking profiles. Ginger D'Amico was almost terminated following a bachelorette party. Her colleagues posted a picture of her and a male stripper (Sostek, 2010). She was consequently suspended from her job although she had immediately requested the removal of the picture upon discovering it.

A special education teacher was penalized by her school district for posting a comment on her profile that said, "You're a retard, but I love you" (Shapira, 2008). Other teachers have been dismissed for posting sexually suggestive pictures (Di Marzo, 2012). Additionally, educators can fall into otherwise innocent traps in this new age of electronic media. June Talvitie-Siple, a math teacher, was forced into retirement after posting a comment (easily viewable by the public) stating that the people in her community were "snobby" and her students were "germbags" (Manning, 2010).

SOCIAL MEDIA AND SCHOOL COUNSELORS

You have always been told by other educators to refrain from having a Facebook site. Now all around you schools and school counselors are doing just that. You are always struggling with ways to increase outreach with students on critical timely information about career and college admissions. You have decided to develop a Facebook page. What are the legal and ethical advantages and the legal and ethical pitfalls you need to address, if any?

Points to Consider

Many school counselors have embraced technology. With Facebook, Twitter and MySpace having billions of members, it comes as no surprise that educators are among those users (Smith, 2013). Out of necessity and problem behavior, school districts are implementing policies and regulations controlling social interactions between educators and students (Lehrer, 2011). A number of states have passed laws or policies limiting student/educator contact in cyberspace to avoid improper student/educator relationships (Puzio, 2013; Amy Hestir Student Protection Act, 2011). The Association of American Educators (2011) proposes that professional educators must "act with conscientious effort to exemplify the highest ethical standards (p.1)."ASCA members indicate that they infrequently interact with students or families using social media, but when they do, it is often through Facebook.

If you interact with students and/or families on social media, which do you use for that interaction?

Facebook: . . . . .10 percent
Twitter: . . . . .7 percent
LinkedIn: . . . . .1 percent
Google Plus: . . . . .1 percent
Do not interact with students/families on social media: . .83 percent

(Steele, Ferranti & Stone, 2013)

Findings from an investigation by the Associated Press between 2001 and 2005 reveal that 75 Missouri educators had been stripped of their teaching licenses because of sexual relationships with students and inappropriate online message sharing with students. Missouri implemented the Amy Hestir Student Protection Act, now called Missouri Facebook Statute, which prohibits public school teachers from utilizing any form of social media granting them exclusive access to students. Louisiana has followed Missouri's lead by passing legislation that makes Facebook interaction between educators and students illegal (Miller, 2011).

The American Counseling Association (2005) addresses the use of technology in counseling. It is essential that counselors (a) ascertain the legal and ethical requirements of their jurisdiction and that of the client; (b) assess client's knowledge and ability related to technology; (c) determine client's access to private locations; (d) discuss confidentiality, security and encryption; and (e) provide clients alternate methods of communication in the case of technology failure. ACA requires all confidential communication occur via encrypted channels.

When schools, school counselors, teachers or administrators develop Facebook pages as supportive education outreach to students, they have the added responsibility to ensure that students are technologically literate, understand privacy regulations, are aware of the consequences of building a negative reputation and understand the importance of social awareness (Internet Keep Safe Coalition [iKeepSafe] & American School Counselor Association [ASCA], 2012). Kolmes (2009a, 2009b) suggested school counselors do not friend, follow or be followed by client/students on personal Facebook accounts. Other recommendations by Jencius (2009) are to keep personal and professional Facebook and Twitter pages separate, reserve your professional name for messages sent through professional accounts, refrain from using inappropriate user names on personal accounts, provide client/students with a written policy regarding work hours and approximate response times, avoid frequent visits to students' Twitter feed or Facebook pages and ensure school, agency or institution policies are followed regarding social media.

Do your students or families have access to your personal and/or professional social media accounts?

Professional account: . . . . .12 percent
Personal account: . . . . .1 percent
Both professional and personal account: . . . . .2 percent
Students/families do not have access to my social media: . .56 percent
I do not use social media: . . . . .29 percent

(Steele, Ferranti & Stone, 2013)

It is helpful if school officials work together to ensure all students have access to and are knowledgeable about online educational outreach information. Students know, but it cannot be assumed they understand, that privacy on Facebook or other social media sites is often not secure. The privacy of student posts cannot be guaranteed (iKeepSafe & ASCA, 2012). It is important that schools maintain appropriate professional distance with students, because interacting on Facebook can leave professionals vulnerable to inappropriate conduct.

PROFESSIONAL DISTANCE AND CYBERSPACE

You are a school counselor who is technologically savvy, and you encourage your students to take advantage of your willingness to engage with them more frequently through technology. You find your tweets, texts messages, instant messages, video chats and Facebook postings are more amorous, honest and less formal. You see this as a good mode of communication. A group of parents/guardians has become concerned about some of the content of the postings, which are "way too familiar, more like student-to-student conversations than school counselor-to-student." You are in

trouble with the principal, who tells you to take down your
Facebook pages connecting you to the school. Can this principal
legally demand that you take down your Facebook page?

Points to Consider

"Professional distance is the space a professional must keep between their
professional relationship with another and any other relationship they
have with that person" (Crehan, n.d., p.1). This space is necessary for
school counselors to be able to fulfill their professional obligations in an
impartial way, with a protective boundary between the student and the
school counselor.

Spanierman v. Hughes (2008) is an example of the vigilance and judgment
educators need to use with social networking. Jeffrey Spanierman, a non-
tenured English teacher, was terminated from his position at a high school
in Connecticut. Spanierman tried to reach out to his students by creating
a MySpace account to encourage communication (Belch, 2012). The
school board fired him because Spanierman's communications with students were "peer-like" conversations that impeded the learning atmosphere. Spanierman filed a lawsuit (*Spanierman v. Hughes*, 576 F. Supp. 2d
292, Dist. Court, D. Connecticut, 2008) but lost in court when it was
determined that the destruction of the learning process outweighed the
educational value of the MySpace account.

The school counselor/student relationship is naturally an imbalance in
power and requires vigilance on the part of the school counselor to avoid
exploitation. Professional distance provides a buffer space contributing to
the safety of students and school counselors so the possibility of exploitation is lessened. Consequences arise from crossing into the space between
personal and professional relationships with minors in mandated settings
such as schools. The setting and the relationship between student and
school counselor require a high standard of care. School counselors
should avoid dual relationships with students that engage students in peer-
like conversations.

It is a well-known fact that people say and do things in cyberspace they
would not ordinarily do in a face-to-face conversation. This phenomenon
is called the disinhibition effect (Suler, 2004). The online environment creates a feeling of invisibility and anonymity. This anonymity amplifies the
disinhibition effect, resulting in people dropping their guard and revealing

too much about themselves, such as secrets, fears or wishes. The sometimes asynchronous effect (not interacting in real times, such as e-mail and message boards) seems to contribute to the disinhibition effect. "Immediate, real-time feedback from others tends to have a very powerful effect on the on-going flow of how much people reveal about themselves" (Suler, 2004, p.2). The appearance of authority is minimized in cyberspace, and the tendency and effect is that people are acting as equals, as in the case of Spanierman, who took on the role of peer and apparently dropped the role of teacher as role model. School counselors who engage in peer-like conversations with students have to ask themselves, "Whose needs are being met? Am I trying to meet my own needs in these familiar peer-like exchanges?"

In another case, Stacey Snyder was terminated for posting a picture on her MySpace account as a "drunken pirate" holding a cup. The federal district court ruled in favor of Snyder's removal as a public high school intern and stated that she was acting in the place of a certified teacher (Michels, 2008). Snyder was not able to complete her internship and, therefore, unable to obtain her teaching certificate (*Snyder v. Millersville* WL 5093140 (ED Pa 2008).

PROFESSIONAL DEVELOPMENT AND THE INTERNET

Your principal will rarely allow any school counselors out of the building for professional development and never allows both school counselors to leave at the same time. You are keenly aware that a school counselor's standard of care includes staying abreast of developments in the field and continuing to take care of one's professional development. You worry you are not holding yourself to a high standard. Your principal will not relent. How can the Internet help you?

Points to Consider
School counselors are taking advantage of the surge of online professional development opportunities. Through programs such as ASCA SCENE discussion boards, Twitter school counselor chats (#scchat) and a number of blogs, school counselors have an opportunity to communicate with other school counselors to share their ideas (Sampson, 2013).

Many organizations such as ASCA and American Counseling Association provide school counselors with easily accessible professional development opportunities such as webinars. On the ASCA webinar archive alone they are more than 50 different webinars addressing various issues in school counseling. The National Association of College Admissions Counselors, The National Office of School Counselor Advocacy of the College Board, state school counseling associations and other education organizations provide quality, free webinars. It is possible to attend a first-rate webinar every week.

When given the opportunity to physically attend workshops, bring back something to share with the principal about how the workshop is going to benefit the school. This will hopefully encourage the principal to allow you to continue to grow your standard of care by attending to your professional development.

STUDENT SAFETY ON THE INTERNET

A student comes to you worried about her friend, who plans to meet in person a boy she met online. How do you address this situation on a larger scale to ensure none of your students fall victim to Internet pedophiles?

Points to Consider

Research from Wolak, Mitchell & Finkelhore (2006) suggests that 4 percent of children ages 10-17 are targeted for sex online. One in 33 is aggressively persuaded to meet face-to-face with an online predator, and 34 percent of children are sent unwanted sexually explicit content online. Predators victimize children through sexual abuse or exploitation, cyber-bullying or emotional abuse, corruption or violence abuse and distraction or social abuse (A Better Child, n.d.). Pedophiles use many outlets on the Internet to target and exploit students like blogs, online forums and chat rooms (Penna, Clark & Mohay, 2005).

This situation is one of those times when a school counselor will want to talk to the students to impress on them the danger they are putting themselves in and, depending on what the school counselors learn from the students, it is highly likely that in most cases the school counselor will decide to alert the students' parents/guardians to possible harm.

Burrow-Sanchez, Call, Zheng & Drew (2011) have proposed strategies school counselors can use to help parents/guardians promote Internet safety in their home. School counselors can help parents/guardians improve communication with their children around Internet use and help parents undstand how to establish and reinforce Internet-use rules such as the computer only in common areas of the house. Additionally, Burrow-Sanchez, Call, Zheng & Drew (2011) have also suggested Internet safety strategies for school counselors working with students who may be at risk for online victimization.

Facebook has developed a new initiative called "Facebook for School Counselors" in alliance with The Internet Keep Safe Coalition (iKeepSafe) and ASCA, available as a free download. Facebook and ASCA provide suggested actions for school counselors (Facebook Education Notes, 2012):

- Helping develop school policies
- Responding to online incidents that affect conditions for learning
- Assisting the community in detecting at-risk behavior
- Addressing digital citizenship, technology literacy, privacy, reputation and social awareness

American School Counselor Association	*www.Facebook.com/pages/American-School-School counselor-Association/ 77096899005?ref=nf*
Parenting	*http://www.parenting.com/article/ keeping-your-child-safe-on-the-internet*
SafeKids.com	*http://www.safekids.com/*
Childnet International	*www.Facebook.com/childnetinternational*

INDIVIDUAL COUNSELING ONLINE

You see the need for individual online counseling in your school as a growing percentage of your students are taking virtual classes for the majority of the week. Which data will you present to convince school administration of the effectiveness of having an online school counseling component?

Points to Consider

Online counseling is counseling via the Internet through the medium of e-mail, real-time chat or video conferencing. There are a number of research results on the benefits and disadvantages of online counseling. A survey conducted by Leibert, Archer, Munson & York (2006) found two major advantages of individual online counseling. Leibert et al. found that individual online counseling is advantageous for students who have dealt with emotional disturbances, social alienation and ridicule from others. These students often feel less anxious while disclosing emotionally oriented information electronically.

Additionally, online services give students a greater sense of autonomy and control (Osbern, 2010). According to Internet-based group interviews, adolescent users felt safer and less emotionally exposed in online counseling as opposed to other forms of counseling (King, Bambling, Lloyd, Gomurra, Smith, Reid & Wegner, 2006). Adolescents are comfortable with real-time audiovisual medium. For counselors working with adolescents, cognitive behavioral therapy is most often used. This approach requires homework rather than tunneling into the patient's past and seems to lend itself to the real-time video conferencing of counselors who work online. "Tech-savvy teenagers resistant to office visits might brighten at seeing a therapist through a computer monitor in their bedroom. Home court advantage" (Hoffman, 2011).

Individuals suffering from depression, anxiety and eating disorders can potentially benefit from the therapeutic style of online counseling treatments (Christensen, Griffiths & Jorm, 2004; Leibert et al., 2006). Most online counseling programs are being categorized as "computer-mediated-communication" or to put it simply counselor/clients interaction aided by computers and the Internet (Mallen & Vogel, 2005, p. 762).
A study by Rochlen, Land & Wong suggest that some males find more comfort in online counseling compared with face-to-face counseling (2004). Schultze's (2006) research study found that some students are able to express themselves more freely because of the anonymity online counseling provides. Due to this observation, theorists propose that online counseling has interpersonal components such as anonymity, protection and openness, which promote change in how students relate to school counselors online. Suler's research found that when the boundaries of communication were blurred it produces an "online disinhibition effect" (2004, p. 321), which decreases defensiveness and self-consciousness, thereby allowing students to disclose information more frequently (Alleman, 2002; Chester & Glass, 2006).

In the practical sense, Tracy Steele knows online counseling from her work as a school counselor at Stanford University's Online High School; her students are literally all over the world. Steele recognizes that a certain degree of anonymity holds true with the barrier of a monitor but believes it is less a factor for the students with whom she works because her online counseling is through video conferencing. Granted, video conferencing is not in the flesh, but it is in many respects face-to-face because the school counselor and student can see each other through video conferencing real-time platforms. "Video conferencing is certainly different from chat rooms, e-mail or instant messaging, and it has proven to be a powerful medium for supporting my students" (Steele, personal communication, April 2013).

School counselors in traditional settings are more often using e-mail as an asynchronous communication method where school counselors have to use their counseling skills, and in some ways these e-mail exchanges are applicable to the benefits/drawbacks of the discussion here about online communication with students.

Cook's research found a meaningful therapeutic alliance can be formed over the Internet, even in the absence of nonverbal cues (Cook, 2001; Prado & Meyer, 2006). For example, Cook studied the working alliance (as measured by the Working Alliance Inventory) in Internet therapy. Cook found that a working alliance was strongly established between clients and providers of synchronous and asynchronous e-therapy. Cook and Doyle (2002) found similar results after only one online session. Alleman's research found that students with anxiety disorders, agoraphobia and social anxiety may benefit more from online counseling because they can access it from their homes (2002).

Leibert, Archer, Munson and York (2006) in their study found that clients receiving face-to-face counseling had stronger perceived working alliances than those in e-therapy, but the e-therapy users still had high satisfaction ratings of their experience. In a review of the literature, Mallen, Vogel, Rochlen and Day (2005) noted that, collectively, findings indicate clients are just as satisfied with online counseling as they are with face-to-face counseling (Rummell & Joyce, 2010).

These are just a few of the research studies school counselors can turn to when they are trying to determine if the benefits outweigh the drawbacks of online counseling.

BENEFITS OF ONLINE SCHOOL COUNSELING

You work in the state's virtual high school. You counsel students on various issues just as your brick-and-mortar colleagues do. What are the cautions and benefits for your work as compared with that of face-to-face school counseling?

Points to Consider

The online environment has distinct qualities that draw students: accessibility, simplicity, convenience, flexibility and inexpensiveness are a few of the benefits. Online counseling may be appealing to students who seek the solace of counseling sessions that do not require face-to-face interactions or online situations that allow them to express themselves through writing (Shaw & Shaw, 2006). Online counseling is beneficial for students who do not need persistent counseling sessions but may need to be held accountable for improvements they have made (Mallen & Vogel, 2005). Students can also maintain correspondence with school counselors after moving to another state or region (Mallen, Vogel & Rochlen, 2005). Some school counselors have found the availability of text from previous counseling sessions to be beneficial in focusing sessions on particular issues students may have faced (Mallen & Vogel, 2005). School counselors have also found that communicating with students online provides them with more time to respond appropriately to students' statements, which makes the therapeutic practice more effective (Alleman, 2002).

Do you feel online communication is compatible with your school counseling role?

Extremely compatible: . . . . .7 percent
Very compatible: . . . . .17 percent
Moderately compatible: . . . . .33 percent
Slightly compatible: . . . . .27 percent
Not at all . . . . .16 percent

(Steele, Ferranti & Stone, 2013)

DISADVANTAGES OF ONLINE SCHOOL COUNSELING

The state's virtual school is assessing its online school counseling program, and you are in charge of improving the program. What are some disadvantages of online school counseling the state can address?

Points to Consider

The literature speaks to three major problems in online counseling: not all problems are suitable for online counseling; confidentiality in online counseling is impossible to guarantee; students in crisis are sometimes more difficult to help immediately, and it is harder to secure referrals for them (Osborn, 2010).

Other disadvantages of online counseling are:

- Student issues and identity (suicidal, depressed)
- Informed consent
- Laws differ across states for confidentiality, privileged communication, etc.
- Equality of access
- Technical problems (Osborn, 2010, p.4).

In an unpublished survey by Steele, Ferranti & Stone (2013) ASCA members reported the following barriers in using online communication. These results do not focus just on individual online school counseling, but there is overlap in the implications.

What barriers do you face in using online communications?

Lack of professional development in the area
   of online communications: ....64 percent
Lack of time: ....55 percent
Lack of access to online technologies: ....32 percent
Little or no applicability to my role: ....19 percent
Lack of interest: ....13 percent

The question has also been raised about whether special training is needed for a practitioner to be able to facilitate a meaningful and viable counseling relationship online (Shaw & Shaw, 2006). Communicating warmth, caring, genuineness and openness over the Internet are also considered to be difficult to achieve by some.

From a risk-management perspective, school counselors need to know the true identity and location of their students should an emergency arise (Shaw & Shaw, 2006). It is also important to know the community resources in the student's local area and to make plans for how to respond to an emergency situation during the informed consent process at the outset of the professional relationship.

ETHICS OF ONLINE SCHOOL COUNSELING

You are an online school counselor. You have just been thrown into the role as the state just came up with a virtual high school for students. No one has given you guidance in the ethics of online school counseling. Where do you go for help?

Points to Consider
The new modality of online school counseling brings with it previously undiscovered ethical concerns. Online school counseling should be as ethically orientated as any other counseling being offered to [student]/clients (Lee, 1998, p.2). Ethical codes are what separate the counseling occupation from other professions, and professional codes are needed for the online world of counseling. Counseling by nature can exploit and create harm or provide tremendous good.

Counseling and social work organizations have been proactive in developing Internet regulations. The National Board of Certified Counselors (2012a), the American Counseling Association (ACA; 2005), The National Association for Social Workers (2008), the American Mental Health Counselors Association and The International Society for Mental Health Online (ISHMO) (2000) have all developed ethical codes for online counseling.

STUDENT FIRST-AMENDMENT RIGHTS AND CYBERSPACE

Serena, the school newspaper editor, has a blog she runs from home in which she writes freely about the principal's "heavy handedness in controlling what goes into the newspaper." She says what a "narrow-minded bigot" he is and discusses his "homophobic editing of anything to do with gays." She says, "He is a major douchebag." The principal removes Serena as editor of the school newspaper. Serena sues for violation of her First-Amendment rights. Will she prevail?

Points to Consider

Avery Doninger was junior class secretary and in charge of organizing school events. Doninger created and ran a blog from home in which she vented after a less-than-perfect battle of the bands event that the superintendent got "pissed off" and the school administrators were "douche bags." She also used other offensive language to further berate the school employees. The administrators reacted by barring Doninger from applying for senior class secretary. Her mother brought a lawsuit requesting the court implement a preliminary injunction that would allow her daughter to run for senior secretary. Her motion was denied by the District Court and 2nd Circuit Court (*Doninger v. Niehoff*, 527 F.3d 41 (2d Cir. 2008). After graduating, Avery Doninger became a plaintiff in her own case. She asked for damages from the court claiming that her First- and 14th-Amendment rights were violated. Her case made its way through the court system from the District Court to the 2nd Circuit Court and ended up in the U.S. Supreme Court. The Supreme Court declared that her offensive language revoked her First-Amendment rights (Hader, 2009).

CYBERSPACE SEARCH AND SEIZURE

The principal is technologically challenged and asks you to go through a student's phone and read the student's text messages aloud. What should be your legal concerns in this situation?

Points to Consider

A reasonable search of a student's possession by school officials occurs when school officials are suspicious of a student's activities and have reason to believe the student has violated school regulations and when a conducted search is directly related to the initial suspicion. The principal is drawing the school counselor into a disciplinary situation that could also be a situation of unreasonable search and seizure. This situation is politically fraught with landmines. To refuse is to appear uncooperative, but to oblige might mean you are now an unwitting party to an illegal search and seizure. As astutely as possible, school counselors will extract themselves from searching the phone's text messages. At the very least the school counselor will want to discuss with the principal the reasons for the search. Are the reasons connected to a strong suspicion that the school's code of conduct has been violated, and as the text messages are searched, will school officials only attend to what is directly related to the initial suspicion?

Unreasonable search and seizure has been the topic of many court cases involving school officials. One such case was *Klump v. Nazareth Area School District*. In this case, Klump's cell phone was confiscated by a teacher when he violated school rules and used it in class. The teacher and principal later accessed Klump's personal text messages, voicemails and made phone calls to classmates to inquire about drug activity. A drug-related text message was received while the officials were in possession of the phone. Officials consequently used this information to determine the student had violated the school's drug policy. Klump sued the district stating that his Fourth-Amendment rights, which protect against unlawful search and seizure, were violated. The court agreed and ruled in favor of the student, stating the district "had no reason at the onset to suspect that such a search would reveal that the [student was] violating another school policy" (*Klump v. Nazareth Area School District*, 425 F. Supp.2d 622 (E.D. Pa., 2006).

In a Position to Know: School Counselors Speak

The cases presented at the beginning of the chapter are revisited here by two school counselors. Compare their answers with your own approach.

CONFIDENTIALITY IN A VIRTUAL HIGH SCHOOL

You are the department head at your state's first virtual high school. The administration is looking to you for suggestions regarding procedures the school counseling department will use for the section of the server where all educators are to keep notes on every student. The notes section is to record summaries of e-mails, phone calls, text messages and face-to-face interactions. The principal explains that it is not optional. Every faculty and administrative staff member must use this section so collaboration can happen to optimize each student's education. This means it will be visible to all educators at the school. You are uneasy about the fact that school counselors' notes will be there for all educators to see. You are thinking of suggesting school counselors be allowed to record only codes such as A for academic, P for personal, S for social or E for emotional or, if that is not acceptable, then something vague and generic. Yet, even these approaches might be a breach of confidentiality. What will you advocate for when you meet with the principal?

Points to Consider

It is encouraging that this school counselor is thinking through confidentiality, especially in the cyber-setting where communication occurs differently than in a traditional school setting. If you are in a U.S. school, I would recommend checking state law to see if school counselors have privileged communication in your state (for more information see the Obligations to the Court Chapter). That information will provide important guidance you should share with your administrator. It is not unusual for the legal definition of privileged communication to read something along the lines of "information a student shares in a confidential setting cannot be shared in court unless the student consents." This is privileged communication, which you may or may not have in your state. It is a protection of confidentiality in a legal setting.

Regardless of state statutes, there are limits to confidentiality, and being in a cyber-setting will have an impact on those limits. A school policy requiring you to enter information in a notes section of a database is one limit of confidentiality. Although it may be tricky, I don't think the policy creates an unworkable situation. You can think of these notes in the same way as when, in a brick-and-mortar school, a school counselor sends a request to a teacher to send a student to his or her office or when a school counselor writes an excuse slip when a student returns to class. It is also common for school counselors to follow up with teachers, administrators or parents/guardians about a student concern after holding an individual counseling session with the student, so some information is naturally shared without breaching confidentiality when collaborating with other staff or parents/guardians. School staff members have a need to know some information but definitely not all information. On the positive side, the notes section of the database may be an effective way to communicate and collaborate with teachers, especially at an online school.

Since all of the staff can see your documentation, regardless of whether or not they work with the student, the situation is especially challenging and may have an impact on more than just the school counseling staff. Family Educational Rights and Privacy Act (FERPA) guidelines delineate who may have access to a student's educational record without parent permission. Individuals who have a "legitimate educational interest" can access education records. Would a staff member who does not work with a student have "legitimate educational interest" to their information? If all staff members have access to the student's record, you will want to talk with administrators about how that level of access to student information may not comply with FERPA guidelines.

Next, advocate for a system where teachers and administrators can only see notes on students who are assigned to them. Also, advocate for school counselors to be allowed to keep generic notes in the notes section to avoid creating a major limit on confidentiality. Your notes could include dates and times you met with the student, contacted the parent or consulted with a teacher. Your notes could also include generic information such as academic discussion, college and career readiness, personal/social issue, etc. These notes would be equivalent to what you might say to a parent who questions why you are meeting with his or her child if you were working in a brick-and-mortar school.

Once information is entered into the database, it becomes a part of the education record and will be included with the record if it is subpoenaed in a court proceeding. You will want to write any notes in a manner in which you would feel comfortable if that situation were to occur. You could then create more detailed personal case notes that are not a part of the education record based on FERPA.

It is critical in this situation to make sure students understand the limits of confidentiality. Be sure to include information about your school's policy in your informed consent so students can make a decision about how much information they are comfortable disclosing to the school counselor. But, in most cases, I think you'll find students appreciate you are there for them and will not mind opening up to you. On occasion, you may meet a student who is reluctant to talk with you or may even refuse to meet with you because of this policy, but in any event, you should inform students of your school's policy on this issue. After a particularly sensitive discussion, you could discuss with the student what information you would like to include in the notes section of the database and obtain the student's consent before entering it.

A school policy requiring school counselors to keep notes in the notes section of a schoolwide database may be tricky, but if you work with your administrators to help them clearly understand confidentiality and agree ahead of time as to what information will be included in the notes, you can turn this requirement into a workable situation that will help you collaborate for student success with others staff members.
– *Eric Sparks, Ed.D. assistant director, ASCA, and former school counseling supervisor, Wake County Public Schools, N.C.*

ONLINE SCHOOL COUNSELING AND SUICIDAL IDEATION

Seth, one of your students in your online high school, lost his mother a year ago. As is typical in an online school, Seth lives hours away from you and the school. Immediately after his mother's death he goes into a tailspin academically. He gets back on track only to begin slipping again this semester. Of tremendous concern to you is the fact that his teachers and friends report he has expressed the desire to stop living. These conversations can be found in the students' chat room groups, which were forwarded to you by a concerned friend. The situation is critical, but Seth's father feels his son is being overly dramatic and does not believe Seth would ever harm himself. Then, in a panicked call, Seth describes a rough fight with his father, mumbling how he could use his father's gun or pills and end it all. You keep Seth on the phone while you try to get his father on another line, but Seth informs you his father's cell phone is ringing right next to him as his father forgot to take it with him. He says he must go, and hangs up the phone with you abruptly. What do you do?

Points to Consider
The main concern in this case involves Seth's safety. Given that the school counselor has evidence Seth has discussed his desire to stop living in prior online chats and that he mentioned to the school counselor on the phone

98 • SCHOOL COUNSELING PRINCIPLES

that he may use his father's gun or pills to end it all, it is reasonable to suspect Seth may proceed to attempt suicide. Therefore, in addition to providing immediate counseling to Seth, the school counselor has a legal and ethical obligation to call Seth's father. However, because Seth's father is unreachable and Seth is not sitting in a school office where he can be supervised to remain safe from harm, the online school counselor will need to take additional steps to ensure Seth's safety.

The school counselor may decide to look up emergency contact numbers for Seth and work to get in contact with a relative or family friend who might be able to care for Seth until his father is reached. If this approach fails and the school counselor cannot connect with an emergency contact, the school counselor can choose to call the police in Seth's area to conduct a welfare check. When talking to the police, the online school counselor should let them know he or she fears the student is suicidal, and the father is unreachable. Often, the police may bring a social worker or psychologist to the house to perform an assessment of the individual's psychological condition. In this case, the police, and possibly a social worker or therapist, can determine whether Seth may be such a threat to himself that he requires hospitalization.

It will also be important to encourage the father to seek professional help for Seth and help him get referrals to community agencies in the area. Seth's father should be educated about suicide risk in teens, and he should be strongly encouraged to seek professional help. At the end of the day, if the school counselor believes the father may be contributing to Seth's situation by engaging in what Seth deemed as a "rough" fight and by refusing to get Seth professional help, the school counselor may do well to consult with Child Protective Services in the area where Seth lives. School counselors can contact The Childhelp National Abuse Hotline, which is staffed 24 hours a day, seven days a week, with professional crisis counselors who have access to a database of 55,000 emergency, social service and support resources. All calls are anonymous. A qualified crisis counselor will answer and assist in determining whether a report should be made. The counselor can also connect you to the child welfare agency and the best possible resources in the area where your student lives. After ensuring Seth's safety and having a discussion with the father, it will be important for the school counselor to discuss the situation that occurred with the principal or administrator at his or her school. School policies may differ, but given the fact that Seth's emotional state and behaviors are interfering with his studies, some schools will require that Seth seek mental health treatment and provide a letter from his doctor stating he is healthy before being able to continue in classes.

– *Tracy Steele, Ph.D., director of counseling, Stanford Online High School; and Chloe Benjamin, school counselor, Stanford Online High School*

Making Connections

1. During your classroom guidance lessons you usually take your students to the computer lab to assist them in researching prospective colleges and career options. Describe the websites you will have them research and why you have chosen these sites.

2. You are a school counselor at an urban school where few students have access to the Internet or computers at home. How do you assist students in accessing the information they need for future goals and plans?

3. Explain how ASCA and ACA address school counselors' use of technology.

4. The creative writing teacher wants to create a blog where students can share their opinions of books they read throughout the semester. She is apprehensive about using the Internet to communicate with students because of the many cases she has heard of where teachers have lost their jobs for inappropriate discussions with students. She has come to you for advice. What advice will you give her?

5. Discuss the ethical codes of online counseling.

Key Terms

ASCA SCENE
Blogs
Cross-tabulate data
Cyberspace
Data warehousing
Digital footprint
Disinhibition effect
Facebook

Missouri's Facebook Statute
MySpace
Technologically literate
Twitter
Video conferencing
Virtual
Webinar

CHAPTER 4

Family Educational Rights and Privacy Act

IN THIS CHAPTER

Objectives

By the time you complete this chapter, you should be able to:

- Discuss the exceptions and revisions to the federal legislation Family Educational Rights and Privacy Act (FERPA, 1974).
- Define directory information and describe the precautionary methods that must be used when disclosing it.
- Identify the role of school counselors in protecting the privacy of students' education records and parents' rights to records.
- Identify situations in which FERPA regulations can affect how a school counselor performs his/her duties.
- Adhere to FERPA's rights for noncustodial parents.

Ethical Standards Addressed in This Chapter

Professionalism means knowing your professional associations' codes and adhering to them. The ASCA Ethical Standards for School Counselors most relevant to this chapter are the following:

- Professional school counselors maintain and secure records necessary for rendering professional services to the student as required by laws, regulations, institutional procedures and confidentiality guidelines. (A.8.a)
- Professional school counselors take appropriate and reasonable measures for maintaining confidentiality of student information and education records stored or transmitted through the use of computers, facsimile machines, telephones, voicemail, answering machines and other electronic or computer technology. (A.10.c)
- Professional school counselors inform parents/guardians of the school counselor's role to include the confidential nature of the counseling relationship between the school counselor and student. (B.2.a)
- Professional school counselors make reasonable efforts to honor the wishes of parents/guardians concerning information regarding the student unless a court order expressly forbids the involvement of a parent(s). In cases of divorce or separation school counselors exercise a good-faith effort to keep both parents informed, maintaining focus on the student and avoiding supporting one parent over another in divorce proceedings. (B.2.e)

- Professional school counselors understand about the "release of information" process and parental rights in sharing information and attempt to establish a cooperative and collaborative relationship with other professionals to benefit students. (C.2.d)
- Professional school counselors conduct appropriate research and report findings in a manner consistent with acceptable educational and psychological research practices. School counselors advocate for the protection of the individual students' identities when using data for research or program planning. (F.1.c)

The full text of the ASCA Ethical Standards for School Counselors is available at *www.schoolcounselor.org.*

Introduction

The 1974 Family Educational Rights and Privacy Act (FERPA) is federal legislation governing education records and dictating how all written information regarding a student is handled and disseminated for the protection of students and their families (Alexander & Alexander, 2011). The U.S. Department of Education (USDOE) Family Policy Compliance Office (FPCO), administers FERPA, which gives parents the opportunity to inspect and review their children's education records and have a voice in how that information is shared with others (USDOE/FPCO, 2011a). Managing the school's education records does not fall within the appropriate roles of a school counselor (ASCA, 2012), but it is important to have a working knowledge of FERPA guidelines to advocate for the legal and ethical protection of a school counselor's case notes and any other written information kept on a student (American School Counselor Association, 2010). Each school day represents multiple challenges school counselors and other educators must negotiate in complying with FERPA. FERPA's changes and challenges are addressed in the cases throughout this chapter.

FERPA changes with U.S. Supreme Court cases, new statutory acts such as the USA Patriot Act and tragic school events such as the Virginia Tech shooting. On Jan. 8, 2009, the USDOE enacted changes to FERPA regulations. Three of the changes involved attendance, peer grading and emergency situations. Attendance was redefined to include various forms of distance learning. The new changes also stated that grades on peer-graded papers are not education records until recorded in the grade book. This new statement in FERPA codifies a U.S. Supreme Court Case (*Owasso v.*

Falvo 534 U.S. 426 (2002). The new regulations broaden the authority of the institution to define a health and safety emergency and, therefore, give more latitude to take the totality of an emergency into consideration when deciding whether or not to release student information.

When changes are made to FERPA, it is important that school counselors are informed, but sometimes they are left out of the information loop. A case in point is the Uninterrupted Scholars Act (2012), which became law in January 2013. This act amended FERPA to permit schools to disclose a student's education records, without parental consent, to a representative of a state or local child welfare agency or tribal organization that has the right to access a student's case plan (as defined and determined by the state or tribal organization), is engaged in addressing the student's education needs and is authorized by the agency or organization to receive such records, when such agency or organization is legally responsible (in accordance with state or tribal law), for the care and protection of the student. Only 8 percent of surveyed ASCA members indicated they had been informed about the change by their school district (Stone, 2013c).

FERPA's primary purpose is to ensure parents' rights to view their children's education records, to seek to amend inaccurate information in the records and to decide, within certain parameters, which entities or individuals can access their child's records. Eligible students, those who reach the age of 18 while in secondary school, have access to their records (USDOE/FPCO, 2011b; USDOE/FPCO, 2011c). Noncustodial parents also have rights under FERPA (1974, 34 C.F.R. § 99.3). According to FERPA, a parent or eligible student must provide written consent before personally identifiable information is disclosed from a student's education records. Following is a partial list of the exceptions that do not require a parent or eligible student's permission:

- School officials with legitimate education interest (school counselors employed by or under contract to the school are considered school officials along with teachers and others)
- Other schools to which a student is transferring
- Federal, state or local education officials for purpose of audit or evaluation
- Those conducting specific studies for the school
- Organizations involved in accreditation
- Holders of a judicial order or lawfully issued subpoena
- Appropriate parties in connection with a health or safety emergency

■ Local and state authorities in the juvenile justice system, in compliance with specific state law

■ An agency caseworker or other representative of a state or local child welfare agency or tribal organization in relation to a foster child's case

FERPA affords parents and eligible students the right to seek to amend information in education records the parent or eligible student believes to be inaccurate or misleading. Once the request is made, the school must decide whether to amend the record as requested within a reasonable time after it receives the request. If the school decides not to amend the records as requested, it must inform the parent or eligible student of its decision. The parent/eligible student has a right to a hearing under FERPA. In an February 2013 survey of ASCA members, 72 percent responded said in the last 36 months no parent had asked for information to be removed or amended from his/her child's education record (Stone, 2013c), and 13 percent said this request had happened only once.

FERPA further allows for the dissemination of "directory information," without parent or eligible student consent. Directory information typically includes basic contact information about a student such as name, address and telephone number. However, FERPA allows school districts to determine the items they will consider directory information, within certain parameters. School districts can establish policies and procedures regarding the release of directory information, including having a limited directory information policy, and they may decide not to participate in releasing directory information at all. Parents also have the right to request their student's directory information not be released by opting out of the disclosure.

In this chapter, we will look at the many ways FERPA legislation affects students and families in schools. The cases presented will lead school counselors through the primary FERPA guidelines that will help protect student confidentiality under the FERPA legislation.

Getting Started: What Would You Do?

The following case is answered for you at the end of this chapter by two school counseling administrators. Before you read their responses, formulate in your own mind how you would approach this ethical dilemma.

REPORTING STUDENT INFRACTIONS TO COLLEGES

You gave a student a strong letter of recommendation regarding his character, service, leadership and academic record. The student, Mark, was accepted by his first-choice college, which subsequently received Mark's midterm report showing all A's. In April, school officials discovered Mark and two others had exchanged papers during a test in the first semester of trigonometry. The school disciplined all three students, and once the zero grade was factored into the final grade, the result was a drop to a letter grade of B. Are you under any legal or ethical obligation to report the cheating incident to the college? Will you be breaching any legal or ethical obligation if you do report the cheating incident to the college? How would you handle this ethical dilemma?

Working Through Case Studies

DIRECTORY INFORMATION

Ms. Sheffield fled several cities away from her abusive husband, bringing her children with her. She enrolled her fifth-grade son, Richard, in a nearby elementary school without disclosing their situation to any of the faculty or staff. Richard performed well at his new school and made the honor roll. The school published a list of the honor roll students in the newspaper, and Richard's name was included. Mr. Sheffield saw Richard's name in the paper and started contacting his estranged wife. Ms. Sheffield is furious; she feels she must uproot her family once again and seek a new town in which to hide. She maintains the school acted inappropriately by publishing her child's name without her permission. Is she correct?

Points to Consider

Schools or districts are encouraged to designate specific information as "directory information" or information about a student that would generally not be considered harmful or an invasion of privacy if disclosed. Directory information may include:

- Name
- Address
- Telephone number
- E-mail address

- Photograph
- Date and place of birth
- Dates of attendance
- Grade level
- Participation in officially recognized activities and sports
- Weight and height of members of athletic teams
- Degrees, honors and awards received
- Student ID number, user ID or other unique personal identifier used to communicate in electronic systems that cannot be used to access education records without a PIN, password, etc. (exception: prohibited for whole or parts of Social Security numbers) (USDOE/FPCO, 2011d).

Assuming the school district had a policy in place designating directory information, it was legal for the school to print Richard's name in the newspaper to recognize his academic achievement. FERPA allows for the publication of directory information, which includes the acknowledgment of honors or awards received. In fact, under FERPA, the school potentially could have also legally published Richard's photograph if that were an item designated by the school as directory information (USDOE/FPCO, 2011d). Most school districts use best practice to safeguard privacy rights and prevent this type of situation from occurring by having parents sign a publicity release form agreeing their child's photo or name can be used in the newspaper other media.

FERPA requires school districts to notify parents of their rights under FERPA each year. As part of that notification, schools also include the required notification concerning directory information, including advising parents they can opt out of having their child's directory information made public (1974, 34 C.F.R. § 99.7). In other words, parents can keep their child's directory information private. Schools may use a variety of vehicles for this annual notification to parents of their rights under FERPA, such as the student handbook, PTA newsletters, school calendars, special letters, e-mail, websites or newspaper articles. Schools should offer parents or eligible students who wish to opt out of directory information a reasonable amount of time to respond. School counselors are generally not placed in charge of educational records. In an February 2013 survey of ASCA members, 65 percent said the school counselors in their school were not in charge of receiving and sending education records (Stone, 2013c). Even though school counselors are not responsible as a member of the school community, they will want to know their school is complying with FERPA.

In an April 2013 survey, ASCA members responded to the question:

Which most closely describes your school's practice?

My school or school district complies with FERPA by
    annually giving each family their rights under FERPA
    through some written means such as a special letter,
    PTA bulletin, student handbook: . . . . .47 percent
No, my school or school district does not comply with
    FERPA by annually giving each family their rights
    under FERPA through some written means: . . . . .7 percent
I don't know: . . . . .47 percent

Richard's situation is especially sensitive because of the circumstances surrounding his personal life. Assuming the school district notified parents and eligible students of their right to opt out of the disclosure of directory information under FERPA, and Ms. Sheffield did not take advantage of the opportunity to opt her son out of directory information disclosures, the school was not in violation of FERPA by publishing the information about the student. However, an overburdened parent like Ms. Sheffield may be too consumed with creating a safe home for Richard to read the fine print regarding FERPA. Additionally, if the school counselor was made aware of the family situation, this would have provided an opportunity for the school counselor or other school personnel to discuss FERPA and its implications concerning directory information with this parent. Unless there is a court order specifically severing the father's rights, then Ms. Sheffield is breaking the law by hiding her children. The school counselor might be able to help Ms. Sheffield with a call to legal aid if she and her children need protection in the form of legal documents. Additionally, the school counselor could provide information on other community resources for survivors of domestic violence and their children. The school counselor might also increase contact with Richard and check in with his teachers periodically. Keeping the lines of communication open with Richard can foster a beneficial comfort level between the school counselor and him, cementing a trusting relationship where both Richard and Ms. Sheffield know they can turn to school officials and the school counselor in the future.

The Ann Arbor (Mich.) Public Schools district has established a website for parents to help them understand their rights under FERPA:

www.a2schools.org/aaps/parents/ferpa_information. School counselors may want to advocate that their school district establish a user-friendly website, and this might be a helpful model.

ACCESS TO DIRECTORY INFORMATION

A local business owner, Mr. Achinson, was denied a request for the class lists, names and addresses of the students in the local high school for a targeted marketing campaign. He works for a cruise line that offers special cruises for graduating seniors. Mr. Achinson knows the local school district gives the information to cap and gown and class ring vendors and colleges and the military. He believes the school district is acting capriciously and arbitrarily in denying his request and that school officials do not have the legal right to deny him the information. Is the school district acting within FERPA guidelines?

Points to Consider

While marketing campaigns like Mr. Achinson's offer students relatively harmless products or opportunities, this is not always the case. Students are targeted by programs and services promising everything from a quick and easy high school diploma to helping provide for a fee support for filling out the Free Application for Federal Student Aid (FAFSA, 2012), taking advantage of vulnerable students. FERPA permits schools to adopt limited directory information policies allowing the school district to limit the disclosure of directory information to specific parties or for specific purposes or both. Schools can choose to adopt policies prohibiting certain for-profit companies from accessing the information. Class ring companies, yearbook companies and other entities considered necessary to the graduation process that have a history of not abusing class lists are usually provided information.

Any school district receiving federal money must allow military recruiters the same access to students as college admissions counselors or business recruiters. Colleges and recruiters often are allowed access to students to discuss admissions, employment opportunities and so on; frequently, this takes place with the involvement of school counselors. Thus, if a school has a policy allowing colleges, college recruiters and employment recruiters on campus, then military recruiters must be allowed as well. Additionally, under the military recruiter provision under the Elementary and Secondary Education Act (ESEA) schools are required to provide recruiters with student directory information, such as names, addresses and phone numbers, unless a parent or student has opted out.

IDENTIFICATION BADGES AND DIRECTORY INFORMATION

Mrs. Hall, the mother of one of your students, comes to your office with a concern about her son, Andrew, who is new to your school this year. Andrew was the victim of severe bullying at his previous school, and at his parents request, the district allowed him to transfer to another school. Due to the harassing phone calls her son received at home, Mrs. Hall has changed the family's home phone number and has opted out of releasing Andrew's directory information. She is concerned about the school policy that requires all students to wear their ID badges, with their name and photo visible, at all times on campus. She worries friends of her son's bullies who attend the school will realize who her son is and that Andrew will now be bullied at his new school. Mrs. Hall feels that because she has opted out of releasing Andrew's directory information Andrew should be excused from following this policy. Is she correct?

Points to Consider

Information displayed on ID badges typically includes items usually considered directory information: a student's name, grade level and photograph. However, December 2011 changes to FERPA regulations state that opting out of directory information does not exempt students from school or district policies requiring students to wear or present identification cards or badges. Under FERPA, schools are not required to establish policies requiring students to wear ID badges, nor are they prohibited from having a ID badge policy (U.S. Department of Education, 2011b).

It is a common practice in schools throughout the United States to require all students to wear ID badges on campus. This allows intruders on campus to be more easily identified and is often intended as a measure to ensure student safety. As such, "The need for schools to implement measures to ensure the safety and security of students should not be impeded by a parent or student using FERPA's directory information opt-out provisions" (USDOE, 2011b). While Mrs. Hall's concern for her son's safety is legitimate, her choice to opt out of directory information does not excuse him from school policy. The fact that he is not wearing a badge might bring more attention to Andrew than fellow students paying attention to the badge he wears.

LEGITIMATE EDUCATIONAL INTEREST

Your cousin coaches Little League baseball and would like information on a student in your school whom he coaches. The child seems to be having difficulty with his vision. The coach asked the boy's parents about his problem, and the parents dismissed it by saying, "He can see; he is just uncoordinated." Your cousin would like you to look at the vision screening results in this child's education record to see if a problem has been noted and report back to him. Is there an ethical or legal dilemma here?

Points to Consider

FERPA guidelines delineate who may have access to education records without parental permission. School counselors and other educators who have "legitimate educational interest" (National Forum on Education Statistics, 2006, p. 4) can access education records. Legitimate educational interest generally means you may access an education record for the purpose of:

- Performing appropriate tasks within your job description
- Performing a task related to a student's education
- Performing a task related to discipline
- Providing a service or benefit related to the student or to the student's family such as counseling, health care or job placement.

School counselors typically have legitimate educational interest, not by virtue of their title but in the context of their work. However, school counselors do not have unrestrained, unlimited access to education records. When a school counselor legitimately needs to access a record, it can be done without parental permission. Examining an education record out of curiosity, however, to figure out what that new next-door neighbor does for a living or to see how many people live in the house is not a legitimate educational interest. Professional school counselors take great care to read records only if the action is within the parameters of legitimate educational interest (Stone, 2001; National Forum of Education Statistics, 2006).

In an April 2013 survey, ASCA members responded to the question:

If you keep electronic records can others who have legitimate educational interest (LEI) in your school enter the student management system and see what you have written in your case notes?

Yes, anyone with LEI can see my case notes: . . . . .5 percent
Yes, but only the educators with LEI who are
    directly working with the student such as
    the student's teacher and administrators: . . . . .9 percent
No, no one can see my records unless I give them
    access as they are password-protected: . . . . .16 percent
Not applicable: . . . . .70 percent

As the school counselor, you may not give the coach information on the vision screening results as this is outside the boundaries set by FERPA, unless the parents give consent for you to share this information. However, it is legitimate for you to take the information learned from the coach and review the student's education record to note if there are vision screening results, and contact the student's parents if the student needs attention. Advocacy is important, but even hinting to the Little League coach what you have learned is a FERPA violation.

School districts must "use reasonable methods to ensure that school counselors, teachers and other school officials (including outside service providers) obtain access to only those education records – paper or electronic – in which they have legitimate educational interests. School districts must ensure their administrative policy is effective and that they remain in compliance with the legitimate educational interest requirement for accessing records. In particular, if a parent or eligible student alleges a school official obtained access to the student's records without a legitimate educational interest, the burden is on the district or institution to show the school official had a legitimate educational interest in the information. Reasonableness depends ultimately on what are the usual and customary good business practices of similarly situated institutions, which, in turn, requires ongoing review and modification of methods and procedures as standards and technologies change" (USDOE/FPCO, 2008, p. 6-7).

CHILD WELFARE AGENCIES AND ACCESS TO EDUCATION RECORDS

A child protection caseworker is at your school to examine the education records of a child who was recently placed in foster care. The principal is requiring a subpoena, court order or parent signature before allowing the worker to see the education records. Is the principal acting legally?

Points to Consider

The Uninterrupted Scholars Act (2013), enacted Jan. 15, 2013, allows for the release of school records without prior written parental consent and notification to foster care agencies investigating a case. Under the Child Abuse Protection and Treatment Act (CAPTA), Child Protective Services workers have had access for decades to all school records without prior written parental consent if they are investigating a case of child abuse, neglect and maltreatment. Now with the Uninterrupted Scholars Act foster care case workers also have access. You can find CAPTA at *www.acf.hhs.gov/programs/cb/resource/capta2010* and the Uninterrupted Scholars Act at *www.govtrack.us/congress/bills/112/s3472.*

POTENTIALLY VIOLENT STUDENTS: EDUCATION RECORDS

Clifton is a student you have been counseling. He is a quiet, brooding young man who will not make eye contact with others and seems sullen and withdrawn. On the occasions he does speak, his comments are negative and sarcastic. His remarks are often related to others' "incompetence." Clifton appears to have little or no positive contact with his peers at school. He brags considerably about his prowess in martial arts. Clifton is a skilled fighter who scares people who are much larger and stronger. He has been known to become violent when he feels "pushed." Students say, "Don't mess with Clifton. He is crazy." You are also convinced this young man is seriously troubled and become alarmed when he names Lee as a student that he is particularly repulsed by, "I just hate him." Where if anywhere do you go with this information?

Points to Consider

The school counselor must share the concern with administration, as administration must act to protect Lee. The administration may choose to call a meeting of Clifton's teachers to get a collective sense of what others are seeing and may call the parents of both boys.

In informal polls at more than 200 legal and ethical workshops, a large number of attendees raised their hands when asked if they could name a student whom they feared could be a violent member of society (Stone, 2008). While this may seem discriminatory to predict something so vile, the unfortunate truth is that school counselors often see signs and symptoms in certain students that cause them grave concern but experience uncertainty in determining where to go with the information. Beyond the support school counselors regularly exercise in trying to shepherd students like Clifton through the referral process to secure the most intensive counseling services, there are still the nagging questions about who and at what point someone should be notified about your fears. Clifton is not threatening any particular person, but he is nonetheless a potential source of concern given his explosive, brooding behavior.

When deciding the best course of action, many believe educators' hands are often tied due to federal statutes protecting students' privacy rights and antidiscrimination laws restricting how schools can deal with students who have mental health problems (Jones, 2012; Lewin, 2007). Caught between privacy rights and school safety, educators look for support from the FPCO. "FERPA is not intended to be an obstacle to school safety" (USDOE, 2007). In an emergency situation, FERPA permits school officials to disclose, without consent, education records, including personally identifiable information from those records, to protect the health or safety of students or other individuals. In 2009, this was expanded to move from "strict construction of a health and safety emergency" to a "rational basis test for disclosure of education records in an emergency." At such times, records and information may be released to appropriate parties such as law enforcement officials, public health officials and trained medical personnel. This exception is limited to the period of the emergency and generally does not allow for a blanket release of personally identifiable information from a student's education records (FERPA 34 CFR § 99.31(a)(10) and § 99.36). The most up-to-date information on FERPA and school safety can be found at: *http://www2.ed.gov/policy/gen/guid/ fpco/ferpa/safeschools/index.html*. FERPA empowers school officials to act decisively and quickly when issues arise (USDOE/FPCO, 2007).

In the case of Clifton, his actions may not fit the health and safety emergency exception in FERPA. It has to be an "emergency" for it to fit. Don't fail to have the conversation with administration about Clifton. The first step for the administration might be to meet with Clifton's parents and provide them with a school counselor-generated list of mental health agencies for Clifton's family. Educators keep a careful watch, and if this escalates, the school will have to contact the police or mental health agency.

FERPA "does not prohibit a school official from disclosing information about a student if the information is obtained through the school official's personal knowledge or observation and not from the student's education records. For example, if a teacher overhears a student making threatening remarks to other students, FERPA does not protect that information, and the teacher may disclose what he or she overheard to appropriate authorities" (USDOE/FPCO, 2007, p. 1).

PURGING EDUCATION RECORDS

A first-grader has just been adopted by her stepfather. The student's natural father agreed to the adoption. Her mother requests that all information regarding the natural father be purged from the cumulative folder. The principal has appointed you to handle this situation. Can the record be purged?

Points to Consider

Records are not meant to be kept absolutely intact. FERPA allows for purging of records. If the entry on the record no longer has a legitimate purpose and the parent wants you to alter the record, then the designee can comply and amend the record. Maintaining the integrity of education records is important but not more so than respecting the parents' right to advocate for the privacy and accuracy of their child's educational record. The main point is that FERPA does not require a school to maintain any records, and records may be destroyed unless a parent or eligible student has an outstanding request to inspect and review the records or the records have been subpoenaed.

There will be times, however, when parents or eligible students will have their request to have an item purged from an education record denied. FERPA states: "An educational agency or institution shall give a parent or eligible student, on request, an opportunity for a hearing to challenge the content of the student's education records on the grounds that the information contained in the education records is inaccurate, misleading or in violation of the privacy rights of the student" (1974, 34 C.F.R. 99.21). "If, as a result of the hearing, the educational agency or institution decides the information in the education record is not inaccurate, misleading or otherwise in violation of the privacy rights of the student, the parents will be informed of the right to place a statement in the record commenting on the contested information in the record or stating why he or she disagrees with the decision of the agency or institution or both" (1974, 34 C.F.R. 99.21).

You can learn more by reading "Excerpts from a Letter to Parent re: Amendment of Special Education Records," in the FERPA Online Library at *www2.ed.gov/policy/gen/guid/fpco/doc/hastings82004.doc.*

CASE NOTES AND EDUCATION RECORDS
You have been seeing Stephen off and on for the first six months of the school year. His mother is in a battle with the school district about her son's educational opportunities. You have received a request from Stephen's mother for copies of your case notes. Are you legally required to provide her with your case notes?

Points to Consider
Not all the information collected and maintained by schools and school employees about students is subject to the access and disclosure requirements under FERPA. One of the six categories exempt from the definition of "education records" under FERPA is records made by teachers, supervisors, school counselors, administrators and other school personnel that are kept in the sole possession of the maker of the record and are not accessible or revealed to any other person except a temporary substitute for the maker of the record. A sole-possession record is a memory jogger note, not your official case records, and only memory joggers fall under sole-possession records. This is found under 99.3, "education records," at the following link *http://www2.ed.gov/policy/gen/reg/ferpa/index.html.*

"For example, a teacher or school counselor who observes a student and takes a note to remind himself or herself of the student's behavior has created a sole-possession record, so long as he or she does not share the note with anyone else" (Federal Register, 2000).

Parents have rights to education records. Therefore, if our case notes are not sole-possession records, meaning they meet the criteria, then we are legally required to respect the spirit and intent of FERPA and provide these case notes as education records to the requesting parent. School counselors in noneducational settings do not have to filter what they write through the lens of FERPA, as their records will not cross the line into education records. FERPA cast a blanket over every word written and maintained on a student in a public school and also a private school if the private school receives even one dollar of federal funds.

School counselors do not usually keep prolific notes, as the reality in the course of a school counselor's day is that they do not have time to write detailed case notes. In an February 2013 survey of ASCA members, 83 percent of the respondents said they do not keep detailed case notes on every student they see. Five percent do not keep notes at all, and only 12 percent responded that they consistently keep written case notes on the majority of the students they counsel and the notes are detailed (Stone, 2013c). Often, case notes simply record the student's name, time and a few details to jog the school counselor's memory. However, when we do write case notes, in the case of a child-abuse situation, a student who is self-mutilating or a student who has suicidal ideations, we take great care to write professionally and with caution because we know our notes can be subpoenaed in most states, and parents can access the case notes if they are demanded.

AMENDING CASE NOTES

A parent just demanded your case notes on her son, and you complied. This incident has caused you to rethink all your notes and second-guess yourself on information you have kept in notes. You want to go back in on a number of students and review and revise your notes to remove information you would not want parents to see. Can you rewrite or purge case notes?

Points to Consider

In absence of a district policy or a subpoena or court order (or the hint that one is coming) it is appropriate and acceptable to review notes from the past and amend or even delete the entire note. Again, if your case notes have been subpoenaed or you think they are about to be, you would not amend or purge your case note on the case at hand as you would be interfering with a rule of evidence.

PROTECTING GROUP MEMBER IDENTITY

Your case notes contain multiple names of children in your group. Reginald May's mother has requested your case notes on the group. You suspect she is gearing up for a nasty custody fight. Do you have to comply with Ms. May's request? Can you eliminate all the names of the other children before complying with her request?

Points to Consider

The school counselor is able to redact all the other names and identifying information pertaining to other students. Under FERPA, parents "have the right to inspect and review only such part of such material or document as relates to such student or to be informed of the specific information contained in such part of such material" (USDOE, 2004, p. 4).

INDIVIDUALS WITH DISABILITIES EDUCATION ACT AND FERPA

Mr. Markett is an attentive parent, whose child Shane is in exceptional student education (ESE). Shane has academic, social and emotional problems that are well-documented by the ESE teacher on the report card under "work habits and personal interactions with others." Mr. Markett disagrees with the evaluations and wants them purged from the education record. The principal has denied the request to purge the report card record and has put you in charge of the due process hearing. Is the principal acting legally by denying the parent's request? Should the school counselor be in charge of the due process hearing?

Points to Consider

Exceptional student education records also fall under FERPA and therefore are governed by FERPA. Additionally, the Individuals With Disabilities Education Act (IDEA), federal guidelines for ESE administered by the Office of Special Education, spells out parents' and students' rights regarding ESE records. Therefore, ESE records are subject to FERPA.

However, this scenario does not involve Shane's ESE records. Therefore a due process hearing under ESE is not necessary in this case. The work habit evaluation part of Shane's education record stands. Parental rights to challenge information are not unlimited. A school is not required by FERPA or IDEA to give parents the right to seek to change substantive decisions made by school officials, such as grades or other evaluations, including decisions regarding special education students (USDOE, 2004, para. 4). Therefore, the work habit evaluation part of Shane's education record stands, and due process is not necessary.

If during a legitimate hearing parents are denied the right to remove or change information, then each time the contested part of the record is given out, the parents can require that their statement of protest be attached (FERPA regulations, 34 CFR § 99.22(c)).

SECTION 504 AND FERPA

Over the past few years, you have noticed an increase in the number of students in your school who have 504 plans. Are these plans considered education records? What should you know about protecting the privacy of these students?

Points to Consider

Under Section 504 of the Rehabilitation Act of 1973, students can receive aids and services if they "have a physical or mental impairment that substantially limits one or more major life activities, have a record of such an impairment or (are) regarded as having such an impairment" (Office for Civil Rights, 2011, para. 20). A student's Section 504 plan is an education record and is protected under FERPA, as would be any other education records. Section 504 plans can be maintained anywhere and by anyone considered a school official and can be destroyed at any time after the student leaves the school or district, as long as there is not an outstanding request for the records. The Office for Civil Rights provides extensive information on Section 504 and students' rights at *http://www2.ed.gov/about/offices/list/ocr/504faq.html.*

STUDENT ACCESS TO EDUCATION RECORDS

One of your 17-year-old high school juniors comes in and asks to review her education records. Can you honor this student's request to review her own education records?

Points to Consider

FERPA permits, but does not require, school officials to share education records with a noneligible student. A request by a student to view her or his records would most likely be addressed under the policies and procedures of a particular school or school district and, if allowed, would probably be conducted under adult supervision. Students who are 18 or older have the right to review their education records.

Under current regulations, all rights of parents under FERPA, such as the right to review education records and consent to disclosure of their child's education records, transfer to the student once the student has reached 18 years of age or attends a postsecondary institution and thereby becomes an "eligible student." Current regulations also provide that, even after a student has become an "eligible student" under FERPA, postsecondary institutions (and high schools, for students over 18 years of age) may allow parents to have access to their child's education records, without the student's consent, in the following circumstances: the student is a dependent for federal income tax purposes (§ 99.31(a)(8) or the disclosure is in connection with a health or safety emergency under the conditions specified in § 99.36 (i.e., if knowledge of the information is necessary to protect the health or safety of the student or other individuals (§ 99.31(a)(10), USDOE, 2008, p. 4.)

MARRIED STUDENTS AND EDUCATION RECORDS

Faye, a 16-year-old married student, wants to deny her parents access to her education records. Can Faye prohibit her parents from obtaining her records?

Points to Consider

If a student is emancipated, the parents still have the right to the student's education records until the student turns 18. The school must provide access to the parents and may provide access to the student under FERPA.

VIDEO IMAGES AND FERPA

A student is in trouble for bullying, and it was caught on a school security camera. Her mother is threatening to sue because she claims the video images are an invasion of her daughter's privacy under FERPA. Is she correct?

Points to Consider

The mother might be correct if the taping violates state law; however, this does not violate FERPA. "Schools are increasingly using security cameras as a tool to monitor and improve student safety. Images of students captured on security videotapes that are maintained by the school's law enforcement unit are not considered education records under FERPA. Accordingly, these videotapes may be shared with parents of students whose images are on the video and with outside law enforcement authorities, as appropriate. Schools that do not have a designated law enforcement unit might consider designating an employee to serve as the law enforcement unit in order to maintain the security camera and determine the appropriate circumstances in which the school would disclose recorded images" (USDOE/FPCO, 2007, p. 1).

VIOLATING THE PRIVACY OF EDUCATION RECORDS

The copy machine is in the nurse's office. You are busy making photocopies of a student's education record when a student begins experiencing difficulty breathing. You drop everything to call 911 and assist school officials in helping the child. Twenty-five minutes pass before you are able to return to the copy machine. In the interim, a student who was ill and waiting in the nurse's office for her parent read sensitive information from the education record about the student's past misconduct and quickly spread the information to other students. The administration was able to trace the source back to the unprotected education record and the student who read it. The offended child's parents are preparing a lawsuit against the district and you. How have the courts responded when confidential information from a student's record has been revealed? How does FERPA apply in this situation?

Points to Consider

FERPA does not give individuals the right to sue educational institutions that violate the law's provisions by divulging confidential student information. In a decision involving a lawsuit against Gonzaga University, the U.S. Supreme Court held that the original purpose of FERPA was not to give individual students and their families the litigious license to bring charges against educational institutions for violating the privacy of education records (*Gonzaga University. v. Doe* (2002)). Rather, FERPA was designed to hold institutions accountable to the federal government for following guidelines involving privacy issues and confidentiality of education records.

The justices held that FERPA intended that the U.S. secretary of education would enforce its privacy provisions, mainly by withholding federal funds to educational institutions that failed to change their policies to comply. Based on this Supreme Court case, the parents in the scenario above would not be able to seek damages for a breach in the confidentiality of their student's record (*Gonzaga University v. Doe* (2002)). The parent could file a complaint with FPCO alleging that the school violated FERPA. School officials should try to work with the parent and explain the situations.

NONCUSTODIAL PARENTS AND EDUCATION RECORDS

One of your students, Justina, has a history of conflicts with her mother, with whom she lives, and is often in your office distraught over their latest verbal bout. You are worried, as Justina appears withdrawn, distracted and depressed. You suggest that you need to involve her mother so she can get some help, but she begs you to call her father instead. You honor her wishes and call her father but explain to her that you must inform her mother also. Her father, the noncustodial parent, immediately comes to the school to discuss the situation and to pick up copies of Justina's education records to take to a psychologist whose help he will seek. Justina's mother is furious that you contacted Justina's father and says she is refusing to allow you or any other school representative to contact the father or give him information about Justina. Were you right to call Justina's father even though she lives with her mother during the school week? Does Justina's father have the right to be included in parent-teacher conferences and to receive education records? Is the school obligated to notify the custodial parent before contacting the noncustodial parent?

Points to Consider

FERPA clarifies that "An educational agency or institution shall give full rights under the act to either parent, unless the agency or institution has been provided with evidence that there is a court order, state statute or legally binding document relating to such matters as divorce, separation or custody that specifically revokes these rights" (99.4).

You may contact and involve noncustodial parents in an academic or emotional issue. In an effort to preserve the relationship with the custodial parent, you may decide to inform the custodial parent that you have called the noncustodial parent. This is a judgment call that would depend on the context, history and the student experiencing the problem.

Consider the court case *Page, Petitioner, v. Rotterdam-Mohonasen Central School District* (1981). First-grader Eric Page lived with his mother, who was legally separated from his father. Mr. Page tried to meet with the educators in Eric's school and to review his son's education records so he could stay involved in his son's academic progress. However, Mrs. Page contended that the courts has awarded her custody of Eric and that, consequently, Mr. Page had "abandoned" any interest he had in Eric's education. She requested that the school deny Mr. Page's access to Eric's records, and the school followed Mrs. Page's directions.

The lawsuit against the Rotterdam-Mohonasen Central School District resulted in Mr. Page being given full access to Eric's teachers and also to his records, in accordance with FERPA, which allows inspection of school records by either parent, regardless of custody issues. According to the court, "Educators and school districts are charged with the duty to act in the best educational interests of the children committed to their care, and although it may cause some inconvenience, those interests dictate that educational information be made available to both parents of every school child fortunate enough to have two parents interested in his welfare" (*Page, Petitioner, v. Rotterdam-Mohonasen Central School District* (1981)).

All 50 states and the District of Columbia have adopted the Uniform Child Custody Jurisdiction Act in an effort to support both parents' involvement in their child's life. When deciding custody using the Uniform Marriage and Divorce Act decisions in part to favor the parent determined to be most likely to keep the other parent involved in the child's life (Uniform Law Commission, 2012).

STEPPARENTS AND EDUCATION RECORDS

One of your seventh-graders, Joseph, is new at school and is having a difficult time adjusting. Joseph has just moved across the country after his mother sent him to live with his father and stepmother. You have worked with Joseph, but you have not been successful in getting his father involved. Joseph's stepmother is receptive and offers to come to the school for a parent conference and to check and sign for his daily progress reports. Can you involve Joseph's stepmother in parent conferences, progress reports, report cards and other education records?

Points to Consider

FERPA defines the term "parent" as "a natural parent, a guardian or an individual acting as a parent in the absence of a parent or a guardian." Additionally, the U.S. Department of Education has stated, "A parent is absent if he or she is not present in the day-to-day home environment of the child." Accordingly, a stepparent has rights under FERPA where the stepparent is present on a day-to-day basis in the home with the child and the other parent is absent from that home. In such cases, stepparents have the same rights to education records under FERPA, as do natural parents. Conversely, a stepparent who is not present on a day-to-day basis in the home of the child does not have rights under FERPA with respect to such child's education records" (USDOE/FPCO, 2004).

RESEARCH INVOLVING STUDENTS

You are the school counselor at Gracian Howell Elementary School. The discipline referral rate is high, and you want to deliver strategies to address the rate. First, you are trying to better understand the problem. A University of the West counselor educator has been working with you to design lessons addressing the discipline problem. First, you and the university counselor educator collected and analyzed aggregated data for the discipline referral rate for all students. Next, you, the school counselor, identified the chronic discipline referrals. You obtained parental notification for the 12 students who were the chronic discipline referrals. You gave the counselor educator the list without any personally identifying information so students remained anonymous. You, the school counselor, meet with the eight teachers who have the 12 students and ask them to track student behavior on a rating chart. You plan to use the disciplinary records of these students to complete the data. In the final report, you will not identify students by name to the university. The university will never know the students' names. Have you followed FERPA laws?

Points to Consider
Yes, you followed FERPA when you completed these steps:

- All the data were collected and analyzed by you, the school counselor, in an effort to learn more about patterns of discipline referrals in your school to address the problem.
- All the data containing identifying information were absent from the file, and nonpersonal identifiers (Student A, B, C...) were used when given to the university counselor educator.
- The students' parents gave consent for the 12 students to have their discipline data disclosed.
- The school counselor gave the counselor educator the list with 12 students with all personally identifying information removed so students remained anonymous.

All universities have internal review boards established to approve research projects in advance so human subjects are protected legally and ethically. Additionally, the school district probably has a research department with whom the school counselor would need to seek permission before starting the study. Also, the final report would pass the FERPA test if all other types of identifying information were also removed. For example, if the report discusses a 14-year-old Asian male in the sixth grade and there is only one student fitting that description, then the study has failed the FERPA test.

In addition to FERPA protection, there is the Protection of Pupil Rights Amendment (USDOE, 2002). PPRA applies to the programs and activities of a local education agency (LEA), a school or other recipient of funds under any program funded by the U.S. Department of Education. It governs the administration to students of a survey, analysis or evaluation concerning one or more of the following eight protected areas:

- political affiliations or beliefs of the student or the student's parent
- mental or psychological problems of the student or the student's family
- sex behavior or attitudes
- illegal, anti-social, self-incriminating or demeaning behavior
- critical appraisals of other individuals with whom respondents have close family relationships
- legally recognized privileged or analogous relationships, such as those of lawyers, physicians and ministers
- religious practices, affiliations or beliefs of the student or student's parent
- income (other than that required by law to determine eligibility for participation in a program or for receiving financial assistance under such program)

PPRA also concerns marketing surveys and other areas of student privacy, parental access to information and the administration of certain physical examinations to minors. The rights under PPRA transfer from the parents to a student who is 18 years old or an emancipated minor under state law.

LEAs must provide parents and eligible students effective notice of their rights under PPRA, which in part explains their right to provide consent before their child participates in a survey concerning one or more of the eight protected areas listed above.

A model PPRA general notification for use by LEAs may also be obtained on FPCO's website at: *http://www2.ed.gov/policy/gen/guid/fpco/index.html.* PPRA requires LEAs to work with parents to develop and adopt certain policies. Also, PPRA requires LEAs to "directly" notify, such as through U.S. mail or e-mail, parents of students who are scheduled to participate in the specific activities or surveys listed below and provide an opportunity for parents to opt their child out of participation in the specific survey or activity.

- The administration of any survey concerning one or more of the eight protected areas listed above if it is not funded in whole or in part with Department of Education funds. (LEAs must obtain active consent, and may not use an opt-out procedure, if the survey is funded in whole or in part with Department of Education funds).
- Activities involving the collection, disclosure or use of personal information collected from students for marketing purposes or to sell or otherwise provide the information to others for marketing purposes.

- Any nonemergency, invasive physical examination or screening that is 1) required as a condition of attendance, 2) administered by the school and scheduled by the school in advance and 3) not necessary to protect the immediate health and safety of the student or of other students. This law does not apply to any physical examination or screening that is permitted or required by state law, including physical examinations or screenings permitted without parental notification (U.S. Department of Education, 2011b).

LETTERS OF RECOMMENDATION

Evelyn is applying to a competitive university, and your letter of recommendation will be a critical part of her admission to that school. Evelyn's freshman year was academically dismal. She confided in you that she was being physically abused by her boyfriend during her freshman year but ended the relationship after seven months. Evelyn has been a stellar student since her sophomore year, and she seems like an almost entirely different person compared with when you first met her as a freshman. You are considering explaining all this in your letter of recommendation in hopes that Evelyn will be judged only on what she has done since leaving the abusive relationship. Legally and ethically, can you include this information in a letter of recommendation?

Points to Consider

School counselors conscientiously work to behave legally in writing letters of recommendation, and they find their guidance primarily in FERPA. On the other hand, ethical considerations involving letters of recommendation are far more complicated for school counselors. In an informal survey of more than 2,000 school counselors (Stone, 2004b), respondents overwhelmingly said they would consider it a breach of confidentiality to put sensitive, confidential information in a letter of recommendation without a student's permission. Most respondents said they would not put Evelyn in the position of having to make that decision but would write the letter to convey triumph without giving the details of her past. Even when it comes to confidential information that, if known, would benefit a student, school counselors would rather get the student's permission.

If the college requires a statement or essay as part of the admission application process this could provide Evelyn with an opportunity to explain about the trauma she suffered in ninth grade. With the school counselor's assistance, Evelyn can also contact the admissions office and speak to an admissions counselor regarding her academic record.

Typically, you write a letter of recommendation because the student or student's parent has asked you to do so. Legally, school counselors can include anything in a letter that is common knowledge and observable such as, "Kennard has never let the fact that he is wheelchair-bound keep him from being an active and high-profile school leader, engaged in numerous school activities such as…" It is best practice to get Kennard and his parent's permission to include his disability, as they might not want this known at this juncture.

Further, under sec. 99.12 of FERPA, a postsecondary institution may prevent a student from inspecting and reviewing "confidential letters and confidential statements of recommendation" if the student has waived his or her right to inspect and review the letters and statements under FERPA and the letter has to do with admission to an institution, application for employment or receipt of an honor or honorary recognition. FPCO interprets this provision to apply to high school students as well. If a high school student has waived his right, the waiver has to be in writing and signed by the student, regardless of age.

In a Position to Know: School Counseling Administrators Speak

The case presented at the beginning of the chapter is revisited here and answered by two school counseling administrators. Compare their answers with your approach.

REPORTING STUDENT INFRACTIONS TO COLLEGES

You gave a student a strong letter of recommendation regarding his character, service, leadership and academic record. The student, Mark, was accepted by his first-choice college, which subsequently received Mark's midterm report showing all A's. In April, school officials discovered Mark and two others had exchanged papers during a test in the first semester of trigonometry. The school disciplined all three students, and once the zero grade was factored into the final grade, the result was a drop to a letter grade of B. Are you under any legal or ethical obligation to report the cheating incident to the college? Will you be breaching any legal or ethical obligation if you do report the cheating incident to the college? How would you handle this ethical dilemma?

Responses from School Counseling Administrators

Ethically, this is a case that must be decided by the individual school counselor, as there are no hard and fast rules governing what a school counselor should do. Legally, the school counselor is under no obligation to call or contact the university to inform it of changes in the status of students who have applied to the school. Knowing this doesn't necessarily help you do what is right. Written below are some considerations to take into account.

The line of reasoning is that this student did not deserve the glowing letter and that it would be wrong to let the recommendation letter stand without adding the new information. However, if we follow this line of reasoning, where does it end? Is it then a school counselor's responsibility to inform potential employers, military recruiters, community colleges, career and technical schools and other postsecondary placements of any new and potentially damaging information that came to light since the writing of any letter or evaluation? And, perhaps more importantly, is cheating the only offense that would trigger a report to any of these agencies? What does a school counselor choose to report or not report after an initial letter of recommendation or evaluation?

On the other hand, school counselors might respond that they do not believe it is their responsibility to notify the university. A school counselor believes the letter was written in good faith based on the information available at the time, and no obligation exists to voluntarily provide additional information to the university. The drop in the grade or any additional discipline issued by the school should be consequence enough without the incident of poor judgment affecting a student's entire future.

A potential downside to not informing the university is that many university admissions counselors believe they should be informed and could devalue future letters of recommendation written by the school counselor should this information come to light. This could adversely affect future college applicants who have letters of recommendation from this school counselor. Nevertheless, a school counselor's role is to be a student advocate, not a university gatekeeper.

School counselors may believe the grade change or cheating incident should be reported to the university in the belief that their own integrity will be called into question. Caution is needed, as this could be a problem with FERPA. Yes, schools can send information to a school that a student is seeking to enroll in (FERPA, 99.31 (a)(2), but an out-of-the-blue call to report a discipline infraction may be problematic. Instead the school or school counselor might choose to send the disciplinary record as part of the final transcript or a transfer of record to the new school. All of this has to meet conditions of disclosure under FERPA. What is needed is careful consideration that parent and student rights are not being violated under FERPA. Through your administration, seek help from the school district's legal arm.

A third approach might work as an effective compromise. Upon the lowering of the grade, the school counselor sends the university a corrected transcript with no explanation. It is then the university's responsibility to call and inquire regarding the change of grade. If the university calls, the school counselor can truthfully explain the grade change. The school counselor should also inform the student that should the university call regarding the grade change, the school counselor is ethically responsible to tell the truth for the reason the grade changed. The student may make the decision to "do the right thing" and inform the university himself before the university inquires with the school counselor.

In any case, it would undoubtedly help the situation if the school district had a policy in place regarding letters of recommendation and updates. A short paragraph to be included with a recommendation form or evaluation could delineate the district policy. This would effectively inform both the student and any recommendation letter or evaluation recipient of the guidelines in place to protect all parties involved.
– *Bob Tyra, Consultant, Tyra Consulting, and retired Los Angeles County Office of Education project director, and Paul Meyers, superintendent, South Bay Union School District in Eureka, Calif.*

Making Connections

1. Based on your knowledge of a school counselor's role regarding education records, identify some personal changes you would make if you have free range.

2. Give examples of current practices by your school that potentially violate FERPA.

3. What is the current method used by your school to tell students and parents about directory information and their rights? Is this a good method? If not, what changes would you suggest?

4. A licensed mental health counselor, whom you know to be a reputable therapist, wants to write a book about student behavioral issues in middle schools. The mental health counselor asks you to identify common behavioral issues in your school and to supply notes about these behaviors for the book. What should you do? Give some examples of best practices.

5. A teacher in your school makes a habit of making her students' grades public in an attempt to motivate them to perform better. You realize this practice is quite hurtful to students and does not produce the aimed outcome. What can you do to advocate for these students?

6. A parent wants to change an "inaccurate" notation in her child's file regarding alleged behavioral issues. The parent wants this because she claims the teacher had personality conflicts with her child. You are the principal's designee for handling this matter. What are the due process procedures you must offer this parent?

7. A 14-year-old student tells you that her biological father, whom she met for the first time recently, has suddenly appeared in her life and wants to be involved in her education. The father's name is on her birth certificate filed in her educational record. The student and the student's mother do not want him to be able to have any access to her education records or her teachers. Can you comply with their request?

Key Terms

Custodial parent
Directory information
Due process hearing
Family Educational Rights and
   Privacy Act
Family Policy Compliance Office
Individuals with Disabilities
   Education Act
Legitimate educational interest

Noncustodial parent
Protection of Pupil Rights
   Amendment
Uniform Child Custody Jurisdiction
   Act
Uniform Marriage Act
Uninterrupted Scholars Act
USA Patriot Act

Negligence

IN THIS CHAPTER

Objectives

By the time you have completed this chapter, you should be able to:

- Define negligence as it pertains to school counseling.
- Understand the definition of malpractice in school counseling.
- Identify the components of standard of care.
- Understand *in loco parentis.*
- Identify the four elements of negligence.
- Discuss practices that may lead to negligence in school counseling.
- Discuss how to prevent negligence in academic advising, suicide prevention and other potentially difficult areas.
- Apply the ethical standards that govern competency in school counseling.

Ethical Standards Addressed in This Chapter

Professionalism means knowing your professional associations' ethical codes and adhering to them. The ASCA Ethical Standards for School counselors most relevant to this chapter include the following:

- Each person has the right to privacy and thereby the right to expect the school/school counselor/student relationship to comply with all laws, policies and ethical standards pertaining to confidentiality in the school setting. (Preamble)
- Professional school counselors are knowledgeable of laws, regulations and policies relating to students and strive to protect and inform students regarding their rights. (A.1.d)
- Professional school counselors adhere to laws, local guidelines and ethical standards of practice when assisting parents/guardians experiencing family difficulties interfering with the student's effectiveness and welfare. (B.1.b)
- Professional school counselors accept employment only for positions for which they are qualified by education, training, supervised experience, state and national professional credentials and appropriate professional experience. (D.1.e)
- Professional school counselors function within the boundaries of individual professional competence and accept responsibility for the consequences of their actions. (E.1.a)

The full text of the ASCA Ethical Standards for School Counselors is available at *www.schoolcounselor.org*.

Introduction

The fundamental basis for exploring legal concepts in this chapter is that school counselors live and work in a litigious society. People sue. Historically, the chances that school counselors would be sued in the course of doing their jobs have been slim (Remley & Herlihy, 2001; Zirkel, 2001).

"Even though various special-interest groups have contributed to skewed perceptions, objective research reveals that K-12 education litigation, in terms of published court decisions, has gradually declined since the 1970s; the outcomes have continued to favor school district defendants; and the outcomes of the student suits, which are of primary concern to school counselors, have shifted significantly further in favor of school district defendants" (P.A. Zirkel, personal communication, Dec. 1, 2008).

This fact may provide little comfort since the emotional and financial burden involved in defending against a lawsuit can be substantial. This chapter is designed to help familiarize school counselors with their obligations to students in issues involving the court system, specifically with regard to negligence.

Constitutional law involves two major categories, criminal law and civil law. A criminal wrong is a crime against society. The degree of the crime can be categorized as either a felony or a misdemeanor, with a felony carrying a longer prison term (Alexander & Alexander, 2011). A civil wrong is a wrong against another person that causes physical, emotional or monetary damage and for which the plaintiffs can seek compensation. An individual can be exonerated of a crime, yet be found guilty of breaching the plaintiff's individual rights (Scheidegger, 2008). School counselors who find themselves in legal difficulty are frequently defending themselves in a negligence or civil wrong case. School counselors charged with job-related criminal activity are usually defendants in a case of sexual abuse of a minor student in their school.

This chapter will focus primarily on negligence and malpractice. Negligence is a civil wrong or tort, in which one person breaches the duty owed to another. Malpractice is the negligent rendering of professional services (Remley & Herlihy, 2007; Watts, 2005).

Negligence: As a general legal principle, civil liability for negligence accrues if a school counselor is found to owe a duty to another person, breaches that duty by not living up to expected standards and, as a result of the breach of duty, causes damages to another person. According to Prosser (1971), all four of the following elements must be present for negligence to be proven:

- The school counselor owes a duty to a student or parent/guardian of a student.
- The school counselor breaches the duty owed.
- There is sufficient legal causal connection between the breach of duty and the injury.
- The student or parent/guardian suffers an injury or damages, and an assessment is made.

Duty: Duty requires the establishment of a relationship whereby the defendant owes the plaintiff a duty to act reasonably (Scharffs, B., & Welch, J., 2005; Cardi, J., & Green, M., 2008; Watts, 2005). A school counselor who sponsors the Foreign Exchange Club and takes the members to the beach for their end-of-the-year party is acting *in loco parentis*. The school counselor owes a duty if a student enters the water and starts to drown whereas a passerby does not in most states even if that bystander is Ryan Lochte, Michael Phelps or Mark Spitz. The stronger the duty, the greater the legal responsibility and concurrent legal liability if something goes wrong (Alexander & Alexander, 2011; Cardi, J., & Green, M., 2008; Imber & Van Geel, 2009).

Breach: The judgment as to whether or not a breach has occurred with regard to the duty owed is centered on the issues of reasonability and an agreed-upon standard of care. Reasonableness includes the precautions you take. When taking the students to the beach, did you have enough chaperones? Did you explain to the students that they could not enter the water for any reason? Did you position yourself so that you would know if any student wandered away? Did you take along someone trained in first aid? Another test of whether one has acted reasonably is the potential for harm and the possible magnitude of harm. There is significant likelihood of harm on field trips to locations with water, and the seriousness of harm, such as potential drowning, is great. School districts across the country have banned field trips to pools, beaches, rivers and lakes because of the likelihood of harm.

Reasonableness: This is difficult to define as it is person-specific and depends on an individual's background, education, profession, culture, nationality and experiences. The court system tries to answer the question, "What would the reasonably competent school counselor do in a similar situation?" The school counselor, as defendant, would have to show that he or she behaved with reasonable care. The ASCA Ethical Standards (2010) provide us with ethical codes, and our school districts provide us with written policies and procedures; out of this is born standard of care to help define the "reasonable man test" or how the reasonably competent school counselor would behave (Alexander & Alexander, 2011; Imber & Van Geel, 2009; Remley & Herlihy, 2007).

Causal connection: There must be a causal connection between the school counselor's breach of duty and the injury suffered by the student. Liability in a negligence case hinges on causation. Proximate cause refers to the foreseeability of harm or whether the school counselor could have predicted the harm (Alexander & Alexander, 2011). Using the example of the educator who takes a student to the beach, this school counselor owed a duty to keep students safe, but another adult chaperone expressly there to watch the students decided to steal away to smoke a cigarette. The school counselor might have been negligent in not properly supervising the students, but if the second adult's job was only to keep a keen eye on the students, then that adult's percentage of fault would be greater. In some states, such as North Carolina, Tennessee, Virginia and Maryland, compensation to the injured party is denied in cases of contributory negligence because the injured party can only recover for his injuries if the injured party did not contribute in any way. Comparative negligence, used by other states, balances the percentage of blame based on the school counselor's negligence with the percentage of blame assigned to others who contributed to the injury. Damages are then assessed by percentage of fault (Alexander & Alexander, 2011).

Injury suffered: Assessment refers to determining monetary damages needed to compensate for the harm an individual suffers, such as injury, lost scholarship or death. Nominal damages can be awarded in cases where actual cost cannot be determined. Punitive damages are awarded in cases where the intent is to punish the defendant and deter similar actions in the future (Imber & Van Geel, 2009; Remley & Herlihy, 2007; Larson, 2007).

The courts have rejected the vast majority of negligence cases against educators (P.A. Zirkel, personal communication, Dec. 1, 2008). Student service educators, such as school counselors, make it even more difficult to prove negligence as "it is not easy to prove that a school counselor deviated from accepted practices and that the school counselor's act or negligence caused the harm that a client suffered" (Remley & Herlihy, 2007, p. 165).

The courts have been reluctant to determine that school counselors owe a duty in areas such as suicide or academic advising. Generally speaking since the courts are reluctant to find that school counselors owe a legal duty, liability for negligence against school counselors is infrequently imposed. Therefore, only a few court cases exist in which school counselors are the defendants, and of the few that do most of them will appear throughout this chapter and book.

In a recent survey, ASCA members responded to the query, "With regard to your professional role as a school counselor, have you been asked to be a witness (not a defendant) in a court case or legal proceeding through a subpoena or a court order in the last five years? One third or 34 percent reported having been involved in legal proceedings in the last five years. Very few school counselors are called on to be a witness in negligence lawsuits. The vast majority of any involvement school counselors have with legal proceedings has to do with custody issues (72 percent) or child abuse by a parent (52 percent). The Obligations to the Court Chapter has more details about school counselors as court witnesses. In comparison, the negligence cases for which school counselors replied they were a witness are few:

Which statement best describes the reason you were subpoenaed or court ordered.	Percentage
Negligence case regarding academic advising	3 percent
Negligence case regarding a student's suicide	1 percent
Negligence case involving failure to report child abuse	1 percent
Negligence case involving failure to protect a child from sexual harassment	1 percent
Negligence case involving failure to protect a child from bullying	1 percent
Negligence case involving a student's sexual orientation	0 percent
Negligence case in writing letters of recommendation	0 percent
Negligence case involving falsifying records	0 percent

(Stone, 2013d)

In this same survey, ASCA members responded to a question as to whether they were ever a defendant in a court case. Only 5 percent of the respondents have ever been a defendant in a legal proceeding.

With regard to your professional role as a school counselor, have you ever been a defendant in a court case or legal proceeding in the history of your role as a school counselor. If so how many times?

No: ....95 percent
One time: ....4 percent
Two times: ....1 percent

(Stone, 2013d)

Educational malpractice: To prove malpractice, there must be a comparison between the acceptable standard of care for the school counseling profession and the specific act or conduct claimed to be malpractice. The testimony of an expert witness, another school counselor or someone well versed in school counseling often helps determine whether or not the defendant met the professional standard.

In addition to expert witnesses, the standard of care is established in a variety of other ways, including adherence to and participation in professional licensing and credentialing entities both locally and nationally and educational degree preparation and continuing education programs (ASCA, 2010). For the school counselor, additional resources for establishing a standard of care include school board policies as well as participation with in-service opportunities on a local level. Using standard of care as the framework, the court will decide if the school counselor acted as the reasonably competent professional would have acted under the same or similar circumstances (Demitchell & Demitchell, 2007). Malpractice claims often result from dissatisfaction with services provided, breakdowns in communications between persons, anger with the professional, and retaliation or personal greed. Claims are not, generally, from substantiated grievances (Alexander & Alexander, 2011).

Historically, school districts have had governmental immunity or protection from civil or tort liability. In most states with regard to negligence, malpractice or civil liability individual employees are protected from personal liability if they are not acting in a willful or wanton way (Alexander & Alexander, 2011). Most states have legislation declaring that public employers must defend, indemnify and hold harmless any employee who is named in a civil suit for an act of omission arising out of the employee's job (Alexander & Alexander, 2011). For example, Montana statute 2-9-305, regarding "immunization, defense, and indemnification of employees," states in part:

(1) It is the purpose of this section to provide for the immunization, defense and indemnification of public officers and employees civilly sued for their actions taken within the course and scope of their employment.
(2) In any noncriminal action brought against any employee of a state ... or other governmental entity for a negligent act, error or omission ... committed while acting within the course and scope of the employee's office or employment, the governmental entity employer ... shall defend the action on behalf of the employee and indemnify the employee (Mt. Code, Ann., Ch. 9, § 305, 2007).

According to the Montana statute and the governmental immunity statute of many other states, the employee cannot be fired because of an unintentional act that has harmful effects. This obligation does not extend to criminal acts or acts where the employee is intentionally, willfully harmful (Alexander & Alexander, 2011). Know your state's statutes, as they vary by state and are constantly changing.

There are limits and exceptions to governmental immunity. Malicious, willful and intentional torts occur when one acts in a determined way to harm another individual (Alexander & Alexander, 2011). Some intentional torts may also be crimes, such as assault, battery, wrongful death, fraud and theft. An example of a malicious, willful and intentional tort involving a school counselor is found in *Doe v. Blandford* (2000). The school counselor sexually abused a student, constituting a willfully harmful act or intentional tort. The student's parents brought a complaint against the school district, claiming the district was negligent in hiring, failing to supervise and failing to fire their child's abuser. In its decision, the court found that the intentional tort exception should be interpreted narrowly and that action in this case should be brought against the government.

Education malpractice has yet to be codified, but the term is failure to render professional service that reasonably should be expected from educators. States are hesitant to recognize educational malpractice. The courts have articulated five reasons. The standard of care for educators lacks specificity and is difficult to define. Financial harm to the complainant is difficult to determine. If a school counselor misadvises a student about a required prerequisite college course, causing the student to lose an awarded scholarship, should the student be awarded the cost of tuition for the first year or for all four years? Courts are aware the floodgates open for other suits when students and families win educational malpractice suits. The list would be long if students could sue for not getting into the college of their choice or they failed because of a bad teacher. The courts do not want to be in the position of making decisions regarding internal operations of schools.

With regard to negligence and school counselors, a unique relationship exists between the school counselor and the minor in school settings. This unique and special relationship is *in loco parentis*, Latin meaning "in place of a parent," in which the person or entity takes on the standard of care attributed to a parent. A school has a duty to provide for its students' physical safety. Teachers and other certified employees may step in as a parent would to discipline and correct a child's behavior or, alternatively, to keep one child safe from another child or adult (*Gammon v. Edwardsville Community Unit School District* (1980)). In addition, a school board may stand in the place of a parent to ban sexually explicit material from the school library (*Bethel School District No. 403 v. Fraser* (1986)). A student's biblical condemnation of homosexual behavior and his assertion that he had a right to do so under freedom of speech was balanced against the school's responsibility to act as parent to protect the rights of other students (*Doe and Doe v. Greendale Baptist Church and Academy* (2003)).

Getting Started: What Would You Do?

The following case is answered for you at the end of this chapter by a counselor educator. Before you read his response, formulate in your own mind how you would approach this ethical dilemma.

NEGLIGENCE IN EATING DISORDERS

Karen has been a regular in your office for the last two years. She has serious problems, and you have implored Karen's stepmother – you can never get her father to respond – to get her some help. Lately, you believe Karen is suffering from bulimia. Her teeth appear pitted, her skin is sallow and pasty-looking, she is losing weight and she appears more nervous than ever. When you confront Karen, she does not answer but rather starts a long diatribe about how you cannot tell her father because he is ready to send her off to live with her birth mother, and this information will give him the ammunition he needs. Karen has all but admitted to you that she is bulimic, and you know her assessment of her father's reaction is probably accurate. You decide to try to help Karen without calling her parents. The unthinkable happens, and Karen suffers heart failure. You are sued for negligence. How do you believe the courts will react? Is it likely that your school district will pay for your defense?

Working Through Case Studies

FORESEEABILITY

You have heard positive reports from several sources about a local counselor, Mr. Stevenson, and his success with difficult teenagers. Ms. Smith seeks your advice about Emily, her truant daughter who is also abusing drugs and alcohol. You give Ms. Smith the name of only one counselor, Mr. Stevenson, even though he is not on the district's approved list for agency referrals. If Mr. Stevenson turns out to be a sexual offender and abuses Emily, are you in any way legally responsible?

Points to Consider

In the case *Smith v. The School Board of Orange County, Fla.* (1994), the parents sued the school district because a school counselor did not follow school board policy for making outside referrals. The school district requires school counselors to give a list of multiple district-approved resources. When K.W.'s mother sought help from the school counselor for her 14-year-old daughter's alcohol and substance abuse problems, the school counselor allegedly gave only one name, that of Ron Markham. Markham ran an outpatient treatment center licensed by the Department of Health and Rehabilitative Services, but his name was not on the school district's approved list. Markham insisted he be given 24-hour custody of the child, although his program was not licensed to have in-patient care or to place children in foster homes. K.W.'s mother immediately had misgivings when she placed K.W. with Markham and sought more information from a school employee, who said if the school counselor thought Markham was "okay" then he must be "okay." Unknown to K.W.'s mother and apparently to the school counselor, Markham "placed" K.W. in his own home, and for two-and-a-half months sexually abused her.

The Florida Court of Appeals dismissed the complaint, but speaking on behalf of the minority vote, a dissenting justice issued this opinion: "The foreseeability of K.W.'s injury – sexual battery by Markham – is a jury issue. In my view, the school had at least a threshold duty to make a referral only to 'approved' programs. ... Further, K.W.'s mother's specific inquiry about Markham, after meeting him, should also have triggered a follow-up by the school counselor, which was not done in this case. Had an additional conversation with K.W.'s mother taken place following her questions about Markham, the school counselor might have discovered that Markham was not licensed to place children in foster homes on a 24-hour custody basis and that the treatment being proposed for K.W. was inappropriate. I do not think the sexual battery of a young female child consigned to the 24-hour custody of an adult male (particularly one with a criminal record) is 'unforeseeable' in the least" (*Smith v. The School Board of Orange County* (1994)).

NEGLIGENCE IN ACADEMIC ADVISING

Bert was lured to your school by the basketball coaches. His school counselor was not able to match his courses from his previous school, and scheduling Bert was a feat. The summer after graduation Bert learned he did not have enough English credits for NCAA eligibility. Are the school counselors liable?

Points to Consider

Before 2001, no jurisdiction had recognized that negligence could occur in the context of a school counselor giving academic advice to a student (Zirkel, 2001). In reversing a lower court's decision and remanding the case to trial, the Iowa Supreme Court in *Sain v. Cedar Rapids Community School District* (2001) determined that a school counselor owed a duty in this situation to advise a student with due care and attention.

Bruce Sain, a senior in Cedar Rapids, Iowa, was a talented all-state basketball player. In 1996, he was awarded a five-year basketball scholarship to Northern Illinois University. However, in the summer prior to his freshman year, Sain was notified in a letter that he did not meet the National Collegiate Athletic Association regulations for incoming freshman athletes at Division I schools. The letter explained that he fell one-third credit short in the required English credits because his one-third English credit in technical communications was not on the list of classes his high school submitted to the NCAA for approval. Sain lost his scholarship, and his family filed suit against the Cedar Rapids School District, citing the school district as negligent and the school counselor, Larry Bowen, as guilty of negligent misrepresentation in his role as an academic advisor (*Sain v. Cedar Rapids Community School District* (2001)). How did a scholarship opportunity for Sain turn into a disaster, with Larry Bowen at the center of a lawsuit?

In his senior year, Sain needed three trimesters of English. Dissatisfied with the second-trimester English course, he turned to Bowen, his school counselor at Jefferson High School, and asked Bowen to place him in another English class. Bowen suggested technical communications and explained to Sain that it was being offered at the school for the first time but that the Initial Eligibility Clearinghouse would approve the high school course. Without further concern, Sain completed technical communications and graduated in spring 1996 with the prospect of a five-year scholarship at Northern Illinois University. Then, the letter arrived from the NCAA Clearinghouse declaring Sain ineligible based on academic grounds. Sain and Jefferson High School requested reconsideration from the NCAA, but their request for a waiver was denied (*Sain v. Cedar Rapids Community School District* (2001); Zirkel, 2001).

With his scholarship offer voided, Sain turned to the courts. He filed suit against the NCAA (a suit he dropped shortly thereafter) and the school district, but not the school counselor, claiming negligence and negligent misrepresentation. He alleged negligence occurred when the school counselor never submitted the course, technical communications, to the NCAA for approval. The suitability of the course was not at issue, since technical communications had been approved for other schools as a core English course. The problem was it had not been approved for Jefferson High School because the school had not included it on the list annually submitted to the NCAA Clearinghouse for approval. Sain claimed negligent misrepresentation by the school district because Bowen gave out erroneous information by telling him technical communications would be an approved course (*Sain v. Cedar Rapids Community School District* (2001)).

The trial court initially rejected Sain's suit. In the past, courts have received a number of educational malpractice lawsuits, but they continually sided with school districts, rejecting the notion that school counselors owe a duty to a student to give competent academic advice. Courts recognize how difficult the role of academic advisor is for school counselors who are routinely required to manage large numbers of students, constantly changing rules and regulations, and fluctuating admissions and financial aid criteria. Courts have therefore been reluctant to determine that school counselors owe a duty in the academic advising arena. Surprisingly, however, when Sain appealed to the Iowa Supreme Court, the court remanded the case for trial (*Sain v. Cedar Rapids Community School District* (2001)).

It is important to note that the Iowa Supreme Court did not determine whether the school district was negligent; that was left for the lower court to decide. Rather, the state Supreme Court found the claim of "negligent misrepresentation" possibly had merit and should not have been dismissed by the lower court. "Never before had any court, let alone one in Iowa, considered the liability of a school counselor for the tort of negligent misrepresentation without the ability to rely upon a tort immunity statute that protected school districts" (Willis, 2004, p. 7).

The Iowa Supreme Court remanded the case to the lower court for trial on the count of negligent misrepresentation. Justice Mark Cady of the Iowa Supreme Court wrote for the 5-2 majority that school counselors could be held accountable for providing accurate information to students about credits and courses needed to pursue post-high school goals (Parrott, 2001). The erroneous advice given by the school counselor was equated to negligent misrepresentation in professions such as accounting, the law and others whose businesses require they give accurate and appropriate information (*Sain v. Cedar Rapids Community School District* (2001); Zirkel, 2001).

The court determined that school counselors have a similar type of business relationship and responsibility of giving accurate advice to students when the student has a need to know. The court explained that just as accountants and lawyers stand to gain financially from giving accurate advice, so do school counselors, since that is what they are paid to do. Therefore, negligent misrepresentation may be applied to the school counselor/student relationship when erroneous advice means a student loses a lucrative scholarship. This kind of lawsuit is more business-oriented than academic and, according to the Iowa Supreme Court, is a classic case of negligent misrepresentation (*Sain v. Cedar Rapids Community School District* (2001); Zirkel, 2001).

The court found that school counselors must use reasonable care in providing specific information to a student when (a) the school counselor has knowledge of the specific need for the information, (b) the school counselor provides the information to the student in the course of a school-counselor/student relationship and (c) the student reasonably relies upon the information in circumstances where the school counselor knows or should know of the student's reliance (Zirkel, 2001). Bowen claims never to have had a conversation with Sain about NCAA course eligibility, which Sain disputes.

Justice Linda K. Neuman, speaking on behalf of the minority, wrote that the Iowa Supreme Court's decision "spells disaster for the law," explaining that the decision will open the "floodgates" and could be applied broadly to students in a variety of situations and not just athletes who need counsel on NCAA rules (Reid, 2001, p. 3). Neuman noted that the decision exalts logic over experience; it might appear logical that school counselors should give correct advice, but the reality of the expectations placed on school counselors makes this logic impossible. School counselors cannot have a command of everything there is to know about colleges and universities, admissions requirements, NCAA rules, financial aid and scholarships and a multitude of other facts that change daily. Neuman wrote, "Instead of encouraging sound academic guidance, today's decision will discourage advising altogether" (Reid, 2001, p. 3).

The majority justices acknowledged that the ruling could have a "chilling effect" on academic advising by school counselors (Reid, 2001, p. 3). However, the court cautioned that the ruling should have limited effect, as negligent representation is confined to students whose reliance on information is reasonable (such as an inquiry as to whether a course meets NCAA eligibility). Additionally, the school counselor must be aware of how vital the information is to the student. This explanation was intended to reassure school counselors and to keep them from overreacting to the principles outlined by the Sain case (*Sain v. Cedar Rapids Community School District* (2001)).

Although the case was never heard by the lower court, the findings of the Iowa Supreme Court in remanding the case to trial serves as a caution to the school counseling profession about providing accurate advice that could have an impact on a student's future financial opportunities. It is unusual for a tort claim of this nature to proceed to court, but, by breaking with tradition, the Iowa Supreme Court has reinterpreted the nature of the school counselor/student relationship (Parrott, 2001).

A court case in California, *Brown v. Compton Unified School District* (1998), further demonstrates the court's reluctance to impose the first element of negligence, a duty owed, against a school district. Brown enrolled in Manuel Dominguez High School as a senior with the express purpose of taking the required classes to satisfy the NCAA eligibility requirements and of participating in the Manuel Dominguez High School basketball program. School counselor Rae Bonner advised Brown to enroll in a particular science course, but the course did not meet the NCAA requirements. After Brown had enrolled at the University of Southern California, the university revoked his basketball scholarship. Brown argued in his lawsuit that a special relationship existed between him and the school district because the district induced him to transfer and assured him that the Manuel Dominguez High School would allow him to satisfy the NCAA requirements for athletic eligibility. Brown further contended that he relied on the promise that he would be placed in courses that satisfied NCAA requirements. Under governmental immunity both Bonner and the school district were immune from liability. "Government Code n1 section 822.2 protects a public employee acting in the scope of employment from injury due to the employee's misrepresentation" (*Brown v. Compton Unified School District* (1998), p. 6).

Another case, in Wisconsin, made its way to the state's highest court, which ruled that school counselors and school districts may not be held liable for giving students erroneous information – even when that information costs a student a full four-year college scholarship. Ryan Scott, a student at Stevens Point Area Senior High, sued the school district after he was declared ineligible for an NCAA student-athlete scholarship. The negligence claim hinged entirely on whether the district was immune from liability for negligence under Wisconsin's governmental immunity statute. The Wisconsin Supreme Court dismissed (but not happily) the lawsuit because of governmental immunity. Although the justices were compelled to follow prior decisions, in their opinion their decision was an injustice. Justice Bablitch stated, "This court should revisit these past cases. ...A doctrine of governmental immunity that has caused such injustice and inequity, in this case and others, cannot, and I predict will not, stand much longer. In light of these sentiments, which appear to have growing support in many state courts, school districts should keep a watchful eye on the seemingly unstable future of the state's government immunity law" (*Scott v. Stevens Point Area Public School District* (2003), n.p.).

Recommendations for Academic Advisors

The *Sain, Brown* and *Scott* rulings should not deter school counselors from career and academic advising, a role that has great opportunity for implementing a social-justice agenda and leveling the playing field for many students. Continue to offer academic advising sessions to students. School counselors can help close the information gap between those students who know what they need to do to successfully access postsecondary education leading to wider economic opportunities and those students who have not received even the most basic information. Students without a significant adult in their lives helping them understand how to access and be successful in postsecondary opportunities need the school counselor to be an advocate.

The following are some recommendations for school counselors who are in the role of academic advisor.

- Act as the reasonably competent professional would. Hold yourself to a high standard-of-care test. The courts are not asking for extraordinary care, only reasonable care. Our ethical codes help professionals aspire to extraordinary care, but the courts do not demand this level. By exercising skill and care in every action taken as a professional, school counselors can demonstrate they are behaving as reasonably competent professionals.

- Stay abreast of information needed for competent academic advising. Demonstrate a working knowledge of procedures, policies, laws, ethical standards and the school district's policies. Seek professional development in the area of academic advising. Demonstrate a good faith effort to stay informed.

- Empower others to take responsibility for having and giving the right information. You can teach students to be their own advocates through classroom guidance lessons in the computer lab, where students can conduct Internet searches and locate information on their own. As a manager of resources, the school counselor can equip others to be a key presence in the career and academic advising roles.

- Widely publicize academic information for all students and parents/guardians. Make use of newsletters, form letters and e-mail groups in your advising role, thus demonstrating a proactive stance to disseminating critical, timely information.

- Require students and parents/guardians to sign off when they receive critical information. When you give seniors their personal credit check for remaining graduation requirements, for instance, have them sign an acknowledgment that they have been told and understand what they need to do, and have parents/guardians sign, too.

- Consult when appropriate. Best practice for school counselors is always to consult whenever they are unsure. School counselors never stand alone unless they fail to consult with others who are in a position to help, particularly school district legal counsel.

NEGLIGENCE IN WRITING LETTERS OF RECOMMENDATION

You are a high school counselor in a diverse public school. One of your seniors, Connie, asks you for a letter of recommendation. You have not worked with Connie other than a brief conversation over a schedule change. You asked a teacher who happened to be in the counseling office what he thought of Connie, and his opinion was that Connie excels academically (as confirmed by her transcript) and athletically but lacks character, "always in it for herself, not a team player." This teacher appeared to know what he was talking about so you sent the university a letter emphasizing Connie's self-centeredness. Are there any legal and/or ethical issues that may arise from this process?

Points to Consider

In a 2010 court case, *McCoy v. Rockwood School District*, Shannon McCoy and her parents brought a civil suit against the district (Harris, 2010). McCoy was a Missouri state champion swimmer and high school graduate. The suit alleged that her school counselor and principal defamed her character, were negligent and purposely caused emotional stress. McCoy's parents maintain that her scholarship was withdrawn due to a libelous and fabricated recommendation letter submitted by her high school counseling department. According to the suit, McCoy was an exemplary student who maintained a 3.0 grade point average and received many athletic accolades such as a school board award four times for being the "epitome of Rockwood spirit" (Harris, 2010, p.1). However, the recommendation by school counselor Beth Brasel emphasized McCoy's deficiency in initiative, character, integrity, leadership and community service. The McCoys contend that Brasel's evident disregard of McCoy's positive traits and later her confession of not having had any personal interactions with McCoy was evidence of a premeditated fabrication. Upon receiving the recommendation signed by Brasel, the Colorado State University withdrew McCoy's acceptance, leaving her without options for a scholarship at any four-year institution. McCoy was later reinstated with her full scholarship to Colorado State, but the family maintained their suit for loss caused by the ordeal (Harris, 2010).

A letter from a high school counselor is recognized by college admissions officers as a powerful statement of accuracy about a student. "Recognize and respect the fact that high school counselors/advisors have the perspective of knowing students in the context of school settings over an extended period of time. Their assessment of students includes academic potential through teacher feedback, as well as observed involvement and demonstrated leadership in campus activities" (Independent College Counselors & Educational Consultants, March 30, 2013).

School counselor recommendations play a pivotal role in the application process. According to the National Association for College Admission Counseling's 2011 State of College Admission report, nearly two-thirds of colleges and universities attribute considerable or moderate importance to school counselor and teacher recommendations in determining which academically qualified students they would choose for admission. "When all else is equal between two applicants, a recommendation from you can pull a lot of weight. Also, for students with mediocre or low scores on college admission tests, your honest assessment of their potential success in college can tip the scales in their favor" (National Association for College Admission Counseling, 2012, p.1).

In an April 2013 survey, ASCA members indicated they are, by and large, expected to write letters of recommendation for all students needing one. Letters of recommendation pose challenges for school counselors as they wrestle with how to be fair to a student while not saying anything the school counselor cannot stand behind. In this survey, 46 percent of the respondents said they work with students who need letters of recommendation. Of this 46 percent, 80 percent said, "It is the expectation that I write a letter for all students needing one."

These school counselors also described their letter-writing practice.

Which best describes your practice regarding writing letters of recommendation? Choose only one.

I only agree to write a letter if the student is someone
    for whom I can write a positive letter: . . . . .12 percent
If I cannot write a positive letter I explain to the
    students they would be in a better position to seek
    a letter from someone else: .37 percent
I will write letters and include negative comments
    from my own first-hand knowledge: . . . . .4 percent
I will write letters and include negative comments, but
    I make certain I can back up the statements with other
    reliable sources as well as first-hand knowledge: . . . . . .6 percent
Not applicable as I do not have students who need
    letters of recommendation: .41 percent

(Stone, 2013d)

If, for some reason, the school counselor believes he or she must go forward with a letter that includes negative comments, then have anecdotal information from more than one reliable source to back up your remarks. It is hard to justify negative comments when there is no first-hand knowledge and the only engagement with the student was a schedule change. The only anecdotal information in the case scenario was from a brief chance conversation with one teacher.

Some admissions officers say, "Be candid and comprehensive; include negatives if you are comfortable doing so" (Cowdrey, 2013). However, the Stone 2013c survey revealed that school counselors are not comfortable including negatives in letters. Rather, they will stick to a student's strengths, but what their letters omit or say minimally conveys that there might be some weaknesses simply by omission, e.g., the school counselor does not mention service or character as maybe these are not strengths. If a letter focuses on negative information instead of mentioning it in a minor point, then school counselors ask a student to seek someone else to write them a letter.

The survey supported the widely held belief that school counselors who agree to write letters of recommendation are using time-saving, efficient techniques to learn all they can about the student. Techniques school counselors use for documentation and help with information include: teacher checklists about student strengths/weaknesses; student responses to a school-counselor-generated form about information they would like shared in a letter, such as their strengths and challenges they have overcome with examples to support their claims; and a small percentage use parent or guardian questionnaires. The College Board has samples of all of these at *http://professionals.collegeboard.com/guidance/applications/school counselor-tips.*

Which best describes your practice regarding writing letters of recommendation? Choose all that apply:

I give teachers a form to fill out regarding a
    student's strengths/weaknesses: . . . . .7 percent
I give students a form to fill out on their strengths,
    challenges they have overcome, examples
    of information about their character, etc.: . . . . .37 percent
I gather information from parent or guardian
    questionnaires: . . . . .2 percent
I write letters but I do not do any of the above: . . . . .16 percent
Not applicable as I do not do letters of
    recommendation: . . . . .39 percent

SUICIDE AND DUTY OWED

A student tells you her friend Jocelyn, one of your students, is threatening suicide. When you call Jocelyn into your office, she vehemently denies any consideration of suicide, scoffing at the idea that she would ever harm herself. You are convinced there is no basis for concern, and you drop the issue without discussing it with anyone else. Do your actions pose an ethical or legal dilemma?

Points to Consider

The threat of teenage suicide is an unfortunate reality for school counselors. In addition, school counselors know all too well the damage to their effectiveness if they have the reputation of breaking confidences and calling parents/guardians. The ambiguity of protecting a student's trust in the school counselor as a confidant and the need to respect parents' rights to be the guiding voice in their children's lives are a constant source of tension for school counselors. This case underscores the conflict school counselors face in trying to behave legally and ethically toward students, parents/guardians and their school district.

The law of negligence involves injury or damage to another through a breach of duty owed to that person. Duty owed is a legal responsibility one person has to another, such as a legal responsibility to drive with care so you do not injure another person (Alexander & Alexander, 2011). As we noted earlier, negligence requires the presence of four elements: (1) a duty is owed, (2) the duty owed was breached, (3) there is a causal connection between breach of duty and injury, and (4) an injury has occurred. Until the *Eisel v. Montgomery County Board of Education* court case (1991), courts consistently found that school counselors did not "owe a legal duty" to prevent a student's suicide. *Eisel* strengthened school counselors' legal obligation to students by satisfying for the first time the primary element of negligence, declaring school counselors have a special relationship with students and owe a duty to try to prevent a student's suicide.

The Maryland Court of Appeals in the *Eisel* case ruled that school counselors had a duty to notify the parents of a 13-year-old student who made suicidal statements to her classmates. Nicole Eisel allegedly became involved in Satanism and told several friends and fellow students of her intention to kill herself. Some of these friends told their school counselor of Nicole's intentions, and this school counselor in turn informed Nicole's school counselor. The two school counselors questioned Nicole about the statements, and Nicole denied making them. The school counselors did not notify either the parents or the school administrators about these events. Shortly thereafter, in a public park, Nicole and her friend tragically consummated their suicide pact.

The court in the *Eisel* case cited as critical the *in loco parentis* doctrine, which states that educators, including school counselors, legally stand in the place of parents. Furthermore, school counselors owe a special duty to exercise reasonable care to protect a student from harm. The court concluded school counselors have a duty to use reasonable means to attempt to prevent a suicide when they receive notice of a student's suicidal intent. With the Eisel ruling, the court redefined the school counselor/student relationship and declared school counselors have a duty of care when placed on notice of a possible suicide. The court recognized the fact that school counselors hear a great amount of suicidal ideation and have the complicated task of trying to determine which threats are real, yet the court stated, "The consequence of the risk is so great that even a relatively remote possibility of a suicide may be enough to establish duty" (*Eisel v. Board of Education of Montgomery County* (1991), n.p.). In other words, the court stopped just short of declaring school counselors have an affirmative duty to notify parents in each and every case involving a suicidal threat.

Does the *Eisel* ruling take away school counselors' ability to exercise judgment with regard to student suicide? Eisel did not argue for absolute duty as in the case of child abuse reporting, in which school counselors must report any and all suspected situations. The court stopped just short of declaring an absolute duty. However, the tenets established in *Eisel* set a precedent that school counselors now have a legal obligation to try to prevent suicide. School counselors should not be paralyzed by the *Eisel* ruling. Rather, the ruling should serve to help school counselors realize the importance of seeking supervision and carefully deliberating decisions about breaching student confidentiality, as well as protecting parental rights. The duty of care is critical, as is the enormous consequence of breaching confidentiality. You should feel considerable discomfort with the weight of the decision to breach; if not, examine carefully your level of commitment to confidentiality.

The *Eisel* case did not deliver the final word. Following the *Eisel* case, courts in at least five states have rejected these kinds of cases. An Illinois appellate court in 1997 absolved a school counselor of legal liability when the school counselor failed to tell the student's parents about his threats of suicide (*Grant v. Board of Trustees of Valley View School District* (1997)). "But courts in three other cases have ruled that in certain circumstances school employees' failure to act can make them or the school legally responsible for a student's suicide" (Simpson, 1999, p. 12). All of the cases that imposed liability, however, involved employees who failed to notify parents that their children had written or talked to others about killing themselves (Portner, 2000; Simpson, 1999).

Where does a school counselor's legal liability end? It ends when you have notified school authorities or parents that a student is at risk, and you have recommended appropriate actions. Be sure to document your notification. The courts do not expect school counselors to do the impossible and prevent all adolescent suicides. Rather, the court's message is that the consequence of the risk in not involving parents is too great and that parents must be allowed to try to intervene. However, a school counselor's ethical obligation to a suicidal student may extend beyond parental notification if the parents do not enroll the student in counseling. If they do not arrange counseling when the suicidal student is first identified, the probability of attempts and completion increases. School counselors must make every attempt to supply parents or guardians with counseling referrals until placement is secured for that student (Capuzzi, 2002; National Association of School Psychologists, n.d.). In most cases, the school counselor will need to notify Child Protective Services of a possible neglect situation if the parents do not pursue counseling.

Ethical standards provide guidelines regarding protecting students and others from potentially dangerous situations, but it is ultimately the school counselor's responsibility to negotiate the rights and privileges of students and parents regarding issues of duty to care. The courts continually vest parents with legal rights to guide their children (*Bellotti v. Baird* (1979); *H.L. v. Matheson* (1981); American Bar Association, 2004). The ASCA Ethical Standards for School Counselors dictate that school counselors have a primary obligation and loyalty to students but that parents need to be involved as appropriate (ASCA, 2010, code A.7.). Community standards, a school counselor's own personal values, school board policy, the school setting, state and federal statutes and school procedures all contribute to the complex nature of working with minors in schools.

GOVERNMENTAL IMMUNITY AND SUICIDE

A student comes to you worried about her friend Jeff. "I think someone needs to check on him. Something is not right. He is not himself. He said he was sick and tired of life." You are pulled to do AP proctoring, and you did not have a chance to check on Jeff. His friend skipped school that afternoon and found Jeff dead from an apparent suicide. Your state has a strong governmental immunity law. Will you escape legal liability under governmental immunity?

Points to Consider

Andrew was a freshman at St. Croix Falls High School in January 1996. Mr. McMahons drove his son to school, but Andrew did not attend classes that day. A district policy provides that if a student is absent from school, the school will call the parents/guardians at home or work to verify the absence, but the school did not call the McMahons. A classmate, Jamie Stocker, told a school counselor that Andrew "was planning to skip school that day," that he was probably at her house and that someone should check on him or contact his parents. Stocker further said she thought Andrew seemed depressed and had said something to the effect that he was "sick and tired of this life." Stocker left school without permission that afternoon to check on Andrew at her home and discovered Andrew's body in her family's closed garage. Andrew had doused himself with gasoline and set himself on fire.

The McMahons' suit was dismissed, but they appealed their wrongful death suit against St. Croix Falls School District for their son's suicide. The McMahons argued that the circuit court erred when it established that a school district has absolute governmental immunity for its negligent acts when a student commits suicide. The McMahons contend that, contrary to Wisconsin tort law, the circuit court erroneously established that, under no conceivable circumstances, no matter how egregious a school district's negligence, could a school ever be found liable for a minor student's suicide. They contended that the district breached its duty to call them and to follow up after a school counselor learned that Andrew was despondent and absent from school. The district disputes the facts of Stocker's affidavit but states that it is of no matter as they are immaterial to governmental immunity. The appeals court agreed with the district that such facts would not change the results.

In *Fowler v. Szostek* (1995), the court found that school officials did not owe a legal duty to a student who committed suicide once she left the school campus. Brandi Nelson was suspended and had to face an expulsion hearing based on claims that she sold marijuana to two students while on school grounds. Brandi fatally shot herself on the eve of the suspension. Brandi's mother had implored school administrators to wait until after the impending Christmas holidays before disciplinary action as the suspension would be a devastating blow to Brandi. The appellate court never reached the details of the negligence claim, because in Texas as in many states school officials are protected by governmental immunity except for actions of 1) excessive force in the discipline of students or (2) negligence resulting in bodily injury to students, and in the court's opinion this 1995 case did not rise to either exception (Fossey, R., & Zirkel, P., 2004).

SUICIDE: AN INTERVENING VARIABLE THAT BREAKS THE CAUSAL CONNECTION

Howard is very fragile. You have been unable to get his parents to seek outside counseling help for Howard, but you continue to call and to see Howard whenever you can. It has been three weeks since you have seen him, and you make a mental note to seek him out on Monday. Monday you are hit with the news that Howard committed suicide over the weekend. Howard's parents bring suit against the district and you, citing the depth of their child's distress and suicidal ideation was not told to them. What is the plausible outcome?

Points to Consider

In *Bogust v. Iverson* (1960), the Wisconsin Supreme Court dismissed a wrongful death action brought against a college guidance counselor by the parents of a 19-year-old student who committed suicide six weeks after counseling was terminated. Bogust cited that suicide constitutes an intervening force that breaks the line of causation from the wrongful act to the death, and therefore the wrongful act does not render the counselor civilly liable (*Bogust v. Iverson* (1960)).

The four major elements of negligence (one of which is the causal connection) are:

- duty owed
- duty owed breached
- causal connection between the breach and injury
- injury suffered

For negligence to be determined in the case scenario, there had to be a connection (the third element of negligence) between the counselor's breach of duty (second element) and the injury suffered (fourth element). Most states follow the general rule that suicide is an intervening force. Regardless of what the counselor did or did not do (the wrongful act) before, the suicide is the intervening variable that breaks any chain of causation.

Another ruling provided a similar result. In *Lezner v. Shaw and Gresham School District* (1990), Lezner, an emotionally disabled student, was suspended from school for smoking marijuana on school property. The school unsuccessfully tried to reach the parents by phone to let them know of the suspension, then gave a copy of the suspension papers to the student and mailed the original to his home. The student did not inform his parents of the suspension and committed suicide. The parents claimed the school was negligent by failing to notify them promptly of their son's suspension. Following the *Bogust v. Iverson* (1960) precedent, the court ruled that a delayed suicide was not sufficiently connected to any act of negligence.

Even though case after case throughout the country finds school officials and school counselors do not owe a duty to try to prevent suicide or that suicide is an intervening variable, school counselors take little comfort in the courts' reluctance to hold us to a legal duty. "Do no harm" means school counselors should always err on the side of caution when they think a student may be in danger. Call parents/guardians. The breach of confidentiality is a minor transgression when weighed against the greater harm, the death of a child.

WILLFUL AND WANTON DISREGARD

Millie has made suicidal threats on three occasions this school year. The first time you called her mother you were met with resistance, "She is a drama queen. You are just feeding into her bid for attention." The second time you called there was a weak commitment to seek help for Millie. The third time Millie talked about suicide it was a veiled threat of, "No one understands how hard life is for me. Nothing works in my life so what is the point." You question her, but she clams up. You knew that Millie's mother would hit the roof if you called her with Millie's statement as your evidence that Millie is still struggling with thoughts of suicide. Being absolutely worn down by the conversations you have already had with Millie's mother you decide to wait for the next threat before calling her mother to check on Millie's outside counseling and to report subsequent threats. If this student follows through with her suicide threat are you negligent?

Points to Consider
Parents/guardians have rarely succeeded in establishing liability for student suicide, and none of the known decisions have resulted in an educator being responsible. Certainly, there may be unpublished cases or settle-

ments to the contrary, and the case law is subject to change in the future. Although the precedents to date strongly undercut any undue fear of school counselor liability, awareness of the legal reasoning behind the court decisions serves as guiding principles for school counselors as they make decisions that could prove lifesaving for students in the future.

In *Killen v. Independent School District No. 706* (1996), a ninth-grade student killed herself at home with a firearm. Although the school counselor had warned the parents that their daughter had expressed suicidal feelings and recommended counseling, the parents alleged the school counselor didn't inform them when their daughter subsequently made a more specific statement about committing suicide. The Minnesota appeals court upheld the lower court's dismissal based on governmental immunity provisions.

Similarly, in *Grant v. Board of Trustees of Valley View School District* (1997), a student's friends reported his suicidal ideations and drug use to the school counselor. The school counselor called the student's mother and urged her to take him to a hospital for drug treatment. Later that day, the student jumped to his death from a highway overpass. His mother alleged the school counselor failed to tell her about his suicidal expressions. An Illinois appellate court upheld the trial court's dismissal on the grounds that public schools and their employees have immunity unless their misconduct was willful or wanton.

Schools are acting responsibly when they have suicide prevention and intervention plans in place with regular in-service training sessions that prepare all educators to respond appropriately to suicidal threats. Trainings should include all school personnel: teachers, administrators, security guards, cafeteria employees, custodians, bus drivers, secretaries, paraprofessionals and student services staff. It is necessary to inform these colleagues of the appropriate procedure for referring suicidal students to resources, crisis teams or whatever the intervention plan entails. Although school counselors are not directly responsible for creating and implementing policies, as systemic change agents they advocate for policies and procedures that protect students' physical and mental health needs. Particularly, school counselors help ensure the suicide intervention plan includes contacting the parents/guardians of a suicidal student, not allowing the student to leave campus alone and contacting protective or emergency services if necessary.

Most states protect employees who are not willfully negligent; they often have legislation suggesting employers adamantly defend public employees who are in civil suits because of job omissions. Therefore, employees cannot be dismissed based on unintended acts they commit that may have negative consequences (Alexander & Alexander, 2011). However, there have been cases where school counselors, principals and even districts have been sued for committing actions that had foreseeable negative effects on students.

School counselors strive to be culturally sensitive when working with families to secure additional help. When school counselors and crisis team members meet with unresponsive parents/guardians, they may need to turn control over to other authorities such as protective services for possible neglect or, if the student is at immediate risk, police or emergency services.

School counselors, with their specialized training and *in loco parentis* status, have a high standard of care when a student's suicide is even a remote possibility. School counselors must always contact parents/guardians and refer them to appropriate resources that will allow them to seek help for their child. Confidentiality is trumped when weighed against the death of a child. Calling parents/guardians upholds school counselors' most significant obligation to students: above all, do no harm.

School counselors are clear with parents/guardians about a child's expressed or implied suicidal ideation. When a student makes veiled threats of suicide, school counselors avoid skirting the issue; rather, they ask the tough questions. Wanting their suffering, not their lives, to end, many suicidal students answer "no" when asked if they are considering suicide. However, this answer does not negate the risk. Use open-ended questions, such as "What do you think about life and death?" This approach can serve as the first step in getting necessary help for an at-risk student. Parents/guardians need to understand that expressions of suicide or other warning signs require vigilance. School counselors should document that they contacted the parents/guardians and wherever possible have a witness to the conversation. The principal or another administrator can add needed leverage and urgency to the conversation if parents/guardians are reluctant to act. School counselors use their best judgment in these emotionally charged situations and avoid putting documentation above the parents' and/or guardians' feelings and well-being. However, seek a signature from parents/guardians at the first appropriate opportunity.

NO LONGER IMMUNE FROM LIABILITY

Your colleague Barbara is new to the district. On a recent college trip she shocked you with her horse playing with students, going so far as to jump on one student's back. On the trip home she feigned falling asleep on a student's shoulder. You are dumbfounded, but fearing a scene and unable to get her alone on the crowded bus, you decide to discuss your concerns with her on Monday morning. Before you can even speak to Barbara, a parent who was on the trip calls you to complain that Barbara was "flirting a mile a minute" on the school trip. You approach Barbara, who is offended and dismisses you as someone who does not relate to students and that maybe you should try her approach and "lighten up." You try a second time to discuss the situation, but she stares at you without responding. You feel like you will never get through to her so you contact a colleague from Barbara's previous district to ask for advice. You learn that Barbara was dismissed for sexual behavior toward students. She was never accused of sexual abuse, but "there was inappropriate behavior." You notify your administration immediately, who says, "Let's give her a chance." You see a runaway freight train, but no one is listening. Are there any legal repercussions for the district when and if this school counselor acts on her sexual flirtations?

Points to Consider

In a 1989 ruling, the court found in a case where a teacher molested a student that the school district could not be held liable as the molestation was unrelated to the teacher's job duties. In a major narrowing of the impact of the 1989 case, the California Supreme Court has ruled that a school district may face liability because it hired a school counselor, Roselyn Hubbell, who allegedly was a known child abuser, and then allowed her to interact closely with students without adequate supervision. The case in point is *C.A. v. William S. Hart Union High School District*. C.A., the 14-year-old student, alleges that Hubbell, the head school counselor at his high school, sexually harassed, abused and molested him on a number of occasions. The difference between this case and the 1989 case is the accusation that the school district knew Hubbell had a history of engaging in sexually related conduct with minors and that, despite this knowledge, the school district hired her and gave her unsupervised access to minors. In fact, in 2008, one year after C.A. was abused by Hubbell, Hubbell resigned after being accused of improper conduct with two students. *The Signal*, a local newspaper, said she tried to check into a motel with an underage boy, not the plaintiff, and was required to register as a sex offender (Worden, 2012).

C.A.'s causes of action, rejected by the lower court, were against the school district, the high school and the school counselor for "negligence; negligent supervision; negligent hiring and/or retention; negligent failure to warn, train or educate; constructive fraud; intentional infliction of emotional distress; sexual battery; assault; sexual harassment; gender violence; and unfair business practices" (*C.A. v. William S. Hart Union High School District*, 12 S.O.S. 1151). The lower courts agreed with the 1989 ruling and found in favor of the William S. Hart Union High School District. However, on March 8, 2012, the California Supreme Court noted, "[a] public entity is liable for injury proximately caused by an act or omission of an employee of the public entity within the scope of his employment if the act or omission would, apart from this section, have given rise to a cause of action against that employee or his personal representative. Supervisory personnel have a duty to take reasonable measures to protect students from abuse, including abuse by teachers and school counselors when they know or have reason to know of the potential for such abuse" (*C.A. v. William S. Hart Union High School District*, 12 S.O.S. 1151). School officials "have a duty to protect students from harm, which includes an obligation to exercise ordinary care in hiring, training, supervising and discharging school personnel. An administrator who hires a known child molester as a school counselor and fails to provide adequate training, supervision or termination when faced with ongoing sexual misconduct has failed to perform the duties within the scope of his or her employment" (*C.A. v. William S. Hart Union High School District*, 12 S.O.S. 1151).

In a Position to Know: A Counselor Educator Speaks

The case presented at the beginning of the chapter is revisited here and answered by a counselor educator. Compare his response with your approach.

NEGLIGENCE IN EATING DISORDERS

Karen, one of your seventh-graders, has been a regular in your office for the last two years. She has serious problems, and you have implored Karen's stepmother – you can never get her father to respond – to get her some help. Lately, you believe Karen is suffering from bulimia. Her teeth appear pitted, her skin is sallow and pasty-looking, she is losing weight, and she appears more nervous than ever. When you confront Karen, she does not answer but rather starts a long diatribe about how you cannot tell her father because he is ready to send her off to live with her birth mother, and this information will give him the ammunition he needs. Karen has all but admitted to you that she is bulimic, and you know her assessment of her father's reaction is probably accurate. You decide to try to help Karen without calling her parents. The unthinkable happens, and Karen suffers heart failure. You are sued for negligence. How do you believe the courts will react? Is it likely that your school district will pay for your defense?

Points to Consider

We can learn many lessons from this school counselor's unfortunate predicament. School counselors who want to make sure they are never sued for negligence could avoid such unfortunate experiences by always telling parents or guardians everything students tell them in counseling sessions. Of course, such school counselors might have to find other jobs at some point, because few students would seek them out for help when they realize the school counselors are informing parents and guardians of everything the students say. Every time a school counselor decides not to inform parents or guardians after students have disclosed something in a session that could possibly lead to the student or others being harmed, school counselors take a legal risk. However, if they refuse to take such risks from time to time, they could not possibly be effective school counselors.

In reality, school counselors have to decide on a regular basis when to inform parents or guardians of something students have told them in counseling sessions. When school counselors determine that students may be at risk of endangering themselves or others, school counselors have an ethical and legal duty to inform parents or guardians. But when should school counselors tell parents or guardians, and when should school counselors take a risk and not tell them?

No one knows the answer to that question, and statutes and case law do not offer much help. The general rule is that if a reasonable school counselor with similar education and training in a similar community would have foreseen harm to self or others in a similar set of circumstances, then school counselors should disclose what they know from counseling sessions with their students to parents or guardians. Unfortunately, this is an "after-the-fact" test, and school counselors have to make their decisions on the firing line, often quickly.

The best advice for school counselors is to consult with other professionals if they are unsure whether they should disclose a student confidence to the student's parents or guardians. The more colleagues school counselors discuss the situation with, the better. If a school counselor's decision not to inform parents or guardians is questioned later (as is the situation in this case study), and the school counselor consulted with others who agreed parents or guardians should not be informed, then the school counselor has met the legal test stated above, "What would a reasonable school counselor with similar education and training in a similar community have done?"

Most school counselors reading this case study probably will conclude that the school counselor should have told Karen's father of Karen's suspected bulimia because her condition was life-threatening, even though Karen's father was likely to react negatively in a way that would add more pressure to Karen's life. However, there might be special circumstances to this situation that could have led a reasonable school counselor and the people the school counselor consulted to decide not to inform Karen's father but instead to seek help for Karen in other ways. Telling the father of the school counselor's suspicion of bulimia would have relieved the school counselor of any finding of negligence, but would it have been the ethical, moral and professional action to take? Should the school counselor have taken a risk by not telling the father in this particular situation? No one knows for sure.

Will the school district pay for the school counselor's legal defense in this case study? Probably, yes. In this situation, both the district and the school counselor most likely will be sued. The insurance company holding a liability policy for the school will hire an excellent attorney who specializes in defending professionals in negligence cases to represent the school district. That same attorney probably will represent the school counselor as well, but only if the attorney believes it is in the school district's best interest to do so. In most states, public entities cannot be sued because of sovereign immunity, or there are limits to negligence suits because of the sovereign immunity doctrine. If the attorney believes he or she could get the school district dismissed from the lawsuit but could not get the school counselor dismissed, the attorney would have an obligation to do that.

Getting the school district dismissed from the suit would leave the school counselor in this case study legally and financially vulnerable. As a result, school counselors should always have their own personal professional liability insurance policies that would pay for their defense and any judgment rendered against them individually. If school counselors do not have such a policy as a benefit of their union dues, they should purchase a policy from professional associations such as the American Counseling Association or be sure to maintain their membership in the American School Counselor Association, which provides professional liability coverage at no cost to its members.
– Theodore P. Remley Jr., counselor educator, Old Dominion University

Making Connections

1. Discuss the differences between negligence and malpractice.

2. What are the elements of negligence? Why is it so difficult to find that a school counselor owes a duty to prevent suicide?

3. What is standard of care? Who is the reasonably competent professional?

4. What is foreseeability? How should this guide your behavior?

5. What is governmental or sovereign immunity?

Key Terms

Addressing a known danger
Breach
Causal connection
Civil law
Constitutional law
Criminal law
Duty of care
Educational malpractice
Governmental immunity
Injury suffered

In loco parentis
Intervening, superseding cause
Malicious, willful and intentional
  torts
Malpractice
Ministerial
Negligence
Reasonableness
Willful and wanton disregard

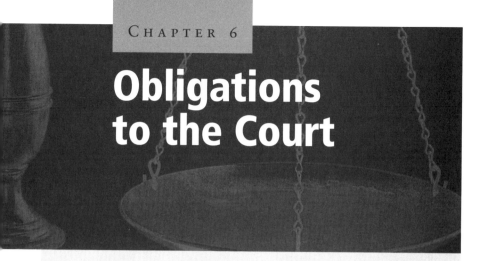

CHAPTER 6

Obligations to the Court

IN THIS CHAPTER

Objectives

By the time you have completed this chapter, you should be able to:

- Understand that schools are governmental agencies and how this fact affects legal behavior for educators.
- Discuss how the Constitution, statutes and case law form the legal foundation on which public schools are based.
- Understand the difference between privileged communication and confidentiality.
- Explain the difference between case notes and education records.
- Determine what to do if you receive a subpoena.
- Discuss how to advocate for your students without becoming involved in the court system.

Ethical Standards Addressed in This Chapter

Professionalism means knowing your professional associations' codes and adhering to them. The ASCA Ethical Standards for School Counselors most germane to this chapter are the following:

- Professional school counselors recognize the complicated nature of confidentiality in schools and consider each case in context. Keep information confidential unless legal requirements demand confidential information be revealed or a breach is required to prevent serious and foreseeable harm to the student. Serious and foreseeable harm is different for each minor in schools and is defined by students' developmental and chronological age, the setting, parental rights and the nature of the harm. School counselors consult with appropriate professionals when in doubt as to the validity of an exception. (A.2.c)
- Professional school counselors request of the court that disclosure not be required when the release of confidential information may potentially harm a student or the counseling relationship. (A.2.g)
- Professional school counselors protect the confidentiality of students' records and release personal data in accordance with prescribed federal and state laws and school policies including the laws within the Family Educational Rights and Privacy Act (FERPA). Student information stored and transmitted electronically is treated with the same care as traditional student records. Recognize the vulnerability of con-

fidentiality in electronic communications and only transmit sensitive information electronically in a way that is untraceable to students' identity. Critical information such as a student who has a history of suicidal ideation must be conveyed to the receiving school in a personal contact such as a phone call. (A.2.h)

- Professional school counselors keep sole-possession records or individual case notes separate from students' education records in keeping with state laws. (A.8.b)

- Professional school counselors recognize the limits of sole-possession records and understand these records are memory aids for the creator and in absence of privileged communication may be subpoenaed and may become education records when they are shared or are accessible to others in either verbal or written form or when they include information other than professional opinion or personal observations. (A.8.c)

- Professional school counselors establish a reasonable timeline for purging sole-possession records or case notes. Suggested guidelines include shredding sole-possession records when the student transitions to the next level, transfers to another school or graduates. Apply careful discretion and deliberation before destroying sole-possession records that may be needed by a court of law such as notes on child abuse, suicide, sexual harassment or violence. (A.8.d)

The full text of the ASCA Ethical Standards for School Counselors is available at *www.schoolcounselor.org*.

Introduction

Schools are governmental agencies. The legal authority of schools is as diverse as the 50 states that enact laws to govern those schools. Even though the United States is composed of a union of states under one central government, America has a "unique education system that is governed by laws of 50 states, with component parts amounting to several thousand local school district operating units. Through all of this organizational multiformity and, indeed, complexity runs the basis for justice on which the entire educational and legal systems are founded" (Alexander & Alexander, 2012, p. 2). The basis of the states' responsibility for schools is the 10th Amendment, which states, "The powers not delegated to the United States by the Constitution, nor prohibited by it to the states, are reserved to the states respectively, or to the people. Therefore, under the "implied powers" of the 10th Amendment, state legislation provides the basis for public school law, and the courts, through litigation, interpret the laws. The Constitution, state statutes and judge-made law (case law), administrative law (rules, regulations, applications, licenses, permits, available information, hearings, appeals and decision-making not usually found in statute) all combine to form the legal structure on which the public schools are based (Alexander & Alexander, 2011).

State legislatures give school boards authority to create their own rules and regulations. School boards must act in accordance with their own requirements (Imber & Van Geel, 2009), and school counselors must be aware of the nature of the school district's obligation to the judicial system. For example, a school district allowing first-offender drug users to seek counseling instead of discipline failed to follow its own policy. The school counselor served as the hearing officer in this case, and the student was expelled. However, the courts overturned the recommendation because the school did not follow the school board's own policies stating that a first offender could seek drug counseling instead of being expelled (*Camlin v. Beecher Community School District* (2003)).

The courts have traditionally maintained and enforced the concept of separation of the different branches of power to enable each division of government to function freely within the area of its responsibility (*Ricker v. Board of Education of Millard County School District* (1964); Beckham & Klaymeier Wills 2009). In short, school districts are not often sued, and when they are, the lower courts are reluctant to rule against school districts.

According to the courts, statutes are the basis for "the most common litigation involving school operation" (Alexander & Alexander, 2011, p. 4). Courts determine the constitutionality of such legislation. If a statute can be interpreted in two ways, one of which will be constitutional, the courts will adopt the constitutional interpretation (*Bonvento v. Board of Public Instruction of Palm Beach County* (1967); *Hobbs v. County of Moore* (1966)).

The United States has court systems at both the federal and the state levels. This book includes court cases involving educators at both levels, although state courts decide most cases (Alexander & Alexander, 2011; Imber & Van Geel, 2009; Beckham & Klaymeier Wills, 2009). From highest to lowest, state court systems include the courts of last resort such as the state supreme courts; intermediate appellate courts; courts of general jurisdiction, otherwise known as district, circuit, superior or juvenile;

and courts of limited jurisdiction, otherwise known as small claims courts, probate or justice of the peace (Harris & Tichenor, 2010).

The highest court in terms of this body of law is the supreme court of a state, called the Court of Appeals or Supreme Judicial Court in seven states. The states' supreme courts are not considered lower courts, even in relation to the U.S. Supreme Court. State supreme courts follow the U.S. Supreme Court's ruling on the meaning of the U.S. Constitution, but the highest court in each state is free to interpret state laws or the state constitution in any way that does not violate principles of federal law (Alexander & Alexander, 2011; U.S. Courts, n.d.).

Intermediate appellate courts exist in 38 states to hear appeals from trial court, to review trial court proceedings and to correct errors in the application of law and procedure (Alexander & Alexander, 2012). Courts of general jurisdiction are major courts in which defendants or plaintiffs can appeal to higher courts. About three-fourths of all cases in the limited jurisdiction courts involve traffic offenses (Alexander & Alexander, 2011; Imber & Van Geel, 2009; Harris & Tichenor, 2010; U.S. Courts, n.d.). In the federal court system, each state has at least one federal district court, with most states having two courts. California, Texas and New York each have four district courts. These federal courts litigate cases involving citizens of several different states and cases involving federal statutes. Appeals go to the district circuit courts of appeals or directly to the U.S. Supreme Court. Beyond the Supreme Court, citizens of the United States have no redress (Alexander & Alexander, 2011; Imber & Geel, 2009).

Court cases begin at the lower or district court level by a plaintiff or petitioner. A plaintiff or petitioner is one who initiates a court action by filing a complaint with the appropriate court. The court serves a summons on the person or persons named as the defendant(s). The next step is the plea, in which the defendant can respond by a denial, by seeking independent relief or by introducing an affirmative defense (Alexander & Alexander, 2011; Imber & Van Geel, 2009; Policarpio, 2007).

Prior to trial, there is a process of discovery in which the attorneys may require an oral or written deposition, written interrogatories requiring written responses to questions, certain documents or materials or a request to submit a listing of facts not in dispute and/or a physical or mental examination of one of the parties of the lawsuit (Alexander & Alexander, 2011; Imber & Van Geel, 2009; Policarpio, 2007). The case may be disposed of before going to trial if the judge dismisses the case or allows a motion for summary judgment if there is no dispute of the facts and a trial is not necessary to establish them. Alternatively, the plaintiff may voluntarily dismiss the case, or the parties may reach an out-of-court settlement. The vast majority of civil suits are settled out of court (Alexander & Alexander, 2011). If the case goes to trial, it would be heard by a judge or a jury. The plaintiff bears the burden of proof.

The majority of the cases in this book involve school counselors as defendants or witnesses. In a survey of ASCA members, 95 percent of the respondents said they had never been a defendant in a legal proceeding in the history of their career. Four percent of the 5 percent who had been a defendant said it was for one occurrence (Stone, 2013d).

When a school counselor becomes a defendant in a case, it is often a civil case: a wrong against a student or his or her parents (see the Negligence Chapter). A criminal wrong might involve sexual misconduct with a minor student. Some of the most common cases in which a school counselor might become a defendant involve defamation and qualified privilege, abortion or birth control counseling, academic advising, failure to report child abuse or unauthorized disclosure of information (Stone & Zirkel, 2010; Lazovsky, 2008).

In a recent survey (Stone, 2013d) 34 percent of the respondents reported having been involved in a legal proceeding during the last five years as a witness.

Regarding your professional role as a school counselor, have you been asked to be a witness (not a defendant) in a court case or legal proceeding through a subpoena or a court order in the last five years? If so, how many times?

No: . . . . .66 percent
One or two times: . . . . .27 percent
Three to four times: . . . . .6 percent
Five to six times: . . . . .1 percent

Court proceedings involving school counselors as witnesses for the court are usually cases of child custody, child abuse or disciplinary action (Hays, Craigen, Knight, Healey & Sikes, 2009). This was proven again to be the primary reason in this Stone survey (2013d). School counselors overwhelmingly responded that custody issues and child abuse were the reason they were being asked to be witnesses in legal proceedings in the course of doing their job.

Which statement best describes the reason you were subpoenaed or court ordered. Indicate how many times for each case. Indicate all that applies in the last five years.

Custody battle . . . . .72 percent
Child abuse or neglect by a parent/guardian . . . . .52 percent
A student was sexually abused by a parent
   or stepparent . . . . .21 percent
Foster care or parental rights case . . . . .17 percent
A student was accused of criminal behavior . . . . .16 percent
A parent was accused of criminal behavior . . . . .16 percent
A student was sexually abused by a neighbor,
   babysitter or friend of the family . . . . .15 percent
A student was hurt while on school grounds, on the
   way to school or a school-sanctioned function . . . . .4 percent
A student was sexually abused by a fellow educator
   or administrator . . . . .3 percent
Electronic communication on social media . . . . .2 percent
A student was sexually abused by a stranger . . . . .1 percent

Negligence case regarding academic advising (3 percent), suicide (1 percent) and six other areas for whom school counselors were minimally engaged (0 percent to 1 percent) are discussed in the Negligence Chapter.

Percentages add up to over 100 percent because respondents indicated all that applied to capture all reasons for witnessing in court proceedings (Stone, 2013d).

Generally speaking, school counselors are required to testify in a court proceeding. Although school counselors have confidentiality requirements, school counselors cannot deny the courts their testimony unless the students of school counselors are given privileged communication in state statutes (Stone, 2006; Remley & Herlihy, 2009).

The ASCA member respondents who said they have been subpoenaed or court ordered in the last five years indicated their level of
involvement as follows:

I had to give a deposition only. .42 percent
I had to give a deposition and testify in court. . . . . .68 percent
It ended up that I did not have to give a deposition
   or testify in court because my school district
   intervened. . . . . .22 percent
The case was settled without my testimony. . . . . .57 percent
I was able to explain to the attorneys that they did not
   want my testimony as it would likely damage their
   client's case . . . . .19 percent

Percentages add up to over 100 percent because some members were
involved in more than one court case and respondents were asked to
indicate all that applied to them (Stone, 2013d).

Privileged communication is a creature of statute and only applies to
court proceedings. Privilege is given to students in a few states. Privileged
communication renders the school counselor incapable of testifying in
court about the student's confidential communications unless the student
gives the school counselor permission to do so. In this same survey by
Stone (2013d), 49 percent of the respondents were not sure about their
state statutes and privilege communication. The question of privilege is
one for the school district attorney and should really be answered before a
school counselor receives a subpoena, as it is helpful to know this information in daily work. Check your state statute.

In most states where statutes give privileged communication, there are
many caveats about when a judge can decide that the needs of the state
outweigh the right to privileged communication.

There is judicial reluctance to extend the privilege to students of school
counselors because of the age of their clients and the setting in which they
work (Bodenhorn, 2006; Lazovsky, 2008). Another problem with privilege
is the definition of what constitutes counseling. The court's tendency is to
interpret privileged communication statutes for school counselors very narrowly (Glosoff & Pate, 2002; Lazovsky, 2008). For school counselors,
counseling takes place everywhere. For example, some places counseling

can occur are the playground, in the bus-loading zone or in the hallways. Currently, there are no court cases to give authoritative guidance on this matter (Stone, 2005b). A school counselor may believe that an exchange with a student in the cafeteria is counseling, intending all communication in that meeting to be counseling, and thereafter the student tries to invoke privilege. However, the judge may or may not rule that privilege applies in the situation. Whereas, if an attorney and client exchange any information anywhere – the subway, sauna, tennis court – every utterance is privilege. For the school counseling profession, the interpretation is much more confined, with nearly every state statute offering exceptions to school counselor-student privilege to be interpreted as the judges see fit.

Kentucky offers an example of privileged communication with exceptions in Kentucky Revised Statutes, 2004, § 506:

> "A 'counselor' includes ... A certified school counselor who meets the requirements of the Kentucky Board of Education and who is duly appointed and regularly employed for the purpose of counseling in a public or private school of this state ...
> (b) General rule of privilege. A client has a privilege to refuse to disclose and to prevent any other person from disclosing confidential communications made for the purpose of counseling the client, between himself, his counselor and persons present at the direction of the counselor, including members of the client's family. ...
> (d) Exceptions. There is no privilege under this rule for any relevant communication. ... (2) If the judge finds:
> (A) That the substance of the communication is relevant to an essential issue in the case; (B) That there are no available alternate means to obtain the substantial equivalent of the communication; and,
> (C) That the need for the information outweighs the interest protected by the privilege. The court may receive evidence in camera to make findings under this rule" (Kentucky Revised Statutes, 2004, § 506).

State statutes granting the students of school counselors privileged communication with exceptions are:

Indiana: "A school counselor is immune from disclosing privileged or confidential communication made to the counselor as a counselor by a student..." "[Privilege] is not a ground for excluding evidence in any judicial proceeding resulting from a report of a child who may be a victim of child abuse or neglect or relating to the subject matter of the report or failing to report as required by IC 31-33" (Ind. Code Ann., 2004a, 2004b, § 31-33).

North Dakota: Elementary and secondary school counselors in North Dakota have confidential communication unless the student or counselee requests that the information provided be disclosed (North Dakota Century Code, 2003, § 31-01-06.1).

Oregon: In Oregon, school counselors are listed among those being granted privilege. "Section 40.245, Rule 504-3. School employee-student privilege. ... (2) A certificated school counselor regularly employed and designated in such capacity by a public school shall not, without the consent of the student, be examined as to any communication made by the student to the counselor in the official capacity of the counselor in any civil action or proceeding or a criminal action or proceeding in which such student is a party concerning the past use, abuse or sale of drugs, controlled substances or alcoholic liquor. Any violation of the privilege provided by this subsection may result in the suspension of certification of the professional school counselor as provided in ORS 342.175, 342.177 and 342.180. However, in the event that the student's condition presents a clear and imminent danger to the student or to others, the counselor shall report this fact to an appropriate responsible authority or take such other emergency measures as the situation demands" (Oregon Rev. Stat., 2003).

South Dakota: South Dakota has privileged communication between students and elementary or secondary school counselors with the following exceptions: privilege is waived in writing by the student; the information was disclosed to the counselor for the purpose of being publicized; the counselor has cause to suspect that the student or other individuals have been abused or their physical or mental health is at risk (South Dakota Code, 2003, § 19-13-21.1, Rule 508.1).

Idaho: Idaho seems to leave little doubt that the students of school counselors have privileged communication. When listing all the professionals who cannot be forced to testify against their clients, number six of the list reads: "Any certificated counselor, psychologist or psychological examiner, duly appointed, regularly employed and designated in such capacity by any public or private school in this state for the purpose of counseling students, shall be immune from disclosing, without the consent of the student, any communication made by any student so counseled or examined in any civil or criminal action to which such student is a party. Such matters so communicated shall be privileged and protected against disclosure" (Idaho Code, 2001, § 9-203).

Getting Started: What Would You Do?

The following case is answered for you at the end of this chapter by practicing school counselors. Before you read their responses, formulate in your own mind how you would approach this ethical dilemma.

COURTS, CUSTODY AND THE SCHOOL COUNSELOR'S ROLE

Irene's father, Ronald Carter, asked you to work with his daughter as he and Irene's mother are going through a bitter divorce. You can plainly see Irene needs extra support during this time. Her grades have been spiraling downward, and she seems sad and worried. However, you also think the father has an ulterior motive. Mr. Carter continually calls and feeds you information against Irene's mother. You have negotiated these calls fairly well by always bringing the conversation back to Irene. You stress how Irene might need to visit her pediatrician, and the family might need additional support from an outside resource to make sure Irene is not part of the war. You speak in broad generalities about Irene and skillfully cut off complaints about Ms. Carter. However, the calls keep coming, and you feel certain you are being primed by Mr. Carter to testify against Ms. Carter. What is your role when the subpoena comes?

Working Through Case Studies

PRIVILEGED COMMUNICATION APPLIED

Richmond's mother and father have each separately requested you work with their son as his grades and emotional well-being have been spiraling downward. Both parents give you reasons for their son's downward spiral, and it is always the other parent's fault. Each parent wants you as an ally in the custody battle. You can plainly see in Richmond's grades and affect that he needs extra support during his parent's divorce; however, you are unwilling for your counseling office to become their sparring ground. You try to stick to the subject of student success when they call, but try as you might the mudslinging starts. The mother's attorney has subpoenaed you to testify. You live in North Carolina. Can you refuse to testify if you have Richmond's blessing to do so?

Points to Consider

Yes, Richmond can render you incapable of testifying about him in court in North Carolina. In North Carolina, school counselors cannot "testify in any action, suit or proceeding concerning any information acquired in rendering counseling services to any student ... and which information was necessary to enable him to render counseling services; provided, however, that this section shall not apply where the student in open court waives the privilege conferred" (North Carolina Gen. Stat., 2004, § 8-53.4).

You and Richmond live and work in Montana. His mother demands you testify. Can you refuse?

Maybe. In Montana both the minor student and the parent must give permission to testify, or both must render you incapable of testifying. What if one parent says it is okay for you not to testify, and one parent says he/she wants your testimony? A thorough search failed to reveal a court case to give guidance; it stands to reason that the student's wishes would prevail if they coincide with the wishes of one parent as long as that parent's rights have not been severed by the courts. Because the Montana statute is designed to protect a student's confidence and one parent agrees to do so, then judges would most likely protect the confidence.

"A counselor, psychologist, nurse or teacher employed by any educational institution cannot be examined as to communications made to him in confidence by a duly registered student of such institution. However, this provision shall not apply where consent has been given by the student, if not a minor, or, if he is a minor, by the student and his parent or legal guardian" (Montana Code Ann., 2003, § 26-1-809).

The answer to how the school counselor should behave in this case resides solely in the state statutes. In absence of a statute giving the school counselor's student/clients privileged communication, school counselors legally owe the state their testimony. Ethically, the school counselor may continue to try and get out from under a subpoena, which is the topic of a case in the section, "Confidentiality When There is No Privileged Communication."

COURTS AND ADMINISTRATIVE HEARINGS

A school counselor was accused of sexually abusing a student. The courts cleared him of any wrong doing. Subsequently, the school district conducted an administrative termination hearing. Can the school district fire an educator who was exonerated of wrong doing by the courts?

Points to Consider

In a 2004 case, a school counselor was cleared in a criminal case for allegedly sexually abusing one of his female students. The school board subsequently voted to dismiss him based on the same incident. Unlike criminal trials where prosecutors must overcome the much-higher reasonable doubt standard to secure a conviction, school boards may rely on "substantial evidence" to terminate employees (Shapira, 2005, p. 1). Additionally, evidence is permitted in a school district hearing that is not permitted in a criminal trial. For example, the results of a polygraph test showing deception were allowed in the school district hearing; however, the results were inadmissible in Virginia criminal courts. The board was also able to consider the discovery of pornography on the school counselor's school computer although this information was inadmissible in the court hearing because it was not possible to determine who had downloaded the material (Shapira, 2005).

CONFIDENTIALITY WHEN THERE IS NO PRIVILEGED COMMUNICATION

You have been the primary advocate and confidant for Hansen, who has been in and out of foster homes all his life. He has been in three foster homes in the two years you have known him. Hansen has a difficult time trusting adults, communicates only when necessary and is guarded and suspicious. You have painstakingly built a bond with Hansen, albeit a fragile bond. One of the foster families Hansen lived with for eight months is being investigated for receiving and selling stolen property. You receive a subpoena from the prosecution to give testimony about your confidential conversations with Hansen. Students in your state do not have privileged communication. Hansen, who has already been deposed, was vague and guarded in his responses, and the attorneys are hoping you learned more from him about his time in this home. Hansen told you little about this foster family. What are your legal responsibilities to the court? What are your ethical responsibilities to Hansen?

Points to Consider

Ethically school counselors can try to protect their students' confidences and stay out of court. Legally, as explained in earlier discussion in this chapter, because this state does not extend privileged communication to students, the school counselor has to try to find other ways to keep her students' confidences.

The school counselor should consult the school board attorney to see if he or she can help by getting a motion to quash the subpoena. A motion to quash makes the subpoena null and void, therefore canceling the requirement to testify. The school counselor should inform the attorney who sent the subpoena that there is no information to help the case (if this is true). The school counselor should explain that his or her obligations are to the student. Cite ethical codes, which support the student's confidences, and stay out of court if possible. Advocate. Explain that the relationship is too fragile and too much at risk if you as the school counselor, like all the other adults in Hansen's life, cannot be trusted to stand with him and protect his confidence. Seek research on abandonment issues, foster care and other children in Hansen's situation if further work is needed. Draw attention to the fact that you as the school counselor should not be called on to breach Hansen's confidence, but volunteer to attend court with him if this support seems important to Hansen.

Another approach if unable to get out of the testifying is to ask the judge to use only notes that are pertinent, thereby sealing documents and excusing you as the school counselor from the court proceedings, or requesting an informal conference with only the lawyers and the court in chambers. Failing this approach, the school counselor must testify unless the student has privileged communication under state statute, rendering the school counselor incapable of testifying about him or her.

PROTECTING SOCIETY VS. CONFIDENTIALITY

A teacher asks you to talk to a student who is too preoccupied with sexual matters and displays overtly sexualized behavior. The teacher suspects this child has been or is being sexually abused. You counsel with the student, and she unravels a horrifying story. Physical evidence is collected, the perpetrator arrested, and the trial is about to start. You have been subpoenaed. Do you want to contact the lawyer who sent you the subpoena to try and get the lawyer to quash the subpoena? Should you testify?

Points to Consider

Generally speaking in custody matters and other court proceedings school counselors do not want their case notes or testimony in court. School counselors' loyalty is to their students, and they owe them confidentiality. School counselors advocate to protect their case notes and to be excused from testifying.

However, there will be times such as child abuse situations in which school counselors will want to testify and share their records to help bring a pedophile to justice. School counselors want to protect students' privacy as much as possible. However, the greater good to society will outweigh student confidence.

COURT ORDER VS. SUBPOENA

You have been subpoenaed by the prosecution's attorney. Is a subpoena different from receiving a court order from a judge?

Points to Consider

A court issues a court order requiring a person to do a specified act, such as producing material or appearing in court (Kennedy, 2008; Stone, 2006). If a court orders a school counselor to provide it with information, that person must provide the necessary documents or oral information unless the school counselor's students are protected by a privileged communication statute in that state. The government has the right to obtain a person's information by court order.

A subpoena *duces tecum* (Latin meaning "under penalty you shall bring with you"), on the other hand, is a court order issued by a clerk of court, justice of the peace, notary public or lawyer, usually signed by a lawyer. It requires the recipient to perform a specified act, such as appearing in court to answer questions about something he or she has witnessed or heard, or producing records as evidence (Kennedy, 2008; Stone, 2006). Upon receiving a subpoena, the school must balance student confidentiality and its duty to respond to the court order. There are two different types of subpoenas. One is a subpoena to testify in the courts, and the other is to produce documents (Kennedy, 2008). Although both documents require a response from the school counselor, legal counsel may be more successful with a motion to quash a lawyer-signed subpoena than a motion to reverse a court order. Always seek help from the local school board attorney before responding to a court order or lawyer-signed subpoena. There are penalties for failing to respond to a subpoena or court order, so try to submit a motion to quash (A. L. Colvin, Esq., personal communication, January 2009; Alexander & Alexander, 2012).

In a study by Hermann, Legett & Remley (2008), they found that although school counselors are being trained in the legal and ethical issues, such as when to report child abuse and what to do when a student is suicidal, almost half of the participants felt they were poorly prepared to respond to a subpoena. Increased professional development nationwide is needed in subpoena responses as school counselors want to be knowledgeable in how to guard the safety and privacy of students from court intrusion. The answer to this case resides solely in statute. In absence of a statute giving your student/clients privileged communication, school counselors owe the state their testimony.

DUAL LICENSURE AND THE COURTS

Your colleague Risty is a licensed professional counselor practicing as a school counselor in a state that grants privileged communication for clients of licensed professional counselors but not for students of school counselors. Risty is called to testify regarding one of her students. If the student in question does not give Risty permission to testify, will she be able to successfully respect the student's privileged communications?

Points to Consider

Currently, there are no court cases that give the school counseling profession a clear answer as to dual license and how this will be used by a judge in deciding privileged communication. Risty is working as a school counselor, and her students are not granted privileged communication in her state. However, Risty holds a license as a mental health counselor whose clients do have privilege. So what is the judge to do? Risty argues she cannot be made to testify as her license as a professional licensed mental health counselor grants her clients privileged communication. In absence of a court case that conclusively answers this question, it seems intuitive that the role in which counselors are functioning defines the rules by which they must practice. However, since a judge has not addressed the issue in a published court case, the profession has only conjecture with the exception of a couple of states which asked their attorneys general for an answer.

The Texas Counseling Association asked the state's attorney general to give an interpretation of what would likely happen if a school counselor tried to invoke privilege while practicing in a profession (school counseling) that did not grant students privileged communication. The attorney general believes the Texas statute for privileged communication for clients of licensed mental health professionals would extend to students/clients in schools if these dual licensed counselors were practicing as school counselors even though the Texas counselor is not working in the job for which the license is held. However, this has not been tested in court.

Amy Colvin, Esq., has a different take: "I would think a judge would not let a school counselor fall back on privileged communication as they are acting as a school counselor and not as a licensed counselor with a private client. If I were a judge in a complicated custody case and my whole decision rested on the testimony of the school counselor, I would not want to let them off the hook because I was unlucky enough to get the one school counselor who is also licensed. It is not fair to the justice system ... that some counselors do have to break confidentiality and some do not. The legislature should make these rules so it is fair to all" (A.L. Colvin, Esq., personal communication, January 2009).

J. Freidan, practicing school counselor, said, "I believe the role in which you are functioning defines the rules by which you must practice; this is the law. The law considers 'intent' when considering the truth of the matter." (J. Freiden, NCSC, LPC, personal communication, Jan. 13, 2005).

School counselors lean toward believing your job defines your legal imperatives but not by a sizable margin. In an April 2013 survey, 15 percent of the responded said they hold dual credentials as both a licensed mental health professional and a certified school counselor. These ASCA members were asked to respond to this query:

Which best describes your position if your mental health license allows your clients/student to have privilege communication but students of certified school counselors do not have privilege in your state?

A. I believe the requirements of both my license and my certificate are applicable in my job as a school counselor, and when there is a conflict such as privilege communication, I can choose the license or certificate that best advantages my program or students and adhere to the tenets of that license or certificate.

B. I believe the requirements of my certificate for my current job as a school counselor supersede my license in mental health, and I defer to the requirements of the certificate in the job I am actually performing. In others words my school counseling certification credentials trump any requirements of my mental health license when there is a conflict.

A: . . . . .40 percent
B: . . . . .60 percent

(Stone, 2013d)

INTERPRETING STATE STATUTES ON PRIVILEGED COMMUNICATION

Your state statute says it allows "privileged communication for licensed professional counselors, marriage and family therapists, social workers and chemical dependency specialists (Wyoming Code, 2004, § 33-38-113). You have a student who needs you to respect his confidence, but now you have been subpoenaed. You are not certain your student can render you incapable of testifying about him via state statute. It does not sound like your student can invoke privilege because you are a certified school counselor, not a "licensed professional counselor," as indicated in statute, but this is the third time you have been unsure if students in schools have privileged communication and can render you incapable of testifying, and you are getting conflicting answers. What do you do?

Points to Consider

As Texas did in the previous case, state counseling or school counseling associations can ask the state's attorney general to give an opinion. California gives an excellent example of how an attorney general can bring clarity to ambiguous state statutes. "Any information of a personal nature disclosed by a pupil 12 years of age or older in the process of receiving counseling from a school counselor, as specified in Section 49600, is confidential. The information shall not be revealed, released, discussed, or referred to, except as follows:... (c) Reporting information to the principal or parents of the pupil when the school counselor has reasonable cause to believe that disclosure is necessary to avert a clear and present danger to the health, safety or welfare of the pupil or the following other persons living in the school community: administrators, teachers, school staff, parents, pupils and other school community members (California Education Code, 2004).

School counselors were especially concerned about Education Code section 49602(c), and California attorney general Kamala Harris gave an interpretation on Dec. 29, 2011, in answer to the following questions:

Under Education Code section 49602(c), is a school counselor required to disclose pregnancy-related or abortion-related personal information received from an unemancipated student age 12 or older to the student's parents or school principal when the school counselor has reasonable cause to believe disclosure is necessary to avert a clear and present danger to the student's health, safety or welfare? And, to the extent that the statute allows disclosure of a student's pregnancy-related or abortion-related information to be made under any circumstances, is it invalid on its face as violating the student's constitutional right to privacy?

Kamala D. Harris, attorney general for the state of California, rendered an opinion on Dec. 29, 2011. "Education Code section 49602(c) permits, but does not by its terms require, a school counselor to disclose personal information (including pregnancy-related or abortion-related information) received from an unemancipated student age 12 or older to the student's parents or school principal when the counselor has reasonable cause to believe that disclosure is necessary to avert a clear and present danger to the student's health, safety or welfare. The statute does not, on its face, violate a student's constitutional right of privacy."

In a Position to Know:
School Counselors Speak

The case presented at the beginning of the chapter is revisited here and answered by practicing school counselors. Read their opinions carefully to see what you can learn. Compare their answers with your approach.

COURTS, CUSTODY AND THE SCHOOL COUNSELOR'S ROLE

Irene's father, Ronald Carter, asked you to work with his daughter as he and Irene's mother are going through a bitter divorce. You can plainly see Irene needs extra support during this time. Her grades have been spiraling downward, and she seems sad and worried. However, you also think the father has an ulterior motive. Mr. Carter continually calls and feeds you information against Irene's mother. You have negotiated these calls fairly well by always bringing the conversation back to Irene. You stress how Irene might need to visit her pediatrician, and the family might need additional support from an outside resource to make sure Irene is not part of the war. You speak in broad generalities about Irene and skillfully cut off complaints about Ms. Carter. However, the calls keep coming, and you feel certain you are being primed by Mr. Carter to testify against Ms. Carter. What is your role when the subpoena comes?

Points to Consider

Middle School Counselor's Response
The child is always the primary client in the school setting. However, parents (both of them) are secondary recipients of care. My response to the father would be candid and honest about his voiced concerns. When he criticizes the mother, my response would be to validate his concern on

behalf of the child and to invite both parents into the problem-solving process on the child's behalf. To that end, my efforts would be to engage them in assisting Irene's progress in school and getting her the emotional support needed through this turbulent period. I also would engage the school support process on the child's behalf (response to intervention, small-group counseling, etc.) to improve her progress in school and/or her emotional status. If called to testify I can only speak to the child's performance in school; her observable affect and reports from teachers are all that can be discussed. I will endeavor to respect all other conversations, including any conversations with Irene, her father and her mother.
– *Christy A. Clapper, Ph.D., Quaker Valley School District (retired); Sewickley, Pa., ASCA School Counselor of the Year finalist, 2010*

Elementary School Counselor's Response
As a school counselor, it is my obligation to work with students whose problems at home are affecting their school experience. There may be times, like a divorce situation, in which a parent might desire to use the knowledge gained from my responsive services to influence an outcome in a court case. Because of this danger it is important to go over confidentiality with the student, who needs to know that if asked to share information from our sessions in a court of law I do not have the ability to decline. It is also important to remember that when sharing in a court case I should only relate examples of behaviors I have seen. It is up to the court to determine what these things mean because they will be able to more fully see the whole picture of the situation.
– *Katrina Beddes, Holt Elementary/Davis School District, West Point, Utah, ASCA School Counselor of the Year finalist, 2013*

District Supervisor and Adjunct Counselor Educator's Response
Following is a typical statement I have frequently made to parents appearing to alienate the other parent. "Mr. Carter, I am honored that you would trust me with the details of your hurt over the divorce; however I feel I need to be open and honest with you, as I have been with other parents going through similar difficulties. My role is to help you find additional help for your child. I want to provide you with a list of some wonderful counselors in the community who have received positive feedback from other parents who have sought their help. Based upon our collaborative history together when working with your daughter, I also feel a need to be honest with you about my professional ethics, which prohibits me from taking sides or forming opinions regarding divorce and parenting styles. My role is to be here for your daughter to provide excellent school

counselor support and interventions and not become involved with family mediation issues."
– *Ken Elliott, Coordinator of Testing Services, Director of the Violence Prevention Project, Adjunct Professor, University of Central Oklahoma; ASCA School Counselor of the Year finalist, 2012*

Making Connections

1. Discuss the federal and state court systems and your understanding of them.

2. Determine if your state extends privileged communication to students in schools. How does the statute giving your student privilege read? If your students do not have privileged communication in statute, is there any language that gives you confidentiality to protect their confidences?

3. Read and discuss the responses in the section, "In a Position to Know: School Counselors Speak." Which response do you particularly agree with and why? Which response do you disagree with and why?

4. Under what circumstances can school counselors deny the courts their testimony?

Key Terms

Case notes
Court of Appeals
Court order
Defendant
Deposition
Duces tecum
Federal court
Guardian *ad litem*
Plaintiff

Privileged communication
Process of discovery
Separation of power
State legislature
State court
Subpoena
Testimony
Witnesses
Written interrogatories

Child Abuse

IN THIS CHAPTER

Objectives

By the time you have completed this chapter you should be able to:

- Identify the signs and symptoms of child abuse.
- Understand both short-term and long-term effects of abuse on students.
- Discuss why suspicion of abuse is enough to establish duty to report.
- Understand school counselors' legal and ethical obligations in child abuse reporting.
- Understand good faith reporting and how it protects school counselors.
- Discuss laws and regulations regarding rape, statutory rape and child abuse.

Ethical Standards Addressed in This Chapter

The ASCA Ethical Standards for School Counselors most relevant to this chapter include the following:

- Professional school counselors adhere to laws, local guidelines and ethical standards of practice when assisting parents/guardians experiencing family difficulties interfering with the student's effectiveness and welfare. (B.1.b)
- Professional school counselors are sensitive to diversity among families and recognize that all parents/guardians, custodial and noncustodial, are vested with certain rights and responsibilities for their children's welfare by virtue of their role and according to law. (B.1.c)

The full text of the ASCA Ethical Standards for School Counselors is available at *www.schoolcounselor.org*.

Introduction

Child abuse is not uncommon. Each year, thousands of abused youngsters come through the halls of America's schools and interact with other students, teachers and school counselors. Many of these students are silent victims; educators do not know their pain. Child abuse is severely underreported. School counselors, using their observational skills and ability to deliver professional development, help all under the schoolhouse roof detect, report and prevent child abuse and neglect. This chapter will help school counselors recognize signs and symptoms of child abuse or neglect and understand the legal and ethical dimensions of this often-hidden problem.

Child maltreatment includes all types of abuse (physical, emotional or sexual) and neglect. Minimum standards for what constitutes child abuse and neglect are defined in federal law, and the standard of what constitutes abuse is further stipulated in each state (U.S. Government Accountability Office, 2011). Statutes defining what constitutes abuse or neglect in each state are available at: *www.childwelfare.gov/systemwide/laws_policies/state*. This website also describes the statute of limitations and other important information such as the penalty for failure to report.

Anyone who suspects child abuse or neglect of any kind can report it by calling the police, by contacting the Childhelp USA National Child Abuse Hotline at (800) 4-A-CHILD or by contacting their local child abuse hotline. Educators in all states are mandated to report suspected abuse under penalty of criminal charges. Federal law requires school counselors to report any reasonable suspicion of abuse, even in the absence of hard evidence. In most states mandated reporters (such as school counselors) are immune from legal proceedings brought by parents or guardians who have been erroneously reported to Child Protective Services (CPS). Good-faith reporting is assumed. State-specific information about child abuse reporters, policies and hotline numbers is available at *www.childwelfare.gov*. This site includes not only extensive information about specific state guidelines but also about the level of incidence for child abuse and neglect.

In October 2012, Florida passed what is being described as the most stringent mandatory reporting law in the nation. The new law states everyone is a mandated reporter, "Any person who knows, or has reasonable cause to suspect, that a child is abused, abandoned, or neglected ... shall report such knowledge or suspicion to the department." The new law also makes reporting of child-on-child abuse mandatory for the first time. Children 12 and under who are deemed perpetrators will be referred for treatment and therapy, but those 13 and up will be referred to law enforcement (Fla. Stat. § 39.201- 1a (2012)).

According to the National Child Abuse and Neglect Data System (NCANDS), an estimated 1,560 children died in 2010 as a result of abuse or neglect. Thirty-two percent of child maltreatment fatalities were associated with neglect alone. Physical abuse was cited in almost one-half (45.1 percent) of reported fatalities. Another 40.8 percent of fatalities were the result of multiple maltreatment types (Children Welfare Information Gateway, 2012). "In more than 80 percent of all cases, one or both parents were involved" (U.S. Department of Health and Human Services, Children's Bureau, 2010, p. 42).

As horrific as these numbers are they probably do not tell the whole story. Child welfare officials in 28 states thought the official number of child maltreatment fatalities in their state was probably or possibly an undercount (U.S. Government Accountability Office, 2011). Schnitzer, Covington, Wirtz, Verhoek-Oftedahl and Palusci (2008) found that child welfare agency data in California, Michigan and Rhode Island underestimated child maltreatment fatalities by 55 percent to 76 percent.

In a September 2012 survey, ASCA members weighed in on how often they have made child abuse reports. On average these school counselors reported making eight child abuse reports in the last 24 months (Stone, 2012c).

How many child abuse reports have you called in during the last 24 months?

The average answer was:
Physical 4.9
Neglect 2.6
Sexual abuse 1.1
Emotional abuse 1.4

Abuse may take many different forms: physical abuse, neglect, sexual abuse and emotional abuse. More often than not, these types of abuse occur in combination with one another. Children who are physically abused, for example, often face emotional abuse at the same time. In another example, a child who is sexually abused may also be neglected (Child Welfare Information Gateway, 2007b). Individuals who are working or plan to work in schools should be prepared to recognize the signs of child abuse and neglect. The presence of just one of these signs is not typically indicative of child maltreatment. Rather, alert professionals should consider abuse as a possibility when these signs occur repeatedly and in combination. The following are warning signs of physical abuse, neglect, sexual abuse and emotional abuse taken from the Child Welfare Information Gateway (2007b) fact sheet.

Consider the possibility of physical abuse when the child:
- Has unexplained burns, bites, bruises, broken bones or black eyes
- Has fading bruises or other marks noticeable after an absence from school
- Seems frightened of the parents and protests or cries when it is time to go home
- Shrinks at the approach of adults
- Reports injury by a parent or another adult caregiver

Consider the possibility of physical abuse when the parent or other adult caregiver:
- Offers conflicting, unconvincing or no explanation for the child's injury
- Describes the child as "evil" or in some other very negative way
- Uses harsh physical discipline with the child
- Has a history of abuse as a child

Consider the possibility of neglect when the child:
- Is frequently absent from school
- Begs or steals food or money
- Lacks needed medical or dental care, immunizations or glasses
- Is consistently dirty and has severe body odor
- Lacks sufficient clothing for the weather
- Abuses alcohol or other drugs
- States that there is no one at home to provide care

Consider the possibility of neglect when the parent or other adult caregiver:
- Appears to be indifferent to the child
- Seems apathetic or depressed
- Behaves irrationally or in a bizarre manner
- Is abusing alcohol or other drugs

Consider the possibility of sexual abuse when the child:
- Has difficulty walking or sitting
- Suddenly refuses to change for gym or to participate in physical activities
- Reports nightmares or bedwetting
- Experiences a sudden change in appetite

- Demonstrates bizarre, sophisticated or unusual sexual knowledge or behavior
- Becomes pregnant or contracts a venereal disease, particularly if under age 14
- Runs away
- Reports sexual abuse by a parent or another adult caregiver

Consider the possibility of sexual abuse when the parent or other adult caregiver:
- Is unduly protective of the child or severely limits the child's contact with other children, especially of the opposite sex
- Is secretive and isolated
- Is jealous or controlling with family members

Consider the possibility of emotional abuse when the child:
- Shows extremes in behavior, such as overly compliant or demanding behavior, extreme passivity or aggression
- Is either inappropriately adult (parenting other children, for example) or inappropriately infantile (frequently rocking or head-banging, for example)
- Is delayed in physical or emotional development
- Has attempted suicide
- Reports a lack of attachment to the parent

Consider the possibility of emotional abuse when the parent or other adult caregiver:
- Constantly blames, belittles or berates the child
- Is unconcerned about the child and refuses to consider offers of help for the child's problems
- Overtly rejects the child

In a September 2012 survey, school counselors responded to the type of abuse reports they had to make in the past 24 months (Stone, 2012c).

Please check the primary symptom that led to the report.

Reported injury by a parent or another
    adult caregiver: . . . . .68 percent
Had unexplained burns, bites, bruises, broken bones
    or black eyes: . . . . .41 percent
Was frequently absent from school: . . . . .30 percent
Stated there is no one at home to provide care: . . . . .30 percent
Lacked needed medical or dental care, immunizations
    or glasses: . . . . .28 percent
Had fading bruises or other marks noticeable after
    an absence from school: . . . . .24 percent
Seemed frightened of the parents and protests or
    cries when it is time to go home: . . . . .24 percent
Was consistently dirty and had severe body odor: . . . . . .23 percent
Reported sexual abuse by a parent or another
    adult caregiver: . . . . .21 percent
Showed extremes in behavior, such as overly compliant
    or demanding behavior, extreme passivity
    or aggression: . . . . .14 percent
Lacked sufficient clothing for the weather: . . . . .13 percent
Demonstrated bizarre, sophisticated or unusual sexual
    knowledge or behavior: . . . . .13 percent
Had attempted suicide: . . . . .13 percent
Ran away: . . . . .8 percent
Begged or stole food or money: .8 percent
Reported a lack of attachment to the parent: . . . . .8 percent
Was either inappropriately adult (parenting other
    children, for example) or inappropriately infantile
    (frequently rocking or head-banging, for example): . . . .7 percent
Abused alcohol or other drugs: . . . . .4 percent
Was delayed in physical or emotional development: . . . . .4 percent
Was fearful at the approach of adults: . . . . .2 percent
Became pregnant or contracted a venereal disease,
    particularly if under age 14: .1 percent

Child maltreatment has both long-term and short-term consequences.
Negative physical, cognitive, psychological and/or behavioral outcomes
may appear at any time during an abused individual's lifespan. These
effects range in consequence from minor physical injuries, low self-esteem,

attention disorders and poor peer relations to severe brain damage, extremely violent behavior and suicide. Research consistently shows that any and all forms of maltreatment increase the risk of lower academic achievement, juvenile delinquency, teen pregnancy, drug use and mental health problems (Child Welfare Information Gateway, 2007b). Such dire potential long- and short-term consequences emphasize the need for adults in schools to identify the symptoms of maltreatment and intervene appropriately. Early identification and intervention for these students may reduce the consequences of the abuse.

The ASCA position statement on the Professional School Counselor and Child Abuse and Neglect Prevention reads in part: "ASCA recognizes it is the absolute responsibility of professional school counselors to report suspected cases of child abuse/neglect to the proper authorities. Responsible action by the professional school counselor can be achieved through the recognition and understanding of the problem, knowing the reporting procedures and participating in available child abuse information programs. Professional school counselors are instrumental in early detection of abuse. The association also recognizes that the abuse of children is not limited to the home and that corporal punishment by school authorities can be considered child abuse."

Professional school counselors commit themselves to providing strategies to help break the cycle of child abuse. Professional school counselors can help children and adults cope with abusive behavior, facilitate behavioral changes and develop positive interpersonal relationships, which may reinforce appropriate parenting skills. Professional school counselors coordinate team efforts on behalf of the child, provide support to staff and other school personnel, work to re-establish trust and provide follow-up counseling or refer to ongoing counseling services outside of the school community, provide developmental workshops and/or support groups enhancing parenting skills, and coordinate or provide programs and in-services designed to help prevent child abuse" (ASCA, 2003, p.1).

Unfortunately, child abuse persists in a cycle. Research indicates that about one-third of abused or neglected children will go on to subject their own children to maltreatment (Child Welfare Information Gateway, 2008a). School counselors commit themselves to providing coping strategies and promoting healthy relationship skills to abused children to help break the cycle of child abuse. School counselors can initiate appropriate behavioral changes and help students to develop positive interpersonal relationships, which may reinforce appropriate parenting skills in the future.

When working with a student for whom abuse is suspected, school counselors have an opportunity to use their facilitative counseling skills to make the student feel supported. It is paramount for school counselors to provide validation and encouragement to a child who is maltreated (Dezen, Gubi and Ping, 2010). Listening attentively, reassuring the student that the abuse is not his/her fault and explaining that reporting is what you have to do to protect the student are all ways to use facilitative skills to comfort the student.

School counselors are mandated legally and ethically (ASCA, 2010) to report child abuse. The Keeping Children and Families Safe Act of 2003 (P.L. 108-36) provides minimum standards for defining child physical, sexual, emotional abuse and neglect that all states must incorporate into their statutory definitions to receive federal funds. These statutes outline who must report, to whom the abuse or neglect must be reported, and the form and content of the report. Given the diversity of statutes, educators should obtain a copy of the law in their state and familiarize themselves with it. At least 17 states currently require anyone who has reason to suspect child abuse or neglect to report. Statutes lay out penalties for those who do not act accordingly. Penalties can range from paying a small fine to imprisonment (Price, 2005).

Being directed by law to report means being aware and alert to the potential of abuse, deciding whether abuse is present and being brave enough to take action. Some cases are simple, because the evidence is irrefutable and conclusive. Physical and sexual abuse can fall into this category. Professionals simply see it, hear about it and report it. Other cases fall into a gray area, where pinpointing neglect, mental or emotional harm or threat requires making judgments. Most ethical dilemmas confronting school counselors do not involve a simple "right" or "wrong" answer (Remley & Huey, 2002). The ethical dilemma lies in choosing a course of action. These are occasions where a school counselor has to weigh the facts and consider any extenuating circumstances. In matters of family and the sanctity of the home, school counselors need to give due diligence, acknowledging that their individual perceptions and personal beliefs will influence their choices.

Abused children are our most vulnerable citizens, and our mandate is to use courage to care for them. Sikes, Remley and Hays (2010) found that it is common for school counselors to fear that reporting abuse may have a negative impact on the child. Numerous questions may arise:

"What really constitutes child abuse?"
"What's the difference between bad parenting and abuse?"
"Whom should I call?"
"Do I need to tell my principal I am reporting the case?"
"Will I be legally liable in any way if the case is found to be untrue or unsubstantiated?"
"What specific information do I need to report?"
"What will happen after I file a report?"
"How will I feel in my future interactions with the suspected parents?"

School counselors who reported negative experiences in Child Protective Services commonly worried that their reports would not be properly investigated or that the report would end up having a negative impact on the child (Sikes, Remley and Hays, 2010).

In a 2012 survey of ASCA members, 61 percent of the respondents reported feeling fear, anxiety or indecision while contemplating reporting abuse in the past two years (Stone, 2012c).

The reasons given for the feelings of fear, anxiety or indecision were as follows:

Child Protective Services would not take the report
    seriously or properly investigate: . . . . .71 percent
Child Protective Services might take actions that would
    make the situation worse for the child: . . . . .61 percent
Breaking confidentiality with the child and harming
    our trusting relationship: . . . . .49 percent
I was unsure whether I had enough evidence to file
    a report: . . . . .43 percent
Harming the family's relationship with me
    or the school: . . . . .37 percent
The family would move to another school, and the
    situation would worsen or stay the same
    for the child: . . . . .24 percent
The perpetrator would contact me or harm me or
    someone else at the school: . . . . .23 percent

Sikes et al. (2010) found elementary school counselors are more likely to report suspected abuse cases than middle or high school counselors; their report explains that this is due to high frequency of direct student contact. The school counselors they surveyed were familiar with child abuse laws and procedures in their state. "Years of counseling experience and post-master's degree training events significantly predicted frequency of negative reporting experiences among school counselors" (Sikes et al., 2010, p. 19).

ASCA members responded that they felt "very prepared" or "prepared" to make different types of child abuse reports. Regarding physical abuse, 95 percent of respondents felt confident to report, 83 percent for sexual abuse and 86 percent for neglect. The confidence level declined to 68 percent regarding reporting emotional abuse.

State statutes vary slightly in language, but there are common themes in most state's statutes. Educators and school counselors are mandatory child abuse reporters, which means they:

- Have an absolute duty to report.
- Do not have to be certain; suspicion is enough to establish a duty.
- Have a duty that is not discretionary; it is inextricably clear.
- Have an obligation to report within their state's specified time period.
- Are protected, since good faith reporting is assumed.
- Understand there is not a statute of limitations on child abuse reporting.

State statutes are available at
www.childwelfare.gov/systemwide/laws_policies/state.

The information reported to CPS generally includes the following: (a) the name, address and gender of the child; (b) the name and address of the parent, guardian or caretaker; (c) the name and age of any other children/adolescents living in the home; (d) the child's condition, including the nature and extent of the injury; (e) an explanation of the injuries as given by the child; (f) any information regarding the presence of weapons, alcohol and/or drug abuse or other factors affecting the social worker's safety; (g) actions taken by the reporter, such as detaining the child; and (h) any other information the reporter believes may be helpful in establishing the cause of injuries and/or protecting the child (Child Welfare Information Gateway, 2009).

Getting Started: What Would You Do?

A response to the following case by a school counselor appears at the end of this chapter. Before you read her response, formulate in your own mind how you would approach this ethical dilemma.

RAPE, STATUTORY RAPE AND CHILD ABUSE APPLIED TO A STATE STATUTE

A 15 year old tells you he is having sex with his 19-year-old girlfriend. A 14-year-old student tells you she is having sex with her 17-year-old partner. Is either scenario considered statutory rape in your state? Are you required to report in either scenario to CPS, the police and/or the sheriff? This is examined by leaders in the school counseling field as applied to their particular state.

Working Through Case Studies

FAILURE TO REPORT CHILD ABUSE

A student told you her father walked around the house naked. You told her to talk to her mother. She came back and told you her father touched her breast. Because she did not have breasts, you dismissed it and told her to tell her mother about things with her body that concerned her. She came back a third time and told you her father asked her to touch his penis. Again you dismissed it because this student fabricates stories. Is there a legal or ethical problem with your behavior?

Points to Consider

In *Hughes v. Stanley County School District* (1999), an elementary school counselor was fired for not reporting alleged child abuse. M.B., a third-grade girl, told Mary Hughes, the school counselor, that in 1994 her father, G.B., walked around the house naked after a shower. In another conversation, M.B. told Hughes that G.B. "touched her in the area of her breast during a playful wrestling match," and in a third conversation Hughes learned that M.B. walked in on her father while he was masturbating. M.B., however, had a history of fabricating and exaggerating facts, so Hughes was unsure about how seriously to take the allegations. Accordingly, she spoke with the high school counselor to get a second opinion, and both felt Hughes should speak with the girl's parents. So, going against school policy to report suspicion of abuse, Hughes contacted the parents in an attempt to validate or dismiss the allegations. The parents told her the allegations were essentially true, and G.B. had taken steps to avoid reoccurrence in the future. While Hughes did check up on the situation with M.B. daily, she never reported the allegations to the authorities.

The failure to report came to light in July 1996 when the police questioned Hughes in connection with a complaint that G.B. had sexually assaulted a neighboring girl. G.B. pled guilty to the sexual assault charge with the neighboring child, and Hughes was fired for failure to report the previous allegations (Swinton, 2005).

PERSONAL JUDGMENT IN REPORTING CHILD ABUSE

You work in a school in which the principal uses his own judgment about whether or not to call CPS. The principal decides if the case is a possible child abuse situation or if "over-discipline" has occurred. There are many times when black eyes and bruised cheeks go unreported because the principal knows the child's parents and has asked they not be reported. The reasons he gives for not reporting vary: The parents just got carried away; the child seems fine and is not really hurt; we are just beginning to get the parents to trust us and a report will destroy all that; these parents will uproot their child and go to another school if we report, and we know the child is better off in this school. The principal says he can do far more good by preserving and building relationships with families and by calling parents himself and explaining they must not continue to mistreat their child. The principal works hard to help the children in this troubled community, and the school has a reputation of being an oasis in a community fraught with a high incidence of problems, including child abuse. How should a school counselor address this principal's practices?

Points to Consider

When the question of administrative support have been raised in workshops by the author, school counselors have routinely reported their administrators have given reasons similar to the above when putting up roadblocks to reporting child abuse. Most of these school counselors report their principals are well-meaning and trying to do the right thing by students and families.

"Donavan, the longtime principal at Kell High School who suddenly announced her retirement earlier this month, was booked into the Cobb County Jail on Thursday night on a charge of failing to report child abuse, a misdemeanor. Donavan turned herself in about 7 p.m. Thursday and was released just before midnight that night on $1,000 bond. ... is the second Cobb principal charged this year with failure to report suspected abuse. In March, former Tapp Middle School principal ... and a counselor at that school were charged with failure to report suspected sexual abuse of a student. Both were fired by the district in April. If convicted, ... faces a maximum sentence of 12 months in jail and a $1,000 fine" (*Marietta Daily News*, June 22, 2012).

Incidences where administrators have created obstacles are more than obstructive; they are illegal. School counselors and administrators are ethically, morally and legally responsible to report suspected child abuse. In this same survey of ASCA members (Stone, 2012c), 6 percent of the respondents said that in the last 36 months they have been asked by an administrator not to call in certain situations they suspected were child abuse. While this is frightening, the good news is the converse; 94 percent of the respondents said this has not happened to them in the last 36 months. In a related question, school counselors were asked if their administrator(s) were supportive when they made child abuse reports. Eighty-seven percent of the respondents said they felt "completely" supported, and 13 percent said they felt "somewhat" supported. Only 1 percent said they were "rarely" supported (Stone, 2012c).

In this all-too-real case scenario, child abuse has been underreported because of the principal's approach to handling child abuse. Legally and ethically, a school counselor is required to report this abuse, even if it goes against individual school practice. Politically, this situation is fraught with land mines as the principal may view your reports to CPS as interference and insubordination. Talk to the principal about the legal mandate to report child abuse. The discussion might well protect him, you and the teachers involved from legal liability. Undermining the principal's decision in such a situation is likely to cause turmoil between you and the principal; however, the reasons to report far outweigh any political fallout from administration.

Kentucky's Supreme Court strictly adhered to the state's reporting statute in *Commonwealth v. Allen* (1998) by holding a teacher and a school counselor criminally liable for failing to report suspected child abuse to proper authorities, despite making a report to their supervisor. Two sixth-grade girls attending an elementary school in Kentucky reported to Betty Allen, one of the teachers, and Pamela Cook, the school's counselor, that another teacher, Donald Mullins, sexually assaulted them earlier that fall. Both Allen and Cook then reported the matter to the school's principal, feeling, in good faith, that doing so discharged their legal duty to report. Yet none of the three reported the suspected abuse to state or local law enforcement officials. In March 1993, another sixth-grade girl, along with several eyewitnesses, reported to an assistant principal that Mullins had recently sexually abused her. At that point, the school reported all three instances to the proper authorities. Shortly thereafter, the state charged the teacher and the school counselor with a Class B misdemeanor for failure to properly report suspected child abuse in violation of the Kentucky child abuse reporting statute.

This case demonstrates that school counselors cannot abdicate their responsibilities unless the state statute specifically says they can. Wyoming statute states that a person must report the abuse to a designated agent, who will then be responsible for making the report; however, this statute does not relieve the person of his or her responsibility to make certain that the report is made (Child Protective Services Act, Wyoming Code. § 14-3-2 (1999)). In Wyoming, as in many states, the teacher and the school counselor are just as responsible as the assistant principal to make certain a report is made.

UNCERTIFIED SCHOOL COUNSELORS AND CHILD ABUSE REPORTING

You are not yet certified in your state to be a school counselor, yet you are hired on a teacher contract and placed in a school counseling position. You are not certain of the child abuse laws or any other law governing schools, and you have two more years in your school counselor preparation program. Is there a legal or ethical dilemma for you in this situation?

Points to Consider

Principals and school counseling supervisors increasingly face the unfortunate choice between hiring an uncertified school counselor or leaving a position unfilled for months or, in some cases, years. Educators typically understand that hiring an out-of-field or uncertified person leaves the school district more vulnerable in the event of a breach of ethics or law. However, the shortage of educators makes the practice commonplace in some parts of the United States and, rather than having a school counseling vacancy, many school districts want their students to have the benefits of a school counseling program. When a school district hires an uncertified school counselor, both the school counselor and the school district must ensure that the school counselor understands the affirmative duty to report child abuse.

If you take a position for which you are not certified, it is in your best interest and that of the school district that you do all you can to educate yourself about the law for mandatory reporting of child abuse, as well as school board policy and practice. There are no excuses if a school counselor does not know the law about child abuse reporting. The school district is even more vulnerable if an uncertified school counselor commits an offense as the school district lowered its standard of care by placing an uncertified person in a counseling position.

WHEN REPORTING DOESN'T YIELD RESULTS

A student comes to school with severely bruised arms, legs and a black eye. The student freely tells you that her parents beat her for sneaking out of the house last Saturday night. After the beating, she heard her parents discussing the possibility of school officials calling in an abuse report to CPS, and they decided to go on the offense. Her parents called the police and reported her for running away. The police came to the house and took pictures of her bruises, telling her parents they did not have to worry about charges because it would be viewed as over-discipline. You call CPS, and the responding caseworker comes to school, appears sympathetic and takes the student home to meet with the parents. The next day the student reports to you that the caseworker "turned on her" and told the parents she should have to earn everything, including the clothes she wears and the door on her bedroom, and treated her like a criminal. What would you do?

Points to Consider

Black eyes and bruises down arms and legs are clear signs of abuse, according to the Child Welfare Information Gateway (2007b). You can follow up with CPS to see whether or not the case was labeled abuse. It may well be that the caseworker and parents reached an agreement in which future incidences in which the child misbehaves would be handled with lost privileges and the need to earn privileges back. Just because the student is not satisfied with the resolution of the case does not mean that the case was not handled properly. If you have doubts, you can call CPS.

Keeping a close watch on the student can help allay your fears. If signs of abuse reappear, speak to a supervisor in CPS to discuss your concerns. Stress that you want it on record that you are frightened for this child. Explain to the supervisor that you are taking careful notes because you are afraid your notes may be needed one day in the event this child is severely hurt. Putting pressure on others to act is appropriate and necessary when you are concerned and must rely on CPS to intervene on behalf of the student's safety.

Sometimes potential reporters believe nothing will be done if they report, so they choose not to do so. This is faulty reasoning. A record of the report will be made, the educator's legal obligation will be fulfilled, and the investigative process will begin. Maltreated children cannot be protected unless they are first identified, and the key to identification is reporting. While some calls do not result in an investigation, educators may not know what information was previously or subsequently reported about the child or the family. The cumulative effect of all the reports may allow CPS to substantiate a case and to provide help and intervention (Humphreys & Stanley, 2006). Some educators also find it frustrating that CPS will not let them know whether the case is being investigated. Confidentiality laws and policies often make follow-up impossible (Humphreys & Stanley, 2006).

ANGRY PARENTS/GUARDIANS AND A CHILD ABUSE REPORT

You recently reported a case to CPS. The case was deemed unfounded and closed. The parents easily figured out it was you who called, and they take issue with you for discussing "private, personal issues" with their child. They tell your principal they do not want you to ever work with their child again. Can the parents forbid you to work with their child?

Points to Consider

CPS doesn't tell parents or guardians who made the child abuse report, but parents/guardians can often surmise who the reporter was from details they are given or by simply asking their child whom he/she talked to about the abuse. This scenario is repeated many times in households across America, often placing the reporting counselor in a difficult position. School counselors can refuse to talk to perpetrators about child abuse reports, or school counselors may use the opportunity to try to collaborate and help parents/guardians develop better approaches in working with their children. The call is the school counselor's as to how to respond.

If the parents/guardians are in conflict with you over reporting, working with their child can be complicated. In many school districts, parents/guardians can refuse counseling services for their child even if the student still wants to come for counseling. Just as the math teacher and English teacher can do their jobs without parental permission, generally speaking, so can school counselors. However, since counseling involves the personal, social and emotional arena, it is considered best practice to have parental permission for individual counseling.

When parents/guardians expressly state they do not want counseling for their child, it is best not to dismiss their wishes. However, if you believe the child is in danger, and the parents/guardians are trying to hide their behavior by keeping you from having contact with their child, alert everyone to keep a keen eye out for signs of abuse. You can still work with the child if you think it is imperative to do so, but the fallout and strain on all may be too much. If the child needs help, implore the parents/guardians to allow someone else to help, perhaps by referring the student to another school counselor in the school.

LIABILITY IN CHILD ABUSE REPORTING

A teacher brought a case of child abuse to your attention. The teacher noticed a horrible slash mark across the back of a child's neck and, upon inspection, saw that it extended far down the child's back. The mark closely resembled a belt mark. You report the incident to the Child Abuse Registry. The subsequent investigation by CPS reveals a fall from a piece of playground equipment, witnessed by the child's soccer coach and team members. The parents deduce the report came from the school and specifically from you. The parents are livid and are threatening to sue you. Can you be sued?

Points to Consider

Good-faith reporting is assumed when a professional reports child abuse. "The term good-faith reporting refers to the assumption that the reporter, to the best of his or her knowledge, had reason to believe that the child in question was being subjected to abuse or neglect. Even if the allegations made in the report cannot be fully substantiated, the reporter is still provided with immunity. There is a 'presumption of good faith.' All states, the District of Columbia, Puerto Rico, American Samoa, Guam, the Northern Mariana Islands and the U.S. Virgin Islands provide some form of immunity from liability for persons who in good faith report suspected instances of child abuse or neglect under the reporting laws. Immunity statutes protect reporters from civil or criminal liability that they might otherwise incur. This protection is extended to both mandatory and voluntary reporters" (Child Welfare Information Gateway, 2012, p. 2).

A mere suspicion of abuse is all that is necessary when reporting child abuse. By reporting the slash mark, the school counselor acted legally and ethically and earned immunity from all liability in most states. Every state and U.S. territory provides various degrees of protection from liability for persons who in good faith report suspected instances of abuse or neglect under the reporting laws. Immunity statutes protect reporters from civil or criminal liability that they might otherwise incur (Child Welfare Information Gateway, 2007a). For a complete listing of state-by-state child abuse reporting laws, see the website for Child Welfare Information Gateway, which gives state statutes for immunity for reporters of child abuse and neglect at *www.childwelfare.gov*.

In *Zamstein v. Marvasti* (1997), the Supreme Court began an examination of this issue as it related to health care providers and determined safety from civil and criminal liability in its interpretation of the child-abuse-reporting statutes. In *Zamstein*, the report of child abuse arose out of a bitter divorce and custody dispute in which Sharon Zamstein accused her husband, Jacob, of sexually abusing their children. Sharon Zamstein retained a psychiatrist for the express purpose of evaluating the children to determine whether or not the father had abused them. Custody of the children was granted to Sharon Zamstein. A criminal prosecution against Jacob Zamstein ended in an acquittal. He then sued the psychiatrist, Dr.

Marvasti, claiming the prosecution against him and the alienation of his children only occurred because of the psychiatrist's report of suspected sexual abuse. The Supreme Court had no difficulty in deciding that, following the statutory guidelines, providers who make a report in good faith are immune from any liability, civil or criminal. Almost all health care attorneys will advise a client that it is far better to be faced with defending a civil action for reporting suspected abuse, rather than defending a civil action when a child is injured or killed after failing to make a report of suspected child abuse. Failure to report suspected child abuse can result in criminal and civil liability.

CHILD ABUSE AND STATUTE OF LIMITATIONS

You are a high school counselor. One of your students confides in you that five years ago she was the victim of sexual abuse by her mother's boyfriend. Four years ago the perpetrator left the home and moved to another state. She tells you she never told anyone, not even her mother. She begs you not to tell anyone. What are your obligations?

Points to Consider

A statute of limitations is a law that sets the time within which criminal charges or civil claims can be filed and after which one loses the right to sue or make a claim (Child Welfare Information Gateway, 2007b). The statute of limitations of child abuse in most states is between five and 10 years. However, for some states, such as New Jersey, there is no statute of limitations (Aronson, 2002). A summary of the statutes of limitations for each state for offenses against children can be found at www.sol-reform.com/index.php.

The legal determination of the statute of limitations, however, is not part of the duty to report to which counselors must adhere. If a situation of abuse is reported, the professional must contact the authorities, which will then pursue the matter and make the necessary legal determinations. In your advocacy role, you can and should support this student through any subsequent legal proceedings and help her in any way possible, but you are not able to honor her request "not to tell anyone."

DOMESTIC VIOLENCE AND CHILD ABUSE

A teacher is worried about a student who is always either sleeping or crying in class. You talk with the student, and she tells you that for the last week she has listened to her mom and stepfather argue. Her eyes fill with tears as she tells you that the yelling and sounds of things breaking keep her awake all night. Is this considered child abuse? Should you report it?

Points to Consider

Over the past few decades, there has been a growing awareness of the concurrence of domestic violence and child abuse. An estimated 3.3 million to 10 million children a year are at risk for witnessing or being exposed to domestic violence, which can produce a range of emotional, psychological and behavioral problems for children (Humphreys & Stanley, 2006). Research also indicates that children who are exposed to domestic violence are at an increased risk of being abused or neglected. Because of the overlap between domestic violence and child maltreatment, CPS is working closely with services related to domestic violence to ensure more comprehensive assistance to both the child and victim (Child Welfare Information Gateway, 2008a).

"The witnessing of domestic violence can be auditory, visual or inferred, including cases in which the child perceives the aftermath of violence, such as physical injuries to family members or damage to property" (Child Welfare Information Gateway, 2009, p.1). Although witnessing domestic violence can result in severe emotional and developmental difficulties similar to those of children who are direct victims of abuse, the statutes for reporting these types of incidences are far less clear than for other situations of child abuse. The legal system is beginning to recognize the need to protect and care for these children. Approximately 22 states and Puerto Rico currently address in statute the issue of children who witness domestic violence in their homes" (Child Welfare Information Gateway, 2009, p.1).

Children often face harm during violent attacks on the adult victim. Some perpetrators intentionally physically, emotionally or sexually abuse their children in an effort to intimidate and control their partner. While these scenarios explicitly constitute child abuse or maltreatment, other cases may not be so clear. In many states, a conviction for domestic violence committed in the presence of a child may result in harsher penalties than a conviction for domestic violence without a child present. Eight states (Alaska, Arizona, California, Hawaii, Mississippi, Montana, Ohio and Washington) consider an act of domestic violence committed in the presence of a child an "aggravating circumstance" in their sentencing guidelines. This usually results in a longer jail term, an increased fine or both. An additional five states (Arkansas, Florida, Idaho, Louisiana and Oregon), while not using the term "aggravating circumstance," require more severe penalties. In five states (Delaware, Georgia, North Carolina, Oklahoma and Utah), committing domestic violence in the presence of a child is a separate crime that may be charged separately or in addition to the act of violence.

In addition to any criminal penalties, Illinois, Louisiana and Nevada require perpetrators of domestic violence to pay for any counseling a child victim may require. Ohio and Oklahoma require the offenders to undergo counseling. Indiana requires supervised visitation of a noncustodial parent who has been convicted of domestic violence in the presence of his or her noncustodial child for a period of one to two years (Child Welfare Information Gateway, 2009).

The case of *Nicholson v. Williams* (2001) challenged the practice of New York City's Administration for Children's Services. This service was removing the children of battered mothers solely on the basis that the children saw their mothers being beaten by husbands or boyfriends. Judge Weinstein ruled the practice is unconstitutional, and he ordered it to be stopped. The expert witnesses in the case testified that observing domestic violence is "sometimes, but not always, harmful to children. Even when witnessing domestic violence does harm, removing the child from the non-offending parent can be more harmful. Indeed, one expert testified that a removal under such circumstances 'is tantamount to pouring salt on an open wound'" (*Nicholson v. Williams* (2001)). Another witness testified, "When a child is separated from a mother because of domestic violence, the separation is even more traumatic, because the child 'is terrified that a parent might not be OK, may be injured, may be vulnerable. ... They feel that they should somehow be responsible for the parent, and if they are not with the parent, then it's their fault'" (*Nicholson v. Williams* (2001)).

Especially cruel is when siblings are treated differently. For instance, "abusers target one child and not another – e.g., sexually abusing a daughter, while trying to buy a son's loyalty with special privileges"

(Parry, 2007, p. 1). Children who live in households plagued with domestic violence often suffer physical, emotional, verbal abuse and many other forms of abuse:

- 90 percent of children from violent homes witness their fathers beating their mothers.
- 63 percent of all boys, age 11-20, who commit murder, kill the man who was abusing their mother.
- Children in homes where violence occurs are physically abused or neglected at a rate 1,500 percent higher than the national average
- Research has shown that the more severe the abuse of the mother, the worse the child is abused.
- Nationally, 75 percent of battered women say their children are physically or sexually abused.
- Daughters of abused women are six times more likely to be sexually abused as girls from non-abusive families.
- Research has found that 13 out of 20 incestuous fathers were also physically violent to their wives and to their family members.
- More than half of the child abductions in this country occur within the context of domestic violence.
- Child victims of severe violence have two to four times higher rates of trouble making friends, temper tantrums, failing grades in school, having problems in school and at home.
- Abused children are arrested by the police four times more often than nonabused children (Turning Point, n.d.).

Supporting children of domestic violence at school, helping families find resources, and placing the child with a caring adult such as a school mentor are just a few of the ways school counselors can provide these children with a safe haven.

CHILD NEGLECT REPORTING

You are concerned about a 12-year-old student who is a loner. You notice he appears to be underweight and about half of the time comes to school wearing filthy clothing, with hair that is lifeless and dirty. You speak to his teacher about your concerns, and she tells you the student is withdrawn, only speaks when absolutely necessary and frequently appears fearful and furtive. You arrange a conference with the student and his parents. When the parents arrive, you notice a strong smell of alcohol on their breath. Their eyes, mannerisms and slurred speech convince you they are under the influence of alcohol. What do you do?

Points to Consider
This case highlights the "grayness" often occurring when deciding to report suspected child neglect. Neglect is lack of care that risks or causes harm to a child, including lack of food, clothing, supervision or medical attention.

These are some fairly subjective conditions and descriptions of potential areas of abuse. Good protocol in this situation might include discussing your concerns with the school principal and the school counseling director. It is never wrong to call the abuse hotline and discuss your concerns with one of the supervisors or caseworkers for an opinion. Err on the side of caution. It is better to have an angry parent than to let a child in danger escape your attention. It is important to remember that a mandated reporter does not have to prove abuse has taken place; reasonable grounds for suspicion are sufficient. A reporter does not need the permission of the school, parents or caregivers to make a report, and it is not necessary to tell them the report was made (Mattingly, J.B., 2007).

HEARSAY AND SECONDHAND INFORMATION
Two girls come to you saying their parents told them to come talk to you about their friend Shania. The girls tell you that they think Shania's stepfather is sexually molesting her. The girls seem sketchy and confused when you ask why they believe their friend is being abused. They insist that Shania says "things," but they cannot recall any particulars of the conversations. What will be your next step?

Points to Consider
School counselors often receive possible child abuse reports through hearsay or secondhand information. Authorities, such as the police and child protection workers, caution educators against investigating child-abuse reports because we may inadvertently ask leading questions of the student, thus hindering the investigation or subsequent trial of alleged perpetrators. However, the courts support us in asking questions of Shania

and others such as her teachers, who may be in a position to help us determine if we should file a child-abuse report. In *Picarella v. Terrizzi* (1995) the court concluded that a student's constitutional rights were not violated when school officials questioned the student about suspected abuse (LaMorte, 2001; *Picarella v. Terrizzi* (1995)). Likewise, in *Landstrom v. Illinois* (1990), courts supported school officials who had a student remove her dress and underwear to examine her buttocks for signs of abuse. Know your state statutes and whether your state has granted mandated reporters immunity from liability in cases of more intrusive investigation. It is also appropriate to decide to make the call to CPS without any investigation or consultation. If you have reasonable suspicion, certainty is not required, and you have enough to call in a report to CPS. What we do not do is to simply sweep away the report.

A recent court case involved a school counselor who allegedly told a student to "stop lying" and go back to class when she reported to the school counselor that her teacher, Michael Alexander, was touching her inappropriately. "The teacher, Michael Alexander, pleaded guilty in July 2012 to taking indecent liberties with a child and first-degree sex offense with a child" (Marsh, 2013, p 1). He is serving a 40-year sentence. Court documents indicate that abuse by Alexander to the students of his classes probably went on for more than 10 years. "Alexander copied videos of young girls having sex with each other and with adult men, the documents revealed, and he took illicit pictures of young girls wearing T-shirts printed with the school's name" (Marsh, 2013). We never ignore a report from a student. We take additional steps to have authorities refute or substantiate a child's claim. How many other students may have reported incidences and were ignored? Nonmaleficence means, above all, do no harm.

In *Jane Doe v. Unified School District, School Counselor, and Elementary School Principal* (2003), a mother alleged that school personnel negligently failed to report information concerning the suspected sexual abuse of her child. Three classmates told the school counselor that Doe told them of alleged abuse by her stepfather. The school counselor told the school principal, but neither investigated nor reported allegations of abuse. The Kansas courts have followed up on many cases and found educators guilty of not reporting child abuse, but because this was from a third party, Kansas courts have yet to determine duty owed by school district, principal or school counselor after receiving information from a third party that a child is being sexually abused by a parent.

CHILD-ABUSE REPORTS AND RELATIONSHIPS WITH PARENTS/GUARDIANS

Benjamin, who is in fourth grade, is continuously in trouble with his teacher for defiant behavior. You have been working with Benjamin and his mother and have noticed improvements in his behavior. You have worked hard to establish a good relationship with Benjamin's mother based on mutual respect. Lately, she seems less defensive and appears to be relaxing her guard and cooperating fully with you. One day Benjamin comes to school with ugly red welts on his arms and face. His mother voluntarily comes in to tell you that she lost control the night before and hit him with a belt. How would you respond?

Points to Consider

As difficult as it may be to do so, you must make a report to CPS. As school counselors, we are not able to take matters into our own hands. We have a black-and-white mandate with no room for negotiating with parents/guardians. You may choose to take the opportunity to tell Benjamin's mother that you need to make the call to CPS, either before or after you call them, to keep the lines of communication open. It is also understandable to choose not to say anything to Benjamin's mother about making a report. Individual school counselors can decide how they would choose to try to preserve the relationship, but ugly red welts on a child require a report to CPS.

UNREPORTED TEACHER-ON-STUDENT SEXUAL ABUSE

You coach soccer in the school where you are a school counselor. You have heard rumors the softball coach is having an affair with one of her students. After an unscheduled practice with two of your students, you enter the coaches' office and hear the frantic rustling of clothes and hushed whispers. After five minutes, this coach and student emerge from behind closed doors. The coach mumbles something about looking for equipment, and they hurry out. You are certain your unscheduled appearance in the coaches' office has interrupted a sexual encounter. Now what do you do?

Points to Consider

The case of *Doe v. Rains Independent School District* (1994) was a situation in which a teacher was involved in a sexual relationship with a student, and another teacher, Dana White, had knowledge of the relationship but waited several months before making a report. Dana White was told by Sarah Doe, a student, about her sexual relationship with a teacher at a neighboring school, which was hidden under the guise of babysitting for his children. White did not report the incident when she learned about it in June 1992 because of her promise of confidentiality to Sarah.

Upon learning of the abuse, Sarah Doe's parents sued Dana White for violating Texas law requiring teachers to report child abuse within 48 hours. The court found White did not have supervisory control over the other teacher in question. Therefore, the court found no causal connection to Sarah's constitutional injury and determined White's delay in reporting was not "action under color of state law" (*Doe v. Rains Independent School District* (1994)). You do not want to find yourself party to a lawsuit involving non-report of sexual abuse. Even if the court finds in your favor, you will have suffered the strain of court proceedings, not to mention the realization of harm to a child.

EDUCATORS AND STATUTORY RAPE

You are a school counselor, and it comes to light that your 23-year-old colleague, who is new to the school counseling profession, has been having a three-month sexual relationship with one of her 17-year-old students. Will she be criminally charged with statutory rape?

From October–December 2009, a Florida high school counselor was engaged in a sexual relationship with a 17-year-old student. Once discovered, she was immediately fired; however, the school counselor was not guilty of statutory rape. Florida, like the vast majority of states, deems a 17-year-old to be within the "age of consent." In Florida, a 23 year old can legally enter into a sexual relationship with a 17 year old. The school counselor was 23 years old, so the difference in age was not enough to trigger a statutory rape charge (Sanders, 2010).

Florida statute: The age of consent is 16. s.794.05 Unlawful sexual activity with certain minors.— (1) A person 24 years of age or older who engages in sexual activity with a person 16 or 17 years of age commits a felony of the second degree ..."

For some states, specific laws have been passed to criminalize educator-student relationships, even when the students are at the age of consent. Alabama, Arizona, Connecticut, Ohio, New Hampshire and Texas all have specific laws aimed at educators who prey on students. For example, without equivocation the Texas statute makes it clear that educators cannot have sex with their students regardless of the student's age.

Texas Statute: § 21.12. IMPROPER RELATIONSHIP BETWEEN EDUCATOR AND STUDENT.
(a) An employee of a public or private primary or secondary school commits an offense if the employee engages in sexual contact, sexual intercourse or deviate sexual intercourse with a person who is enrolled in a public or private primary or secondary school at which the employee works and who is not the employee's spouse. (b) An offense under this section is a felony of the second degree.

However, even with such laws, states find it difficult to prosecute when the student is an adult, or 18, as in the case of a 25-year-old former Miss Texas contestant who was arrested for having a sexual relationship with an 18-year-old in the high school where she taught. Under the law, the improper relationship warranted a second-degree felony charge and a possible 20-year prison sentence. However, in October 2006, a grand jury refused to indict the teacher, and the second-degree felony charge against her was dismissed.

Perhaps if Florida had a specific statute like Texas, then there would have been a law with which to charge the 23-year-old perpetrator. Instead, she was able to leave one district and secure a job in a counseling agency, which repositioned her into a high school so within weeks she was back working with minors. The school counselor was eventually arrested and charged under a more-difficult-to-prosecute Florida statute regarding government employees who have sexual relations with a minor over whom they have custody and control.

Florida statute (943.253) for Government Employees. (g) When the offender is ... a person in a position of control or authority in a probation, community control, controlled release, detention, custodial, or similar setting, and such officer, official, or person is acting in such a manner as to lead the victim to reasonably believe that the offender is in a position of control or authority as an agent or employee of government.

CHILD ABUSE IN A COUNSELING SESSION

Your colleague appears to be too familiar with students. Students have shared a few comments he has said to them, and you believe he is walking a narrow line with some of the topics he addresses during individual counseling sessions. Today a girl tells you he asked her about her menstrual periods and her sexual relationship with her boyfriend. You are stunned. Is this child abuse?

Points to Consider

The differential in power between school counselor and student is considerable. Although school counselors have influence over their vulnerable minor students, they rarely abuse this power. Occasionally school counselors abuse their position of trust. Although it may or may not be a reportable offense by CPS, it is grounds for dismissal.

A 28-year-veteran Maryland high school counselor is not the first school counselor to be dismissed because of inappropriate sexual comments to students. Circuit Court Judge David Bruce said that the school counselor went far beyond acceptable limits by asking the junior about her sex life with her freshman boyfriend, whom the student complained "treated [her] like crap." Judge Bruce noted the school counselor had a legal obligation to determine if the girl was a victim of sexual abuse, but the school counselor stepped far beyond the limits when he asked her how many times she and her boyfriend had sex, which sex acts she liked, whether certain sex acts hurt her and whether she knew any gay or lesbian students in the school (Capital-Gazette Communications, 2004).

SCHOOL COUNSELOR COMMITS CHILD ABUSE

What if a school counselor's conduct is not necessarily criminal but teeters on the precipice, as in the case of the school counselor who was charged with the criminal offense of indecent liberties with a child?

Points to Consider

A fifth-grade girl, A.U., was referred to the school counselor because she was struggling academically. Allegedly her parents were not responsive to A.U.'s needs, and the school counselor was meeting with her to try and motivate her. The school counselor allegedly try to show A.U. personal attention by letting the student sit on his knee while they talked; hugging her; stroking her back, arms and legs when she cried on his shoulder. On one occasion, she complained of a lump on her hip, and the school counselor felt the lump both inside and outside her pants. The school counselor admitted on the witness stand that he had become emotionally involved with A.U.'s problems more as a parent than a school counselor. He denied he had any sexual contact with her. Although supported by a number of teachers and former students who testified on his behalf, he was dismissed for taking indecent liberties with a student, using highly improper counseling techniques to the detriment of the students and demonstrating immoral and unprofessional conduct resulting in irreparable loss of confidence in his ability to perform his duties as a school counselor.

On appeal, the appellate court reversed the judgment of the circuit court and held that the board of education for the Tonica schools did not have good cause for dismissing the school counselor. While the school counselor's conduct was unethical and unprofessional, the court did not consider it a criminal activity (*Board of Education of Tonica Community High School District v. Adelbert E. Sickley* (1985)).

As discussed in the Negligence Chapter, William S. Hart Union High School District (2012) was found liable for hiring a school counselor with a record of child molestation. Hubbell, the school counselor, subsequently molested a 15-year-old student. School districts whose employees hire, retain or supervise individuals known to be child molesters face vicarious liability for their conduct, meaning they assume the responsibility when these employees molest students in their charge. The 15-year-old student stepped forward after the school counselor was forced to retire after being caught checking into a motel with another minor.

PERMISSION FROM PARENTS TO IGNORE AGE OF CONSENT

A 15-year-old student tells you she lives at home with her parents and her 21-year-old boyfriend. Do you have to report this?

Points to Consider

It depends on the state and its definition of age of consent as to whether or not a crime is being committed. In some states, the age differential of three or more years for minors makes sexual relationships a crime, such as the 14 year old and the 17 year old having a sexual relationship. In some states it is illegal for two minors to have a sexual relationship. Depending on the state, an adult who is 18 or older having a sexual relationship with a minor of certain ages is statutory rape. The age of both victim and perpetrator are variable depending on the state. Even when parents/guardians are aware and blessing a union, this is still considered statutory rape if one party is an adult and the minor is under a certain age. Some educators believe that if parents/guardians know, then it is not our place to report illegal sexual relations. However, law enforcement agencies and CPS do not agree. To find how your state statutes describe age of consent go to the website Age of Consent at *www.ageofconsent.us*.

There is contradiction in the literature as to whether school counselors have to report statutory rape. This is one of those situations where a school counselor should err on the side of caution. Dr. Bernard James, professor of constitutional law at Pepperdine University, states, "Legislation in all 50 states makes school officials mandated reporters of all factual and suspected conditions that compromise the safety and development of children, including rape. Reporting for all acts is a ministerial duty, not a discretionary one, with immunity for the reporting educator and a penalty for the under-reporter" (personal communication, September 2012). Further, James states, "The laws of the 50 states on child protection preempt the common law confidentiality exception of clear and imminent danger. It is a misunderstanding in the field of counseling to think that reporting statutory rape is a choice. In law, a codified statute controls the question under discussion and reshapes common law (as well as professional guidelines for a field of endeavor such as counseling). Reporters, including counselors, are given immunity purposefully to emphasize the point that discretion (and possible failure to report) is not to be exercised by the reporter. Only a federal law would place counselors above the law of the states on this matter (personal communication Sept. 12, 2012).

To determine if a specific situation constitutes statutory rape, seek help from your school board's legal counsel, CPS, sheriff's office and/or police headquarters. A school counselor who is in a position of trust cannot ignore something as serious as a student being victimized by a perpetrator who according to the law is committing statutory rape. Seek supervision.

In a Position to Know:
School Counselors Speak

The case presented at the beginning of the chapter is revisited here and answered by two school counseling leaders. Leslie Anderson is a Middle school counselor and is chair of the Ethics Committee and president-elect of the Michigan School Counselor Association. Karen Gannon Griffith, Ph.D., is an elementary school counselor in Gwinnett County, Ga. Check your state statute at *http://aspe.hhs.gov/hsp/08/sr/statelaws/summary.shtml.*

RAPE, STATUTORY RAPE AND CHILD ABUSE APPLIED TO A STATE STATUTE

A 14 year old tells you he is having sex with his 19-year-old girl-friend. A 13-year-old student tells you she is having sex with her 17-year-old partner. Is either scenario considered statutory rape in your state? Are you required to report in either scenario to CPS, the police and/or the sheriff? This is examined by leaders in the school counseling field as applied to their particular state.

I work in a Georgia elementary school so this situation wouldn't happen exactly as described since the oldest of my students would be 10, 11 or possibly 12 (if the student had been retained). However, if a student in my school reported sexual activity with another young person, I would consult with trusted colleagues, county supervisors and/or the Department of Family and Children Services (DFACS). My school system provides annual staff development on legal updates, including all mandatory reporting issues. In addition, we have staff development on sexual behaviors and when it is or is not considered normal developmental behavior. For elementary-aged children, our county lawyer advises that any molestation or rape reported by a child, regardless of when it occurred, is to be reported to DFACS. When the allegations involve child-on-child sexual behavior, consultation is expected. Georgia has a Romeo and Juliet law. House Bill 1059, enacted April 26, 2006, creates an exception to the mandatory minimum sentences for sex offenders in cases where the victim is 13 to 15 years old, the offender is 18 years old or younger, and the age difference between the two is no more than four years. Consensual sexual acts between teenagers meeting the age criteria above are a misdemeanor, to which no mandatory minimum sentences are attached. *http://law.justia.com/codes/georgia/2006/16/16-6-3*
Karen Gannon Griffith, Ph.D., Gwinnett County, Ga.

Following is a chart outlining the legal consequences in Michigan of cases similar to the one on the previous page.
Leslie Anderson, Michigan

Sample Situation	Legal Application	Legal Consequence
14 year old and a 19 year old having sexual contact (not intercourse)	Fourth Degree Criminal Sexual Contact: The younger participant is at least 13 but under 16 years of age and there is an age difference of five or more years	Misdemeanor punishable by imprisonment for not more than two years or a fine of not more than $500, or both.
13 year old and a 17 year old having sexual contact (not intercourse)	Although the legal age of consent is 16 years old in Michigan, this would not be considered illegal. The Romeo and Juliet Law (Close-in-Age) applies here.	Because the younger participant is at least 13 but not more than 16 years of age and the age difference is less than five years, this would not be illegal as a result of the Romeo and Juliet law.
14 year old and a 19 year old having sexual intercourse	Third Degree Criminal Sexual Conduct: Sexual penetration occurs and the younger person is at least 13 and under 16 years of age.	Felony punishable by imprisonment for not more than 15 years.
13 year old and a 17 year old having sexual intercourse	Third Degree Criminal Sexual Conduct: Sexual penetration occurs and the younger person is at least 13 and under 16 years of age.	Felony punishable by imprisonment for not more than 15 years. The Romeo and Juliet Law is not applicable when sexual penetration has occurred.

continued on the next page

Sample Situation	Legal Application	Legal Consequence
Having sexual intercourse with a 12 year old	First Degree Criminal Sexual Conduct: Sexual penetration with any person under 13 years of age	Felony punishable by imprisonment in the state prison for life or any term of years.

Making Connections

1. If, after you make a child abuse report, the perpetrator shows up at your office door the next day wanting to take issue with you, what will you do? This is not a person whom you fear but someone who is angry and confused about why you would consider their "discipline" as child abuse.

2. You are a school counselor in a school where child abuse and neglect are prevalent. You want to develop programs to inform parents/guardians, teachers and students about child abuse and neglect, but your principal does not support your endeavor. What can you do to get your principal on board?

3. You need to make a child abuse report, and your principal, instead, wants to call the parents/guardians in and talk to them about better approaches to discipline. Write up how you would make your principal feel heard and supported and yet at the same time meet your statutory obligations.

4. Call Child Protective Services in your area and inquire whether they consider domestic violence to be child abuse for your state. Gather resources they suggest might help if you have a student in this situation.

5. Visit the state statutes search at *http://nccanch.acf.hhs.gov/general/ legal/statutes/search/*, and write a summary of the information about child abuse and reporting that applies to your state. What constitutes abuse? Who are the mandated reporters? How are they protected?

6. Although a CPS investigation did not yield any evidence of abuse, you are still uncomfortable about the way Jacob comes to school. He is unkempt and never eats lunch. His parents refuse to allow him to get free lunch, and he never has lunch money. The other students shun him, and

he is a frequent target of bullying at the school. Besides contacting CPS again if necessary, what other strategies might you employ to assist Jacob and his family?

7. A student comes to you to discuss her sexual relationship with her boyfriend. He is 16 years old, and she is 14 years old. Their relationship is unsanctioned by their parents. Do you know the law regarding statutory rape in your state? What would be your advice to this student?

Key Terms

Child abuse
Child neglect
Child maltreatment
Child Protective Services
Domestic violence
Emotional harm
Expert witness
Immune from liability

Mandated reporter
Nonmaleficence
Over discipline
Reasonable suspicion
Statute of limitations
Statutory rape
Threat of harm

CHAPTER 8

Individual and Group Counseling

IN THIS CHAPTER

Objectives

By the time you have completed this chapter, you should be able to:

- Describe the meaning and limits of confidentiality in individual and group counseling.
- Define the process of informed consent.
- Apply the ASCA Ethical Standards for School Counselors (2010) for individual and group counseling.
- Understand the responsibility of group leadership for small-group counseling.

Ethical Standards Addressed in This Chapter

Professionalism means knowing your professional associations' codes and adhering to them. The ASCA Ethical Standards for School Counselors most relevant to this chapter are the following:

- Professional school counselors inform students of the purposes, goals, techniques and rules of procedure under which they may receive counseling. Disclosure includes the limits of confidentiality in a developmentally appropriate manner. Informed consent requires competence on the part of students to understand the limits of confidentiality and, therefore, can be difficult to obtain from students of a certain developmental level. Professionals are aware that even though every attempt is made to obtain informed consent it is not always possible and when needed will make counseling decisions on students' behalf. (A.2.a)
- Professional school counselors protect the confidentiality of students' records and release personal data in accordance with prescribed federal and state laws and school policies, including the laws within the Family Educational Rights and Privacy Act (FERPA). Student information stored and transmitted electronically is treated with the same care as traditional student records. Recognize the vulnerability of confidentiality in electronic communications and only transmit sensitive information electronically in a way that is untraceable to students' identity. Critical information such as a student who has a history of suicidal ideation must be conveyed to the receiving school in a personal contact such as a phone call. (A.2.h)

- Professional school counselors make referrals when necessary or appropriate to outside resources for student and/or family support. Appropriate referrals may necessitate informing both parents/guardians and students of applicable resources and making proper plans for transitions with minimal interruption of services. Students retain the right to discontinue the counseling relationship at any time. (A.5.a)
- Professional school counselors screen prospective group members and maintain an awareness of participants' needs, appropriate fit and personal goals in relation to the group's intention and focus. The school counselor takes reasonable precautions to protect members from physical and psychological harm resulting from interaction within the group. (A.6.a)
- Professional school counselors recognize that best practice is to notify the parents/guardians of children participating in small groups. (A.6.b)
- Professional school counselors establish clear expectations in the group setting and clearly state that confidentiality in group counseling cannot be guaranteed. Given the developmental and chronological ages of minors in schools, recognize the tenuous nature of confidentiality for minors renders some topics inappropriate for group work in a school setting. (A.6.c)
- Professional school counselors provide necessary follow up with group members and document proceedings as appropriate. (A.6.d)
- Professional school counselors respect the rights and responsibilities of parents/guardians for their children and endeavor to establish, as appropriate, a collaborative relationship with parents/guardians to facilitate the student's maximum development. (B.1.a)
- Professional school counselors inform parents/guardians of the school counselor's role to include the confidential nature of the counseling relationship between the school counselor and student. (B.2.a)
- Professional school counselors recognize that working with minors in a school setting requires school counselors to collaborate with students' parents/guardians to the extent possible. (B.2.b)

The full text of the ASCA Ethical Standards for School Counselors is available at *www.schoolcounselor.org*.

Introduction

The legal and ethical complexities of working with minors in schools require school counselors to remain vigilant about the rights and responsibilities of students and their parents/guardians, as well as the implications of these rights on school counselors' work (American Counseling Association, 2005; ASCA, 2010; Imber & Van Geel, 2009). The numerous responsibilities school counselors have in schools and the complexities of delivering counseling services in a setting designed to deliver academic instruction further complicate the legal and ethical realm of school counseling (Baker & Gerler, 2007; Galassi & Akos, 2004; Gibson & Mitchell, 2007; Moyer, Sullivan & Growcock, 2012; Sink, 2005). These complications are acutely present in both individual and group counseling (Smead, 1995; Thompson & Henderson, 2010; Vernon, 2004).

There is additional concern in group counseling, where confidentiality cannot be guaranteed, and sensitive information about the private world of students and their families is often discussed (Corey, 2011; Greenberg, 2003; Venkatesh, 2006). Groups are powerful tools school counselors can use to reach more students. Group counseling is an essential method for school counselors and other human service personnel (Conyne & Bemak, 2004, p. 8). Counseling, especially group counseling, "can be an effective outlet for promoting [a student's] welfare at both individual and systemic levels" (Hays, Arredondo, Gladding & Toporek, 2010, p 179). The astute school counselor will use caution to guard what is said in the group to prevent students from harm due to a breach of confidentiality.

Confidentiality, which is addressed in Standard A.2 of the ASCA Ethical Standards, means school counselors provide informed consent, i.e., disclosing the terms at or before entering the counseling relationship or at the beginning of counseling sessions to provide the counselee the purposes, goals, techniques and rules of procedure under which he or she may receive counseling. The school counselor explains the meaning of confidentiality in developmentally appropriate terms and helps the student understand school counselors will try to keep confidences, except when the school counselor determines serious and foreseeable harm is present. The use of serious and foreseeable is a shift from the previous idea of "clear and imminent" danger, which, after several incidents, was found to be insufficient to cover situations in which school counselors may know of a danger that could not be classified as "clear and imminent" but still needs to be addressed. Therefore, the term "serious and foreseeable" was adopted to provide a larger blanket of protection for students and school counselors.

In brief, confidentiality in school settings is complicated because of the school counselor's competing interests and obligations that extend beyond the students to parents/guardians, administrators and teachers. Working with minor clients always poses special considerations with the client's parents/guardians, but never more so than when the minor client is a student in a setting designed for academic instruction rather than clinical counseling. In some instances, parents/guardians may demand and obtain "maintained" information on their child including case notes (see FERPA Chapter). In *Parents v. Williamsport Area School District* (1991), a psychologist could not use his professional confidentiality as a basis for refusing to reveal to parents/guardians what was said in an individual counseling session and recorded in individual case notes.

Other court cases have supported the school counselor's confidentiality to the greatest extent possible; however, the courts tell us to be ready to defend our behavior and to show we are competent to address sensitive subjects with students in isolation from their parents/guardians. Generally speaking, school counselors should feel free to discuss relevant but controversial issues with students, such as drug and alcohol abuse, pregnancy, abortion and birth control. However, when counseling a student about these sensitive topics, we must carefully consider the student's developmental and chronological levels and the legal status of minors, as well as parents' and/or guardians' rights to be the guiding voice in their children's lives, especially when it comes to value-laden issues.

This chapter gives us an opportunity to revisit and highlight some of the basic principles of legal and ethical issues for individual and group counseling. In this chapter we will discuss confidentiality, informed consent, best practice for group leadership, parents' and/or guardians' rights, administrators' and teachers' need-to-know, serious and foreseeable harm and no-harm contracts.

Getting Started: What Would You Do?

The following case is answered for you at the end of this chapter by a school counselor educator who is a past president of the Association of Specialists in Group Work. Before you read her response, formulate in your own mind how you would approach this ethical dilemma.

SMALL-GROUP COUNSELING:
SCREENING POTENTIAL MEMBERS

You develop a small group in response to complaints from seventh-grade teachers who say some students are having difficulty getting along with their peers and are interrupting classroom lessons. The teachers also say they believe the behavior is affecting the students' grades. You establish a set of goals for the group that includes learning ways to get along with others while improving group members' own grades. The teachers recommend eight students for the group; the principal requests you also include two other students who are repeatedly in trouble for fighting. After you secure parental permission, you conduct your first meeting to discuss the ground rules, confidentiality and goals for the group. By the third session, bickering escalates. The two students the principal recommended are not benefiting from the group and are fueling the group's negativity by making threatening comments to the other members. Are there ethical issues with the small group?

Working Through Case Studies

CLEAR AND IMMINENT DANGER OR SERIOUS AND FORESEEABLE HARM

You are working with a student you suspect might be clinically depressed. Parts of her life are spiraling downward due to a recent breakup with her boyfriend, who dumped her and put cruel postings about her "chronic moodiness and depression" on Facebook. Her friends say these posts are causing her tremendous anxiety, and they are worried about her. In your professional judgment, this young woman is in trouble. You wish you could reach out to her parents, but in your view, this student's situation does not meet the threshold of clear and imminent danger. Therefore, you feel your hands are tied. You have always operated under the belief that unless a suicide is about to happen (a clear and imminent danger) you would not breach confidentiality. You have never defined any circumstance except suicide as triggering a breach under the clear-and-imminent-danger test. Are you behaving within the profession's standard of care?

Points to Consider

School counselors' test for breach is not that of the proverbial uplifted knife poised to plunge in the heart. The revised 2010 ASCA Ethical Standards for School Counselors replaced clear and imminent danger with serious and foreseeable harm, as did the 2005 American Counseling Association Code of Ethics.

What is clear and imminent danger for a minor who is in a setting designed for academic instruction and in most cases is mandated to be there? Webster defines imminent as about to happen, looming. Clear and imminent danger has always been a concept that was defined by most school counselors as broader than looming, as they are acutely aware that their obligation extends beyond their minor students to the parents/ guardians who have retained their right to be the guiding voice in their children's lives. Is clear and imminent danger a 7 year old smoking cigarettes? A 17 year old smoking cigarettes? If you substitute the concept of clear and imminent danger with serious and foreseeable harm, does this help you make the decision as to whether or not to notify the 7 year old's parents/guardians or the 17 year old's parents/guardians?

Serious and foreseeable harm also describes a concept used in negligence (tort) law to limit the liability of a party to those acts carrying a risk of foreseeable harm, meaning that a reasonable person would be able to predict or expect the ultimately harmful result of his or her actions. The legal and ethical complications of any human-service profession are daunting, but on any given day a school counselor puts into play the "reasonable person" approach and navigates such charged, delicate subjects as abortion, harassment and suicide. School counselors exercise professional judgment when a reasonable person would know a student has reached the limits of being able to negotiate a situation in isolation from parental involvement.

Serious and foreseeable harm is more appropriate in the case of a student in a downward spiral into a dangerous zone. No, we cannot say with conclusiveness that this situation is clear and imminent danger and that this student is going to succumb to the temptation of suicide today. However, if it is evident that it is serious and foreseeable harm, then the school counselor will want to consult, seek supervision, work with this student to involve the parents and if need be, make the decision to call the parents. The Association of Specialists in Group Work states, "Group workers process the workings of the group with themselves, group members, supervisors or other colleagues, as appropriate" (2007, C.1).

Trust is a crucial hallmark of the school counseling profession. The ASCA Ethical Standards emphasize the balance that must happen between minors' rights and the rights of their parents/guardians. The school counselor's primary obligation and loyalty is to students, but it does not end there. Our setting dictates responsibility beyond the student. School counselors should always feel off balance when negotiating between the rights of parents/guardians and those of students as it is a tug of war we must skillfully negotiate with the help of our partners in consultation – colleagues and supervisors.

CONFIDENTIALITY AND A TEACHER'S NEED-TO-KNOW

A math teacher stops you in the hall and launches in with, "Why is Roberto out of my class all the time? It has been at least four times in the last two months. What can be so important that he has to miss my class? He is barely hanging on to a D, and missing class is not helping him." What is your response?

Points to Consider

The politically astute school counselor will figure out how to defuse the teacher's frustration. The teacher's concerns are quite legitimate, even if the method of relaying this information seems accusatory rather than collaborative. It may be tempting to respond in-kind and to jump right into defending yourself, but politically it is better to figure out how to keep the lines of communication open. A good place to start is honoring the teacher's frustrations with an acknowledgement that you should have staggered the times you are seeing Roberto so he would not be missing the same class. An offer to come by later during the teacher's planning would be helpful to discuss what the teacher has been observing with the student. It might be necessary to find a private spot immediately and get the teacher to talk about what he or she has been observing. The benefit to using this technique is that if the teacher is talking then you do not have to, so confidentiality is respected, and you can skirt the pressure to give the teacher information that should be kept confidential. There are many times when teachers need to know what is going on with one of their students. They should know at least enough information to be able to optimize this student's education and well-being. Two professionals working to advantage a student is not a breach when, if informed, the teacher can be a more powerful support to the student. Providing information to the teacher in general terms will sometimes be enough, but the judgment is on the school counselor to determine need-to-know information and how much to involve the teacher in a student's confidential communications. The test is always to balance how to advantage the student by collaborating with other educators in the school while keeping a trusting relationship. Sometimes teachers are just curious. School counselors try to determine the teacher's motive for knowing the information. School counselors usually know better than anyone which teachers are operating high on the personal-social consciousness continuum and will easily discern between a caring teacher's need-to-know and pure curiosity. If in doubt as to the teacher's motives, the school counselor errs on the side of keeping the information confidential.

> In a December 2012 survey, 86 percent of school counselor respondents indicated they had been asked by teachers at least once in the last 36 months for the contents of their counseling sessions. The average number of times these school counselors had been approached for information from teachers in this three-year period was 29.7 times.

CONFIDENTIALITY AND PROTECTIVE PARENTS/GUARDIANS

You are working with Esther in a small group on student success skills. Esther has trouble getting along with others, but some individual work with you has paid off. You believe she is ready to move to a small group being formed on school success skills. You informed the parents in advance and, after many questions, they seem satisfied. However, despite your explanation that you would give them a periodic update as to Esther's progress, they call every week wanting to know how she did in the group. What do you do?

Points to Consider

Parents/guardians often ask questions about the contents of counseling sessions. School counselors' primary loyalty is to maintain the confidentiality of students as outlined in the profession's ethical practices and standard of care. School counselors want to protect student privacy to the extent they are able to do so while walking the precarious tightrope of negotiating the political landscape with parents/guardians who will request information from individual counseling sessions.

> In a December 2012 survey of school counselors, respondents indicated they had been asked by a parent at least once for the content of their counseling sessions. The average number of times these school counselors had been approached for information from parents/guardians in the most recent three-year period was 17.9 times.

Iyer and Baxter-MacGregor (2010) recommend that a school counselor always remind both parents/guardians and students about confidentiality and its limits. This approach helps to give parents/guardians comfort that they will be informed if there is serious and foreseeable harm to their child and may help them maintain realistic expectations when making requests of their child's school counselor.

Maintaining positive relationships with parents/guardians is important as this enhances the school counselor's ability to provide services to students (Huss, Bryant & Mulet, 2008). Parents/guardians are protected by statute and the courts to be the guiding voice in their children's lives, and school counselors support parents/guardians in this role to the greatest extent possible. "The conflict for professional school counselors is that parents/guardians need to be an integral part of a student's educational experience, yet students expect they can talk freely with a school counselor without the fear that the information will be shared. Finding a balance between protecting the information shared and collaboratively working with parents/guardians and other educators to do what is best for the student is a key issue for professional school counseling program success" (Huss, Bryant & Mulet, 2008, p. 362). Although confidentiality must be breached in cases where there is serious and foreseeable harm to the student, such as in the cases of suicidal students or those suffering from eating disorders, situations such as this one have many more gray areas.

In some cases, it is not appropriate to break confidentiality, even at the parent's request. Again, while allowing parents/guardians to be the guiding voice in their child's life is important, your primary obligation is to the student. However, there are appropriate actions school counselors can take in these situations to help both the student and the parent while still maintaining their ethical and professional obligations.

In Esther's case some general responses might be enough: "She is working hard in the group" or "She is making progress." You can back up statements with facts by allowing Esther to take her completed work home to share what she did with parents/guardians, opening up conversations and allaying concerns.

CONFIDENTIALITY AND A PARENT'S AND/OR GUARDIAN'S NEED-TO-KNOW

Two teachers approach you and share their concerns about Katie, whom they believe is suffering from an eating disorder. You have only worked with Katie a few times, usually around scheduling issues, but you do know that she is cautious about sharing personal information and seems closed-off emotionally. You have no medical proof Katie has an eating disorder, but based on the teachers' reports and your professional observations during counseling with Katie, you believe she is in trouble. Katie vehemently denies having an eating disorder and, in so many words, asks you to stay out of her life. What do you do?

Points to Consider

You may be wrong in your assessment, but err on the side of caution. It is better to be wrong and have a student mad at you than to turn a blind eye simply because you cannot be certain she really has an eating disorder. Do not ignore it and hope someone else will address it (Smith, Robinson & Sega, 2012).

School counselors cannot assume Katie's parents are aware of her behavior or that they even know what an eating disorder is. Whether you are right or proven wrong, the ethical school counselor will confront the student (Carney & Scott, 2012). Several factors complicate confronting a student about having an eating disorder. On one hand, a person's weight and eating habits are considered private and personal. Additionally, personal appearance and weight have significant links to self-esteem (Veazy Morris, Parra & Stender, 2011), which the school counselor does not want to negatively affect in any way. Generally speaking, students with eating disorders are often secretive or ashamed of their behavior; hence, school counselors usually hear about eating disorder issues from concerned friends (Carney & Scott, 2012). Regardless, these students do not often welcome what they would consider school counselors interfering in their lives.

Insist that the student involve his or her parents and offer your help in telling them. Make the student aware of your concerns, and get in touch with the parents. Too much hangs in the balance. Given the highly sensitive nature of eating disorders, the student will likely become upset, or the parents/guardians may become angry and complain about you to administration. However unpleasant the consequences and fallout to your relationship with this student, not involving the parents/guardians poses a greater risk to the student. Only in an extraordinary circumstance where more harm than good comes from involving the parents/guardians would the school counselor choose not to contact them. Bardick, Bernes, McCulloch, Witko, Spriddle and Roest (2004) stress making "honest, objective statements defining the behaviors of concern followed by insistence on obtaining the opinion of a trained professional" (p. 170) in situations such as notifying parents/guardians of their child's potential eating disorder. Telling students that you care about them but believe they are not fine and need help is the brave thing to do. Even if the parents/guardians are also in denial, you have forced them to discuss the situation and perhaps have planted some seeds so they will at least consider the possibility their child is not well.

Can you be charged with negligence for not acting? There are no court cases at this point charging a school counselor for negligence in not reporting a student's suspected eating disorder. It would be hard to charge a school counselor with negligence for not reporting a student with anorexia. In the case of a bulimic student, there is more tangible evidence you might observe, such as purging. Anorexia is harder to determine. This situation is really less about avoiding a lawsuit and more about bravely facing the fallout by refusing to look the other way when you think a student may be in danger.

ADMINISTRATORS AND THE NEED-TO-KNOW

Your principal has asked you to keep him informed about all the students you see, including their presenting problem. He is a strong child-advocate and a good administrator, but on this directive you disagree. You have explained your ethical confidentiality imperative, and he listens intently but does not relent except to say he will also respect the students' confidences unless there is a compelling reason why he must involve their parents or teachers. You do not believe he means any ill will, but you have not been successful in getting him to understand how his insistence on knowing all "the issues our students bring to school" is causing you an ethical dilemma. Can you legally and ethically refuse to cooperate?

Points to Consider

This is a familiar scenario to many school counselors. Administrators, more than teachers or parents/guardians, want to know the contents of counseling sessions.

> In a December 2012 survey, 86 percent of school counselor respondents indicated they had been asked by administrators at least once for the content of their counseling sessions. The average number of times these school counselors were approached for information from administrators in the previous three-year period was 36.5 times (as compared with 29.7 times from teachers and 17.9 from parents/guardians).

School counselors fulfilling both ethical principles and negotiating political landmines face challenges not easily solved as demonstrated in the case of *Woodlock v. Orange Ulster B.O.C.E.S.* (2006/2008). In this case, a school counselor found herself in a conflict with her principal that ended with the loss of her employment and a federal civil rights lawsuit. N.W., a school counselor at a special education center, tried to advocate with her administrators for gym and certified art instructors for her students as indicated on their individualized educational programs. Administration did not respond to her calls and faxes, so she started keeping a log of her attempts and eventually went over her principal's head to the district's pupil services administrator. The principal responded by sending N.W. a letter of reprimand for "going out of process." In what appears to have morphed into a full-blown power struggle, the principal subsequently sent N.W. two disciplinary letters for performance problems N.W. contended were unfounded. The principal recommended against N.W. receiving tenure, and N.W.'s response was to file a civil rights suit in federal court alleging adverse administration actions that violated her First Amendment freedom of expression.

In deciding if N.W. would get a jury trial, the court concluded that N.W.'s repeated requests for special education compliance was a matter of public concern, so the case moved forward on N.W.'s request for a jury trial. The school district appealed to the Second Circuit Court of Appeals, which ruled in favor of the school district and set aside N.W.'s hope for a jury trial (*Woodlock v. Orange Ulster B.O.C.E.S.* (2008)). The Supreme Court's ruling in *Garcetti v. Ceballos* (2006), a completely separate case, dealt the fatal blow to N.W.'s case. The Supreme Court held in *Garcetti* that First Amendment freedom of expression does not protect statements public employees make pursuant to their official duties, as compared with those they make as citizens on a matter of public concern. The Second Circuit Court of Appeals concluded that N.W.'s repeated communications were made pursuant to her official duties as a school counselor at the special education satellite center and therefore did not fall under her First-Amendment rights.

The case shows how legal protection does not necessarily accompany ethical imperatives. The responsibility is on the politically astute school counselor to minimize the conflict between political compliance and ethical behavior, as the option of legal recourse is not a promising one. Negotiating the politics with administrators can at times be complex or even fruitless work, but adhering to ethical standards requires that school counselors find alternate routes to compromise without going to battle with administrators.

N.W. was trying to be an advocate for her students, but she approached the administration in what resulted in a self-defeating way. School counselors use their best political and collaborative skills to demonstrate respect for the position of authority that has been entrusted to school administrators, while carefully determining the most effective way to adhere to the school counseling profession's obligation to protect and advocate for students.

So what is the answer to the question posed at the beginning, "Can you legally and ethically refuse to cooperate?" The balance of power is in the principal's favor, and courts tend to rule in the favor of school districts when administration and other educators collide in the legal arena (Gavin & Zirkel, 2008). School counselors engage in both political acumen and legal awareness to effectively advocate.

TEACHERS AND ADMINISTRATORS AS ALLIES IN INDIVIDUAL COUNSELING

During individual counseling, Marcus brings up Sarah, a classmate, with chilling anger, "All she does is talk, talk, talk," he said. "I intend to take her big mouth and shut it once and for all. I am done with listening to her constant dribble." You have been able to make progress with Marcus, but your relationship is fragile. He has cut back on creating daily chaos in the classroom. You know if you breach his confidence he will turn his back on the progress you have made, but Sarah may be in danger. What do you do?

Points to Consider

The school counseling profession is built on trust, and confidentiality is an ethical imperative the profession guards with great care. In a case like this, school counselors struggle to balance protecting the trusting relationship while making sure we err on the side of caution regarding student safety. Marcus has a long way to go, but the fact remains that positive change is happening for Marcus, and the classroom is calmer because of collaborative work between you, his teachers and his parents/guardians. Yet, this outburst could be a real threat and cannot be ignored. Marcus' comments indicate the possibility of serious and foreseeable harm to Sarah. The school counselor will want to explore further with Marcus his venomous statements and see how deep his anger goes. Regardless of what Marcus conveys in further discussion, confidentiality must be breached. School officials have to err on the side of caution to prevent harm to Sarah and to place the adults in the school on watch for Sarah's safety. The extent to which action is needed would be determined by the extended conversation the school counselor has with Marcus, which will help dictate if the school counselor chooses to advocate. If, after further exploration, the school counselor believes Marcus' statement was more bluff than an actual threat and if there is nothing in Marcus' past to make the school counselor believe he would actually harm Sarah, then the school counselor may choose to try and work out a plan with administrators and teachers to protect Sarah and, to the greatest extent possible, protect the relationship the school counselor has built with Marcus. It will take a delicate balance of doing the right thing for Sarah while watching Marcus like a hawk to make sure Sarah is safe. Depending on the circumstances and what comes next, it may be necessary for administration to change Marcus' classroom, involve his parents, suspend Marcus, contact outside authorities and/or meet with Sarah's parents. How it plays out will depend on Marcus' behavior toward Sarah. If he actually bullies Sarah this is a very different scenario than just blowing off steam about her to the school counselor.

Teachers can be a tremendous force in helping us keep that tenuous relationship with Marcus moving in a positive direction. There is nothing quite as powerful as a school counselor/teacher team fighting to make positive changes in a child's life. The setting in which counselors work, more than any other factor, defines our role differently than that of school counselors in other settings. We are in a setting in which we have the added benefit of one or more teacher(s) who may have Marcus anywhere from four to 35 hours a week. If Marcus' teachers and administrators are operating high on the personal-social consciousness continuum, we have perfect allies to fight for Marcus' well-being while also keeping Sarah safe by monitoring Marcus' interactions with her. Armed with need-to-know information, teachers and administrators who are skilled and trustworthy can help monitor Marcus' behavior through the appropriate lens and, more importantly, orchestrate opportunities for Marcus to have positive peer-to-peer and student-to-adult interactions. All school counselors can name the teachers and administrators with whom they collaborated to gain positive changes in students' lives. Orchestrating an environment in the school that positively intervenes in Marcus' life and keeps Sarah safe is the ultimate plan.

School counselors occasionally struggle to provide unconditional positive regard to more challenging students. School counselors have to affirm all students, but we certainly are not expected to affirm all of their behaviors. Unconditional positive regard may be more difficult to realize for students like Marcus, who can spew venom and prejudicial statements, but if we revisit why we went into the field of school counseling in the first place, we recall it wasn't to work with perfect students. It was to work with all children, affirm them and help them grow into productive citizens (ASCA, 2012). Helping Marcus develop empathy helps both Marcus and society.

NO-HARM CONTRACTS IN INDIVIDUAL COUNSELING

Heather has been referred to you because she was overheard saying she was going to take her dad's gun and blow her brains out. You immediately react by bringing her into your office for counseling. Heather seems fine and expresses to you that she is not going to kill herself. You call Heather's mother and explain what has been going on and you tell her you believe there is nothing to it and she does not have to come and get Heather. You also explain to Heather's mother that you have completed a suicide or no-harm contract with Heather. You had Heather write on the contract the name of a friend she could turn to if she ever felt like harming herself. She listed another student in your school. Are there any legal or ethical concerns in your handling of this case?

Points to Consider

In *Mikell v. School Administrative Unit #33* (2009), a middle-school student allegedly told a teacher's aide that he "wanted to blow his brains out" (p. 1053). The aide informed the school counselor, who met with the student and told the parents the student was fine to remain at school. Then the school counselor had the student sign a "contract for safety." The school counselor took no further action regarding the suicide threat, and about two months later the student hanged himself.

Mikell, the plaintiff, argued that the school counselor, Moule, voluntarily took custody and control of Mikell's child when Moule told Mikell Joshua's threat was the result of a learning disability, and he was okay to stay at school. Moule also completed a no-harm contract with Joshua and did not advise Mikell to have Joshua examined by an outside professional. In other words, the school counselor was accused of overstepping *in loco parentis*, making a decision about the stability of Joshua's condition that belonged solely to Joshua's parents. The plaintiff asserted that "[t]his series of actions effectively shielded Joshua from the benefit of parental or other professional assistance while [in] school." The New Hampshire Supreme Court disagreed, ruling that school authorities could be liable for the student's death only if they had custodial care of the student, which exists in a special relationship like a hospital setting, or if they had engaged in "extreme and outrageous" conduct that "resulted in an uncontrollable impulse to commit suicide, or prevented the decedent from realizing the nature of his act" (p. 1054). In the New Hampshire court's view, the school counselor did not have custodial care and had not engaged in the requisite outrageous conduct, thus precluding liability.

Even though the school counselor escaped legal liability, the outcome gives school counseling professionals little comfort. Risk assessments and suicide contracts are controversial practices in suicide prevention in school settings. No-harm contracts are simple, and many school counselors believe the contracts will help them avoid lawsuits, which results in an over-reliance on them. However, little empirical evidence supports the effectiveness of these contracts (Centre for Suicide Prevention, 2002; Goin, 2003; Leenaars & Wenckstern, 1995; Mandrusiak, Joiner & Rudd, 2006). Additionally, use of a suicide contract in some parents'/guardians' minds might imply the school counselor is ensuring the student's safety. The word "contract" can give the impression of a binding agreement. However, a suicidal person is in no way trustworthy to uphold the promise made in signing a contract due to the delicacy of the person's mental and emotional state. If a school counselor believes it is necessary to have the student put something on paper, a better approach might be to ask the student to identify personal goals, write hopeful comments, list what is going right or what adult the student can turn to for help.

In some cases, well-intentioned school counselors may recruit a student's friend as a helper and name the friend as someone a suicidal student can turn to for help when having suicidal thoughts. However, doing so burdens a peer with too much responsibility for another minor's life or death. It would, however, be a wise decision to make the entire student body aware of what to do when a classmate shares suicidal thoughts with them (King & Smith, 2000). Few students know what to do; yet, students reported being more likely to report suicidal ideations to a friend than to an adult (Granello, 2010).

School counselors who rely on suicide assessments for definitive answers are risking danger for themselves and their students. Using a suicide assessment to negate the possibility of a suicide is faulty practice at best and dangerous at worst. If used at all, a suicide assessment should be a tool to underscore to parents/guardians the urgency of the need to monitor their child and get the child professional help. The school counselor's role is to help parents/guardians find available resources to help suicidal students. Part of Mikell's argument was that the school counselor did not recommend that she take her child to an outside counselor for further evaluation. A network of referral resources is a valuable tool school counselors should have in place prior to an emergency situation (Granello, 2010). When working with suicidal students, a school counselor should make every attempt to supply parents/guardians with counseling referrals until placement is secured for that student (ASCA, 2010; Capuzzi, 2002).

INDIVIDUAL COUNSELING AND DRUG AND ALCOHOL ABUSE

Ernie just revealed to you that he is using marijuana and asked you not to tell his parents. In your district he is not breaking the Student Code of Conduct. Are there any federal laws that inform school counselors about confidentiality and drug counseling? In absence of a law forbidding a breach of confidentiality is drug use an automatic call to parents? Under what circumstances would you inform or not inform Ernie's parents?

Points to Consider

If written case notes are kept on the student's drug use and parents/guardians want to access those case notes, then they have a right to do so (see the FERPA Chapter for more details). The Family Policy Compliance Office (FPCO), which governs FERPA, provided this guidance, "There may be another federal law and regulation (such as SAMSA's Student Assistance Program) that addresses student confidentiality matters, but you would have to check with those agencies and offices. However, I am not aware of any other laws or regulations that supersede FERPA's requirement that parents be provided access to their children's records upon request. Under FERPA, school counselors are generally considered 'school officials,' assuming they are school employees or contractors. As such, they have a responsibility to comply with FERPA. The term 'education records' in FERPA is broadly defined to include any record that is directly related to a student and maintained by a school or by a party acting for the school. There is no exemption in the definition for counseling records. Also, it doesn't matter if the student is breaking the student code of conduct or not. If a school official creates a record on a student (that is not a simple memory jogger for the official), then it is an 'education record' under FERPA, and a parent has the right to inspect and review that record. The school does not have to 'announce' to the parent what is in their child's education records, but they can't deny the parent if the parent asks to see the record or makes a request for 'all education records'" (personal communication, Oct. 22, 2012).

The Healthy Students Group, Office of Safe and Healthy Students (OSHS), U.S. Department of Education has as its mission to provide "useful and timely information that will enhance your knowledge of safe and supportive schools; health, mental health, environmental health and physical education; drug-violence prevention; character and civic education; and homeland security, emergency management and school programs administered by OSHS and of issues that are important to the Elementary and Secondary Education Act as reauthorized by the No Child Left Behind (NCLB) Act" (U.S. Department of Education, Office of Safe and Healthy Students, n.d. p 1).

Norris Dickard and Paul Kesner of OSHS were subsequently contacted with this question. "If a student comes to a school counselor for help with alcohol or drug use and wants the school counselor's help but does not want his or her parents/guardians to know, is there anything in federal statute or regulations addressing a student's right to seek confidential help from a school counselor for drug or alcohol use? Again, the question is not about a written case note, just about a school counselor having the knowledge that a student is using drugs and the student is requesting confidentiality. Does this student have a right to confidentiality in federal statute?" Paul Kesner responded, "To the extent that we know, there is nothing in federal language that gives guidance to the issue we've been presented" (personal communication, March 18, 2013).

School counselors have wrestled with these questions, especially regarding whether Federal Statute 42 CFR Part 2 extends to students of school counselors. Federal Statute 42 CFR Part 2 protects the records of students and patients "who have applied for, participated in or received an interview, counseling or any other service from a federally assisted alcohol or drug abuse program, including someone who, after arrest on a criminal charge, is identified as an alcohol or drug client during an evaluation of eligibility for treatment" (Substance Abuse and Mental Health Services Administration & U.S. Department of Health and Human Services, 2010, p 5).

Public education receives federal funds, but school counselors do not offer federally assisted alcohol or drug abuse programs. Once again, this complicated issue rests on school counselors' shoulders to consult and exercise judgment to determine if they need to involve parents/guardians. Confidentiality with students for whom we have knowledge of their drug and/or alcohol use falls under the complications of confidentiality (see the Introduction Chapter). It is difficult to determine whether or not we should breach confidentiality. In absence of a state statute giving students confidentiality for drug and alcohol counseling from a school counselor, school counselors have to continue to wrestle with each individual case in context of the student's developmental levels, home situation and parents' and/or guardians' rights. The type of drug, the student's age, the student's family support and the frequency of drug/alcohol use all come into play as school counselors wrestle with whether or not the student is engaged in serious and foreseeable harm.

STUDENT CODE OF CONDUCT AND ALCOHOL AND DRUG ABUSE

Ernie is a student who is obviously under the influence of some illegal substance when he comes to school one day. When you confront him, he admits to smoking marijuana on his way to school. In your school district Ernie is breaking the student code of conduct for admitting to using drugs and also for being under the influence of drugs. Do you report Ernie to the administration?

Points to Consider

In some school districts, it is written into the student code of conduct that even the admission of the use of alcohol or drugs is a code of conduct violation whether or not the substance is currently in the student's system. School counselors in these districts may be contractually required to report student code of conduct violations.

For example, Duval County Public Schools (DCPS) in Jacksonville, Fla., is a large school district (125,000 students, 20th largest in the nation). Its student code of conduct has four classifications of offenses. Drug and alcohol is a Class III violation. "Major Offenses – Class III: Alcohol – Possession, use of alcoholic beverages, being under the influence of alcoholic beverages or admitting to using alcoholic beverages. Drugs – Unauthorized possession or use of drugs, admitting to such use or possession or being under the influence of drugs, inhalants or any other substance with a potential for abuse, which might create a hazard to the user's health or the safety of another" (Duval County Public Schools, 2011, p. 16). However, there appears to be nothing in the DCPS's collective bargaining agreement (contract) that specifically says all school personnel must uphold the student code of conduct. However, school boards are given the right to establish policies and laws, and in absence of a conflict with a state or federal statute, school board policy stands. Therefore, all school personnel are required to uphold the student code of conduct. Here is one clause from the DCPS's collective bargaining agreement supporting the power of the school board to establish and to expect its policies are followed. "It is the right of the employer to determine unilaterally the purpose of each of its constituent agencies, set standards of services to be offered to the public and exercise control and discretion over its organization and operations. It is also the right of the employer to direct its employees, take disciplinary action for proper cause and relieve its employees from duty because of lack of work or for other legitimate reasons."

INDIVIDUAL COUNSELING AS ENTRAPMENT

You receive a phone call from Mr. Wilson, whose daughter Gabby is on your caseload. Mr. Wilson is concerned because his daughter was caught stealing wine from the grocery store. Gabby claimed an older neighborhood child who wanted the wine put her up to it and that she had no intentions of drinking any of the wine. Gabby's father does not believe her story. Alcoholism runs in his family, and he is worried that Gabby may be putting herself at risk by drinking. He asks you to please gain his daughter's trust and learn if she is drinking as he is worried sick about possible alcohol dependency. How would you handle this situation? Are there any ethical issues to consider?

Points to Consider

Our professional standards dictate that "School counselors have a primary obligation to the students" (ASCA, A.1.a). Mr. Wilson has a legitimate concern, and he needs help investigating it. This is a case of balancing keeping confidence with the student and helping the father help his child. This case focuses on the delicate question, "Is it ethical to establish a relationship with students to help them while informing their parents/guardians of their activity?" While it may be founded with good intentions, the end goal of individual counseling is not so parents/guardians can acquire evidence about their children.

Being open with both parents/guardians and students and being a facilitator of communication between them is a far better option for everyone involved. The school counselor may want to explore different avenues to facilitate communication between the student and parent. Ask Mr. Wilson's permission to allow you to be upfront with Gabby about his concerns. You are then able to be forthcoming with the student and hopefully open the line of communication between father and daughter. Perhaps both parties will agree to a meeting that you help facilitate (Iyer & Baxter-MacGregor, 2010). If the student admits she is consuming alcoholic beverages, the school counselor can then connect the student and father to an outside agency specializing in alcohol use and abuse. It is important the school counselor not be deceitful when working with the student and parent but to take the opportunity to help the two confront the issue. The school counselor does not want to be untrustworthy in this student's eyes or in the eyes of all her peers with whom she will share how she was duped by you. Working to help open communication between the father and the student also helps you maintain a relationship with the father and let him know you hear and validate his concerns as a parent.

Maintain a close consultation network to seek supervision and advice from colleagues (Iyer, Baxter-MacGregor, 2010). Given the many gray areas in this case, a supervision and peer consultation will be beneficial in arriving at positive solutions. The Association of Specialists in Group Work states, "Group workers process the workings of the group with themselves, group members, supervisors or other colleagues, as appropriate" (2007, C.1).

CONFIDENTIALITY IN GROUP COUNSELING

A mother asks you to work with her daughter who, for three years, was a victim of incest. The perpetrator has been through the legal system, is no longer in the home and, until recently, provided financial support for the victim's counseling. You are already working with another incest survivor. When talking about forming the group, you learn from a teacher about a third student. You ask all three girls individually if they would like to be part of a group. They all readily agree and sign your consent form to be in the group and to agree to respect confidentiality. At the first meeting you spend a great deal of time on confidentiality and its limits. The students sign a second pledge for confidentiality in the form of a contract promising never to reveal anything said in the group. You are comfortable that the students understand the imperative to keep all revelations confidential and how harmful it would be if they did not honor their pledge. Are there any ethical dilemmas in this situation?

Points to Consider

The reality of working with minors in groups requires school counselors to come from the posture that confidentiality will, with no doubt, be breached. Filtering working with students through the lens that whatever is said in the group will be tweeted, on Facebook or at the lockers down the hall within minutes helps school counselors take the necessary precautions to watch what they allow one student to talk about in front of another student. What is said in the group can and most likely will be repeated. School counselors risk the emotional safety of students when they expect that developmentally maturing students will respect confidentiality. The ASCA Ethical Standards (2010) specifically state that confidentiality might be compromised in a group setting. School counselors must "establish clear expectations in the group setting and clearly state that confidentiality in group counseling cannot be guaranteed. Given the developmental and chronological ages of minors in schools, recognize the tenuous nature of confidentiality for minors renders some topics inappropriate for group work in a school setting" (ASCA, 2010, A.6.c). The Association for Specialists in Group Work also addresses the complexity of guaranteeing confidentiality in group work setting: "Group workers maintain awareness and sensitivity regarding the cultural meaning of confidentiality and privacy" (ASGW, 2008, A.6.).

Since there is no guarantee of confidentiality in groups, even adult groups, best practice dictates to avoid putting young people together in groups where highly sensitive and personal material may be discussed. Some minors frequently change friends and loyalties, and with this fluid behavior, there is the danger of a student wanting attention, seeking revenge or just acting thoughtlessly in revealing another student's personal pain. For every group school counselors form, regardless if the topic is as innocuous as school success skills or as serious as children in divorce situations, children of alcoholics or victims of date rape, it is imperative to remember confidentiality will be breached. Before bringing students with like issues together to explore their family troubles or personal issues, school counselors must ask themselves if the potential emotional cost to students and their families is worth the gains that could result from having a topic group.

INFORMED CONSENT AND GROUP COUNSELING

Revisiting the incest group in the prior case, you asked all three girls individually if they would like to be part of a group, and they all readily agreed and signed your consent form to be in the group. Did you really get informed consent from these students?

Points to Conside

Informed consent delineates the limits of confidentiality (ASCA, 2010, A.6.). Informed consent has major implications in this case. Is the school counselor in this situation running a group in which a student may later regret participating? Is a student really competent to give informed consent to participate in this group whose common thread is a very heinous act perpetrated on vulnerable children? Competence, voluntariness and knowledge are necessary elements if students are to give us informed consent to participate in a group (American Counseling Association, 2005). An adolescent may be developmentally unable to understand the ramifications of discussing painful personal information in the presence of other students. Are these students able to comprehend that they will be discussing a sensitive topic and that their private revelations may be repeated in the halls and locker rooms? What happens when a student participates in a group focused on a sensitive topic, and the next year (or the next minute) his or her revelations are fodder for school gossip? Given these risks, it is highly unlikely that a student's developmental level is sufficient to constitute informed consent. Voluntariness is also an issue in running this group. Yes the students volunteered, but parents/guardians were not informed and did not get a chance to talk to their child about the implications for being in this group. This case is a real case in which confidentiality was breached. This breach resulted in a student being grievously harmed and, as a result of the harm, ended up refusing to return to her school. The district, as it should have, gave the child a special assignment to a new school since this child was harmed at the hands of a district employee. School counselors have to be the keeper of informed consent when they cannot get informed consent from a student. The school counselor has to weigh the risks and make the decision to proceed or avoid putting students in groups with others who may breach confidentiality down the road.

SKILL LEVEL IN SMALL-GROUP COUNSELING

Revisiting the incest group in the prior two cases, do you have the skill level to conduct a group in school that is therapeutic and clinical in nature?

Points to Consider

Topics for group counseling in schools require careful consideration, as schools are not the place for many topics. The reason being is certain topics cannot be addressed properly in a setting designed for academic instruction. Can school counselors be expected to adequately address difficult therapeutic issues such as incest, whose victims are at varying degrees of healing (and maybe even in the midst of legal cases against perpetrators)? Smead (1995) indicated that "group work is more suited for children whose psychological needs are equally balanced" (p. 49). For example, school counselors can use curriculum that teaches children the difference between good touches and bad touches for the benefit of all students, but there are some topics that can't be adequately addressed in schools.

It is not that school counselors are less talented or less competent than their colleagues in agency or community settings; it is that topics such as incest need a counselor who has the time and expertise to work with students toward healing from this issue. This is a skill level requiring intensive work on the part of the counselor who specializes or at the very least stays abreast of all the research as to best practices in this area (ASCA, 2009b). It is unrealistic for members of the school and larger community to expect that school counselors should have all the skills, knowledge and time required for group work when topics involve such serious clinical issues.

Children and adolescents who have been the victim of incest will need intensive support in individual counseling and family therapy. As a consultant, a powerful school counselor intervention would be to help connect these students to resources for themselves and their families (ASCA, 2009b; Kaffenberger & Seligman, 2003).

School counselors can support students who have been victims of incest or other traumatizing events in a number of ways. Generic small groups are one technique to use to help students whose social development may have been stunted or even regressed due to broken promises with people they once trusted most such as family. Other ways to support student victims of trauma would be to connect them to clubs, activities, mentors or carefully made teacher placements.

This case sets up possible conflicts between students' rights to privacy and parents' and/or guardians' rights to decide what they want their children exposed to in the personal counseling arena (ASCA, 2010). A school counselor's primary objective is to support all students to be successful learners (ASCA 2010; Huss, Bryant & Mulet, 2008).

"Professional school counselor roles have changed over time in response to societal needs and professional initiatives. Although school counselors consistently have been involved in group work, the intent of that involvement has changed. New ways of viewing group work can enable school counselors to engage in roles related to leadership, advocacy and collaboration while continuing to provide direct services to students" (Paisley & Milsom, 2007, p. 9).

MULTICULTURAL CONSIDERATIONS
AND SMALL-GROUP COUNSELING

You are running a school success skills group, and you have carefully planned out your group by looking at school data on who is in danger of failing again for the second year in a row. You have pre-screened participants, determined appropriate techniques and resources, obtained parental permission and are ready to go. One group member, Lilith, lived in a refugee camp for 17 months before being resettled in America. All students will need consideration, but what do you need to know or consider about Lilith's refugee status in particular?

Points to Consider

The Association for Specialists in Group Work (ASGW) developed the Multicultural and Social Justice Competence Principles for Group Workers (ASGW, 2012). The school counselor in this case followed guidelines of ASGW (2007) by carefully "identifying group needs and goals, determining type of group to be implemented, selecting group leadership and membership, pre-screening and preparing group members, and determining techniques, leadership styles and resources needed to conduct a group" (ASGW, 2007, p.1). Adequate and thorough preparation time when building a small group allows the school counselor to learn as much as possible about Lilith's background in compliance with ASGW statement, "Seek to possess specific knowledge and information about the life experiences, cultural heritage and sociopolitical background of group members who have been displaced as a result of trauma, violence and/or other overt forms of oppression with whom they are working (ASGW, 2012, p.1).

One solution to aid Lilith's comfort and feeling of belonging to the group is to add a group member or two who shares Lilith's background or situation. ASGW states, "Determine if group membership needs to be expanded or altered to allow for a greater level of connection and support for group members who are isolated in the group due to one or more dimensions of multicultural identity or experience. This collective strength helps 'validate and reframe members' experiences to foster their resilience" (Chen, Budianto & Wong, 2010, p. 256). Group workers ensure a framework exists for members to feel supported for their diversity in the group" (ASGW, 2012, p.1).

Promoting multiculturalism in small groups is to design and facilitate a support group for newly immigrated students. "In this group the school counselor helps members recognize their individual and collective strengths by validating and reframing members' experiences to foster their resilience, which they have demonstrated in continuously overcoming educational, psychological and social barriers against a challenging, if not harsh, social backdrop" (Chen, Budianto & Wong, 2010, p. 256).

PARENT PERMISSION FOR SMALL-GROUP COUNSELING

There are five students in your school who are so isolated from their peers that it is affecting their attendance, class participation, academic success and, from all appearances, their happiness. You think a small group would be a good intervention. You completed pre-screening interviews with students, and they are all interested in participating. However, parental involvement is an issue at your school, and getting parents to get permission forms back would be time-consuming. Do you need to get written or oral permission from parents before starting this group?

Points to Consider

School counselors want to build, not erode, credibility and maintain a strong working relationship with parents/guardians. This mission is forwarded when school counselors seek parental permission for students to be a group member. The ASCA Ethical Standards say it is best practice to seek parental permission for a child to participate in group counseling (ASCA, 2010, A.6.b). Parents/guardians send their children to school for classroom academic instruction. Some parents/guardians may view small-group counseling as moving away from classroom instruction to a personal, social and/or emotional focus; therefore, it is best practice to notify parents/guardians. This notification gives school counselors a chance to explain the connection small groups have to academic success, and it gives parents/guardians a chance to opt out. The Association for Specialists in Group Work's Best Practice Guidelines (ASGW, 2007) state, "Group workers obtain the appropriate consent-assent forms for work with minors and other dependent group members." It is imperative to always check school district policies first, as some school districts have policies regarding how often a child can see a school counselor before a parent must be notified.

According to ASCA's Ethical Standards for School Counselors (ASCA, 2010), "Professional school counselors respect the rights and responsibilities of parents/guardians for their children and endeavor to establish, as appropriate, a collaborative relationship with parents/guardians to facilitate students' maximum development" (B.1.a). School counselors may find that by communicating the purpose and goals of the small-group programs, they strengthen partnerships with parents.

"It is therefore imperative for professional school counselors to develop a good working relationship with parents/guardians to promote the importance of privacy, confidentiality and privileged communication and to ensure that these principles will be managed in a manner that ensures students receive the counseling services they need" (Huss, Bryant & Mulet, 2008, p. 362). While, legally, a school counselor can provide individual or small-group counseling to a minor student without parental consent (Hansen, 2012), it is an ethically sound practice to gain written or oral parental permission for a student to participate in a small group (ASCA, 2010).

A review of the ASCA Ethical Standards reminds school counselors the importance of involving the family, acting in the best interests of students, working collaboratively with parents/guardians, adhering to laws and local guidelines and obtaining consent when working with minors.

GROUP WORK WITH DISCIPLINE REFERRALS

You are conducting a small group with five students accused of sexual harassment. The principal is responsive to issues of bullying and harassment and believes these five students have the potential to change their behavior and hopes they will be able to provide testimonials to other students about how sexual harassment harms victims. Is it appropriate to run a group designed to correct a discipline problem? If so, what are some things you may want to consider before starting the group?

Points to Consider

Smead (1995) states, "Counseling is a voluntary effort to improve oneself. Change and personal growth cannot be legislated" (p. 14). It is a risky move to involve oneself in discipline issues. If a school counselor agrees to conduct groups in accordance with administrator-identified discipline issues, then the school counselor may be viewed as an arm of the administration and identified as a disciplinarian.

The principal and school counselor would want to make certain they agree that students have to be voluntarily involved in small groups created by the school counselor. The danger would come if a student chose not to be involved and the alternative for that student is discipline; this forced participation would not meet the criteria of voluntariness. Competence, voluntariness and knowledge are necessary elements if students are to give us informed consent to participate in a group. The conflict is positioned that, "Because of increased student misconduct in academic institutions, school counselors have had to use traditional voluntary counseling models with involuntary disciplinary clients" (Kiracofe & Wells, 2007, p. 259). Even though school counselors are being asked to work with involuntary students, it is the ethical and astute school counselor who carefully moves through this landmine with administration to ensure students have the option. An option would be to let the students try the group for a time or two, and then if they make the decision not to continue, the principal would not use an alternative discipline against the students. The school counselor might be able to persuade the students to keep coming. Then the students can work on their issues, and the school counselor retains his or her identity as a helper rather than a punisher.

There is a key consideration in referring to the students as "accused" of sexual harassment. If a student has not participated in sexual harassment, then an incorrect accusation and subsequent group for something he or she may not have actually done further complicates the matter. In a case like this, the school counselor should stress that this group should be for students who have had founded accusations brought against them, not just suspected accusations.

As addressed in other cases in this chapter, confidentiality cannot be guaranteed, so the school counselor must stress, but never rely on, participants not to breach confidentiality (see the section Confidentiality in Group Counseling). School counselors can help students by informing them about the principal's belief that the students can make positive change, stressing that for change to happen students must come prepared to work and to take ownership of their behavior. Some school districts, such as Duval County Public Schools in Jacksonville, Fla., have special programs for drug abusers where they can attend lessons and small groups for a first-time drug offense. "The in-school suspension may not exceed 10 school days and shall end upon both the parent/guardian agreeing to enroll in the Night-time Substance Use Prevention Counseling Education Program" (Duval County Public Schools, Student Code of Conduct, 2011, p. 16). This group cannot be viewed as a voluntary group, but it has a place in the complicated world of trying to help students succeed.

CASE NOTES KEPT OUTSIDE OF THE SCHOOL

You have been told that if you keep your case notes in the trunk of your car then they will not be considered education records as defined by FERPA. Is this true?

Points to Consider

Refer to the FERPA chapter for a complete explanation of school counselor case notes. In answer to this one facet of case notes, "Education records may include materials that are physically located outside the school. For example, education records have been held to include documents in the possession of a school psychologist as in the case of *Parents v. Williamsport Area School District*, in the possession of a school district's attorney as in the case of *Belanger v. Nashua, N.H., School District* and in the home of a classroom teacher as in the case of *Warner v. St. Bernard Parish School Board*" (Hughes, 2001). In the *Belanger* opinion it was noted that, during the public comment period prior to the issuance of regulations for FERPA, there were many requests to replace the term "education records" with "school records" but that the U.S. Department of Education instead stated that "[t]he statute does not provide for a differentiation between records ... based on the source of those records" (*Belanger*, 856 F. Supp. at 49). The location of an education record is not what defines it as an education record as it is any record a school district "maintains" on a student, with some exceptions such as records educators keep when they report child abuse.

SAFETY IN CLASSROOM GUIDANCE

A school counselor was delivering a series of classroom guidance lessons when a lesson took an unexpected turn. When students were asked when they felt sad, a student new to the school offered, "My dad just killed my mom and then killed himself." The school counselor, trying to do the right thing, asked the student if he would like to share his story. He then graphically described the story of his parents' murder/suicide. What is your reaction to this situation? Are there any ethical issues to be considered? Does informed consent play a role?

Points to Consider

While in the classroom setting, the emotional safety of all students is primary (ASCA, 2010, D.1.). School counselors cannot possibly predict what students are going to say, so being prepared to skillfully intervene without dismissing the student or making him feel devalued is an important tool to be able to use. By honoring the student with a sincere acknowledgement that his parents death is indeed a situation that would make you feel sad, the school counselor has to move on to the next person. To do more than sincerely acknowledge and move on opens up the possibility of more trauma for the child who lost his parents and the other children hearing details. Clearing the calendar and bringing the student in immediately after the classroom session would be a good approach. Connecting with the student regularly or seeking outside resources for the student would be the next step.

Given the age and developmental levels of the students, it might be necessary to notify parents and give them suggestions on how to talk to their child about what they heard in the class, especially since the student revealed, in this very real case, the details. The teacher and school counselor might need to collaborate to talk to the class as a group. A skillful teacher could help groom the classroom to accept and support the new student. Students frequently ask unanticipated questions. Predicting questions and spotting potential land mines is part of the overall preparation school counselors undertake before providing a counseling lesson. The events of a similar classroom guidance lesson and the fallout are described in the following newspaper article:

School Forming Death Talk Protocol

A panel of school officials wants to avoid a repeat of a recent incident in which a student graphically described his parents' murder/suicide to his sixth-grade classmates. The Mesick Middle School principal and three school counselors are setting a protocol to follow whenever discussing the deaths of a student's immediate family members.

Meanwhile, school counselor Linda B., who school officials said asked the boy if he wanted to share his story with classmates, was suspended for two days during an investigation, Superintendent Ron Ford said. The board then took "appropriate remedial action," he said, though he would not be more specific. The school counselor since has returned to work.

The panel's efforts were spurred by a student's talk in Carole R.'s sixth-grade class on Oct. 6 regarding his parents' deaths downstate in September. The boy moved to Mesick to live with relatives and enrolled in classes here. Both teacher and school counselor declined to be inter-viewed, Principal Deann Jenkins said. Several parents, including Jay Clough, whose 11-year-old daughter was in the class, told the school board and administrators of the incident. "My first impression was that it should've been brought to the parents' attention before they talked about it in the classroom," Clough said. "So now, instead of one kid that needs counseling, you've got a whole classroom of kids that need counseling." (Carr, 2003)

In a Position to Know:
A School Counselor Educator Speaks

The case presented at the beginning of the chapter is revisited here and answered. Read the school counselor educator's opinion carefully to see what you can learn. Compare her answer with your own approach.

SMALL-GROUP COUNSELING AND SCREENING POTENTIAL MEMBERS

You develop a small group in response to complaints from seventh-grade teachers who say some students are having difficulty getting along with their peers and are interrupting class lessons. The teach-ers also say they believe the behavior is affecting the students' grades. You establish a set of goals for the group that includes learn-ing ways to get along with others while improving grades. The teachers recommend eight students for the group; the principal also requests you also include two other students who are repeatedly in trouble for fighting. This brings your group to 10 students. After you secure parental permission, you conduct your first meeting to discuss the ground rules, confidentiality and goals for the group. By the third session, bickering escalates. The two students who were recommended by the principal are not benefiting from the group and are fueling the group's negativity by making threatening comments to the other members. Are there ethical issues with the small group?

Points to Consider

The school counselor's intent for this small group is commendable, and the group goals are worthy. Despite the well-intended actions of the school counselor, there are ethical issues related to this case.

Ethical guidelines call for appropriate screening of potential members. "Professional school counselors screen prospective group members and maintain an awareness of participants' needs, appropriate fit and personal goals in relation to the group's intention and focus. The school counselor takes reasonable precautions to protect members from physical and psychological harm resulting from interaction within the group" (ASCA, 2010, A.6.a).

School counselors are the front-line professionals responsible for creating an experience that ultimately fulfills the goals of the group and of each member. Screening prospective group members is an essential ethical practice. In this case, the school counselor relied on teacher referrals and complied with the principal's request. Group membership was based on others' perceptions of students who might benefit from the small-group experience, rather than the professional school counselor adhering to best practices (ASGW, 2007) and following ethical practices for group leaders (ASCA, 2010). In this case study, the school counselor did not meet with group members until the first session; thus, assessing the suitability of each student for the group and formulating individual goals with each student did not happen. Therefore, the degree of commitment and investment of each student to the group experience and fellow members of the group is at best questionable.

Sink, Edwards and Eppler (2012) described criteria and pre-group screening approaches indicating appropriateness to participate in small groups. Typically, the more preferred method of screening is an individual interview. While individual meetings may be dismissed because of time constraints, school counselors need to remember that screening is an ethical practice for conducting small groups in schools and will contribute to the effectiveness of the group experience. Smead (1995) suggested individual meetings (a) afford the group leader the opportunity to discuss the "purpose and goals of the group" (p. 287), (b) confirm the student's willingness to participate, (c) check for "compatibility" (p. 287) with other group members and (d) check that the student is indeed interested in and committed to participating in the group. Sink et al. suggested that prescreening need not be considered a lengthy, formal process and offered suggested questions that may be completed informally and in a reasonable time frame. In the case presented, students were drafted as members of the group and only in the first meeting can we assume that expectations were discussed.

A second issue related to screening is the selection of members and the number of members for a group. Typically, a group size for middle school would range from six to eight members. This group had 10 members, all of whom were in the group because of unacceptable and aggressive behaviors. Because of the homogeneity of the group, the potential for appropriate modeling behaviors between group members significantly decreased. The size and composition of this group would potentially pose challenges for any group leader.

The school counselor did follow ethical practices of obtaining parental consent to participate in the group. The school counselor, however, omitted an important step in the informed consent process. By not screening the students, the school counselor did not inform or seek consent from the students themselves for participation. Young adolescence is such a pivotal developmental period. Students at this age seek adult approval, but they also search to develop identity and autonomy (Kaplan, 2004; Stevenson, 2002; Dinsmore, 2009; Mullins, 2008). To be an ethical practice, informed consent should be done with both students and parents/guardians.

In this case, following ethical practices might have increased the odds for a successful group experience for students. Unfortunately, this case had a number of pitfalls. One, appropriate screening of the students referred to the group did not occur. Two, the composition of the group was potentially too homogeneous (too many like-behaviors and not enough students to model appropriate behaviors) and contained too many students. Three, there was no indication that students voluntarily joined this group or had an opportunity to express their thoughts and feelings about participation.

This case was described as "some students" having "difficulty getting along." Before leaping into a small group based on referrals, the school counselor would want to review and try to determine more objectively, "how many students" are indeed "not getting along." It would be good practice to first review the data on grades and the discipline referrals for seventh grade. What do the grades show? What are the grades of students in the different subjects? Breaking down or disaggregating the data could prove more enlightening and supplement teacher comments. If each class the students attend is a separate subject, look to see which students in which classes have low grades. What about discipline referrals? Where do most discipline referrals occur, and who are the students being referred? A host of questions can be explored around data.

Rather than singling out "some students" for small groups, the school counselor might find it beneficial to conduct classroom lessons, using the same goals developed for the small-group counseling. One can assume that the "interruptions," as described by the teachers, affect every seventh-grader. It is reasonable then to believe that every student could benefit from developing an understanding about relationships and skills for resolving conflicts. By delivering classroom lessons on peer relationships and skills for better working relationships, the school counselor is not only addressing an immediate issue within the seventh grade but contributing to the learning climate of the seventh-grade classrooms and educating students in a topic that will be beneficial for adult life.

Group work for the two boys "repeatedly in trouble for fighting" is not appropriate for the boys or potentially for other members in the group because of the risk of physical harm to others. The school counselor may find a collaborative consultation more helpful for changing behaviors. For example, developing a behavioral contract with each boy that enlists support from parents/guardians, teachers and the principal may be more likely to change the negative behaviors.

Small-group work is a complex and difficult process that has the potential for effectively helping students in schools. It is the responsibility of school counselors to be informed and knowledgeable of the ethical, legal and professional standards of group work. Developing knowledge and skills for leading groups with children and adolescents is a continual process that calls for professional development, supervision and practice.
– *Rebecca A. Schumacher, assistant professor and school counseling program director, University of North Florida*

Making Connections

1. You are considering running a small group for children of alcoholics. Are there any ethical issues you should consider regarding this topic?

2. You are considering running a small group for children whose parents/guardians are going through a divorce. Are there any ethical considerations you must consider regarding this topic?

3. You would like to enlist a group of parent volunteers to help you follow through on a behavior management program for a group of seven students who are having difficulty finishing their work every day. The volunteers will stop by five classrooms and check to see if the participants have finished their work and, if so, bring them to the school counselor's office to put stickers on their charts. Are there any legal or ethical issues you must consider before involving parent volunteers in this behavior management program?

4. When is it best practice to get parental permission for individual and group counseling?

5. If a parent wants to know what his or her child is saying in individual counseling sessions with you, must you share the information? What are some techniques for making the parent feel included without breaching a child's confidence?

Key Terms

Anorexia
Bulimia
Classroom guidance
Clear and imminent danger
Confidentiality in group counseling
Foreseeable harm
Group counseling sessions

Informed consent
Multiculturalism
No-harm contract
Parental permission
Screening members
Suicide assessment
Unconditional positive regard

CHAPTER 9

Sexually Active Students

IN THIS CHAPTER

Objectives

By the time you have completed this chapter, you should be able to:

- Discuss the complications of confidentiality regarding sexually active students.
- Define your own values regarding sexually active students.
- Recognize when and if your values interfere with your ability to work effectively with students.
- Understand the rights of pregnant students.
- Understand how the school setting complicates school counselors' efforts to respect confidentiality.
- Understand parents' and/or guardians' rights to be the guiding voice in their children's lives in value-laden issues.
- Discuss the prevalence of sexual activity among teens.

Ethical Standards Addressed in This Chapter

Professionalism means knowing your professional association's ethical codes and adhering to them. The ASCA Ethical Standards for School counselors most germane to this chapter are the following:

- Professional school counselors inform students of the purposes, goals, techniques and rules of procedure under which they may receive counseling. Disclosure includes the limits of confidentiality in a developmentally appropriate manner. Informed consent requires competence on the part of students to understand the limits of confidentiality and, therefore, can be difficult to obtain from students of a certain developmental level. Professionals are aware that even though every attempt is made to obtain informed consent, it is not always possible and when needed will make counseling decisions on students' behalf. (A.2.a)
- Professional school counselors recognize the complicated nature of confidentiality in schools and consider each case in context. Keep information confidential unless legal requirements demand that confidential information be revealed or a breach is required to prevent serious and foreseeable harm to the student. Serious and foreseeable harm is different for each minor in schools and is defined by students' developmental and chronological age, the setting, parental rights and the nature of the harm. School counselors consult with appropriate professionals when in doubt as to the validity of an exception. (A.2.c)

■ Professional school counselors inform parents/guardians and/or appropriate authorities when a student poses a danger to self or others. This is to be done after careful deliberation and consultation with other counseling professionals. (A.7.a)

The full text of the ASCA Ethical Standards for School Counselors is available at *www.schoolcounselor.org*.

Introduction

This chapter deals with the highly sensitive and value-laden issue of sexually active students. The consequences of sexual activity can place school counselors in vulnerable positions with students and parents/guardians. Through a series of case studies, this chapter examines the difficulties of working with minors around this delicate topic.

School counselors regularly face ethical dilemmas of confidentiality for which there are few definitive answers. The American School Counselor Association (2010) provides guidelines for ethical behavior, but it is ultimately the school counselor's responsibility to negotiate the rights and privileges of students and parents/guardians with regard to disclosing information to parents/guardians (Stone, 2001). Parents' and/or guardians' legal rights to guide their children, community standards, a school counselor's personal values, school board policy and the school setting all contribute to the complex nature of working with sexually active students. Difficult decisions involving value-laden issues must always be made against the backdrop of parental rights. School counselors have the complicated task of figuring out when it is time to involve parents/guardians so they can exercise their right to guide their children.

Court decisions give school counselors some guidance in issues involving abortion counseling. However, the answers to complex questions involving sexually active students elude the profession in absence of clear-cut school board policies. Of all the topics school counselors tackle, sexually active students pose the most nail-biting, tense moments regarding confidentiality. As a school counselor, sometimes your best defense is to seek supervision and consultation with other professionals who are in a position to understand the context-specific world in which you are operating, including the prevailing community standards and school board policies.

Many people report having their first sexual experiences during adolescence (Fortenberry, Herbenick, Sanders, Dodge & Reece, 2010). Responding to a 2008–2010 survey, 42 percent of females and 43 percent of males aged 15–19 reported having had sexual intercourse. This statistic marked a sharp decline since 1988, when 51 percent of adolescents reported having had intercourse, although rates have stayed about the same since 2002 (Martinez, Abma & Copen, 2010). In a Youth Risk Behavior Survey conducted in 2009, 34.2 percent of students from ninth to 12th grade reported being sexually active (had intercourse during the three months before the survey), and 46 percent of students reported having had sexual intercourse (Centers for Disease Control and Prevention, 2012).

The majority of high school students are not regularly engaging in oral sex; however some students do begin to experiment with oral sex during their teenage years. Fewer than 12 percent of women and 8.5 percent of men this age reported having performed oral sex on an other-sex partner in the past year. The prevalence of oral sex increases with age: 18.3 percent of 16- to 17-year-old males and 22.4 percent of 16- to 17-year-old females reported having performed oral sex on an other-sex partner in the previous year (Fortenberry, Schick, Herbenick, Sanders, Dodge & Reece, 2010). Although most men and women have not yet given or received oral sex by the time they turn 18, research shows students may not understand the possible consequences of this behavior.

One study conducted by Brady and Halpern-Felsher (2007) showed that teenagers generally expect fewer negative consequences to result from oral sex than vaginal sex, including physical, health, social and emotional consequences. This study showed that adolescents who report only having oral sex are less likely to report experiencing a pregnancy or STI, feeling guilty or used, having their relationship become worse or getting in trouble with their parents/guardians as a result of having sex. This study illustrates a gender gap in consequences of sex, showing girls are much more likely than boys to experience negative social and emotional consequences of both oral and vaginal sex. The gender gap persists, showing that adolescent men are much more likely than women to report experiencing popularity and feeling good about themselves as a consequence of sexual behavior.

In a different survey, conducted by Widdice and Halpern-Felsher (2006), 528 ethnically diverse and sexually inexperienced ninth-graders were surveyed about hypothetical situations such as the likelihood of sexually transmitted diseases (STD) or pregnancy with or without condoms. Males and females believed there was a higher chance of getting pregnant than contracting an STD regardless of whether a condom was used. The data from this study show teens are more concerned about getting pregnant than they are about contracting an STD.

Casual relationships (friends with benefits) are not uncommon among sexually active students. Although the majority of sexually active teens (70 percent of females and 56 percent of males) report their first sexual experience was with a steady partner, a sizeable minority (16 percent of females and 28 percent of males) report their first sex was with "someone they had just met or who was just a friend" (Martinez, Copen & Abma; 2011).

Approximately 750,000 women younger than 20 become pregnant each year (Kost & Henshaw, 2012). Thirty-one percent of teenage pregnancies end in abortion, down from 46 percent in 1986 (Kost & Henshaw, 2012). Eighteen percent of U.S. women having abortions are under the age of 20 (Jones, Finer & Singh; 2010).

Getting Started: What Would You Do?

The following case is discussed for you at the end of this chapter by a school counselor educator. Before you read her response, formulate in your own mind how you would approach this ethical dilemma.

DEVELOPMENTALLY DELAYED, PREGNANT STUDENTS

Sharon is slightly developmentally delayed. Chronologically Sharon is 14, but developmentally she is more like an 11 or 12 year old. Sharon is pregnant, and her mother is aware of the pregnancy. Sharon has long been a concern of many in the school. She is unkempt, explosive and violent. Her developmental problems mean she is always out of sync with her age group. Her peers avoid her because they are afraid of her. You are concerned she will now be responsible for a baby. Sharon seems incapable of taking care of herself, and you fear for the safety of her child. She tells everyone that having this baby will bring the father of the baby back to her. Sharon says her mother will help her raise the baby. She talks excitedly and animatedly about how she has "always wanted a baby." She talks about her cousin, who is also 14, has a baby and "dresses it up in beautiful clothes." What steps if any need to be taken in this case?

Working Through Case Studies

HELPING A STUDENT GET CONTRACEPTIVES

In your school, student pregnancy is common. Jessica comes to you distraught over a fight she had with her boyfriend, Michael. In the course of the counseling session, the student reveals she and Michael are sexually active, and she is terrified of getting pregnant. You encourage Jessica to seek help from her parents or a close relative, but she says that is out of the question. Jessica refuses to meet with the school nurse, explaining she trusts only you. You are convinced that without your help, Jessica will never visit a clinic. You make an appointment for her, and with Jessica's approval, call Michael's mother to take her to the clinic. When Michael's mother refuses, you agree to transport Jessica to the clinic. Can you transport a student to a clinic for the purpose of receiving birth control? Are you required to notify the parents/guardians of students who are engaged in unprotected sex?

Points to Consider

Taking Jessica to get birth control risks potential repercussions from her family, and in many communities in America, you would be stepping on family values. Transporting a student to get any kind of medical attention is risky even with parental permission, and it is out of the question without parental involvement in most parts of the country.

School counselors must also consider the parents' and/or guardians' position and how Jessica's mother might react if she found out you had contacted Michael's mother. Your actions could affect the relationship between the mothers, their children and you. As a school counselor it is up to you to work with Jessica and help her figure out a way to involve her mother. As you counsel Jessica, keep in mind what the policies regarding sexual activity are in your school district. For example, in some school districts a school counselor may be mandated to inform parents/guardians when a child talks about sexual activity.

With the exception of four states, there are statutes giving students guidance as to whether or not they can seek contraceptive help in absence of parental involvement. Guttmacher conducted a study in 2013 of the state statutes involving minors and contraceptive information. In summary,

MINORS' ACCESS TO CONTRACEPTIVE SERVICES

State	Explicitly Allows All Minors To Consent To Services	Explicitly Affirms Certain Minors May Consent To Services §					No Explicit Policy
		Health	Married	Parent	Pregnant or Ever Pregnant	Other	
Alabama			X*	X*	X*	High school graduate* or 14 years*	
Alaska	X						
Arizona	X						
Arkansas	X						
California	X						
Colorado	X						
Connecticut			X†				
Delaware						12 years‡	
District of Columbia	X						
Florida		X	X	X			
Georgia	X				X		
Hawaii						14 years‡	
Idaho	X						
Illinois		X	X	X	X	Referral	
Indiana			X†				
Iowa	X						
Kansas						Mature minor	
Kentucky	X‡						
Louisiana			X†				

State	Explicitly Allows All Minors To Consent To Services	Explicitly Affirms Certain Minors May Consent To Services §					
		Health	Married	Parent	Pregnant or Ever Pregnant	Other	No Explicit Policy
Maine		X	X	X			
Maryland	X‡						
Massachusetts	XΩ						
Michigan			X†				
Minnesota	X‡						
Mississippi			X	X		Referral	
Missouri			X†				
Montana	X‡						
Nebraska			X†				
Nevada			X†	X*		Mature minor*	
New Hampshire						Mature minor*	
New Jersey			X*		X*		
New Mexico	X						
New York	XΩ						
North Carolina	X						
North Dakota							X
Ohio							X
Oklahoma			X‡		X‡		
Oregon	X‡						
Pennsylvania			X*		X*	High school graduate* or 14 years*	

State	Explicitly Allows All Minors To Consent To Services	Explicitly Affirms Certain Minors May Consent To Services §§					
		Health	Married	Parent	Pregnant or Ever Pregnant	Other	No Explicit Policy
Rhode Island							X
South Carolina			X†			16 years or mature minor	
South Dakota			X†				
Tennessee	X						
Texas			X†			Φ	
Utah			X†			Φ	
Vermont			X†				
Virginia	X						
Washington	X						
West Virginia						Mature minor	
Wisconsin			X†				X
Wyoming	XΩ						
TOTAL	21 + DC	3	21	6	6	11	4

§§ US Supreme Court rulings have extended privacy rights to include a minor's decision to obtain contraceptives.

* State policy does not specifically address contraceptive services but applies to medical care in general.

† State law confers the rights and responsibilities of adulthood to minors who are married.

‡ Physician may, but is not required to, inform the minor's parents/guardians.

Ω The state funds a statewide program giving minors access to confidential contraceptive care.

Φ State funds may not be used to provide minors with confidential contraceptive services.

"Twenty-one states and the District of Columbia explicitly allow all minors to consent to contraceptive services. Twenty-five states explicitly permit minors to consent to contraceptive services in one or more circumstances. Three states allow minors to consent to contraceptive services if a physician determines the minor would face a health hazard if not provided with contraceptive services. Eleven states allow a minor to consent if the minor meets other requirements, including being a high school graduate, reaching a minimum age, demonstrating maturity or receiving a referral from a specified professional, such as a physician or member of the clergy" (p.1). Find the complete report at *www.guttmacher.org/state center/spibs/spib_MACS.pdf*.

NOTIFYING PARENTS/GUARDIANS WHEN THEIR CHILD IS SEXUALLY ACTIVE

Seventeen-year-olds Rachel and Bradley have been having sexual relations for more than a year. In the course of working with Rachel, she tells you this information. You try to determine if she is using protection against pregnancy and STDs. She says she is but with much hesitation, shifting in her seat and equivocation. Your gut tells you she is not using protection. Are you required to notify the parents/guardians of students who are engaged in sexual activity? Does the situation change for you if the student is not using protection?

Points to Consider

At 17, how prepared is Rachel to understand the potential repercussions of having sex, either unprotected or protected? Is this a girl who has a strong handle on what she is doing? Find out what she thinks about how her decisions will affect her future, and help her think through the issues with a sequential problem-solving approach. Encourage this student to involve her parents/guardians.

The National Survey of Family Growth showed that more than two-thirds of male teenagers and almost four-fifths of female teenagers had spoken with their parents/guardians about at least one of six sex education topics, which included how to say no to sex, methods of birth control, STDs, where to get birth control, how to prevent HIV/AIDS and how to use a condom (Martinez et al., 2010). Studies associate parental communication and sexual education with delayed initiation of sex and healthier sexual behaviors (Lindberg & Maddow-Zimmet, 2011; Martinez et al., 2010). In general, the younger the child, the more rights are vested in the parents/guardians – a concept that applies to both physical maturity and, in a court of law, also mental maturity.

You can avoid scrambling in a crisis by being prepared. Know your community's prevailing opinions about minors and pregnancy as these opinions have an impact in some respects on how you will respond. Know which resources in your community can help your students with issues involving their sexual activity.

Essential to establishing a network of support is developing a relationship with the school principal and staff members, including teachers, the school nurse, cafeteria workers, janitors and secretaries. One of the secrets of being an investigative reporter in the world of journalism, for example, is to cultivate sources on the front lines; these are the people who see and hear everything and can be the most useful to you. Teachers and other educators can be your front line if you empower your "investigators" to responsibly gather and use sensitive information to help you support students. You can widen your influence by delivering professional development around topics such as suicidal ideation, signs of abuse and available community resources and help each educator be an extension of the school counseling program.

The following are recommendations for the school counselor when counseling students in the area of sexuality or abortion:

Know your school board policy. School counselors can sometimes find guidance in school board policy and must adhere to the stated policy. School counselors behaving as advocates work appropriately to change policies they believe have an adverse impact on students.

Know your state's age-of-consent laws. The Romeo and Juliet law was first created in Florida during the 2007 legislative session to address concerns about high-school-age youth being labeled as sexual offenders or sexual predators as a result of participating in a consensual sexual relationship. The pedophile registry provides no clear distinction between the young sex offenders who had consensual sex and the offenders who harm children and pose a risk to society. Under Texas' version of the law, if a young adult over the age of 17 has consensual sexual relations with someone under the age of 17 but at least 15 years old with no more than a four-year age difference between the two, the new law will not require the older party to register as a sex offender if convicted of statutory rape. Texas and other states have used a petition process for sex offenders to clear their name and to get off the pedophile registration if they were charged as sexual offenders having engaged in consensual sex with a close-in-age partner. States set up what the close-in-age is, and this is often labeled a Romeo and Juliet law. Notify your principal, call Child Protective Services, and/or the police or sheriff (Findlaw, 2012).

Consider developmental issues. If Rachel had been 14 you would act with greater caution for her well-being in possible risky behavior. It is especially important to consider the developmental level to determine whether an intervention(s) is needed and how much is required. School counselors promote the autonomy and independence of a minor by carefully considering how much to support students in making their own decisions without interference or breach of confidentiality. Primary to the school counselor's decision-making is the seriousness of the minor's behavior, his or her developmental level and the minor's history of making informed decisions (Stone, 2001).

Consider the impact of the school setting and parental rights. Parental rights are complicated since parents/guardians send minors to school for academics, not for personal counseling. Therefore, when a minor seeks counseling in a value-laden area such as abortion, which may be related to the parents'/guardians' morals or religious beliefs, consideration must be given to the wishes of parents/guardians and their rights to be the guiding voice in their children's lives. The onus is not on the school counselor to know the religious beliefs of all the students and their families. However, if a student confides that religion is at issue or if the school counselor learns this information from another source, then it is appropriate to consider this information when determining how to proceed with the student.

Consider diversity issues. Each decision must be made in context and must consider a minor's ethnicity, socioeconomic status, gender, race and sexual identity.

Consult with a supervisor or respected colleague, examining the good and bad consequences of each course of action. Strive to minimize the risk to the student while respecting parents'/guardians' inherent rights. It is ethical, lawful and beneficial to inform and consult with supervisors and colleagues. After the school counselor implements a course of action, it is important to process the results to strengthen the probability of making appropriate decisions in the future.

Know yourself and your values. School counselors should understand their own values in sensitive areas such as abortion and teen pregnancy and understand the impact of those values on their ability to act in the best interest of their students. Professionals know they cannot divorce themselves from their values and exercise caution when their values could inappropriately interfere with promoting a student's autonomy. School counselors will want to refer students to a colleague when they can no longer be objective.

Avoid involvement in a student's medical care. Referring students to birth control clinics should be avoided, and a school counselor should never agree to take students for any kind of medical procedure, especially a procedure as controversial as abortion (Stone, 2004).

PREGNANT STUDENTS AND ADMINISTRATORS' REQUEST FOR INFORMATION

Your assistant principal comes to you and asks you for a list of all students in the school that you know are pregnant. He explains he wants to notify these students about an alternative school for pregnant and parenting teens and encourage them to go there. Do you have any concerns about this request? Must you comply with this request?

Points to Consider

In a 2002 California court case, *Holt v. Bellflower Unified School District*, school counselor Mary Beth Holt filed suit against the district for wrongful termination. The school's vice principal ordered Holt to disclose the names of students who were pregnant so they could be transferred to another school specifically designed to handle pregnant students' circumstances. The vice principal told Holt the school board did not want pregnant girls on the school campus, and they had adopted a policy of transferring pregnant students out of the regular school program. Holt explained the information was confidential, having been disclosed during private counseling sessions and protected under California statute for school counselors and confidentiality. Holt contacted the department of education about the situation. The district then informed her that her employment would not be continued the following year. She was told there was "no cause" for her firing.

Holt sued the school district, the principal, the vice principal and each member of the Bellflower Board of Education. The case was initially dismissed. On appeal, it was ruled Holt could proceed with her complaint in the lower court. The results of the lower court's decision are not published and may have been settled.

Holt's willingness to put her students above the system is admirable. However, once an educator takes employment in a system designed for academic instruction there needs to be a recognition that the rules are more complicated than in a system designed exclusively for counseling. The best approach is to avoid a power struggle with your administration. Perhaps, tell your principal you will consult with the students and seek their permission to be included on a list to administration. There are a number of other techniques to get the job done, protect confidentiality and to avoid going to war with administration. It would be ethical to also tell administration that you will make certain these students know transferring is not mandatory but optional and, depending on the context of the situation, give your opinion on the academic program provided by the alternative school. Title IX explicitly protects pregnant students' rights to equal access to educational opportunities and states that participation in separate programs for pregnant or parenting students must be optional, not mandatory. In fact, the law prohibits schools from urging or pressuring pregnant or parenting students into separate programs (National Women's Law Center, 2012a). The bottom line is that confidentiality is much harder to respect with the competing interests in a school setting. The case took place in California, one of the states where it is easiest to keep confidentiality. Digging in your heels with administrators is one of those no-win situations. School counselors need to balance promoting respect for students' autonomy while also showing administrators they are listening to administration's requests. Holt sounds like a student-centered school counselor, and it is always unfortunate to lose good people because a compromise could not be found.

PARENTAL NOTIFICATION POLICIES AND STUDENT PREGNANCY

Your school district was challenged by an angry parent who felt her daughter's school counselor should have informed her when her daughter sought counseling about her pregnancy. In response the district has issued a new written policy saying school counselors must try to get students to inform their parents/guardians about their pregnancy, and failing to accomplish this the school counselors themselves must inform parents/guardians. Are there any legal or ethical concerns regarding this policy?

Points to Consider

School counselors are faced with the issue of whether or not to inform a pregnant student's parents/guardians. The majority of school counselors work overtime to try and help students find a way to inform their parents/guardians. School counselors sometimes understand they have to let the student take the lead in deciding what is best.

Parental involvement can be supportive and beneficial; however, it can also be punitive, coercive or abusive (Griffin-Carlson & Mackin, 1993). It is the unpredictability of parental reaction that makes it impossible to develop a hard and fast rule on school counselor behavior in parental notification of student pregnancy. School counselors also cite incidences in which a student has valid reasons or legitimate fears that prevent her from involving her parents/guardians. Studies show minors who choose not to discuss their abortion decision with their parents/guardians cite one or more of the following reasons for not confiding: fear of rejection, fear of disappointing their parents/guardians, fear of violence at home, fear of being forced to leave home, wanting to spare their parents/guardians from the problem, wanting to handle it on their own and/or fear their parents/guardians will force them to have an abortion (Griffin-Carlson & Mackin, 1993; Henshaw & Kost, 1992). In cases where such fears are legitimate, parental notification policies stand to cause physical and psychological harm to girls who are already highly vulnerable.

In an October 2012 survey of ASCA members, school counselors were divided about whether or not they think students accurately predict their parents' reaction to their pregnancy.

"In your experience, do your students accurately predict their parent/guardians' reaction to their pregnancy?"

Yes: . . . . .42 percent
No: . . . . .58 percent

(Stone, 2012d)

In this same survey, the majority of school counselors who have worked with pregnant students responded they are working diligently to get the student to involve her parents.

Respondents indicated the statement that most closely matched their practice:

I do not inform her parents, but I always work
diligently to get her to inform her parent/guardians: . . . .41 percent
I will sometimes make the decision to inform her
parent/guardians if she does not: . . . . .21 percent
I let the student take the lead as to whether she
wants her parents to know: . . . . .5 percent
I never inform parents about a student's pregnancy
(under any circumstances): . . . . .1 percent
I have never worked with a student regarding
pregnancy: . . . . .32 percent

(Stone, 2012d)

A district policy eliminates school counselors' capacity to help students weigh the facts, grapple with the issues and determine when, how or whether to involve parents/guardians. A one-size-fits-all policy reduces the school counselor's role to a trigger to be pulled regardless of circumstances and is not in keeping with the intent, nature and function of school counseling. School counselors avoid quick, easy answers in the form of policies but rather rise to the challenge of supporting students and wrestle around the issues in context of students' personal circumstances, fears, developmental levels and parents' and/or guardians' rights.

New York's Port Washington School District in 2002 enacted a written policy requiring educators to inform parents/guardians of a student's pregnancy. In 2005, the district's teachers association failed in court to get an injunction to stop the implementation of the policy (*Port Washington Teachers' Association v. Board of Education of the Port Washington Union Free School District* (2005)). It was hoped that the messiness of the Port Washington court case would dissuade other districts from policy making around pregnancy and minors' confidentiality rights. The courts ruled in favor of the district but not without serious concerns about how the policy affects federal law. Unfortunately, districts do not seem deterred; Port Washington-style policy continues to surface and be implemented in other districts (Stone, 2012b).

On the surface, parental notification policies might appear as a reasonable approach to protecting minors, their parents/guardians and unborn children. In practice, however, such policies are too drastic as they completely eliminate the discretion needed for caring educators to work in context on behalf of individual students. Notification policies treat each student the same whether she is a competent, mature 17 year old or a developmentally delayed 14 year old. Port Washington's policy eliminates the educators' and health workers' discretion to do complex work with sexually active students.

A districtwide parental notification policy is likely meant to protect the district from angry parents/guardians should they threaten to flex their legal muscles when not informed about their child's pregnancy. Other proponents of such a policy hold the view that parental notification requirements will result in parents/guardians persuading their children to carry their baby to term when studies show the opposite appears to be true (Blum, Resnick & Stark, 1990; Prober, 2005). One-fifth of minors whose pregnancy was revealed by a third party were forced by their parents/guardians to have an abortion, and more than 90 percent of the parents/guardians expressed the stance that an abortion is in their minor child's best interest (Henshaw & Kost, 1992; Prober, 2005). Minors whose pregnancy was revealed by a third party were more likely to report physical violence between them and their parents/guardians or concerns that there might be such violence (Henshaw & Kost, 1992).

Whatever the motivation for such policies, legal opponents view them as a violation of students' federal and state rights and explain they actually work against the public interest by deterring students from using school-based medical and mental health care providers for confidential counseling and information (Prober, 2005). When school policies protect students' confidentiality, they encourage students to voluntarily involve surrogate parents/guardians or trusted adults in the school in their abortion decision. Blanket notification policies scare students away from taking advantage of school-based resources (Prober, 2005).

In the Port Washington case, the court examined whether the policy was constitutional in light of the fact that in New York a minor has a right to an abortion without parental involvement. The court drew a distinction "between notification of pregnancy and consent or notification for abortion." It reasoned such parental notification "does not intrude on the student's right to ultimately seek an abortion or to carry her fetus to term" (*Port Washington Teachers' Association v. Board of Education of the Port Washington Union Free School District* (2005)). With consideration of judicial bypass, the argument becomes even stronger. Judicial bypass is a process in which minors can get state approval to have an abortion without parental involvement in states requiring parental involvement. School notification policies render the intent of judicial bypass ineffective as it takes away the minor's option to keep parents/guardians from knowing about her pregnancy. All states that have parental consent or parental notification requirements for abortions must allow for a minor to have access to judicial bypass, following the Supreme Court case *Bellotti v. Baird* (1979). "Minors must be afforded the opportunity to go before a neutral, detached decision-maker to seek an abortion free from any sort of parental involvement. Thus, policies that require parental notification of a student's pregnancy, yet do not provide the student with the required judicial bypass procedure, effectuate an unconstitutional regime because they take away the ability of the student to seek an abortion without the involvement of a third-party" (Prober, 2005, p. 4).

What does *Belotti v. Baird* have to do with the daily lives of school counselors? It strengthens school counselors' argument that not only do they have an ethical imperative to negotiate the difficult task of supporting pregnant students but also the legal imperative to support their constitutionally protected rights. It would hold to reason that policies involving minors' reproductive health are made in consultation with the legal arm of the district. Ethical codes carry clout in court, and school district attorneys understand this. However school board attorneys are rightfully more concerned with ensuring the district's policies safeguard students' constitutionally protected rights. When school counselors need to advocate against district policies requiring an automatic parental notification, they should speak not only in terms of their ethical imperative but also of the constitutionality of parental notification. Ask the district to carefully weigh the possibility that a challenge to the policy might cause the next big court case.

Professional school counselors do what they have always done: encourage and support a student to involve her parents/guardians but with the freedom to use their judgment when it is time to let a mature minor make her own decisions. School counselors function best when given the freedom to exercise their responsibility to negotiate the rights and privileges of students and parents/guardians with regard to disclosing information to parents/guardians regarding pregnancy. Difficult counseling decisions involving value-laden issues must always be made against the backdrop of parental rights and the trusting relationship and not quick and easy policies eliminating all judgment. It would be far easier for the school counselor to have a policy, but resist such as it takes away the wonderful, messy, confusing, troublesome job of helping a student move toward independence and autonomy by wrestling with the nuances of what is best for each student on each day given the context of her life. School counselors choose this messy role not because it is easy but because it makes a difference in children's lives, even those children carrying children.

It is still the exception and not the norm for school districts to establish policies requiring school counselors to inform parents/guardians of a student's pregnancy, and the majority of school counselor respondents in a 2012 survey do not think it is a good idea for district to implement policies that dictate that they must call parents.

In a 2012 survey of ASCA members by Stone, respondents said:

"Does your school or school district have a policy requiring school counselors who learn of a student's pregnancy to inform the student's parent(s)/guardian?"

Yes, the district has a written policy: . . . . .8 percent
No, there is no policy: . . . . .78 percent
It is not a written policy, but it is verbally conveyed
that the expectation is to inform parents: . . . . .14 percent

"In your opinion, should all school districts have policies requiring school counselors to call parent(s)/guardian if a student reports being pregnant?"

Yes: . . . . .30 percent
No: . . . . .70 percent

(Stone, 2012d)

PREGNANCY AS A TEMPORARY DISABILITY

Your administration asked you to "convince" Erika, a pregnant student, to attend the pregnant and parenting teens alternative school. You have a relationship with Erika, and you have been helping her stay on track, as she is often absent due to her morning sickness and doctors appointments. It has been a struggle; her teachers are reluctant to give her make-up work because they believe she should not let morning sickness keep her from her obligations. Teachers are condemning her absences with comments such as, "Well I had four kids, and I never missed a day of work because of my morning sickness." You are growing weary of nudging, begging, cajoling the teachers into providing work, and you are beginning to agree it would be better for all if she did go to the alternative program. Up to this point Erika has expressed a desire to stay in her current school. You are considering using your relationship with Erika to influence her to change schools. What are you legal and ethical obligations to Erika?

Points to Consider

Title IX, the equal access law, is not just about equity in sports. Title IX affords students protection from discrimination based on their "actual or potential parental, family or marital status" and based on a student's "pregnancy, childbirth, false pregnancy, termination of pregnancy or recovery there from" (20 U.S.C. §§ 1681 et seq. (2006). All public schools and private schools must comply with Title IX if they receive even $1 of federal funds following the court's response in *Russo v. Diocese of Greensburg and Greensburg Central Catholic High School* (2010).

School officials must treat pregnant and parenting students as they would all able or disabled students and "provide equal access to school for pregnant and parenting students and treat pregnancy and all related conditions like any other temporary disability" (National Women's Law Center, 2012b, p. 1).

School officials:

- Cannot require a doctor's note for pregnant students to participate in activities unless the school requires a doctor's note from all students who have conditions requiring medical care.
- Must excuse absences due to pregnancy or childbirth for as long as the student's doctor deems medically necessary and provide make-up work or opportunities for catching up.
- Must reinstate students to the status they held when the leave began.
- Must ensure any separate programs or schools for pregnant and parenting students are voluntary and offer opportunities equal to those offered for non-pregnant students.
- Must avoid encouraging students to attend inferior programs.
- Must provide access to homebound instruction if medically necessary. (National Women's Law Center, 2012b, p. 1)

The facts demonstrate that it is in the best interest of Erika, her child and the community if Erika is supported and encouraged to finish high school. Otherwise, her economic prospects look dim. Females who drop out of high school are more likely to be unemployed than male high school dropouts (Bureau of Labor Statistics, 2012). A study by Perper, Peterson & Manlove (2010) revealed that only about one-half of teen mothers get a high school diploma by the age of 22, compared with 89 percent of women who do not have a child during their teen years. Hoffman (2006) found that less than 2 percent of young teenage mothers attain a college degree by the age of 30. Teen mothers are more likely to rely on public assistance than are older mothers and more likely to experience family turbulence, even after accounting for their tendency to come from disadvantaged backgrounds (Perper et al., 2010). As Erika's school counselor and possibly her only advocate in the school, it is your job to present the alternative program to her in a way that empowers her to make the best decision about her future, not the most convenient or expedient decision for the adults in the school.

ABORTION COUNSELING AND THE COURTS

Regina is 16 years old and pregnant. She comes to you seeking help as she considers getting an abortion. Regina tells you she really needs to explore her options with an adult who is "outside of her family." Can you discuss with Regina her pregnancy and her options, including abortion? Does this scenario automatically trigger for you the need to inform Regina's parents/guardians about her pregnancy?

Points to Consider

The legal and ethical complications of working with minors in schools pose daily dilemmas. Among the most delicate of these are value-laden issues such as abortion, contraception and sexual activity, which involve a family's religious beliefs and values about sexual conduct. Respecting students' confidences requires school counselors to balance the rights of minors with the rights of their parents/guardians (Isaacs & Stone, 2001; Kaplan, 1996). "Legal Rulings and the Ethical Standards for School Counselors" (ASCA, 2010) offers suggestions and guidance in the complexities of confidentiality. However, it is ultimately the school counselor's responsibility to determine the appropriate response for individual students who put their trust in the security of the counseling relationship. School counselors need to be advocates and a source of strength for the individual students who come to them for help in confronting and navigating areas such as sexual activity and pregnancy.

Students who do not want their parents/guardians to know about their pregnancy frequently have substantial fears of abuse. This same population demonstrates a strong overlap with students who were victims of incest, in which case notifying parents/guardians might mean notifying their rapist or rapist's partner or relative (Prober, 2005).

Under what circumstances could a school counselor be held liable for giving abortion advice? In *Arnold v. Board of Education of Escambia County* (1989), Jane and John, two high school students, filed suit along with their parents/guardians against the School District of Escambia County, Ala., alleging the school counselor, Kay Rose, and the assistant principal, Melvin Powell, coerced and assisted Jane in getting an abortion. Further, they accused Powell of paying someone $20 to drive Jane to the abortion clinic and Powell and Rose of hiring Jane and John to perform menial tasks to earn money for the abortion. John, the baby's father, and Jane claimed their constitutional rights were violated, including involuntary servitude and free exercise of religion. Their parents/guardians claimed their privacy rights were violated when the school counselor and assistant principal did not inform them Jane was pregnant and when school officials urged the students not to tell their parents/guardians. The trial court dismissed the suit and plaintiffs appealed (*Arnold v. Board of Education of Escambia County* (1989); Zirkel, 2001).

The U.S. 11th Circuit Court of Appeals partially reversed the decision of the trial court and found Jane's privacy claim and both students' religious claim as worthy of further consideration by the courts. In other words, if Jane and John's religion prohibited abortion and Rose and Powell coerced Jane and John to proceed with Jane's abortion, then their constitutionally protected right of freedom of religion might have been violated. Further, Jane's constitutionally protected right to choose to carry or abort a pregnancy had been violated if she was coerced into having an abortion. Jane's parents/guardians claimed their privacy rights were violated when the school counselor and assistant principal coerced Jane into having an abortion and urged her and John to refrain from discussing her options with a parent. The case was remanded back to the lower court for a trial to take place (Zirkel, 2001).

In fact finding, the trial court found Jane visited a physician who confirmed she was pregnant and provided her with abortion information upon her request. John and Jane told Rose they did not want their parents/guardians to know about the pregnancy as they were not supposed to be seeing each other, and Jane left home because she was being abused by her stepfather. Rose presented various alternatives, but the students rejected all alternatives except abortion. Rose repeatedly urged Jane and John to consult with their parents/guardians. Rose reported the alleged abuse by the stepfather to the Department of Children's Services Resources, which sent a representative to meet with Jane. The representative urged Jane to consult with her mother and offered alternatives such as foster care and adoption. When Jane rejected all alternatives, the representative assisted Jane in trying to obtain financial assistance and Medicaid. Jane and John said they felt pressured to have an abortion by Rose when she asked them how they planned to care for the baby and where they were going to take the baby. During the process of discovery, Jane admitted Rose's questions were valid. She conceded that she alone made the decision to have an abortion and that she was not coerced by Rose or Powell. John admitted he had chosen not to tell his mother. The trial court concluded that the students were not deprived of their free will, had chosen to obtain an abortion, had chosen not to tell their parents/guardians and that there was no coercion on the part of school officials (*Arnold v. Board of Education of Escambia County* (1989); Zirkel, 2001).

After the *Arnold* ruling, the question remains: Can school counselors be held liable for giving abortion advice to pregnant minors? School counselors may assist students with value-laden issues such as abortion if they are competent to give such advice and if they proceed in a professional manner. School counselors must consider their responsibilities extend beyond the student to parents/guardians and take great care in abortion counseling. Fischer and Sorenson (1996) stated: "If an immature, emotionally fragile young girl procures an abortion with the help of a school counselor, under circumstances where reasonably competent school counselors would have notified the parents/guardians or would have advised against the abortion, liability for psychological or physical suffering may follow. The specific facts and circumstances must always be considered" (p. 60).

Are school counselors providing students with information about acquiring an abortion? The results of an October 2012 survey may come as a shock as 17 percent of the respondents said they do just that.

Which best describes your practice? If a student seeks your help to obtain information about acquiring an abortion:

I support, listen, but I do not provide them with
  information: . . . . .31 percent
I support, listen and give accurate information
  about how to obtain an abortion: . . . . .17 percent
I do not listen: . . . . .1 percent
None of the above: . . . . .47 percent

(Stone, 2012d)

School counselors assess the student's developmental age and the student's ability to make informed, sound decisions. School counselors must continually ask themselves what the reasonably competent professional would do under similar circumstances. Consider if Jane Doe had been 13 years old. Would Rose have responded differently? Stadler's (1990) test of universality is a good gauge because the test asks professionals to consider the advice they would give to a colleague in the throes of a similar ethical dilemma. If the school counselor would advise the colleague to take a different path, then this begs the school counselor to further examine his or her proposed actions. Perhaps the school counselor is planning action that is too conservative, too risky or outside the bounds of what the reasonably competent professional would do.

Can school boards adopt a policy forbidding school counselors to engage in any discussions with their students about contraception, abortion or sexual activity? School boards can (and some do) adopt policies forbidding school counselors to address certain topics or instructing them to immediately call parents if students bring up such topics. Ethical school counselors work responsibly to change policies that are harmful to students, such as mandates for schools to notify parents if their children bring up such topics as pregnancy, abortion, contraception and sexual activity.

ABORTION COUNSELING AND SCHOOL COUNSELORS' VALUES

Regina, 16, comes to you seeking help as she is pregnant and considering an abortion. Regina's situation engenders strong emotions for you as you are vehemently opposed to abortion (or the opposite, vehemently opposed to children having children). Regina tells you she really needs to explore her options with an adult who is "outside of her family." Can you discuss with Regina her pregnancy and her options since you have an especially strong reaction to abortion? How will your personal feelings about teenage pregnancy and abortion affect your response and behavior with Regina? How will you know when you can address a value-laden issue with a student and when your own values will require you refer this student to someone else?

Points to Consider

To avoid ambiguity when counseling students and to delineate the limits of your pledge to preserve confidentiality, you must give informed consent to students, letting them know when you believe they are in danger you may need to contact their parents. You should also inform students of any district policies requiring you to contact their parents, whether or not you feel they are in danger. You have a strong ethical responsibility to Regina at a time when she may be most vulnerable. Your choice of words, body language and tone carry enormous weight as Regina decides what to do about her pregnancy. If possible, encourage Regina to confide in her parents or a close relative, explaining that discussing her problem with loved ones can benefit her.

Assist Regina in exploring her options without imposing your own views or giving her advice. Generally speaking, it is best practice to let her suggest possible courses of action and the good and bad consequences of each. If you supply her options, you may inadvertently be blessing a choice that until now she had considered completely out of the question, such as abortion. Maybe abortion is not one of her considerations because of religious values or family pressure, and you just planted the idea that it should be a viable option for her.

School counselors must be prepared to argue they behaved as the reasonably competent professional would have. Coercion and imposing one's values on a minor student would not be appropriate actions of a reasonable and professional school counselor (Stone, 2004a).

A school counselor who is vehemently opposed to abortion could not work ethically with a minor in the throes of an abortion decision. The ethical and responsible course of action would be to refer Regina to another school counselor if at all possible. Sometimes an outside agency or a school nurse will be a good choice to help her with the medical questions she may have.

Although school counselors may not voice their opposition to abortion, values may be revealed in voice tone, a raised eyebrow, a heavy sigh or a diverted glance. Such nonverbal cues can inadvertently impose a school counselor's values on a vulnerable student. The influence a school counselor can have on a pregnant minor cannot be understated. The compounding factors of the school counselor's authority over the student, the student's inexperience or lack of awareness of her rights, the student's lack of confidence in her own beliefs and the emotions she may be experiencing related to the pregnancy can result in a heightened state of vulnerability for the client.

HELPING A STUDENT GET AN ABORTION

One of your counselees is pregnant, distraught and unwilling to involve her parents. She turns to you for help. You believe your relationship is such that you can support the student to acquire the abortion she desperately wants. You have worked with this student to help her realize her dreams of a college education, and now she is uncertain if she can take the scholarship and go forward. You give her all the information she needs to have this procedure in a neighboring state, as your state requires parental consent. Have you done the right thing?

Points to Consider

A couple in the Hatboro-Horsham School District in Pennsylvania sued their daughter's high school counselor after she revealed her school counselor advised her to obtain an abortion, a violation of Pennsylvania state law (Sanchez, 2000). The school counselor allegedly advised the student to get the abortion, helped to excuse her from school for the procedure, cashed the checks written by her boyfriend for the abortion and created a map to an abortion clinic in the neighboring state of New Jersey. Pennsylvania state law requires the consent of a parent or guardian before a minor can undergo an abortion procedure; however, New Jersey state law does not. The parents' suit centered on their right to be the guiding force in matters of family life and the upbringing of their children (U.S. Const., amend. XIV). The Hatboro-Horsham School District was named as a co-defendant in the suit, and the parents/guardians sought to prevent the school district from counseling students about abortion or helping students obtain medical procedures or information without parental consent.

School counselors work is influenced by community standards as well as school board policy, local and state laws. For example, although many U.S. school districts have "abstinence-only" sex education that forbids teaching of contraceptives, some public high schools in New York City are able to administer Plan B (known as "the morning-after pill") to female students (Associated Press, 2012). State laws on contraceptive services and abortions, while not directly dictating how school counselors will behave, certainly influences their approach. School counselors who are in a state allowing minors to make medical decisions about their reproductive life will find their work with minors different than in a state or community that believes parents/guardians should decide if a child takes birth control or has an abortion.

STATES' STANCE ON PARENTAL CONSENT
OR NOTIFICATION FOR MINORS' ABORTION

Consent Laws Not in Effect	Notice Laws Not in Effect	States Requiring Consent	States Requiring Notice	States With No Laws
California	Illinois	Alabama	Alaska	Connecticut*
New Mexico	New Jersey	Arizona	Colorado	Hawaii
District of Columbia*		Arkansas	Delaware (if under 16)	Maine*
		Idaho	Florida	New Hampshire
		Indiana	Georgia	New York
		Kansas	Iowa	Oregon
		Kentucky	Maryland	Vermont
		Louisiana	Minnesota	Washington
		Massachusetts	Nevada	
		Michigan	South Dakota	
		Mississippi	West Virginia	
		Missouri		
		North Carolina		
		North Dakota		
		Ohio		
		Oklahoma		
		Pennsylvania		
		Rhode Island		
		South Carolina (if under 17)		
		Tennessee		
		Texas		
		Utah		
		Virginia		
		Wisconsin		
		Wyoming		

*Connecticut, the District of Columbia and Maine have laws explicitly allowing minors to consent to abortion services without parental notification or consent.

The entire report and additional critical details are available at *www.guttmacher.org/pubs/spib_PIMA.pdf.*

Judicial bypass is a process in which minors can get state approval to have an abortion without parental involvement in states requiring parental involvement. The process varies greatly among the states. Generally speaking, minors seeking judicial bypass must demonstrate the maturity to make the decision to have an abortion without parental notification. The minor must show that she understands the health risks involved in getting an abortion, that she has considered alternatives to abortion and, finally, that she is aware of the psychological and emotional consequences that may occur as a result of the abortion, including how the abortion may affect her family relationships in the future (American Lawyer Newspapers Group, Inc., 2000). A judge may grant a judicial bypass after determining an abortion is in the best interest of the teen.

PERSONAL PRIVACY RIGHTS

A school counselor hears a rumor that a certain young woman is pregnant. The school counselor calls the student in and asks her to confirm or deny the rumors. The student said she was unsure but thought she might be pregnant. The school counselor provided a pregnancy test and strongly urged the student to take it in the staff restroom, which the student did. Is this school counselor's behavior problematic?

Points to Consider

Discretion and judgment are vital school counselors' daily lives, and if it is true a school counselor gave pregnancy tests to students in school then the school counselor failed to use either. In the actual court case, *Gruenke v. Seip* (2000), the culprit was a coach who suspected one of his swim team members was pregnant and required her to take a pregnancy test while at practice. This teacher abused his power and intruded on the student's privacy in a way that violated her Fourth-Amendment rights (unreasonable search and seizure) and her familial and personal privacy rights (*Gruenke v. Seip* (2000)). It would have been even worse had the actual intrusion been at the hands of a school counselor because school counselors are held to a higher standard of care. This school counselor in this fictional case needed better instincts to steer her away from doing something that is truly violating the standard of care for the profession.

SAFE-HAVEN LAWS

In an effort to protect newborns from being discarded, such as the cases of babies being found in dumpsters and public restrooms, most states have passed laws allowing birth mothers to leave their newborns at hospitals, fire stations, police stations and other select safe havens for abandoned babies. The understanding is that no questions will be asked, and the mother is relinquishing any legal rights to the child. Your sister works with social services and continually tells you about the incidents in your community of abandoned babies left in harm's way. You want to advertise the state law on bulletin boards throughout your school in an effort to protect the unborn. Your principal will not allow any reference to this law to be displayed in the school. Her concern is that this law sends the message to students that they can be irresponsible, have unprotected sex and then fix an unwanted pregnancy by abandoning their "problem." The principal says the only involvement your school will have with the subject of teenage sexual relations is to promote and implement the district's abstinence-based curriculum.

Points to Consider

Each state has some form of safe-haven laws to prevent such tragic abandonment. These laws, sometimes called "Baby Moses laws," allow the birth mother or agents designated by the birth mother to leave an infant in designated "safe places" (such as hospitals, churches, police or fire stations) anonymously, mostly with no questions asked and mostly with no legal repercussions (Child Welfare Information Gateway, 2010). More information on state-specific state laws is available at the National Safe Haven Alliance website (*www.nationalsafehavenalliance.org/states/*). That alliance also operates a confidential toll-free crisis hotline, which can be reached at 1-888-510-BABY (2229).

Research, delicate diplomacy and probably a collection of compromises could help school counselors inform their students about this law. A school district advocating an abstinence-based curriculum makes thorough sex education a battle; the issue has ignited arguments between community groups as well as the international scientific and religious communities. Even when limited by district's policy it is the responsibility of the school counselor, as explained in ASCA Ethical Standards for School Counselors (codes D.1 and D.2), to work with the administration and

292 • SCHOOL COUNSELING PRINCIPLES

community to develop programs in your students' best interest (ASCA, 2010). Gather information from local and national organizations, such as the Guttmacher Institute, Planned Parenthood and the Centers for Disease Control and Prevention, that provide statistics concerning teenage pregnancy and the practice of abandoning unwanted children in your area. Maybe you can invite a local nurse, emergency medical technician or firefighter to share a success story in which a child was saved because of the Safe-Haven Law.

Explain to your principal that the goal of such laws is not to encourage teenage pregnancy or irresponsibility but to protect the life of a newborn in the event of a mistake. If public-service posters detailing the Safe-Haven Law are out of the question, perhaps the principal would be more amenable to informing students through classroom talks or an assembly. Including your principal in a think tank composed of health care workers, district officials, educators, parents/guardians and school counselors might be a way to spearhead ideas on how to educate teens about sex while preserving the spirit of district policy.

In a Position to Know: A Counselor Educator Speaks

DEVELOPMENTALLY DELAYED, PREGNANT STUDENTS

Sharon is slightly developmentally delayed. Chronologically Sharon is 14, but developmentally she is more like an 11 or 12 year old. Sharon is pregnant, and her mother is aware of the pregnancy. Sharon has long been a concern of many in the school. She is unkempt, explosive and violent. Her developmental problems mean she is always out of sync with her age group. Her peers avoid her because they are afraid of her. You are concerned she will now be responsible for a baby. Sharon seems incapable of taking care of herself, and you fear for the safety of her child. She tells everyone having this baby will bring the father of the baby back to her. Sharon says her mother will help her raise the baby. She talks excitedly and animatedly about how she has "always wanted a baby." She talks about her cousin, who is also 14, has a baby and "dresses it up in beautiful clothes." What steps if any need to be taken in this case?

A Counselor Educator Speaks

Legal, ethical and clinical issues related to teenage pregnancy are problematic for school counselors. Sharon's case is particularly challenging because of her chronological age compounded by her developmental delay. Furthermore, a school counselor would be likely to have concerns about how Sharon's violent tendencies may create an unsafe environment for the baby and how Sharon will care for a baby if she seems incapable of caring for herself.

Staying mindful of the evidence that a baby in the care of this student may be in danger, it is still important to explore one's own values related to teen pregnancy. It is often difficult to separate one's values from the clinical, legal and ethical issues involved in these cases. However, the ASCA Ethical Standards for School Counselors (ASCA, 2010) state school counselors respect "students' values, beliefs and cultural background and do not impose the school counselor's personal values on students or their families" (A.1.c). The standards clarify that a school counselor's primary obligation is to the student and that each student is to be treated with respect (A.1.a). A school counselor is also expected to address the personal and social needs of students and encourage maximum student development (A.1.b). Thus, even though a school counselor may be horrified that Sharon will be responsible for a baby, the school counselor has an ethical duty to address the issues presented by the student's pregnancy and act in the student's best interest without making value judgments.

The fact that Sharon's mother knows about the pregnancy and is willing to help raise the child eliminates the dilemma of whether or not to breach confidentiality and tell a parent about the student's pregnancy. Thus, in this situation, respecting a student's ethical right to privacy while balancing parents' and/or guardians' legal rights is probably not as challenging of an issue. Yet the parental rights of Sharon's mother still need to be considered. The ASCA Ethical Standards for School Counselors (ASCA, 2010) explain that professional school counselors respect the rights of parents/guardians (B.1.a). School counselors are also advised to develop a collaborative relationship with parents/guardians when it is appropriate (B.1.a). In Sharon's case, discussing the pregnancy, the reality of raising a child and options such as adoption with Sharon and her mother may be an appropriate course of action. As previously indicated, such an intervention should be approached with care and consideration of the values of the student and her mother.

If the school counselor decides to meet with Sharon and her mother, the school counselor may want to express concerns about Sharon's view of parenthood. Sharon, like many teenagers, appears to have an idealized view of what caring for a baby will be like. Her references to looking forward to buying clothes for the baby and dressing the baby up support the notion that Sharon has little idea of what caring for a baby really involves. Furthermore, her idea that the pregnancy will bring the baby's father back to her is a common belief among pregnant teenagers that usually is not based in reality.

Several other issues could be addressed in a conversation with Sharon and her mother. A school counselor may want to explore if Sharon's unkempt appearance could be indicative of depression. Her lack of grooming could also be linked to an inability to take care of herself. Her violent tendencies could put the baby at risk. Sharon's age and developmental delay will make caring for a child difficult. Involving Sharon's mother may help Sharon and her mother make a wise decision about whether keeping the baby is in Sharon's and her baby's best interests. If Sharon and her mother decide Sharon should keep her baby, discussing these types of issues could help Sharon and her mother create a plan for caring for both Sharon and the baby.

Many schools are implementing groups for teenage parents/guardians; thus group counseling may be another option for students like Sharon. From an ethical standpoint, the school counselor is expected to screen each potential group member and ascertain whether the student would benefit from the group and be an appropriate fit for the group (ASCA, 2010, A.6.a.). The school counselor would have to assess if Sharon's violent tendencies might be exhibited in a group session and pose a danger to other group members. The school counselor would also want to consider if Sharon's lack of peer support would have a negative impact on the group process. Yet, if the school counselor decides Sharon would be an appropriate group member, attending such a group could help Sharon become better aware of the realities of raising a child. Group settings also provide additional support from peers who are struggling with the harsh realities of teenage parenthood.

The school counselor's legal duty is to act as a reasonable school counselor would act under similar circumstances. Sharon's mother is aware of Sharon's pregnancy and has agreed to help take care of the child. However, school counselors need to remain cognizant of their legal duty to report suspected child abuse. Accordingly, a school counselor needs to determine if Sharon's unkempt appearance is indicative of abuse or neglect. Furthermore, if Sharon keeps her baby and the school counselor suspects the baby is being neglected or harmed, the school counselor would be legally required to report that suspected abuse as well.

Stone (2002) provided guidelines for school counselors who are counseling students in situations like Sharon's. Stone suggested that school counselors look to school board policy for guidance, consider the student's developmental level when providing interventions and remain cognizant of parental rights and values. Stone also recommended consulting with a colleague or supervisor when faced with issues related to a student's pregnancy. Finally, Stone cautions school counselors to avoid involving themselves in a student's medical care.

Sharon's case presents yet another example of the legal, ethical and clinical complexities of working with minors in school settings. Attending workshops and other continuing-education opportunities on legal, ethical and clinical issues is vitally important in remaining competent, practicing in an ethical manner and minimizing legal liability. And, because school counselors face such challenging issues in a litigious society, school counselors are wise to maintain professional liability insurance.
– *Mary A. Hermann, J.D., Ph.D., professor, Virginia Commonwealth University*

Making Connections

1. Do you believe you have an obligation to tell a parent that his or her child is pregnant if the child refuses to involve her parents/guardians?

2. Under what circumstances if any would you help a pregnant student get medical care of any kind?

3. How do your state statutes read regarding minors and abortion?

4. How do the standards of your state and community affect your behavior regarding pregnant students?

5. How do your state statutes read regarding age of consent? What are the implications of your state's age-of-consent laws for you as a school counselor?

Key Terms

Abortion
Age of consent
Developmentally delayed
Judicial bypass

Safe-haven law
Sexually active students
Value-laden counseling

CHAPTER 10

Lesbian, Gay, Bisexual, Transgender and Questioning Students

Objectives

By the time you have completed this chapter, you should be able to:

- Discuss your leadership and advocacy role in creating a safe and inclusive school environment for lesbian, gay, bisexual, transgender and questioning (LGBTQ) students.
- Discuss the cost of dangerous school climates to LGBTQ students.
- Discuss case law, statutes and federal guidelines that can influence positive change for LGBTQ students.
- Give specific strategies for acting as a systemic change agent to improve school climates.
- Identify the legal and ethical ramifications for school counselors and school districts that do not intervene on behalf of LGBTQ students who face harassment or bullying.

Ethical Standards Addressed in This Chapter

Professionalism means knowing your professional associations' codes and adhering to them. The ASCA Ethical Standards for School Counselors most relevant to this chapter are the following:

- Each person has the right to be respected, be treated with dignity and have access to a comprehensive school counseling program that advocates for and affirms all students from diverse populations including: ethnic/racial identity, age, economic status, abilities/disabilities, language, immigration status, sexual orientation, gender, gender identity/expression, family type, religious/spiritual identity and appearance. (Preamble)
- Professional school counselors respect the rights and responsibilities of parents/guardians for their children and endeavor to establish, as appropriate, a collaborative relationship with parents/guardians to facilitate the student's maximum development. (B.1.a)
- Professional school counselors are knowledgeable and supportive of their school's mission and connect their program to the school's mission. (D.1.c)
- Professional school counselors assist in developing: (1) curricular and environmental conditions appropriate for the school and community; (2) educational procedures and programs to meet students' developmental needs; (3) a systematic evaluation process for comprehensive,

developmental, standards-based school counseling programs, services and personnel; and (4) a data-driven evaluation process guiding the comprehensive, developmental school counseling program and service delivery. (D.1.g)

■ Professional school counselors monitor and expand personal multicultural and social justice advocacy awareness, knowledge and skills. School counselors strive for exemplary cultural competence by ensuring personal beliefs or values are not imposed on students or other stakeholders. (E.2.a)

The full text of the ASCA Ethical Standards for School Counselors is available at *www.schoolcounselor.org*.

Introduction

School counselors are committed to facilitating and promoting the fullest possible development of each individual by reducing the barriers of misinformation, myth, harassment and discrimination based on sexual orientation (ASCA, 2007c; Stone, 2003a). Recognizing the unique responsibility of school counselors for the social and emotional well-being of students, this chapter seeks to inform school counselors of the particular vulnerabilities of LGBTQ students and to empower school counselors to advocate for these students when working with school administrators or on school policies. School counselors acting as advocates know there are many languages with which to plead their case on behalf of vulnerable students. Research data related to academic achievement and case law precedents discussed in this chapter seek to inform and to strengthen the advocacy of school counselors working in environments where emotional language appealing to the heart may fall short.

The LGBT acronym is increasingly used to describe a community of people who identify as non-heterosexual and non-cisgender (cisgender describes an individual whose gender self-perception matches the sex they were assigned at birth). This acronym has grown longer in recent years, to include young people who increasingly question binary descriptions of gender and sexuality. Variations on this acronym might add an "I" ("intersex," someone who is not anatomically male or female exclusively), "Q" ("queer," an umbrella term, or "questioning") and A ("ally," or "asexual," someone who experiences an absence of sexual attraction) (Schulman, 2013).

LGBTQ individuals are the only cultural minority group to typically grow up in families outside of their cultural group. Often there are only few, if any, LGBTQ men or women visibly available to aid these youth in learning how to cope with the societal realities of being a sexual minority. This lack of role models creates a situation, most clearly seen in schools, where the LGBTQ youth are not developmentally capable of dealing effectively with the pressures to conform (Frank & Cannon, 2009). Additionally, the societal condemnation of sexual minorities contributes to identity confusion in LGBTQ students and often influences them to keep their orientation a secret. This results in a tendency to hide non-heterosexual feelings, and the negative emotions associated with them such as guilt, fear of stigmatization and fear of rejection may affect the student's home and school life (Frank & Cannon, 2009).

A fair and inclusive education is not possible for a student whose physical and emotional safety is routinely compromised. School climates can have an adverse impact on educational opportunities for LGBTQ students by being, at best, indifferent to the vulnerability of this at-risk minority and, at worst, hostile and dangerous (GLSEN, 2007; Stone, 2003b). The Gay, Lesbian and Straight Education Network (GLSEN) conducts a national biennial survey of experiences of LGBTQ students in America's schools. In 2003, The National School Climate Survey shed new light on the experiences of LGBTQ students in America's schools and clearly demonstrated that despite modest measurable gains, "violence, bias and harassment of LGBTQ students continues to be the rule, not the exception, in America's schools" (GLSEN, 2004). In 2005, 2007 and 2009 GLSEN's National School Climate Survey validated the reality that anti-LGBTQ bullying and harassment remain a common occurrence throughout America's schools (GLSEN, 2005b, 2010).

Unfortunately, GLSEN's 2011 National School Climate Survey did little to reassure that LGBTQ students were safe from harassment (GLSEN, 2012). The majority of LGBTQ students continue to be verbally, sexually or physically harassed at school because of their sexual orientation or gender expression. Of the 8,584 students surveyed aged 13 to 20, 84.9 percent reported experiencing verbal harassment, and 38.3 percent reported physical harassment (e.g., pushing or shoving) at school in the past year because of their sexual orientation. Meanwhile, 18.3 percent reported experiencing physical assault at school in the past year because of their sexual orientation. Additionally, 63.9 percent reported verbal harassment, 27.1 percent reported physical harassment, and 12.4 reported physical assault at school in the last year because of their gender expression. More than three-fifths (63.5 percent) felt unsafe at school because of their sexual orientation, and about a third (29.8 percent) skipped a day of school in the past month because of feeling unsafe (GLSEN, 2012).

School-based bullying and harassment research most often places the focus on physical or overt acts of aggressive behavior (GLSEN, 2010). However, it is also important to examine the many other types of victimization events occurring in schools. According to GLSEN's 2011 survey, relational aggression, or harm caused by damage to peer relationships, is experienced by a large majority, being the target of mean rumors and lies (89.5 percent) and being purposefully excluded by peers (84 percent) (GLSEN, 2012). More than half (55.2 percent) reported experiencing some form of electronic harassment (cyberbullying) in the past year (GLSEN, 2012). Cyberbullying is addressed further in the Bullying, Cyberbullying and Sexting Chapter and also the Violence and Criminal Activity Chapter.

Policymakers have an opportunity to improve school climates. Comprehensive bullying and harassment policies should specifically include sexual orientation and gender identity/expression; 59.5 percent of students in schools with comprehensive policies heard homophobic remarks often or frequently, compared with almost 75 percent of students in schools with generic policies or no policies (GLSEN, 2012). However, policies need support of school staff to be effective. "Anti-harassment policies without publicity and administrator support are not likely to produce change" (Hansen, 2007). When school counselors advocate for a safe, harassment-free environment, they need to give time and attention to this population. Schools need advocates and change agents to promote a safer, more inclusive school climate (Hansen, 2007; Ratts, DeKruyf & Chen-Hayes, 2007).

Although laws and court cases have protected the educational issues of inequality by gender, race or handicapping conditions for years, the courts remained largely mute regarding LGBTQ students until the latter half of the 1990s, which culminated with *Davis v. Monroe County Board of Education* (1999). This ruling, coupled with interpretations of the Title IX statute, strengthens the position for a more humane school environment. School districts are liable in cases where harassment is so "severe" and "pervasive" that it denies equal access to education. In these cases, it must be proven the school district knew about the harassment and was deliberately indifferent (for more details, see the Sexual Harassment Chapter).

In 2010, the Office for Civil Rights of the U.S. Department of Education released new guidelines for educators on Title IX (Ali, 2010). Title IX (1972), the federal statute barring sex discrimination in schools that receive federal funding, supports LGBTQ youth as well as heterosexual youth when the harassment creates a hostile environment. Although a student's LGBTQ status is not specifically included under Title IX, harassment of LGBTQ students frequently also constitutes gender discrimination and/or sexual harassment, which are included under Title IX. For example, "It can be sex discrimination if students are harassed either for exhibiting what is perceived as a stereotypical characteristic for their sex or for failing to conform to stereotypical notions of masculinity and femininity" (Ali, 2010, p. 7-8). Additionally, Title IX requires schools to protect all students from harassing conduct of a sexual nature, "regardless of the actual or perceived sexual orientation or gender identity of the harasser or target" (Ali, 2010, p. 8).

State and local laws may prohibit discrimination on the basis of sexual orientation. In its first State of the States Report in 2004, GLSEN found that 75 percent of students in America's schools do not have legal protection in state statutes against anti-LGBTQ harassment (GLSEN, 2005a). Currently, 19 states and the District of Columbia have comprehensive safe school laws to protect students from bullying and harassment based on sexual orientation and gender identity. The law covers only sexual orientation in one state; five additional states have school regulations or teacher codes prohibiting discrimination based on sexual orientation. However, that leaves 18 states (with 25 percent of the LGBTQ population) with no laws specifically protecting LGBTQ students (Movement Advancement Project, 2013). An individual who is harassed for his or her gender identity or gender expression encounters a form of sexual harassment, which, if treated with deliberate indifference by the school, creates liability for the school under Title IX. This harassment constitutes sex harassment because it is based on gender stereotypes (Sohaili, 2011).

A significant case in Arkansas involving harassment of a gay student, Willi Wagner, changed the interpretation of a Title IX violation with regard to how the courts view harassment of LGBTQ students (Fischer, Schimmel & Kelly, 1999; Lambda Legal, 1998; Title IX, 1972). After Wagner filed a complaint stating he had endured two years of abuse from other students, the Fayetteville (Ark.) School District signed an agreement with the U.S. Department of Education to hold sexual harassment workshops to raise educators' awareness of their legal obligations to protect students from sexual harassment and to take disciplinary action against any student engaging in sexual harassment (Courson & Farris, 2012; Fischer et al., 1999). This case is significant because it opened the door for students to seek legal remedy under Title IX for sexual harassment (Courson & Farris, 2012). Several other early court cases also contributed to increased legal support for LGBTQ students:

- Wisconsin, 1996: The court awarded Jamie Nabozny $962,000 for injuries he suffered while in middle and high school. *Nabozny v. Podlesny* (1996) used the federal equal protection law to challenge public school officials' failure to take action against anti-gay abuse in a school.

- Illinois, 1996: The Riverside-Brookfield School District settled a lawsuit filed by the family of a gay student who alleged school officials did not act on the student's complaints of abuse from his peers (Fischer et al., 1999).

- Kentucky, 1998: A jury awarded $220,000 to Alma McGowen against the Spencer County Public School district for violating Title IX by failing to act to stop severe harassment that stopped Alma McGowen from getting an education (National Center for Lesbian Rights (NCLR) & GLSEN, n.d., p. 8).

- California, 2004: Alana Flores and five other students received $1.1 million from the Morgan Hill Unified school district for harassment the six students faced all through high school. The court said, "The guarantee of equal protection...requires the defendants to enforce District policies in cases of peer harassment of homosexual and bisexual students in the same way that they enforce those policies in cases of peer harassment of heterosexual students" (NCLR & GLSEN, n.d., p. 7).

A consortium of national organizations under the leadership of the National School Boards Association has issued a resource document to help school leaders address legal issues surrounding students' sexual orientation and gender identity. Aimed at school policymakers and administrators yet a valuable resource for school counselors, the guide, "Dealing with Legal Matters Surrounding Students' Sexual Orientation and Gender Identity," provides practical guidance on the legal rights of lesbian, gay, bisexual and transgender students (National School Boards Association, n.d.). The guide is significant, not just for the important information it contains but because more than 20 professional organizations, including the American School Counselor Association, sponsored and contributed to it. This guide makes a strong statement about the need for advocacy for these heretofore largely neglected minorities.

Each chapter in this book has brought court cases to the discussion of the school counselor's legal and ethical role with special populations. However, this chapter is distinct in that there are few court cases involving school counselors as defendants. Most of the cases in this chapter involve equal access, First-Amendment rights and harassment, all areas under the purview of administrators.

Getting Started: What Would You Do?

The following case is discussed at the end of this chapter by a school counseling candidate. Before you read her response, formulate in your own mind how you would approach this ethical dilemma.

A SCHOOL COUNSELOR'S ATTITUDE

Alexia Huart had been taught in religious training and at home that homosexuality is a choice, and people who make the choice to be homosexuals are misguided. She never really questioned her beliefs, and she thought as a school counselor in training it really did not matter how she felt about gays. Huart's preparation program pushed her to examine her biases. Must school counselors continuously take inventory and confront their own prejudices and beliefs about others regarding diversity issues such as sexual orientation and gender identity? At the end of the chapter you can read Huart's words describing her own self-analysis. "I was so challenged and moved by all that has transpired in this graduate program that it pulled at my heart to really take personal inventory of my attitudes, values and prejudices on homosexuality" (A. Huart, personal communication, August 2003).

Working Through Case Studies

HARASSMENT OF LGBTQ STUDENTS

A 15-year-old openly gay student asks you to help stop the daily harassment she has been enduring from other students. She tells you she receives approximately 25 anti-gay remarks a day and at least twice in the last five months she has been kicked and punched while on school grounds. She tells you the harassment is especially bad in Mrs. Smith's class, where students call her a "she-he," but Mrs. Smith pretends not to hear. She tells you she has gone to the assistant principal for support and provided the names of the students who have verbally and physically attacked her. What do you do?

Points to Consider

A safe and respectful school climate is a mandate for all students and is part of the No Child Left Behind legislation. Part A of Title IV issues a directive for safe and drug-free schools and communities (No Child Left Behind Act, 2002).

School counselors can be at the forefront of diversity training for students and staff to raise awareness of the LGBTQ population. Raising awareness in the school community by holding seminars, assemblies or other functions can go a long way toward creating the type of environment in which all students can learn and feel safe. Indeed, the school counselor might implement effective yet simple measures like prominently posting rights and responsibilities of students as citizens of the school to help one another learn and grow in an accepting climate (ASCA, 2007c; Stone & Isaacs, 2002a). By creating and delivering anti-bullying programs and inviting speakers who have been bullied to present at assemblies, school counselors can convey the message the school community will not permit intolerance for any group within it (ASCA, 2011; Stone & Isaacs, 2002b).

In the case of *Walsh v. Tehachapi Unified School District* (2011), the Department of Justice (DOJ) and the Department of Education (DOE) found Seth Walsh's school did not fulfill its duty to protect him after two years of anti-gay harassment led to his suicide in 2010. The school district's settlement included the implementation of a series of specific policies, procedures and training designed to better protect students from sexual harassment and harassment based on gender stereotypes (ACLU, 2011a). This case helped to bring about the 2012 Seth's Law, which requires California schools to "specifically address harassment based on sexual orientation, gender identity and gender expression in their antidiscrimination policies" (Repa, 2012, n.p.).

Other ways to support LGBTQ students include presenting research and data in faculty meetings demonstrating LGBTQ students are at greater risk than their peers for suicide, as well as for physical and emotional abuse in schools. School counselors can partner with administrators to create disciplinary committees to handle discipline referrals and oversee punitive action for offenders of anti-harassment policies (Hansen, 2007; Stone, 2003a).

Expanding awareness and sensitivity to the consequences of homophobia and heterosexism is an important aspect of working toward a harassment-free environment. This education, directed to both offenders and non-offenders, encourages everyone to re-examine thoughts and beliefs and recognizes that respecting human dignity rises above prejudicial feelings (Stone, 2003a; Satcher & Leggett, 2007).

Heterosexist climates certainly have a role to play in the degree to which LGBTQ students are harassed and the degree to which they internalize this harassment. These climates influence academic experiences and developmental outcomes (Chesir-Teran & Hughes, 2009). Different from but related to homophobia, heterosexism refers to a system of attitudes, biases, assumptions and discrimination in favor of opposite-sex relationships and attractions. Chesir-Teran & Hughes (2009) found that less inclusive (heterosexist) school programs and policies have a significant effect on students' perceived prevalence of anti-gay harassment. Students from schools with more inclusive programs and policies reported less frequent anti-gay harassment. Being sensitive to heterosexism is important, since heterosexism is manifested in various ways in school. Heterosexism is seen when LGBTQ issues, history and culture are not included in school curricula; school rules or polices regarding name calling, harassment or bullying are not enforced for anti-gay incidents; students' rights laws or policies do not include sexual orientation as a protected category; school functions are organized around assumptions of heterosexuality; and same-sex displays of affection in school are not tolerated or are treated differently than opposite-sex displays of affection (Adams, Bell & Griffin; 2007).

Homophobic behavior displayed by students toward those identifying as or perceived to be LGBTQ might include bullying, verbal or physical aggression, ostracizing, ignoring or gossiping about LGBTQ students. This type of behavior is not exclusive to just students; adults in schools sometimes make homophobic comments. School counselors need to be aware of the implicit, covert and unintentional demonstrations of homophobia and heterosexism that surface through presumptions of heterosexuality. When this occurs the result is that LGBTQ students, many of whom desperately need the school counseling program and its services, become alienated from it (Curry & Hayes, 2009).

School counselors can make the school counseling program feel more inclusive to LGBTQ students simply by using language accurately and respectfully. The best ways to do this include using gender-neutral language when speaking about relationships and attractions, asking individuals which terminology they prefer for themselves and asking transgender students which pronouns they prefer (GLSEN, 2009).

The ASCA LGBTQ position statement (modified, 2007c) states, "The professional school counselor works with all students through the stages of identity development and understands this development may be more difficult for LGBTQ youth. It is not the role of the professional school counselor to attempt to change a student's sexual orientation/gender identity but instead to provide support to LGBTQ students to promote student achievement and personal well-being."

Professional school counselors:
- are aware of their own beliefs about sexual orientation and gender identity
- are knowledgeable of the negative effects that result from stereotyping individuals into rigid gender roles
- are committed to the affirmation of youth of all sexual orientations (ASCA, 2007c).

Considering that LGBTQ youth are not typically raised with parents/guardians, siblings and extended family members that share their minority status these youth are left with little support, experience and wisdom to draw upon from their family regarding how to navigate a minority identity within a heterosexist and gender-normative culture. In many schools, this leaves these youth intensely isolated with minimal resources. School counselors can become powerful advocates and begin to actualize social justice advocacy for their LGBTQ students by taking incremental, tangible and concrete steps toward supporting these students (Bidell, 2011).

SCHOOL COUNSELOR'S MISGUIDED ADVOCACY

Reggie comes to your office complaining he is being harassed in his classes. Since he began telling classmates he was gay last year, he has started wearing makeup and painting his nails. Another school counselor is also in your office as you were doing credit checks together, and she suggests Reggie tone it down. "Your classmates understand that you're gay," she tells him. "Why don't you make it easier for them to accept you by not flaunting it in their faces all the time?" Are there legal or ethical concerns with her advice?

Points to Consider

In 2002, The Washoe County School District in Nevada settled a lawsuit with Derek Henkle for $451,000 for bullying and physical attacks he experienced in two district schools. The settlement also required the district to adopt a new anti-harassment policy including sexual orientation and to train staff and students on sexual harassment and intimidation. Although school officials were aware of the ongoing, severe harassment and physical assaults, they repeatedly told Derek to keep his sexuality private. This case says, "Students have a constitutional right to express their sexual orientation in school without harassment or discrimination" (NCLR & GLSEN, n.d., p. 6).

In 2003, a school district in Arkansas settled a lawsuit with an openly gay student whose school disciplined him for discussing his sexual orientation and, later, for talking about his punishment. Fourteen-year-old Thomas McLaughlin claimed teachers and school officials violated his rights to free speech, equal protection, privacy and freedom of religion by outing him to his parents without his permission, preaching to him and forcing him to read from the Bible as punishment. In a settlement, the school paid $25,000 in damages and attorneys' fees, expunged McLaughlin's disciplinary record, formally apologized and implemented new district policies to protect student speech, student privacy and discrimination on the basis of sexual orientation (ACLU, 2003a; ACLU, 2003b; The New York Times, 2003).

Present court cases, such as *Doe, et al. v. Anoka-Hennepin School District No. 11, et al.* (2012), found the district inadequately responded to persistent physical and verbal harassment based on real or perceived sexual orientation. This school district's Sexual Orientation Curriculum Policy required staff to remain neutral on issues of sexual orientation, which has been argued to attribute to the lack of educator's response to the harassment of LGBTQ students (Baca, 2012; *Doe, et al. v. Anoka-Hennepin, et al.*, 2012; Eckholm, 2011; Karnowski, 2012; Wooledge, 2012). LGBTQ students did not feel safe at school; one high school teacher said students began to internalize the policy to mean being gay is shameful and wrong. Students saw adults in schools adhering to the policy and repeatedly failing to address anti-gay bullying (Karnowski, 2012). In 2010, the Justice Department began a civil rights investigation into the district after eight local students committed suicide in less than two years. Of them, four were either gay or perceived to be gay and reportedly bullied by other students (Baca, 2012; Eckholm, 2011; Wooledge, 2012). The Justice Department found sex-based harassment in the district it said contributed to a hostile environment, as teachers and administrators failed to protect students (Karnowski, 2012).

COMMUNITY STANDARDS AND PARENTS' RIGHTS

You receive a notice that a program called No Name-Calling Week will be implemented at schools across the nation. You want to bring it into your own school, thinking this will be a great kickoff to your own program to create a safe and respectful school climate for all students. You are confident any program aimed at reducing bullying will be highly supported and respected by your administrators, teachers, parents/guardians and community. What criticism could a bully-proofing program encounter, and how might you be informed and prepared for those criticisms?

Points to Consider

Singh, Urbano, Haston & McMahon (2010) present seven overarching strategies school counselors use as social justice advocates: a) using political savvy to navigate power structures, b) consciousness raising, c) initiating difficult dialogues, d) building intentional relationships, e) teaching students self-advocacy skills, f) using data for marketing and g) educating others about the school counselor role of advocate. Additionally, political savvy (knowing when and how to intervene) serves as a prerequisite for and is an integral part of each of the strategies.

Schoolwide and districtwide programs such as No Name-Calling Week can have a strong impact on school climate and culture, helping minority students feel safe at school. Implementing inclusive programming expands the reach of the school counseling program to involve all students and takes a proactive approach instead of a reactive approach to potential harassment. The chart at the end of this case describes several programs school counselors can introduce in their schools, along with some notes on pushback other communities have faced.

As advocates, school counselors educate themselves about the prevailing community standards, and they learn to predict and skillfully negotiate the political landscape. It is easy for school counselors to feel so strongly about the work of advocacy that their responses might be undemocratic; however these responses lead to mistrust, distrust and stalemates that do nothing but maintain the status quo, with students getting lost in the process (Savage & Harley, 2009). It helps to review materials with administrators to ensure their support and to anticipate possible concerns – and be prepared to address them – should they arise.

Although schools are allowed to make exceptions for parents/guardians who do not want their children exposed to discussions of homosexuality, schools are not legally obligated to do so. In 2006, two families in Lexington, Mass., objected to their elementary school children's curriculum, which used a book depicting single-parent families, a family with two dads and one with two moms and the book "King and King," a story depicting a wedding scene between two princes. When the school refused to provide prior notice and allow them to exempt their children from "instruction recognizing differences in sexual orientation," the two sets of parents sued the school district (*Parker v. Hurley* (2007)). The case was dismissed by the district court and the U.S. Court of Appeals. District court judge Wolf, wrote, "Parents do have a fundamental right to raise their children. The Parkers and Wirthlins may send their children to a private school … . They may also educate their children at home… . However, the Parkers and Wirthlins have chosen to send their children to the Lexington public schools with its current curriculum. The Constitution does not permit them to prescribe what those children will be taught" (*Parker v. Hurley* (2007)). That dismissal was unanimously upheld in the U.S. Court of Appeals (*Parker v. Hurley* (2008)).

In 2005, the Alliance Defense Fund represented a group of students and parents who sued Boyd County High School in Kentucky, saying they should be able to "opt out" of a court-ordered, anti-harassment training that violated their religious rights. The training was implemented in response to an earlier ACLU case; the judge in that case found that anti-gay harassment in the school constituted a widespread problem and ordered staff and student diversity training to focus on issues of sexual orientation and gender harassment. U.S. District Court judge David L. Bunning wrote that students and staff have no religious right to opt out of such training, since the training did not force students to change their religious views (ACLU, 2009c; Koschoreck & Tooms, 2009; *Morrison v. Board of Education of Boyd County* (2006)).

As public schools cope with conflicts over homosexuality, they can get some tips from a guide published by the First Amendment Center (2007). Leaders of several professional education organizations have agreed on guidelines for how educators, parents/guardians and teachers should deal with any aspect of school life involving sexual orientation. The guidance is meant to be a framework for dialogue aimed at finding common ground, essentially a way to get people talking (Feller, 2006; First Amendment Center, 2006; Haynes, 2006). View the guidelines at *www.firstamendmentcenter.org/madison/wp-content/uploads/2011/03/sexual.orientation.guidelines.pdf.*

EDUCATIONAL RESOURCES

Program	Past Community Push Back
No Name-Calling Week (by GLSEN) *www.nonamecallingweek.org/* Activities aimed at ending name-calling and eliminating bullying-inspired by the book "The Misfits." All levels	Parents in Iowa prompted the Pleasant Valley School Board to rule that teachers could no longer read "The Misfits" aloud.
Mix it Up Program *www.tolerance.org/mix-it-up/* Promote tolerance and break up cliques by encouraging students to hang out with those they normally would not seek out for company.	The American Family Association (AFA) expressed fear that the project was "a nationwide push to promote the homosexual lifestyle." Parents pressured schools to cancel the event, but other schools came on board. (2,500 schools participated) (Severson, 2012; Shah, 2012).

Program	Past Community Push Back
Day of Silence (by GLSEN) *www.dayofsilence.org/* Students vow silence to bring attention to the name-calling, bullying and harassment, in effect, the silencing, experienced by LGBTQ students and their allies. Middle and high school	The Alliance Defending Freedom and Focus on the Family have sponsored student-led events to respond to the Day of Silence, most recently called Day of Dialogue. These events encourage students to "express faith-based views about homosexuality," and the Alliance Defense Fund offers legal assistance to students who "have their free speech rights violated" (Day of Silence, 2011; Focus on the Family, 2010).
Think B4 You Speak (by GLSEN) *www.thinkb4youspeak.com/* Reduce and prevent the use of homophobic language. Grades 8-12	
It Gets Better Project *http://itgetsbetter.org* Video database of more than 50,000 user-submitted messages of hope to LGBTQ youth: life does get better. Middle and high school	There have been many LGBTQ-identified teens who were involved in the campaign and later committed suicide. Giving youth access to these messages can be powerful, but young people need to be connected with immediate supportive structures in their schools and communities to counteract feelings of isolation and subvert potential emotional devastation (Boyd, 2011)

INVOLVING PARENTS

John has stuffed his desk to overflowing with papers, library books, supplies from the teacher's closets and more. His teacher turns the desk on its side, empties the contents and proceeds to sort through the pile. Some of John's papers catch her eye, and she starts to read his words describing his pain over sexual identity issues and expressing his love for another boy in the school. The teacher immediately brings six papers to you to read. You are convinced this child is in a great deal of pain. How will you proceed in this situation?

Points to Consider

The school counselor in this complex case will need much sensitivity. A child is in pain and possibly suicidal. John's parents need to know their child needs help, but do they need to know about his writings? *Eisel v. Board of Education of Montgomery County* (1991) has shown that if we have any reason to suspect this child might be suicidal we have a duty to warn parents. However, this duty to protect John from harm does not give us the right or duty to "out" him to his parents. Minors in schools do have a right to privacy with respect to their sexual orientation, and they have the right to decide when and if they will come out to their parents/guardians.

The development of sexual identity is a natural process, but it can be much more stressful for same-sex attracted adolescents because of the way society views sexual minorities (The American Psychological Association, 2008; American School Counselor Association, 2007c). Adolescence, as difficult as it is, frequently requires LGBTQ students to negotiate the daily challenges of hiding their sexual identities, resulting in problems of isolation, depression and real or imagined fear of discovery or rejection by their families and friends (Hansen, 2007; Heatherington & Lavner, 2008; Pachankis, 2007).

There is a potential danger for John here, because statistics have shown that lesbian, gay, bisexual and transgender students have a higher rate of depression and are more likely to consider suicide than other students (American Academy of Child & Adolescent Psychiatry, 2006; National Education Association, 2006). Some may believe parents/guardians have the right to know the content of the letters. However, how can we be sure this will make things better for the child? Maybe the parents/guardians are unwilling to accept their child is gay, and perhaps, the child is experiencing pain and confusion because he is afraid his parents will reject him if they find out (American Academy of Child & Adolescent Psychiatry, 2006; Heatherington & Lavner, 2008). Harrison (2003) indicates that prior positive family relations and family cohesion usually predict a good outcome for adolescents who decide to disclose. A safe sibling is often told first, and mothers are disclosed to before fathers (Harrison, 2003).

To support John, the school counselor will need to establish a relationship with him to address the pain he is experiencing (Harrison, 2003). Let John know you are there for him to talk to and share his feelings with. Without labeling him, drop clues that you are prepared to address these issues by saying phrases like "gay and lesbian" or "sexual orientation" as part of your conversation. Accept whatever language he uses to describe himself and move on from there.

After you form a relationship with John, you could inquire how he believes his parents would react to finding out he is gay or bisexual. For students who seek your help in coming out, consider whether they are developmentally able to make that decision. Allow students to explore their parents' likely reaction, and help them to generate strategies for worst-case scenarios. Do not blindside students by telling family members without their knowledge (National Education Association, 2006).

While studies of LGBTQ youth show they recognize their sexual orientation between ages 8 and 11, the age at which they "come out" is between 15 and 17, indicating that for many years they may feel too afraid to be honest about the issue. But the fact is that many students are increasingly coming out while still in high (or even middle/junior high) school, making it more imperative that school counselors consider how to support students (Avert, 2008; Elias, 2007; James, 2008; Kramer, 2011; Lobron, 2007; National Education Association, 2006; PFLAG, 2005). The decision to share one's sexuality with others and the experience of doing so varies greatly from person to person and can depend hugely on the individual's systems of emotional support, both inside and outside of school. In 2011, *The New York Times* published "Coming Out," an interactive feature on its website, telling the stories of youth all over the country in various stages of coming out (Kramer, 2011). It is available at: *www.nytimes.com/ interactive/2011/05/23/us/20110523-coming-out.html?ref=us.*

Unfortunately, in many cases a child's reluctance to disclose his or her sexuality to family has a basis in real and rational fear. LGBTQ youth represent a disproportionate percentage of the homeless youth population. Durso and Gates (2012) found LGBTQ youth represented 40 percent of the clientele of 354 homeless youth organizations across the country. The most commonly cited factor leading to homelessness was family rejection on the basis of sexual orientation and gender identity, with 46 percent of clients reporting they ran away because of family rejection, and 43 percent reporting they were forced out by parents because of sexual orientation or gender identity (Durso & Gates, 2012). Ryan, Huebner, Diaz and Sanchez (2009) found that "greater experiences of family rejection of lesbian, gay and bisexual young adults is associated with poorer health outcomes...Young adults who reported higher levels of family rejection during adolescence were 8.4 times more likely to report having attempted suicide, 5.9 times more likely to report high levels of depression, 3.4 times more likely to report illegal drug use and 3.4 times more likely to report having engaged in unprotected sexual intercourse, compared with peers from families with no or low levels of family rejection" (p. 349-350). Their study concluded "helping families identify and reduce specific rejecting behaviors is integral to helping prevent health and mental health problems for LGB young people" (p. 350).

In a GLSEN study students were asked about their level of comfort talking one-on-one with various school personnel about LGBTQ-related issues. Students reported they would be most comfortable talking with school counselors or social workers and teachers. More than half of the students reported they would be somewhat or very comfortable talking with a school counselor or social worker (58.2 percent) or a teacher (52.8 percent) about LGBTQ issues (2010, p. 59). LGBTQ students who can identify supportive faculty or staff do better in school than those who cannot identify supportive school staff, with grade-point averages that are almost half a grade higher than their peers (GLSEN, 2010).

REPARATIVE OR CONVERSION THERAPY

A school counselor and her student are talking just outside her door. As you walk by, you see the school counselor hand the student a copy of the book "You Do Not Have to Be Gay" and hear her say to the student, "I know where you can go to get better. You do not have to go through life like this." You strongly suspect the school counselor is talking to this young man about reparative or conversion therapy in an attempt to change him. What would you do?

Points to Consider

The term "reparative therapy," also known as "conversion therapy," refers to psychotherapy aimed at eliminating homosexual desires. Reparative therapy is based upon the assumption that homosexuality is a mental disorder, rather than a variation within human sexual orientation. It is important to note that all major health, medical and mental health professional organizations have rejected the view that homosexuality is abnormal or in any way unhealthy (Just the Facts Coalition, 2008). In response to the danger posed to young people by this quasi-scientific "treatment," American Psychiatric Association and a coalition of several other groups issued in 2008 "Just the Facts About Sexual Orientation and Youth" to clarify the appropriate actions by professionals working with LGBTQ youth. You can find it at *www.apa.org/pi/lgbt/resources/just-the-facts.pdf*

Your colleague might be in jeopardy of punitive action by the district for noncompliance or inviting legal ramifications for the school. In a 2009 court case, *Hamilton v. Vallejo City Unified School District*, the most egregious incidents involved a school counselor who required Hamilton to attend a special weekly support group for gay students. Within this group the school counselor berated students for "choosing" to be gay and tried to convince them to change their sexual orientation or gender expression (ACLU, 2009a). This Northern California school district reached a settlement in which the district agreed to adopt a clear policy explicitly prohibiting discrimination and harassment based on sexual orientation or gender identity, develop a specific procedure for harassment and discrimination complaints, provide mandatory training for all teachers and other staff who interact with students in how to identify anti-gay harassment and discrimination (ACLU, 2009a).

Depending on your relationship with your colleague, perhaps you could have a private conversation respectfully reminding her of her ethical and legal obligations with regard to this student. ASCA's (2007c) position statement says, "The professional school counselor works with all students through the stages of identity development and understands this development may be more difficult for LGBTQ youth. It is not the role of the professional school counselor to attempt to change a student's sexual orientation/gender identity but instead to provide support to LGBTQ students to promote student achievement and personal well-being."

As of 2013, conversion therapy itself faces legal challenges in two states (Eckholm, 2012; Gallegos, 2013). In New Jersey, four gay men who underwent the therapy filed a civil suit under the state's Consumer Fraud Act against a counseling group for deceptive practices. The former clients claimed they paid thousands of dollars in fees over time, in exchange for false promises and emotional scarring from degrading, humiliating therapeutic techniques (Eckholm, 2012).

Several organizations have raised serious concerns that reparative therapy is potentially harmful for persons confused about their sexual orientation. The American Medical Association (2006), the American Academy of Pediatrics (2000), the American Psychiatric Association (2000) and the American Counseling Association have all developed position statements opposing reparative therapy and declaring its potential for harm to include depression, anxiety and self-destructive behavior (Chaney, Filmore & Goodrich; 2011).

EQUAL ACCESS AND GAY-STRAIGHT ALLIANCE CLUBS

Johnston, a junior in your high school, asked for your advice on starting a gay-straight alliance club (GSA). Before he talks with the administration he wants to know if you think it is legal. He explains that seven years ago when his brother tried to form the club this same administration told him he could not because it would put him and the other students in danger and substantially disrupt the school. What have we learned in recent years that let educators know they cannot deny students the right to start a GSA club?

Points to Consider

A student's desire to establish a school club for LGBTQ youth and straight students countered by the school administration's reluctance to support the endeavor is a situation that has been addressed in countless school districts across the country. This dilemma presents an opportunity for you to use your knowledge of court findings and legislation to benefit a minority student population.

Legal efforts to ban GSAs have been struck down by federal court rulings based on the protections afforded in the Equal Access Act of 1984, as well as the First Amendment of the U.S. Constitution (Mercier, as cited by Bidell, 2011). The case *Colín v. Orange Unified School District* (2000) marked the first time the Equal Access Act was invoked to order a school to allow a GSA to meet on campus. The Equal Access Act requires schools that receive federal funds to provide LGBTQ clubs the same access to school facilities that other student groups enjoy. This means that, for example, if your school requires parental consent for students seeking to join a GSA, they must require consent for all clubs and extracurricular activities.

These student clubs must be student-initiated. In other words, the Equal Access Act dictates community members outside the school community may not direct, conduct, control or regularly attend activities of student groups. Guests may occasionally attend student meetings, and school faculty and staff may regularly attend and supervise meetings. If a school staff member is provided to monitor extracurricular student clubs, a staff member should be assigned to the gay student association as well (Equal Access Act, 1984).

Certain limitations apply regarding equal access. For example, a limitation would apply if the school denies access based on a substantive possibility that it will interfere with the orderly conduct of educational activities within the school. In cases of equal access and freedom of expression, the burden tends to fall on schools to prove the disruption significantly interfered with education (B. Littrell, personal communication, Oct. 26, 2012). A complete guide on the Equal Access Act can be found at *www.justice.gov/crt/about/cor/byagency/ed4071.php*.

Efforts have not been met with court favor when school districts have tried to finesse legal definitions to defeat GSAs or other clubs addressing LGBTQ issues. In a Georgia district, students attempting to form a GSA were met with resistance, and eventually, the district announced a ban on all noncurricular clubs for the next academic year. Students sued, and a federal judge found that the ban on noncurricular clubs was an attempt to discriminate against Peers Rising in Diverse Education and forced the school to grant them and all other student groups equal access and the opportunity to meet on school campus (*Pacer v. White County School District* (2006)).

In the case of *Yasmin Gonzalez v. School Board of Okeechobee County* (2008) a U.S. District Court judge rejected the school's claim that the GSA was by definition a "sex-based" club and that it violated the school's abstinence-only policy (ACLU, 2008b). The list of cases rolls on and on. The school administration has the legal responsibility of allowing Johnston to form a GSA club. As the school counselor you have an opportunity to advocate by talking to the administration about the Equal

Access Act to avoid a legal misstep. Your advocacy role would serve two purposes: to position you as supporting the principal by drawing his attention to the appropriate federal legislation and to provide support for Johnston and other students who would benefit from a GSA club.

DISCRIMINATION IN DISCIPLINE AND PRIVACY RIGHTS OF MINORS

Your principal continues to bring same-sex couples into his office and call their parents/guardians for code of conduct violations for public displays of affection. You notice heterosexual couples are treated differently. You are considering discussing this with him. Are you overstepping your boundaries by involving yourself in disciplinary actions?

Points to Consider

The courts are more frequently hearing cases involving gay students, who feel they have been discriminated against. In one such court case, *Nguon v. Wolf* (2007), a federal judge in Los Angeles ruled that a high school does not have the right to reveal a student's sexual orientation without the student's permission. The ACLU brought the lawsuit on behalf of Charlene Nguon, a senior in Orange County's Garden Grove Unified School District, who claimed the principal violated her privacy rights by telling her parents she was a lesbian after he disciplined her for being affectionate with her girlfriend (ACLU, 2005; ACLU, 2006; ACLU, 2007). The school sought to have the lawsuit dismissed, but Judge James Selna of the U.S. District Court in the Central District of California allowed the suit to move forward. "We are pleased that the court recognized that the school does not have the automatic right to disclose a student's sexual orientation just because that student is out of the closet to his or her friends at school," said Christine P. Sun, a staff attorney for the ACLU. "Coming out is a very serious decision that should not be taken away from anyone, especially from students who may be put in peril if they live in an unsupportive home" (ACLU, 2005, para. 4). In September 2007, a California federal district court ruled that the principal, Ben Wolf, had not violated Nguon's privacy rights by disclosing her sexual orientation to her parents because it occurred within the context of the official's legal duty under the California Education Code to inform parents of disciplinary measures being taken against their child (*Nguon v. Wolf* (2007)). However, the case is still viewed as important by those fighting for LGBTQ rights as the case was allowed to proceed because educators do not have an automatic right to infringe upon the privacy rights of students.

In the light of *Nguon v. Wolf* (2007) and similar cases, informational privacy as it relates to minors has recently received attention. Cullitan (2011) proposes that informational privacy afforded to minors "should be expanded to better serve the particular vulnerabilities of children" (p. 460). Courts considering such cases, Cullitan (2011) writes, should consider whether the state had a compelling interest to intervene and, if so, whether they utilized the least intrusive means to violate a minor's informational privacy.

LGBTQ youth are at greater risk for substance abuse, suicide and homelessness and are often targets of physical, verbal and psychological abuse; therefore minors have a lot at stake regarding their informational privacy in the context of the family (Cullitan, 2011; Ludeke, 2009; Roberts, Rosario, Corliss, Koenen & Austin, 2012; Potoczniak, Crosbie-Burnett & Saltzburg, 2009). The application of this strict scrutiny to children's informational privacy rights does not mean they are granted more rights concerning their sexual behavior or conduct; it simply means children will be provided the assurance that their private information will remain confidential when expressing themselves in ways that are legal for minors (Cullitan, 2011).

If Cullitan's (2011) proposal were in place, Charlene's outing would have been unconstitutional, in that she considered school to be insulated from home, a reasonable expectation of privacy, and even if the school had a compelling interest in "outing" Charlene, it would not be able to demonstrate it had employed the least intrusive means available for achieving that interest.

We do not want to be disciplinarians and insinuate ourselves into areas administrators should handle. However, equity is always our business, and it is the politically astute school counselor who will figure out how to let his or her administrator know LGBTQ student rights are an increasing topic of court cases. Political astuteness can go a long way in supporting equitable learning environments for all students. Speak up.

SCHOOL COUNSELORS, PERSONAL VALUES AND AFFIRMATION OF LGBTQ STUDENTS

A student confided in his teacher he was a homosexual and that he was having a difficult time negotiating a same-sex relationship. The teacher asked the student if he would be comfortable talking to the school counselor about his relationship difficulties. The student said he would. Your colleague informed the teacher that, due to a conflict in her values, she would be unable to provide counseling services to this student. Are there any legal and ethical concerns regarding your colleague's behavior?

Points to Consider

Julea Ward, a student preparing to be a school counselor at Eastern Michigan University (EMU), was dismissed from her counseling program after she refused to counsel a gay client who requested help with his same-sex relationship. Ward, citing her religious beliefs, said she needed to refer this client as she could neither validate nor affirm homosexual behavior. Ward filed suit against EMU in 2009, citing her constitutional rights to religious freedom were violated. The university said she was dismissed for not following the American Counseling Association's (2005) code of ethics and not for religious expression. After a failed attempt in federal court, The Alliance Defense Fund helped Ward appeal to the U.S. Sixth District Court of Appeals. Ward won the right to a jury trial, and the case was remanded to a lower court to be heard, but a jury trial never ensued. On Dec. 10, 2012, EMU settled with Ward for $75,000. The university president stated, "Eastern Michigan University has made the decision that is in the best interest of its students and the taxpayers of the state of Michigan to resolve the litigation rather than continue to spend money on a costly trial... The faculty retains its right to establish, in its learned judgment, the curriculum and program requirements for the counseling program at EMU" (Kraft, 2012).

Are there those school counseling candidates whose "isms" should cause them and their preparation program to rethink their suitability for the school counseling profession? Can you have religious beliefs that match with Ward's and still seek and become an effective counselor? On Dec. 11, 2012, one day following the announcement that EMU settled its lawsuit, ASCA members were asked to give their opinion on the issues raised in this case, specifically around referring student/clients to other school counselors when school counselors believe their religious values will impede their effectiveness or when they believe they may harm a student. The survey also explored the question raised by the court case as to the suitability for the school counseling profession for those with certain deeply held convictions biasing them against segments of their student population.

ASCA members responded to a survey of 13 opinion prompts using a five-point Likert scale: strongly agree, agree, neutral, disagree, strongly disagree. Their responses give some insight into how school counselors see their profession as it relates to personal, religious and moral values around sexual orientation.

Referring to another professional to avoid harming a student may be an appropriate ethical response in a few select cases, but this should be the exception rather than the rule.

81 percent of respondents agreed or strongly agreed.

A blanket practice of referring all known same-sex attracted students to other school counselors because conversations may turn to their same-sex relationships is appropriate.

81 percent of respondents disagreed or strongly disagreed

(Stone & Glicksteen, 2012b)

Prejudices (racism, sexism, ageism, ableism, etc.) are sometimes grouped together and referred to as "isms." Some people maintain isms as a conscious part of their value system, choosing to believe certain groups of people or behaviors are inferior. Other people may have biases of which they are completely unaware. In a profession such as school counseling, biases and isms are especially troubling because school counselors are assigned a caseload, and students do not choose their school counselor. Ward professed she was unable to work with students around issues of unwanted pregnancies, sexual activity out of wedlock ("fornication") and homosexuality. Referring becomes burdensome when colleagues have to take on the referrals of the school counselor whose biases continue to inhibit the provision of unconditional positive regard for segments of his or her caseload. Troubling is how unrealistic referring can be when there are no other school counselors in the school to whom a student can be referred.

Compounding the issue of the referral approach is a student may come in with a "presenting" problem that is a safe topic, such as academics, to test the school counselor for trust and acceptance before broaching the real presenting issue of same-sex attraction. Working with students only to pull up short to refer to another school counselor would likely read to students as a rejection of who they are as a person. To reject (by referring) a student based on pregnancy or having sex out of wedlock is grave, but this is a rejection of the student's conduct not a rejection of who the student is as a person. Rejecting a student based on sexual orientation is to reject the student as a person, carrying with it far more potential for grievous harm.

Lambda Legal (2012) wrote an amicus brief (an opinion for the court to consider, provided by someone not a party to the action but invested in the outcome) for the *Ward v. Wilbanks* (2012) court case. "Abundant empirical research attests to the vulnerability of LGBTQ youth in school and the potentially devastating consequences, including youth suicide, that may result from repudiation and rejection by school officials." In asking the state to support EMU, the amicus brief stated, "...especially in light of the harm that a counselor could cause to LGBTQ youth if a counselor expressed disapproval of or refused to counsel such a student in a school setting."

> If a practicing school counselor/school counseling candidate has a bias against homosexuals or other sexual minorities, then it is appropriate to refer a same-sex attracted student to another school counselor.
>
> 78 percent of respondents agreed or strongly agreed
>
> (Stone & Glicksteen, 2012b)

"Above all do no harm" (Kitchener, 1984). What about the 100,000 school counselors already in the field, some of who may have deeply held biases that mirror Ward's beliefs? We are our values; we cannot simply drop our values on the way through the schoolhouse door to retrieve them at the end of the day. ASCA members see the value of referring to avoid harming (78 percent), but that this should be the exception not the rule (81 percent). School counselors frequently counsel students who exhibit behavior they do not condone, such as cursing at the teacher, refusing to cooperate with faculty and staff and disrespecting their parents/guardians. School counselors work through these conflicts in values with students, making sure they accept the student if not the behavior. Referral is a drastic step and should be done only as a last resort to avoid harming a student, but the real work needs to happen with the school counselor examining his or her own isms and biases. The onus is on the school counselor to work to eradicate or soften biases so students are not systematically referred to other school counselors to accommodate a litany of topics the school counselor is unwilling to help students negotiate. Certain school settings, grade levels, or even the profession itself, may not be the right choice for those who are unable to work with segments of the student population because their values will too often conflict with students' need for support.

Survey respondents primarily work with high school or middle school students (175 percent). Think about how many of your students you would not be able to counsel if you denied services to anyone having sex out of wedlock, struggling with an unwanted pregnancy or grappling with sexual orientation or gender-identity issues. Even elementary school counselors have students with these needs. School counseling is a position that has power to promote good or do harm to vulnerable minors. Practicing school counselors have to hold themselves accountable with honest, self-examination of their biases and isms and work so their standard of care is to support all students with unconditional positive regard. Ethical school counselors engage in intentional self-examination, professional development opportunities and pointed opportunities for exposure to other opinions and viewpoints.

If a school counselor/school counseling candidate is generally unwilling to work with students who request help with same-sex relationships, then the school counseling profession is not an appropriate choice for this person.

Strongly agree or agree: . . . . .63 percent

A school counselor should be willing to counsel a student if he or she requests help with same-sex romantic relationships.

Strongly agree or agree: ....74 percent

(Stone & Glicksteen, 2012b).

Because school counselors act as door openers for their PK-12 students, the profession bristles at the idea of gate keeping. However, counselor educators have the unenviable but critical ethical imperative of gate-keeping to guard who goes into the profession, making sure to prepare school counseling candidates to be door-openers for all PK-12 students. Is this gate-keeping in the spirit of the profession of school counseling whose tenet is advocacy for all? Absolutely. Counselor educators realize their primary responsibility is not to the school counseling candidate but to this person's future vulnerable, students. Students are mandated to be in the school setting, without legal autonomy over their lives, struggling with identity issues and at the mercy of the adults they should be able to turn to for help, the school counselor they've been assigned to based on identifiers such as their last name or grade level. All these variables and more make it critical that professionals in the field be aware of their power for harm or good and avoid consciously or unconsciously oppressing students. Isms and biases can sabotage objectivity and inhibit a professional school counselor's ability to work productively with all students. Professionals who harbor biases preventing them from working with segments of their population have work to do. Self-awareness work of ethical school counselors should never end in a profession built on advocacy for all students.

PROM AND SCHOOL-SPONSORED EVENTS

A student comes to you seeking advice about whether or not she will be able to bring a same-sex date to the prom. Before she approaches the administration, she wanted your thoughts. Can the student legally bring a same-sex date to the prom?

Points to Consider

In a 1980 decision by a U.S. District Court in Rhode Island, a judge found a student's First- and 14th-Amendment rights were violated when school officials attempted to stop him from escorting another young man to his senior prom (*Fricke v. Lynch* (1980)). Aaron Fricke, a senior at Cumberland High School, requested permission to attend the senior reception with a male date, and Lynch denied his request, citing his prime concern as fear of violence against the couple. Lawyers for the school argued this was "speech activity" and Fricke had chosen an inappropriate time and place for his speech activity. Judge Pettine recognized Fricke sought to express a political message in a social setting; however, he differentiated Fricke's desire to attend and participate in the dance with leafleting or speechmaking, which might legitimately be banned at a dance. He found that Fricke's expression took a form "uniquely consonant with the setting he wishes to attend and participate like everyone else" (*Fricke v Lynch*, 1980, p. 4).

Judge Pettine wrote, "After considerable thought and research, I have concluded that even a legitimate interest in school discipline does not outweigh a student's right to peacefully express his views in an appropriate time, place and manner. To rule otherwise would completely subvert free speech in the schools by granting other students a "heckler's veto," allowing them to decide through prohibited and violent methods what speech will be heard. The First Amendment does not tolerate mob rule by unruly school children" (*Fricke v. Lynch* (1980), p. 5). Fricke and Guilbert were allowed to attend the dance together. The school provided increased security, and the dance was otherwise unremarkable (Associated Press, 1980).

Since 1980, same-sex couples banned from attending their school's prom and other school-sponsored events have used the precedent set by *Fricke v. Lynch* to negotiate permission to attend. In many cases, school districts allow same-sex dates without incident. In one high-profile case, Constance McMillen, a lesbian student, was forbidden from wearing a tuxedo to her school's prom and bringing her girlfriend. School officials told her only boys could wear tuxedoes, and circulated a memo saying all prom dates had to be opposite sex. When the ACLU filed a complaint on her behalf, the school board withdrew their sponsorship from the prom, effectively canceling the event. McMillen sued the Itawamba County School District (McMillen, 2010), and a federal court agreed in a preliminary ruling that McMillen's constitutional right to freedom of speech was violated. The school board encouraged parents to organize a private prom, which was represented to be the official prom for most of the student body. However, parents also organized a second "decoy" prom, which McMillen, her girlfriend and seven other students attended while most of their classmates partied at a private prom 30 miles away.

The ACLU amended their complaint to highlight the humiliation McMillen faced both on prom night, during the school day and at home, as her classmates treated her with hatred and animosity. The court awarded monetary damages to McMillen and required the school district to establish inclusive policies. McMillen's case played out in the national media, and she appeared on several national television shows, including the Ellen DeGeneres show, where she received a $30,000 college scholarship (ACLU, 2010b; ACLU, 2010c; CNN Wire staff, 2010; Johnson, 2010; Jonsson, 2010; Joyner, 2010).

DRESS CODE AND STUDENT EXPRESSION

A student showed up at school with a T-shirt that said "Gay Pride." The principal made her turn the shirt inside out to hide the message. Was the principal's action legal?

Points to Consider

Heather Gillman sought help from school officials when other students were harassing her because she is a lesbian. The principal, David Davis, lectured her that homosexuality is wrong and outed her to her parents (causing her father to threaten to kick her out of the house). When Gillman missed school the following day, a rumor circulated in the school that she had been suspended because she was homosexual. To show their support, numerous students wrote "GP" or "Gay Pride" on their bodies and wore t-shirts supporting gay rights. Davis interrogated 30 students about their sexual orientation, prohibited students from wearing rainbow belts and from writing "GP" or "Gay Pride" on their arms and notebooks. He required students with such writings to wash them from their arms and hands and lifted the shirts of female students to see if there were writings on their bodies. Less than two weeks later, Davis suspended 11 students for five days each for their involvement in the gay pride movement. Gillman and her cousin approached the school board with legal counsel asking for guidance on which phrases and symbols were permitted in school. They asked to display rainbows, pink triangles and slogans such as, "Equal, Not Special Rights," "Gay? Fine By Me," "Gay Pride," "I Support Gays," "I'm Straight, But I Vote Pro-Gay" and "Sexual Orientation is Not a Choice. Religion, However, Is." The school board responded that such speech would "likely be disruptive" and claimed the symbols and slogans indicated students were part of a "secret/illegal organization," which was forbidden by school board policy.

Gillman sued the Holmes County School Board and Davis. The U.S. District Court ruled in favor of the students, agreeing their First- and 14th-Amendment rights were violated. The court said the student expression in question was not "vulgar, lewd, obscene, offensive or violent" but instead it was "pure, political and expresses tolerance, acceptance, fairness and support for not only a marginalized group but, more importantly, for a fellow student." The court explained that political speech on controversial topics such as equal rights for gays was likely to lead to debate, and high school students, many of whom are old enough to vote, shouldn't be left out of that national dialogue (*Gillman v. Holmes County School District* (2008); ACLU, 2008a; ACLU, 2009b; Volokh, 2008).

In 2013, the ACLU also fought for and won a student's right to wear a shirt with anti-gay imagery. Seth Groody was banned from his Connecticut high school for wearing a shirt depicting a rainbow with a slash through it, a man and woman holding hands and the words "Excessive Speech Day." He wore it on a designated day of awareness toward harassment of gay, lesbian, bisexual and transgender people. The Connecticut ACLU said it vehemently disagreed with Groody's views on same-sex marriage, but that he was "absolutely correct about his right to express his opinion." As the ACLU prepared a federal lawsuit, a lawyer from the school contacted it to say the student could wear the T-shirt (Associated Press, 2012; Associated Press, 2013a).

Schools have struggled in recent years with how to address student dress that defies gender stereotypes (Hoffman, 2009). There is substantial case law to caution schools against creating and enforcing dress code policies discriminating on the basis of gender, gender identity or sexual orientation.

Katrina Harrington, a seventh-grade student in Brockton, Mass., faced discipline from her principal for wearing skirts, hair accessories and makeup. Harrington, a biologically male transgender student known in court documents as Pat Doe, had to report to the principal's office daily by the eighth grade to have her clothing approved. If the principal disapproved, he sent her home. This practice forced Harrington to miss so many school days she could not pass the grade, and she eventually quit going to school altogether. Represented by Gay and Lesbian Advocates and Defenders (GLAD), Harrington sued the Brockton School Department for violating her First- and 14th-Amendment rights for preventing her from attending school wearing her choice of clothes. The Superior Court in Massachusetts ruled a middle school may not prohibit a transgender student from expressing her female gender identity and stated, "Exposing children to diversity at an early age serves the important social goals of increasing their ability to tolerate differences" (GLAD, n.d.a). The school had to allow Harrington to wear any clothing the school dress code allowed, feminine or otherwise (*Doe v. Yunits* (2001); GLAD, n.d.a; GLAD, 2000; NCLR & GLSEN, n.d.).

In 2009, graduating senior Ceara Sturgis posed in a tuxedo for her senior photograph. School officials refused to publish her photo in the yearbook with the other seniors and excluded her name from her senior class. Traditionally, female students at the Mississippi high school wear drapes (to give the appearance of a blouse or dress) and male students wear tuxedos. Sturgis, an honor student who was active in band and soccer, habitually dressed in boy's clothing at school and was openly gay. She hadn't previously had any problems at school, and said nobody at school ever made her feel weird or like an outcast. Represented by the ACLU, Sturgis filed a lawsuit against her school, saying it discriminated against her based on her sex and gender expression. After two years, the school settled the lawsuit. Although Sturgis could not be retroactively placed in her yearbook, the high school will include it in her class picture in the school library. The school also agreed to require all students to wear caps and gowns in their senior portraits, instead of gender-specific outfits (ACLU, 2011b; Eng, 2011; Hoffman, 2009; Sturgis, 2011).

In a Position to Know:
A School Counseling Candidate Speaks

The case presented at the beginning of the chapter is revisited here and discussed further by a practicing school counseling candidate. Compare her thoughts with your approach.

A SCHOOL COUNSELOR'S ATTITUDE

Alexia Huart had been taught in religious training and at home that homosexuality is a choice, and people who make the choice to be homosexuals are misguided. She never really questioned her beliefs, and she thought that as a school counselor in training it really did not matter how she felt about sexual minorities. Huart's preparation program pushed her to examine her biases. Must school counselors continuously take inventory and confront their own prejudices and beliefs about others regarding diversity issues such as sexual orientation and gender identity?

Excerpts of comments written by Alexia Huart:

I never had to "confront" my values or what I thought of others' values and lifestyles prior to entering the school counseling program. The more courses I took, the more my values, biases and prejudices were challenged. At first, my reaction was, "So, what's the big deal? My thoughts and opinions are mine and should not matter or affect my ability to become a successful school counselor."

But I began to realize confronting my values was of extreme importance. I learned that when it comes to a student's issues and situations, what I think, my nonverbal behavior (i.e., my reactions: empathy, shock, horror, concern or indifference), as well as what I say, could make a crucial difference in the student's life. I think about students who could be spared pain or brought back from the brink of suicide just by a caring look, empathy or unconditional support from an educator.

My entire life I believed I was trying to be vigilant in respecting beliefs and cultural differences. I had a great desire to learn more about others, regardless of race, ethnicity or religion. Now the professors in my school counseling preparation program were adding to the pot sexual differences, beliefs and lifestyles. I had no idea as to the challenge it would bring to my doorstep. Now I have to look into myself and address my beliefs and biases concerning homosexuality. I felt I respected the rights of others to be different from me, but did I really? Did I ever consider their actual pain? Not until I watched "The Laramie Project," the moving story of Matthew Shepard (Baldwin & Kaufman, 2002).

Matthew was beaten, tied to a fence and left for dead because he was gay. After watching "The Laramie Project" and seeing Matthew's father give his impassioned speech during the sentencing phase of the trail, I was changed. Anyone who has a heart would realize it doesn't matter about Matthew's skin color or sexual orientation. He was a son, a classmate, a neighbor, a friend, a person...a human being. This man and his family suffered pain and devastation, like so many who have experienced the cruelty of hatred, prejudice and ignorance, which will never go away.

After much pondering and soul searching on my own, I have come to the conclusion that there are a plethora of qualities a counselor should possess to do an adequate job in his or her field. Chief among them are fairness, loyalty, and a tolerance and appreciation for diversity. In the world in which we live, one must do a personal inventory of where he or she stands in view of these most necessary attributes. There are some things

that cannot be acquired from a book. One can study forever and still not possess the qualities needed to work with people successfully or compassionately. This takes personal effort and determination to improve your character and view of the world at large. I'm determined to grow daily through my interactions with others regardless of race, creed, ethnicity or sexual orientation. It's not a pat on the back by any means, just a "charge to keep" to myself, personally.
– *Alexia Huart, retired staff development teacher at P.S. 224 in Brooklyn, N.Y.*

Making Connections

1. Discuss 10 strategies you would like to implement to reduce harassment of LGBTQ students in your school.

2. What are the human costs to lesbian, gay, bisexual and transgender students in dangerous school climates? Cite some statistics to show their peculiar vulnerability.

3. View "The Laramie Project." What is your reaction? Pick a character in the movie, and write your reaction about the barriers or contributions that person made to acceptance of diversity. There are recent revelations from the defendants that Matthew Shepard may not have been a victim of a hate crime but a target for robbery; does this change the impact of the re-enactment for you?

4. What are your personal beliefs about sexual orientation? How will your attitudes and beliefs be manifested in your work? Is this a problem? If so, what will you do to minimize harm to your students?

5. Why is it particularly important for school counselors to promote diversity and respect for all students?

Key Terms

Amicus brief
Biological sex
Bisexuality
Cisgender
Community standards
Equal Access Act
Ex-gay ministry
Gay, Lesbian & Straight Education
   Network
Gay-straight alliance club
Gender expression
Gender identity
Gender nonconforming
Heterosexism
Homophobia
Homosexuality
Intersex

Parents, Family and Friends of
   Lesbians and Gays
Physical and emotional safety
Privacy rights of minors
Queer
Questioning
Relational aggression
Reparative or conversion therapy
School climate
School culture
Sexual minority
Sexual orientation
The Safe Schools Coalition
Title IX of Educational
   Amendment of 1972
Transgender

CHAPTER 11

Sexual Harassment

IN THIS CHAPTER

Objectives

By the time you have completed this chapter, you should be able to:

- Discuss the role of the U.S. Department of Education Office for Civil Rights in sexual harassment.
- Discuss the legal implications of ignoring sexual harassment.
- Explain the emotional cost to victims of sexual harassment.
- Develop strategies preventing repeated occurrences of sexual harassment.
- Understand the elements of a sexual harassment policy and how a policy can be put into practice.

Ethical Standards

Professionalism means knowing your professional associations' codes and adhering to them. The ASCA Ethical Standards for School Counselors most relevant to this chapter are the following:

- Professional school counselors support and protect students' best interest against any infringement of their educational program. (D.1.a)
- Professional school counselors inform appropriate officials, in accordance with school policy, of conditions that may be potentially disruptive or damaging to the school's mission, personnel and property while honoring the confidentiality between the student and the school counselor. (D.1.b)
- Professional school counselors assist in developing: (1) curricular and environmental conditions appropriate for the school and community; (2) educational procedures and programs to meet students' developmental needs; (3) a systematic evaluation process for comprehensive, developmental, standards-based school counseling programs, services and personnel; and (4) a data-driven evaluation process guiding the comprehensive, developmental school counseling program and service delivery. (D.1.g)

The full text of the ASCA Ethical Standards for School Counselors is available at *www.schoolcounselor.org*.

Introduction

Sexual harassment has been the focus of much discourse and debate within the context of social and educational policy. Understanding what constitutes sexual harassment and how to respond to it is now as much a part of being an educator as teaching the letters of the alphabet.

Sex discrimination, especially regarding the influence of gender in educational opportunities in education, was outlawed by Title IX, enacted by Congress in 1972 (Title IX of the Educational Amendments of 1972). In 2008, in the pamphlet "Sexual Harassment: It's Not Academic," the U.S. Department of Education Office for Civil Rights defined sexual harassment as conduct that "is sexual in nature; is unwelcome; and denies or limits a student's ability to participate in or benefit from a school's education program" (U.S. Department of Education, Office for Civil Rights, 2008, p. 3). In 2011, the Office for Civil Rights (OCR) issued a Dear Colleague Letter, an important directive, which focuses on the specific requirements regarding sexual violence. Recent court rulings have further clarified the legal definition of sexual harassment and have resulted in legislation aiding school counselors in advocating against student-on-student harassment.

Generally speaking, there are two types of sexual harassment in schools: hostile environment and quid pro quo. "Hostile environment sexual harassment occurs when unwanted sexual touching, comments and/or gestures are so bad or occur so often that it interferes with schoolwork, makes [a student] feel uncomfortable or unsafe at school or prevents [a student] from participating in or benefiting from a school program or activity. This type of harassment does not have to involve a threat or promise of benefit in exchange for a sexual favor. The harassment can be from your teacher, school officials or other students" (Equal Rights Advocates, 2012).

Quid pro quo sexual harassment means something for something, where benefits are conditioned upon the grant of sexual favors. Quid pro quo is when a school employee causes a student to believe he or she must submit to unwelcome sexual conduct to participate in a school activity or that the employee will make an educational decision based on whether or not the student submits to unwelcome sexual conduct (U.S. Department of Education, Office for Civil Rights, 2006). In a school setting, student benefits can include grades, admission to a program, scholarships and grants in exchange for sexual favors" (Perry & Marcum, 2008).

Males and females often look at sexual harassment in different ways. Regardless of which gender or educational institution is defining sexual harassment, three elements are present: the behavior is sexual in nature or at least related to the gender of the person; the behavior occurs in an unequal relationship where one person has more power over another (physical, psychological, authoritative or other), and the behavior is unsolicited or unwelcome (Hyde & Soronen, 2004; James Madison University, 2008).

The Office for Civil Rights provided examples of sexual conduct within the school system. Some examples are: making sexual propositions or pressuring students for sexual favors; touching of a sexual nature; writing graffiti of a sexual nature; displaying or distributing sexually explicit drawings, pictures or written materials; performing sexual gestures or touching oneself sexually in front of others; telling sexual or dirty jokes; spreading sexual rumors or rating other students as to sexual activity or performance; or circulating or showing e-mails or websites of a sexual nature (U.S. Department of Education [USDOE], Office for Civil Rights, 2008, p. 3).

Title IX ensures students are not sexually harassed during any activities associated with schools such as academic, educational, extracurricular, athletic and other programs regardless of where programs take place. OCR believes a single act of sexual harassment can create a hostile environment in schools and hinder academic achievement (USDOE/OCR, 2011a, p. 3). When school officials are aware of student-on-student harassment, Title IX mandates schools take immediate action to eliminate further instances, prevent reoccurrences and address issues that may arise. School must also have a published nondiscrimination policy and a grievance procedure all employees are trained to implement. "Harassing behavior, if ignored or not reported, is likely to continue and become worse, rather than go away" (USDOE/OCR, 2005, p. 2).

The Office for Civil Rights in 2011, with the Dear Colleague Letter, elaborated on what constitutes acts of sexual violence so school districts, colleges and universities are better informed as to acts prohibited by Title IX. Sexual violence, as defined by the OCR, "refers to physical sexual acts perpetrated against a person's will or where a person is incapable of giving consent due to the victim's use of drugs or alcohol. An individual also may be unable to give consent due to an intellectual or other disability. A number of different acts fall into the category of sexual violence, including rape, sexual assault, sexual battery and sexual coercion. All such acts of sexual violence are forms of sexual harassment covered under Title IX" (USDOE/OCR, 2011a, p. 1-2). Sexual violence is not covered in this chapter, but this topic is addressed in depth in the Chapter 13: Violence and Criminal Activity. The implications of the Dear Colleague Letter for lesbian, gay, bisexual, transgender and questioning (LGBTQ) youth are covered in the LGBTQ Chapter. Sexual harassment and bullying can sometimes overlap, but there are important distinctions. For example, there are some state laws against bullying, but serious sexual harassment – at a level interfering with a student's education – is prohibited under the federal gender-equality legislation known as Title IX. "Too often, the more comfortable term bullying is used to describe sexual harassment, obscuring the role of gender and sex in these incidents. Schools are likely to promote bullying prevention while ignoring or downplaying sexual harassment" (AAUW, 2001, p.7).

Prevalence and Targets. In 1993, the American Association of University Women (AAUW) delivered the ground-breaking report "Hostile Hallways" and again in 2001. AAUW recently presented its latest installment of the "Hostile Hallways" reports, "Crossing the Line: Sexual Harassment at School," which studied the 2010–2011 school year (American Association of University Women, 2011). The AAUW study confirmed the continued presence of sexual harassment in schools. Holly Kearl of AAUW's Legal Advocacy Fund said the problem had not eased and may have worsened because of the spread of electronic and online harassment (AAUW, 2011). Of the 1,965 students in grades 7–12 participating in the study, "nearly half (48 percent) of the students surveyed experienced some form of sexual harassment in the 2010–11 school year. In all, 56 percent of the girls and 40 percent of the boys said they had experienced at least one incident of sexual harassment during the school year. Girls were more likely than boys to say that they had been negatively affected by sexual harassment, which confirms AAUW's 2001 research. Girls were more likely than boys to say sexual harassment caused them to have trouble sleeping, to want to skip school or to want to find a different route to or from school.

In 2009, Petersen and Hyde (as cited by Hill & Kearl, 2011) found sexual harassment could begin "as early as elementary school, but the prevalence increases in higher grades as more students enter puberty." Sexual harassment at younger ages is not typically about sex itself but about gender identity (Hill & Kearl, 2011). Young, Allen and Ashbaker (n.d.) explain boys and girls experience different types of sexual harassment. "Girls are more likely than boys to be physically harassed and are also more likely to be harassed by adults. Girls are more likely to be touched, grabbed, pinched or brushed up against in a sexual way (Young, Allen & Ashbaker, n.d.).

The National Women's Law Center (2010) also addressed the issue of sexual harassment in schools. It found "83 percent of female and 79 percent of male students in grades 8 through 11 had been sexually harassed at school in ways that interfered with their lives. One third of the surveyed students (20 percent of boys and 44 percent of girls) said they fear being sexually harassed during the school day" (p. 1).

Consequence of Sexual Harassment on Youth. In the AAUW study, a majority of those students (87 percent) said sexual harassment had a negative effect on them" (Hill & Kearl, 2011, p.2). One-third of the victims said the harassment made them feel sick to their stomach, affected their study habits or fueled reluctance to go to school at all (AAUW, 2011).

Youth targeted by sexual harassment report myriad negative consequences. As a result of sexual harassment, youth describe experiencing negative psychological outcomes such as:
- Feeling moderately to severely upset
- Feeling self-conscious or embarrassed
- Feeling afraid or scared
- Trouble sleeping
- Loss of appetite
- Decreased participation in class
- Less able to focus

In addition, Young, Allen and Ashbaker (n.d.) cite the following as common reactions to sexual harassment:
- Feeling unclean or dirty
- Feeling worthless
- Feeling anxious, distressed and/or confused
- Experiencing depression symptoms (AAUW, 2011)

The National Women's Law Center survey found, "The consequences of harassment are severe. Students who experience sexual harassment are likely to react by talking less in class, not wanting to go to school and finding it hard to pay attention in school. Targets of sexual bullying and harassment experience anxiety, distress, confusion, loss of self-esteem and depression. Preventing and remedying sexual harassment and bullying is essential to ensuring a safe environment in which your students can complete their education" (2007, p. 1).

School Counselors' Role. In their role as advocates for students, school counselors empower and serve as anchors and sources of strength for individual students in dealing with issues of sexual harassment in schools. Educators promote a safe and respectful school climate for all students by providing students with the knowledge and support they need. School counselors are part of that imperative.

As leaders within school settings, school counselors can raise awareness among students and fellow educators as to the problem of sexual harassment. "Sexual harassment can take different forms depending on the harasser and the nature of the harassment. The conduct can be carried out by school employees, other students and non-employee third parties, such as a visiting speaker...The conduct can occur in any school program or activity and can take place in school facilities, on a school bus or at other off-campus locations, such as a school-sponsored field trip or a training program at another location" (U.S. Department of Education, Office for Civil Rights, 2008, p. 3).

School counselors must take into account the legal and ethical complications of working with minors in schools, especially regarding sexual harassment issues. Through the multitude of roles they play in school settings, school counselors primarily serve students. As advocates and human behavior specialists, school counselors serve as a source of strength in confronting and dealing with sexual harassment. They also raise awareness as to the prevalence of sexual harassment and assist their colleagues in formulating school plans for prevention and intervention.

Confidentiality is difficult to keep when students are the target of illegal behavior. School counselors have been given guidance by OCR in the publication "Sexual Harassment: It's Not Academic" (2008) on how to negotiate the confidentiality imperative while addressing our legal obligation to report sexual harassment. This balancing of confidentiality and legal obligations will be addressed in depth in the first case scenario, Sexual Harassment and Confidentiality.

Students Seeking Help. Students continue to avoid telling an adult in the school. "The prevalence of sexual harassment in grades 7–12 comes as a surprise to many, in part because it is rarely reported. Among students who were sexually harassed, about 9 percent reported the incident to a teacher, guidance counselor or other adult at school...Just one-quarter (27 percent) of students said they talked about it with parents or family members (including siblings), and only about one-quarter (23 percent) spoke with friends…Still, one-half of students who were sexually harassed in the 2010–11 school year said they did nothing afterward in response to sexual harassment" (Hill & Kearl, 2011).

Students gave their reasons for not reporting. Students doubt their reports will have any impact and instead of improving their lot in school, students fear their situation will only get worse through retaliation. Students also said they were concerned about the staff member's reaction.

The survey asked students for suggestions on how to reduce sexual harassment at their schools. More than half the student respondents advocated for anonymous reporting (see the Bullying, Cyberbullying and Sexting Chapter for more on anonymous reporting). Students also favored systematic punishments for harassers.

School officials can walk down the hall and see it happening and not even register they are observing sexual harassment. "Sexual harassment from peers is often largely dismissed as normal student behavior by school officials" (Parker-Pope, 2008, p. 1).

Court Rulings. Court rulings have given school counselors support for raising awareness and making positive change for victims of sexual harassment. One important court case is the U.S. Supreme Court decision in *Davis v. Monroe County Board of Education* (1999), based on a violation of Title IX. Davis demands advocacy against known sexual harassment (*Davis v. Monroe County Board of Education* (1999); U.S. Department of Education, Office for Civil Rights, 2001; Yell & Katsiyannis, 2000; U.S. Legal, 2008).

In the Davis case a fifth-grade girl and her mother, Mrs. Davis, repeatedly complained to teachers and the principal for five months regarding sexual abuse behaviors by another student, G.F., but they received no relief of any kind (Sullivan & Zirkel, 1999; Rollini, 2003). In desperation, Mrs. Davis filed a complaint with the Monroe County, Ga., Sheriff's Department, and G.F. pled guilty to sexual battery. Mrs. Davis' subsequent lawsuit under Title IX's prohibition of sex discrimination in schools ended with a Supreme Court decision in her favor (*Davis v. Monroe County Board of Education* (1999); Hyde & Soronen, 2004; Rollini, 2003; Alexander & Alexander, 2011).

Justice Sandra Day O'Connor emphasized a relatively stringent standard of proof for plaintiffs. Liability may be imposed if the harassment is so severe, pervasive and objectively offensive that it deprives a student of an equal educational opportunity (Yell & Katsiyannis, 2000; Rollini, 2003; Alexander & Alexander, 2011). Additionally, school officials must know of and be deliberately indifferent to the sexual harassment (*Davis v. Monroe County Board of Education* (1999); Hyde & Soronen, 2004). The Davis case decidedly supports school counselors in exercising their leadership and advocacy role to help students victimized by their peers.

Teacher-on-student sexual harassment also takes place in America's schools. The U.S. Supreme Court decision in *Franklin v. Gwinnett County Public Schools* (1992) established a legal precedent by drawing a parallel between teacher-on-student sexual harassment and supervisor-to-subordinate harassment in the workplace (Zirkel, 2001/2002). Teacher-on-student sexual harassment was extended to student-on-student sexual harassment in subsequent court cases (Alexander & Alexander, 2011).

The purpose of this chapter is to explore through case study the legal and ethical implications of deliberate indifference to sexual harassment, the emotional cost to youth and the financial cost to school districts if we do not act on students' behalf.

Getting Started: What Would You Do?

The following case is discussed for you at the end of this chapter by a counselor educator. Before you read his response, decide how you would approach this ethical dilemma.

CYBER-SEXUAL HARASSMENT

Using computers at both the school and her home, Ashley has been sending Kenneth provocative pictures of herself and long love letters, not seeming to care he has asked her to leave him alone. Ashley has e-mailed her communications to Kenneth and to her friends, who have also sent them to other friends. She is instant-messaging people as to every move Kenneth makes, what he wears and what his after-school activities are each day. All this attention across electronic media feels creepy to Kenneth. Ashley has made such an issue of her "love" for him Kenneth feels he has become the object of ridicule. Despite his embarrassment, he feels frustrated he does not seem to have any recourse with Ashley and must simply endure, continuing to tell her he is not interested. Is this harassment? Could this be sexual harassment? Could Ashley be breaking any laws or school board policies? What recourse, if any, does Kenneth have?

Working Through Case Studies

SEXUAL HARASSMENT AND CONFIDENTIALITY

Subjected daily to sexually suggestive remarks by a group of boys in the hallway near her economics class, 14-year-old Regina has started to come late to class to avoid the boys' taunts and jeers. Regina's economics teacher, Ms. Lopez, unaware of the situation, has sent Regina to the office for tardy slips, but it has not changed her behavior. Now Regina is in danger of being suspended. Ms. Lopez, sensing something unusual is happening to her conscientious-student-turned-truant, asks you, the school counselor, to talk with Regina. You begin to learn the extent of Regina's attempt to protect herself when she starts to confide in you about the harassment. Regina describes her embarrassment and her attempts at coping by "laughing it off," "avoiding them," "taunting back" (which she said only made her feel more dirty) or "dressing in really baggy clothes." She begs you not to tell anyone, saying, "It [the harassment] will only get worse." Must you report the sexual harassment to the administration of your school? Can you keep Regina's identity confidential? Can the school administration keep Regina's identity confidential when confronting the perpetrators?

Points to Consider

Regina fits the profile of the harassed student. She blames and doubts herself, uses avoidance techniques and wants to be free of the harassment but endures it rather than risking becoming known as an informant or having the boys take their revenge on her for reporting them. Once regarded as harmless, flirtatious or playful, sexual harassment is now widely understood to be destructive, illegal and damaging.

Must you report the sexual harassment to school administration? Absolutely. School counselors are required by law to report sexual harassment to school officials. "Once a school has notice of possible sexual harassment of students, whether carried out by employees, other students or third parties, it should take immediate and appropriate steps to investigate or otherwise determine what occurred and take prompt and effective steps reasonably calculated to end any harassment, eliminate a hostile environment if one has been created and prevent harassment from occurring again. These steps are the school's responsibility whether or not the student who was harassed makes a complaint or otherwise asks the school to take action" (U.S. Department of Education, Office for Civil Rights, 2001, p. 15).

"A school has actual notice of sexual harassment if an agent or responsible employee of the school receives notification" (U.S. Department of Education, Office for Civil Rights, 1997b, p. 12037). Once Regina confides she is being harassed, this constitutes "notice," triggering the school counselor's legal requirement to report the harassment and the school's responsibility to take corrective action.

Conducting a Title IX investigation is unlike other investigations. The school is obligated to investigate the conduct in its own independent investigation. A law enforcement investigation does not hinder an internal school investigation. The steps of a school investigation differ depending on the nature of the allegations, the involved students' ages, the size and administrative structure of the school, etc. (U.S. Department of Education, Office for Civil Rights, 2011a). Schools must also obtain informed consent for students under the age of 18 in K-12 schools and maintain confidentially when necessary. In cases where students request an investigation not be pursued or request identifiable information not be disclosed, schools should take responsible steps to investigate and respond appropriately (U.S. Department of Education, Office for Civil Rights, 2001).

Can you keep Regina's identity confidential? The Office for Civil Rights, the arm of the federal government requiring compliance with anti-discrimination policy and practice for school districts, promotes protecting confidentiality. In its 2008 pamphlet "Sexual Harassment: It's Not Academic", the Department of Education gives an explanation for student requests of confidentiality when reporting sexual harassment: "The school should take all reasonable steps to investigate and respond to the complaint in a manner consistent with a request for confidentiality from a student. If a student insists that his or her name not be disclosed to the harasser, the school's ability to respond may be limited. The school also must consider its responsibility to provide a safe and nondiscriminatory environment for all students. Thus, the school must weigh the confidentiality request against the following factors:
- Seriousness of the alleged harassment
- Age of the harassed student
- Other complaints that the same individual has harassed others"
(Office for Civil Rights, 2008)

OCR understands breaching a student's confidence will often discourage the student from reporting harassment. This reluctance to report has already been identified as a problem for many students in our schools (AAUW, 2001; U.S. Department of Education, Office for Civil Rights, 2001). If a school has a procedure or policy in place in which the victim is identified on the report, then the school counselor's advocacy role can spark a change in this practice. Reporting is critical; identifying the victim in a report is not critical.

The school counselor will need to educate Regina about the legal requirement to report the sexual harassment and, if appropriate, encourage Regina to allow her identity to be known to support addressing it. However, OCR does not require educators breach confidentiality just to ensure the perpetrators are disciplined. Rather, it requires educators to address the harassment, which can take many forms. What OCR advocates as best practice is an important matter.

Can the school administration keep Regina's identity confidential when confronting the perpetrators? Several factors complicate the question of maintaining confidentiality of the sexually harassed student. These factors include the rights of the victim to confidentiality and the due process rights of the accused to face accusers. Maintaining the anonymity of the victim often interferes with the investigation. In an effort to remedy the effects of the harassment and prevent it from reoccurring, school administrators and school counselors must struggle with the victim's confidentiality in terms of identity (USDOE/OCR, 2001).

OCR promotes the protection of a victim's identity during the investigation and discipline of the perpetrator. Sometimes discipline and investigation of the perpetrator must be forfeited to protect the victim's identity. However, OCR allows school officials to address harassment in global ways, such as an assembly or a classroom presentation. The important directive from OCR is to act and not be deliberately indifferent. A strategy to have an adult catch the students in the act could reduce suspicion that the victim told on the perpetrator. As a last resort, you may have to reveal the identity of the sexual harassment victim. In the hypothetical case of Regina, no obvious good reason exists for revealing her identity.

DELIBERATE INDIFFERENCE

Kayla comes to see you about her discomfort with a group of boys from her English class. Kayla explains these boys are throwing nude pictures on her desk and telling her to pass them to a boy who sits on the other side of her. She asks them to stop, pushes them off her desk and refuses to pass the pictures, but the boys laugh, lean way over her desk and pass them in such a way as to make certain she sees them. Kayla tells you she reported the boys' conduct to the teacher who told her to "just ignore them." The teacher has not made any attempts to stop the practice. Kayla seeks your help. With assigned seats she is stuck in the middle of this misery for a year. Is Kayla being sexually harassed?

Points to Consider

Kayla is in what OCR would describe as a hostile environment. "A hostile environment occurs when unwelcome sexually harassing conduct is so severe, persistent or pervasive that it affects a student's ability to participate in or benefit from the education program or creates an intimidating, threatening or abusive educational environment" (USDOE/OCR, 2005, p. 2). The boys' behavior is affecting Kayla's ability to participate in the educational program.

"OCR considers a variety of related factors to determine if a hostile environment has been created, i.e., if sexually harassing conduct by an employee, another student or a third party is sufficiently serious that it denies or limits a student's ability to participate in or benefit from the school's program based on sex. OCR considers the conduct from both a subjective and objective perspective in evaluating the severity and pervasiveness of the conduct" (USDOE/OCR, 2001, p. 5).

OCR considers "the constellation of surrounding circumstances, expectations and relationships" (USDOE/OCR, 2001, p. 5).

"Relevant factors include the following:
- The degree to which the conduct affected one or more students' education
- The type, frequency and duration of the conduct
- The identity of and relationship between the alleged harasser and the subject or subjects of the harassment

- The number of individuals involved
- The age and sex of the alleged harasser and the subject or subjects of the harassment
- The size of the school, location of the incidents and context in which they occurred
- Other incidents at the school
- Incidents of gender-based, nonsexual harassment"

(USDOE/OCR, 2001, pgs. 6-7).

For Kayla's teacher to say, "just ignore them," she is running the risk of meeting the threshold of deliberate indifference to a hostile environment and setting the school district up for legal action and monetary damages. "If a school otherwise knows or reasonably should know of a hostile environment and fails to take prompt and effective corrective action, a school has violated Title IX, even if the student has failed to use the school's existing grievance procedures or otherwise inform the school of the harassment" (USDOE/OCR, 2001, p. 14).

OCR provides an example scenario describing sexual harassment: "A middle school student makes offensive sexual jokes to another student, but the student does not object to the jokes or speak out against them" (USDOE/OCR, 2008, p, 5). Despite the student's lack of objection, the comments may still be unwelcomed.

Sullivan and Zirkel (1999) analyzed 21 cases of sexual harassment involving students and were "startled by the number of people the victims of harassment notified without obtaining suitable resolution. School districts in the cases to date would have difficulty escaping liability due to the number of staff the target notified" (p. 618). The rule of thumb when it comes to litigation is that liability increases when an entity has knowledge of harm and does not take concrete action to protect the person in its care from this harm. School districts are no exception. The imperative to act that comes from the Supreme Court supports school counselors' advocacy role regarding sexual harassment issues.

"If a school determines that sexual harassment has occurred, it should take reasonable, timely, age-appropriate and effective corrective action, including steps tailored to the specific situation. Appropriate steps should be taken to end the harassment. For example, school personnel may need to counsel, warn or take disciplinary action against the harasser, based on the severity of the harassment or any record of prior incidents or both" (USDOE/OCR, 2001, p. 16).

If needed, the OCR regulations under Title IX require schools to have grievance procedures for all parties, students and families of the accused and complainant, applying to all forms of sex discrimination. A school's grievance procedures should:

- Give notice of the procedure, including where complaints can be filed, to students, parents/guardians of elementary and secondary students and employees.
- Assign an impartial investigator to the complainant, and give the parties involved the opportunity to present witnesses and other evidence.
- Set time frames for the major stages of the complaint process.
- Give notice to the parties of the outcome of the complaint.
- Give an assurance that the school will take steps to prevent recurrence of any harassment and that it will correct its discriminatory effects on the complainant and others, where appropriate.

(USDOE/OCR, 2005, pp. 7-8).

YOUNG CHILDREN AND SEXUAL HARASSMENT

A mother comes to you and complains her kindergartener is being sexually harassed by another student. The mother explains that a male student kissed her child on the cheek several times last week. Can young children engage in sexual harassment?

Points to Consider

The U.S. Department of Education, Office for Civil Rights addresses the issue of sexual harassment among minors by stating, "School personnel should consider the age and maturity of students in responding to allegations of sexual harassment. When determining whether a young child has committed sexual harassment, it is important for teachers and school administrators to use good judgment and common sense" (U.S DOE, OCR, 2008, p. 7).

OCR depicts the issues that may be of concern in this area in the following scenarios: "On one occasion, a first-grade student kisses another first-grade student on the cheek in the playground" (U.S DOE, OCR, 2008, p. 8). This situation is not sexual harassment. This other situation is: "On numerous occasions over a period of several months, a fifth-grade student inappropriately touches another fifth-grade student and makes overtly sexual comments and gestures to that student" (U.S DOE, OCR, 2008, p.

8). The perpetrator's conduct is only considered to be sexual harassment when it is unwelcomed by the victim and affects the victim's performance in school activities.

SEXUAL HARASSMENT OR STATUTORY RAPE?

Your school counseling colleague is involved with a 17-year-old, the age of consent for your state. Is this sexual harassment or child abuse? Does consensual sex exist between a school counselor and a student if the student is at the age of consent in his or her state?

Points to Consider

"Sexual harassment includes conduct that is criminal in nature, such as rape, sexual assault, dating violence and sexually motivated stalking. Even if a school reports possible criminal conduct to the police, that does not relieve the school of its responsibilities under Title IX" (U.S. Department of Education, Office for Civil Rights, 011, p.1).

It is considered outrageous when a teacher or school counselor has sexual relations with a student. Yet, it continues to happen. Some states have made teachers preying on students in their school a crime regardless if the student is age of consent in the state (see the Child Abuse Chapter for more details). Other states, such as Arkansas (Reed, 2012), are overturning such laws. Educators can lose their certificate and job and in many states face felony charges. This obvious breach of trust in the school counseling position makes school counselors bristle. The nature of the school counselor's job in the personal, social and emotional arena makes this behavior especially heinous.

STUDENT INCAPABLE OF IDENTIFYING SEXUAL-HARASSMENT BEHAVIOR

You are walking down the hall, and you see Meri pulling away from Marvin, who is trying to kiss her. From the look on her face it is obvious she wants no part of his show of affection. He blocks her by pushing his shoulders into her, and with quick steps and small shoulder pushes he keeps her from wiggling around him. Is this sexual harassment?

Points to Consider

If the conduct is unwelcome by Meri, she did not request or invite it, and she considers Marvin's conduct to be undesirable or offensive, then she is being sexually harassed. Regardless of Meri's past willingness to kiss Marvin, the subsequent kiss is considered unwelcomed. If you speak to Meri and she says the advances were unwelcome, "I broke up with him, and he just will not leave me alone" then you have a sexual harassment situation. OCR explains sexual harassment in its scenario, "A female high school student willingly kisses a male student on one occasion. When the student subsequently attempts to kiss her again, she objects, but he kisses her anyway" (U.S DOE, OCR, 2008, p. 5). "A student's submission to the conduct or failure to complain does not always mean that the conduct is welcome. This scenario clarifies a special situation of unwelcomed advances" (U.S DOE, OCR, 2008, p. 5).

Sometimes the student's age, the nature of the conduct and other relevant factors affect whether a student was capable of welcoming the sexual conduct. Consider a change in the case scenario. The student in question is in fourth grade and is developmentally delayed; she is functioning more on a 7-year-old level. Her age and developmental level make it unlikely she is capable of identifying this behavior as sexual harassment. Again, a student does not have to object or report for a situation to be considered unwelcome and sexual harassment. This case scenario describes what OCR would label an unequal relationship, where one person has more power over another (in this case physical and probably status in the school), may be unable to give consent due to an intellectual or other disability and the behavior is unsolicited or unwelcome (Hyde & Soronen, 2004; James Madison University, 2008).

SEXUAL HARASSMENT AND SCHOOL COUNSELORS

With angst about the fallout, you bravely told administration on two separate occasions about your colleague's frequent tendencies to put her hands all over male students in a suggestive way. It is an understatement when you say your colleague's behavior is way out of line. Your colleague is charismatic, and the vocal parents/guardians and students really like her. She also tends to take better care of the students whose parents/guardians are politically connected. The administration only responds to your reports by defending her and talking about how student-centered she is and that "touching is how she conveys warmth." You clearly explain her behavior is touching of a sexual nature, but the administration is just not willing to deal with it. What do you do?

Points to Consider

Is all physical contact sexual in nature? No. Legitimate nonsexual touching or conduct generally will not be considered sexual harassment. However, it may rise to that level if it takes on sexual connotations. This example further clarifies the difference: "A high school athletic coach hugs a student who makes a goal. This by itself is not considered sexual conduct. However, a coach's hugging of a student could be considered sexual conduct if it is unwelcome and occurs under inappropriate circumstances" (U.S DOE, OCR, 2008, p. 4).

In this scenario, the administration has been warned by the school counselor on more than one occasion, and this behavior would most likely meet the threshold of deliberate indifference. As uncomfortable as it was for the school counselor to have to report her colleague, it was her ethical and legal obligation to do so, or she would have been deliberately indifferent. Demonstrating her colleague's behavior (of course within reason), bringing any proof if possible, getting others to talk who have witnessed this behavior and/or taking the federal and state statutes that apply might be enough to get administration's attention. Three cases follow involving school counselors as the perpetrators of sexual harassment.

A federal district court in *Doe v. Fournier* (2012) WL 591669, refused to dismiss Title IX and other claims against Palmer Public Schools stemming from a male school counselor's sexual relationship with a female high school student. According to the court, the plaintiff sufficiently alleged the required notice and deliberate indifference (Buz, 2012). In particular, the plaintiff alleged that, prior to the school counselor's sexual affair with her, school officials had notice of allegations that he had had sex with another student and were concerned about his tendency to get "too cozy" with students. Yet, he was not disciplined or supervised in any way to protect female students. The only actions school officials did take were stopping a female student from placing her legs on his, directing him to remove pictures of female students from his office wall and "contemplating – but never effectuating – transferring him to the middle school," *Doe v. Fournier* (2012) WL 591669 (D. Mass. Feb. 22, 2012).

In contrast, a federal district court in Washington held that plaintiffs did not sufficiently allege school officials had notice and were deliberately indifferent to signs a school counselor posed a risk to students prior to having molested the plaintiffs. Plaintiffs had argued school officials should have been on notice of this risk because they knew the school counselor had once taken a student away from school during lunch (with the parent's permission) and that the school counselor had once massaged a student in his office (Buz, 2012). These allegations, if true, do not provide a sufficient basis for the court to conclude school officials had actual notice the school counselor was or could become a child molester (*Doe v. Coleville School District* (2012) WL 554430 (E.D. Wash. Feb. 21, 2012).

A federal court in California refused to dismiss a case against a school counselor in Berkeley, Calif., accused of sexual harassment, spanking, stalking, propositioning, etc. School investigation found his conduct "unprofessional, but not harassment or abuse." The school district settled for $57,500 and agreed to place new restrictions, such as requiring school counselors to keep their door or blinds open when counseling students (Najmabadi, 2012).

SEXUAL HARASSMENT DENYING EQUAL ACCESS

A student confides in you that her chorus teacher is promising her the lead in the spring musical. She says every time he mentions giving her the lead it is always after he gets her alone after class, and he brushes up against her. She tries never to be caught alone with him because she feels he is coming on to her and that he wants something in return for her having the chorus lead. What do you do?

Points to Consider

One form of sexual harassment occurs when a teacher or other school employee makes an educational decision or benefit conditional on the student's submission to unwelcome sexual conduct. If this occurs, it does not matter if the student resists and suffers the consequences or submits to avoid the threatened harm. OCR provides guidance to sexual harassment cases where the perpetrator made educational benefits conditional and the student submitted. "A high school drama teacher tells a student that if she engages in sexual activity with the teacher, she will be given the lead part in a school play. The student agrees to participate in the sexual act but without desiring to do so. The drama teacher thus has limited the student's ability to benefit from the school's education program by conditioning the benefit of receiving the lead role in the school play on the student's submission to unwelcome sexual conduct" (U.S DOE, OCR, 2008, p. 6).

SCHOOL COUNSELORS AS ADVOCATES FOR A SAFE, RESPECTFUL SCHOOL CLIMATE

The principal insists every faculty member serve on a committee. This year, as your service, you would like to form a committee to raise awareness about sexual harassment on the campus. Is this an appropriate role? What will be some of your considerations?

Points to Consider

Playing a role in fostering a school climate encouraging students to report sexual harassment, even if there's no evidence of it in your school, is a worthwhile leadership endeavor. School counselors can serve as another set of eyes and ears as they put into place preventive measures to reduce harassment in the school environment before it starts (Stone, 2003b; ASCA, 2005). Schools and school counselors should "encourage reporting of any behavior that makes students feel uncomfortable" (Perry & Marcum, 2008, p. 36). Students will often fail to report incidents of harassment and those that do "often see no effective action taken by school officials. Therefore, it is important that staff members who observe inappropriate behavior among students and/or staff members report their observations so that an investigation and action may be taken" (Perry & Marcum, 2008, p. 36). Listed below are several recommendations to help your committee get started.

1. Have the committee develop a school policy protecting all students from sexual harassment. A sexual harassment policy should include the following elements:

- A strong, no-tolerance policy, included in a student code of conduct, expressly stating a commitment to maintain an educational environment free of fear and intimidation
- Clearly defined disciplinary consequences for sexual harassment behavior
- Identification of specific sexual harassment behavior
- Listing of applicable laws and definitions of legal terms

- A confidentiality statement outlining limits and protections offered to student victims, e.g., duty to protect another or potential individuals from harm
- Policies to prohibit and prevent retaliation
- Provision of a contact person to whom the victim can report incidents (preferably a school counselor)
- Process for grievance procedures
- Provision for training of school personnel and students (USDOE/OCR, 2001; American School Counselor Association, 2005; National Women's Law Center, 2007).

2. Make the policy widely known. Collaborate in disseminating the sexual harassment policy through student gatherings, club meetings, bulletin boards, brochures, codes of conduct.

3. Establish safe places and mechanisms for students to report sexual harassment anonymously.

4. Develop curriculum to support the policy. Provide lessons for teachers to present to their students centering on tolerance and openness toward differences among people.

5. Educate teachers and staff in your school. Deliver faculty in-services to raise awareness of the issues surrounding sexual harassment. Emphasize school district culpability when educators ignore sexual harassment. Include workshops to relay and create strategies to aid in a positive school climate within and outside the classroom. Educate everyone about the court findings in the face of deliberate indifference to harassment that is pervasive, severe and denies a child an equal educational opportunity.

In a Position to Know: A Counselor Educator Speaks

"As more and more young people have access to computers and cell phones, a new risk to teens is beginning to emerge. Electronic aggression, in the form of threatening text messages and the spread of online rumors on social networking sites, is a growing concern" (Decker, 2007, p. 1).

The case presented at the beginning of the chapter is revisited here and answered by a counselor educator. Compare his answer with your own approach.

CYBER-SEXUAL HARASSMENT

Using computers at both the school and her home, Ashley has been sending Kenneth provocative pictures of herself and long love letters, not seeming to care he has asked her to leave him alone. Ashley has e-mailed her communications to Kenneth and to her friends, who have also sent them to other friends. She is instant-messaging people as to every move Kenneth makes, what he wears and what his after-school activities are each day. All this attention across electronic media feels creepy to Kenneth. Ashley has made such an issue of her "love" for him Kenneth feels he has become the object of ridicule. Despite his embarrassment, he feels frustrated he does not seem to have any recourse with Ashley and must simply endure, continuing to tell her he is not interested. Is this harassment? Could this be sexual harassment? Could Ashley be breaking any laws or school board policies? What recourse, if any, does Kenneth have?

Response From a Counselor Educator

Generally, online harassment or cyberbullying involves the use of information and communication technologies such as e-mail, cell phone and pager text messages, instant messaging (IM), defamatory personal websites and defamatory online personal polling websites, to support deliberate, repeated and hostile behavior by an individual or group, that is intended to harm others (Keith & Martin, 2005).

Sexual harassment in particular occurs when the online communications or information dissemination (via a website or listserv) leads to unwanted sexual attention, creates a hostile environment or becomes quid pro quo harassment. Hostile environment harassment occurs when unwelcome conduct of a sexual nature is so severe, persistent or pervasive that it affects a student's ability to participate in or benefit from an education program or activity or creates an intimidating, threatening or abusive educational environment. A hostile environment can be created by a school employee, another student or even someone visiting the school, such as a student or employee from another school.

Quid pro quo harassment occurs when a school employee causes a student to believe he or she must submit to unwelcome sexual conduct to participate in a school program or activity. It can also occur when an employee causes a student to believe the employee will make an educational decision based on whether or not the student submits to unwelcome sexual conduct. When a teacher threatens to fail a student unless the student agrees to date the teacher, it is quid pro quo harassment. In the case described in our scenario, quid pro quo sexual harassment could occur if Ashley promises to stop the online sexual harassment if Kenneth were to go on a date with her or perhaps even "hook up" (see Office for Civil Rights at *www.ed.gov/about/offices/list/ocr/qa-sexharass.html*).

Is Kenneth experiencing online harassment? I think yes. His unpleasant emotions resulting from the persistent and now pervasive comments from Ashley are a key indicator. Is sexual harassment occurring in the scenario involving Ashley and Kenneth? Not sure. It is at the very least inappropriate and irresponsible. If Kenneth's experience, however, meets the criteria of hostile environment or quid pro quo harassment as previously described, it is likely then to be preventing him from participating in or benefiting from his education and could easily be considered a case of sexual harassment.

Ashley is hurting Kenneth with her words and actions, although what she may not realize is that she may also be hurting herself. For instance, each school typically has an acceptable-use policy specifying what a student (or staff member) can or cannot do while using technology, such as the school's Internet service. Increasingly, schools throughout the country have also chosen to deal with online harassment among their students as part of the student code of conduct, even when the harassing behaviors originated from outside of school property. For example, Florida passed a law in 2008, the Jeffrey Johnston Stand Up for All Students Act, (see *http://tinyurl.com/9krbaj* for the entire statute) requiring schools to create policies about cyberbullying and harassment and empowering them to use their disciplinary procedures to confront this problem even when it occurs "through the use of data or computer software that is accessed through a computer, computer system or computer network of a public K-12 educational institution."

In Missouri, as in other states, laws are being passed to better reflect current technologies so bullying/harassment can be considered criminal when it occurs beyond just personal communication, the written word or over the telephone. And, because technology has made stalking easier and more intense, laws are responding by including more serious punishment such as increased jail time (to learn more about state bullying laws, visit *www.bullypolice.org*). So, in this case, Ashley can be subject to a range of consequences from a denial of Internet services by the service provider, to school suspension, to criminal litigation and/or prosecution.

Being harassed, sexually harassed or stalked is a horrible experience for many and has proven to be a difficult issue to prevent. The Internet offers several features that seem to exacerbate the prevalence, incidence and intensity of these offenses. Among them are:

Anonymity: The Internet provides an almost unprecedented opportunity to communicate with others while remaining anonymous. In fact, some websites are set up to help others surf the Web and communicate without being detected (for example, *http://anonymouse.ws*). The relative anonymity of the Internet can create an outlet for outrageous, often sexist or degrading communication that would otherwise be suppressed.

Instantaneous connectivity: Anyone can now proliferate a communication, photo, video or audio over the Internet within seconds without even having to be on a computer. Cell phones, personal digital assistants, even digital cameras have the capability to post information on the Internet from virtually anywhere and at any time. Once posted, the message can be automatically disseminated via blogs, listservs, file transfer and a host of other electronic media.

Lack of nonverbal cues: Face-to-face communication provides a context for the listener, providing the opportunity to balance actual content of a message with the speaker's facial expressions, intonations and volume. Absent the visual clues, telephone communications provide the same features, with the added benefit of timing (for example, a middle-of-the-night phone call vs. a midday call). In contrast, online communication via written text is generally one-dimensional. This problem of text-only communication often leads to misunderstandings and missteps, particularly regarding sexual issues (Bell & de la Rue, 1995).

Pile-on effect: Speed combined with the sheer number of people one can send information to can foster a hostile environment within hours. The advanced technology of the Internet makes it much easier for a cyber-stalker to encourage third parties to join in the harassing or threatening communications of a victim, triggering a pile-on effect whereby viewers of the original message will add their own caustic message to the conversation (also known as a thread), inciting further offenses.

Removal of space, place and time barriers: Offline stalking or harassment generally requires all involved (perpetrators and victims) to be located in the same geographic area; in cyberspace, they may be located across the street or across the planet. The ease of the Internet's availability, where just about anyone can access it, lowers the barriers to harassment. A cyber-stalker does not need to physically confront a victim.

Although dealing with harassment or stalking over electronic media can be frustrating and lead to a level of hopelessness, there are measures one can take to help stop it. Following are strategies you can tell students to adopt if they are being harassed over electronic media.

Get support. Do not deal with this potentially dangerous situation by yourself. You must tell your parents/guardians or another trusted adult (school counselor, teacher, other educator) immediately.

Pay attention to the stalker or harasser – and to yourself. Never ignore the first signs of stalking. You have a creepy feeling about someone? Sit up and take notice. Always, always trust your instincts. It beats someday saying, "I knew there was something wrong; I wish I'd paid attention."

Save every piece of communication relating to the situation. Save every piece of communication you get from this person: e-mails, instant messages, postings, website content. Later you may need to provide copies of each harassing communication to others such as school administrators, Internet service providers, network system administrators or even the police. In addition to your archive of communications, start a log explaining the situation in more detail. Document how the harassment is affecting your life, and document what steps you're taking to stop it.

Tell the harasser or stalker to cease and desist. It's important that you contact the perpetrator directly, telling him or her in simple, strong and formal terms to stop contacting you or communicating to others about you. You must state that the communications are unwanted and inappropriate and that you will take further action if it does not stop. Don't worry about whether your letter sounds too harsh; make sure it's professional and to the point. Copy your postmaster and the harasser's postmaster. Save a copy of the mail you've sent, and note in your log that you saved it.

After you send this mail, your communication to this person must stop. Any further communication can feed the situation. Your attention will reward the harasser, so the behavior will continue. Also, if the case goes to court, your harasser can report that the communication was going both ways, and it could damage your case. It's best to keep quiet no matter how tempted you are to defend yourself. It's important that you tell your friends not to communicate with the harasser in your defense for the same reasons.

Report your experience to the appropriate people. Report the situation to your parent(s)/guardian(s) immediately and, together with them, your school's principal. If appropriate, also work with your local authorities (police, FBI) and file a report with the National Center for Missing & Exploited Children (*www.missingkids.com*). Many states have modified their stalking laws to include electronic communications. Often states will let you file for a restraining order in cases like this, and the courts will often let you ask that your harasser pay for any filing fees. You'll need the person's address if you want to serve them with a restraining order or press charges against them. The police can get this information from the harasser's postmaster if needed. Offline charges such as defamation or libel, invasion of privacy or infliction of emotional distress can apply in an online environment.

Protect your online space. Change your password frequently. Pay attention to your files, directories and last logout information. Monitor information about yourself on the Internet with Google and other search engines.

Protect your offline space. Take all the precautions you would if an old boyfriend or girlfriend were acting inappropriately, especially if you think the harasser can find you at home or at work.
– *Russell A. Sabella, Ph.D., Professor, Florida Gulf Coast University*

Making Connections

1. How can you help determine the extent and prevalence of sexual harassment in your school? What are some of the strategies you can suggest to reduce sexual harassment for your students?

2. See if your school has a sexual harassment policy. Read the policy and highlight parts you think the school could strengthen as well as sections the school is successfully implementing.

3. Sexual harassment is emotionally costly to students. In what other ways does it take its toll on students and schools?

4. How does Title IX support students who are being sexually harassed? Why does the Office for Civil Rights recommend you keep the identity of the victim confidential?

5. Discuss why sex between a teacher and a secondary student is not recognized by boards of education and state statutes as being consensual sex.

Key Terms

Breach of trust
Deliberate indifference
Hostile environment
Liability
Office for Civil Rights
Quid pro quo harassment

Sexual harassment
Sexual harassment policy
Student-on-student sexual
  harassment
Teacher-on-student sexual
  harassment

CHAPTER 12

Bullying, Cyberbullying and Sexting

IN THIS CHAPTER

Objectives

By the time you complete this chapter, you should be able to:

- Discuss the prevalence of bullying in schools
- Classify the different forms of bullying and the different ways others can be included
- Discuss the roles of school counselors regarding discipline as it pertains to bullying
- Describe how bullying can violate a student's civil rights
- Describe a bully-cide incidence
- Cite court cases where the identity of the victim is protected
- Identify anti-bullying policies in schools, and explain how they are implemented
- Describe cyberbullying as it relates to First-Amendment rights
- Identify the complications of substantial disruption
- Define sexting and its negative consequences.

Ethical Standards Addressed in This Chapter

Professionalism means knowing your professional association's codes and adhering to them. The ASCA Ethical Standards for School Counselors most relevant to this chapter are the following:

- Professional school counselors inform parents/guardians and/or appropriate authorities when a student poses a danger to self or others. This is to be done after careful deliberation and consultation with other counseling professionals (A.7.a).
- Professional school counselors are knowledgeable of laws, regulations and policies relating to students and strive to protect and inform students of their rights.(A.1.d)
- Professional school counselors have a primary obligation to the students, who are to be treated with dignity and respect as unique individuals (A.1.a).
- Professional school counselors are concerned with the educational, academic, career, personal and social needs and encourage the maximum development of every student (A.1.b).
- Professional school counselors support and protect students' best interest against any infringement of their educational program. (D.1.a)

- Professional school counselors inform appropriate officials, in accordance with school policy, of conditions that may be potentially disruptive or damaging to the school's mission, personnel and property while honoring the confidentiality between the student and the school counselor. (D.1.b)
- Professional school counselors assist in developing: (1) curricular and environmental conditions appropriate for the school and community; (2) educational procedures and programs to meet students' developmental needs; (3) a systematic evaluation process for comprehensive, developmental, standards-based school counseling programs, services and personnel; and (4) a data-driven evaluation process guiding the comprehensive, developmental school counseling program and service delivery. (D.1.g)
- Professional school counselors collaborate with community agencies, organizations and individuals in students' best interest and without regard to personal reward or remuneration (D.2.a)

The full text of the ASCA Ethical Standards for School Counselors is available at *www.schoolcounselor.org*.

Introduction

School counselors have a great deal of influence and impact in helping create a safe and respectful school climate. Through collaboration with teachers and administrators, school counselors help raise awareness and knowledge about the emotional needs of students (Austin, Reynolds, Barnes, 2012) and teach students needed skills through a variety of proactive measures such as schoolwide behavior modification programs, classroom guidance lessons, small groups and individual work with students. Bullying is the most common form of school violence. Bullying in middle schools appears much more common than at other levels, with 39 percent of middle school students reporting that bullying occurred at school daily or at least once a week, compared with 20 percent of primary and high school students (Neiman, 2011). A higher percentage of males (10 percent) than females (8 percent) reported being physically bullied, such as being pushed, shoved, kicked or spit on (Robers, Zhang & Truman, 2012).

Technology has expanded the social lives of teenagers but has also offered more opportunities for student-to-student bullying and harassment. Bullying is no longer confined to the lunchroom or face-to-face contact, as cyberbullies are online around the clock. Students have taken cyberbullying to new heights, often not realizing the implications of their actions. Technology has brought a disturbing, dark side to bullying because it allows a student to inflict pain with anonymity or perceived anonymity, sometimes even without being forced to see the effect of bullying on the victim. Power balances are different from those in traditional bullying, since such factors as physical strength, energy and courage take on a lesser importance (Sabella, 2012).

The National Center for Education Statistics (2011) presented "Student Reports of Bullying and Cyber-Bullying: Results from the 2009 School Crime Supplement to the National Crime Victimization Survey." These findings illuminate the issue of bullying and cyberbullying. The National Center for Education Statistics (NCES) data show 28 percent of students ages 12 through 18 were bullied at school in the 2008–2009 school year. Approximately 6,500 public and private school students grades six–12 self-reported the following for the school year 2008–09:

- 28 percent reported being bullied at school.
- Bullying decreased as their grade level increased from 39.4 percent in sixth grade to 20.4 percent in 12th grade.
- Bullied students more frequently reported being afraid of being attacked on the way to or from school (10.8 percent) compared with students who were not bullied (1.7 percent).
- About 6 percent of students ages 12 through 18 reported they were cyberbullied (anywhere) during the 2008–09 school year.
- Students who engaged in a fight on school grounds reported a higher percentage of being cyberbullied (15.6 percent), compared with students who were not cyberbullied (5.1 percent).
- A higher percentage of students who reported being cyberbullied skipped school during the 2008–09 school year (4.0 percent), compared with 0.4 percent of students who were not cyberbullied.

In an April 2013 survey, ASCA members responded that they, too, see bullying as a problem in their school. The positive news is that the respondents also felt their school's approach to handling bullying was intentional, methodical and that their school administration was responsive to acts of bullying (Stone, 2013e).

	Strongly Agree or Agree	Neutral	Disagree or Strongly Disagree
Bullying is a problem at my school.	69 percent	20 percent	11 percent
My school has an intentional and methodical procedure for handling acts of bullying.	69 percent	15 percent	16 percent
My school has a practical, well-thought-out, research-based protocol to handle acts of bullying.	44 percent	28 percent	28 percent
My school uses an informal approach when handling acts of bullying.	38 percent	17 percent	45 percent
My school administration is responsive to acts of bullying.	86 percent	9 percent	5 percent
My school district provides professional development for all educators on how to identify and react to bullying.	45 percent	19 percent	36 percent

In this same survey, almost the exact percentage (69 percent) that thought bullying was a problem at their school responded that cyberbullying is a problem in their school (68 percent). About half the respondents (48 percent) thought their administrators' approach to handling cyberbullying was effective.

	Strongly Agree or Agree	Neutral	Disagree or Strongly Disagree
Cyberbullying is a problem at my school.	68 percent	16 percent	16 percent
My school district has a policy addressing cyberbullying.	62 percent	22 percent	16 percent
My school district's policy on cyberbullying is effective.	22 percent	53 percent	25 percent
My individual school has a policy addressing cyberbullying.	46 percent	26 percent	28 percent

	Strongly Agree or Agree	Neutral	Disagree or Strongly Disagree
My school administration is effective at responding to cyberbullying.	48 percent	35 percent	17 percent
Sexting is a problem at my school.	33 percent	30 percent	37 percent

The courts continue to offer disparate judgments and confusion in cases of cyber-speech. "It is exceedingly difficult for a school or court to parse out which bullying happened off campus (and can be ignored so as to protect the bully's First-Amendment rights) and which bullying happened on campus" (National School Board Association, 2011). Three student cyber-speech cases were jointly presented to the United States Supreme Court; "*J.S. v. Blue Mountain School District, Layshock v. Hermitage School District* and *Kowalski v. Berkeley Count School District*. Unfortunately, in January 2012 the Supreme Court announced it was unwilling to accept the cases and allowed the lower courts decisions to stand (Huffington Post, 2012). Six education associations led by the National School Boards Association filed a friendly brief (*amici curiae*) in hopes a Supreme Court ruling would result in standards administrators could follow in addressing off-campus cyber-speech affecting the on-campus learning environment. Administrators have the daunting job of determining when cyber-speech represents a substantial disruption to the educational environment; however, the courts have not provided an operational definition of substantial disruption. (National School Board Association, 2012). The lower court rulings are mixed, and the muddiness continues in determining when off-campus speech creates a substantial disruption to the learning environment. School district officials are obligated under federal laws to seek to remedy bullying and harassment that is severe, pervasive and objectively offensive. These statutes do not distinguish between whether bullying happened on or off campus. The responsibility to act is clear, yet substantial disruption is not clear or in any way standardized.

Identifying traits and characteristics of the bullies and the bystanders has been the subject of many research articles of late. The parties to bullying and their roles have been culled from research by Austin, Reynolds & Barnes, 2012; Barboza, Schiamberg, Ochmke, Korzeniewski, Post & Heraux, 2009; Rivers, Poteat, Noret & Ashurst, 2009; Wei & Williams, 2009; Wolke, Woods & Samara, 2009. Their findings follow:

Bully aides are students who "actively encourage the bullies" (p.285). They can be people who lack the social capital or social leadership to be a bully, but they would enjoy the role if and when they could do it. "They lack empathy for victims and admire bullies" (p.285). They believe they are friends with the bully although this is not the case. Interventions could include encouraging the students to do altruistic activities such as to "participate in leadership roles in food drives" (p.285), which hopefully would also develop empathy.

Bully supporters are students who laugh when bullying is taking place (Rivers, et. al., 2009) and provide the bully with an approving audience. Interventions might include helping the supporters develop confidence in their own decision-making abilities so they are not always prone to just go with the crowd (Austin et.al. 2012).

Defenders are usually females who guard the victims by actively stepping in to stop the bullying, then consoling the victim after (Rivers et al., 2009). Defenders are often friends of the victim or attention seekers who crave the admiration they receive when they are involved in "drama" (Austin et.al., 2012, p. 286). Intervention might include helping them develop strategies to cope with viewing the mistreatment of others.

Bullies are often students with dominant personalities who lack empathy (Wei & Williams, 2009). Bully behavior may be learned or be a mode for manipulation. They are often delinquent students with less involvement in school activities who are prone to criminal tendencies (River, et al., 2009). Interventions might include educators encouraging them to participate in service activities that may help them be more empathetic (Barboza, et.al. 2009).

Victims can be either classified as chronic (always victims) or acute (targeted based on an action), characterized by low self-esteem, social awkwardness, high anxiety and high risk for suicide (Wolke, et al., 2009). Interventions could include classroom guidance and small groups designed to help students build interpersonal skills (Austin et.al. 2012).

Witnesses are students who are aware bullying is taking place, do their best to avoid it and, because they are empathetic, suffer when they know it is happening. These students are prone to depression, post-traumatic stress, drug and alcohol abuse and suicidal tendencies (Rivers, et al., 2009). These risks heighten when their parents are violent. Interventions might include individual counseling (Austin et.al. 2012).

Getting Started: What Would You Do?

The following case is discussed at the end of this chapter by a school counselor. Before reading her responses, formulate how to approach this ethical dilemma.

SCHOOL COUNSELORS AND BULLY PROOFING

The discipline referral rate for bullying in your school is high. You conduct an anonymous schoolwide survey and learn bullying is a problem for many students in fourth and fifth grade. What might you do to try and create a safer school climate for students?

Working Through Case Studies

SUBSTANTIAL DISRUPTION AND CYBERSPACE SPEECH

Rachel, a student, comes to you distraught that she was being called a "slut with herpes" by Ruth, a classmate, on Ruth's MySpace page. Ruth asked others to join her in humiliating Rachel. Rachel is desperate for your help to stop this bullying. You take it to the principal, who expresses concern for Rachel and promises to call in Ruth and her parents, but she says her hands are tied as far as being able to punish Ruth because the cyber-speech did not cause a disruption to the educational environment, and a future disruption is not predicted. You are distressed to think there is no recourse for this student other than asking the bully to behave. Is your principal correct?

Points to Consider

Berkeley County School District in West Virginia disciplined Kara Kowalski for starting a MySpace page that successfully invited others to make offensive comments and bully a student who was called a "slut" with "herpes." The Fourth Circuit court cited *Tinker v. Des Moines Independent Community School District* (393 U.S. 503, 1969), which supported the school district's discipline of the cyberbully. *Tinker*, a U.S. Supreme Court case, defined the First-Amendment rights of students in public schools and supports the conclusion that public schools have a compelling interest in regulating speech interfering with or disrupting the work and discipline of the school, including discipline for student-on-student harassment and bullying. The court in the Kowalski case determined that it was reasonably foreseeable that the speech would reach the school, so it was "satisfied that the nexus of Kowalski's speech was sufficiently strong to justify the action taken by school officials in carrying out their role as the trustees of the student body's well-being" (National School Board Association, 2012).

However, your principal in her assessment of Rachel's situation could also be correct. Why? Courts are issuing decisions in disparate ways, and administrators do not have a clear-cut standard they can use to regulate and punish online speech. School officials cannot and should not feel confident that *Kowalski v. Berkeley County School District* is the last word in online speech and discipline. Rightfully so, the administration is confused by substantial disruption as the courts have found against districts that have tried to intervene in cyberbullying. In *J.C. v. Beverly Hill*, a 13-year-old girl was being cyberbullied. The district tried to intervene and implement discipline against the alleged bully, but the courts sided with the bully and found the district violated the student's First-Amendment rights. The school district failed to meet the burden of establishing a substantial disruption resulting from the cyber-speech and, thus, violated the student's First-Amendment rights. In addressing the issue, the administrator had to dedicate time to address the victim's concerns and the concerns of her parents. Five students missed classes, and the victim remained fearful on-campus bullying and gossip would follow. However, the courts didn't consider all of this attention to the problem to be a substantial disruption.

ASCA; the National School Boards Association; the Gay, Lesbian, and Straight Education Network; the National Association of Elementary School Principals; the National Association of Secondary School Principals; the Pennsylvania School Boards Association; and the School Social Work Association of America all had high hopes when they filed an *amici curiae* brief in the cases *J.S. v. Blue Mountain School District* and *Layshock v. Hermitage School District*. These educational associations were seeking clarity and guidance for online conduct through court resolution (National School Board Association, 2012). Two student cyber-speech cases were jointly presented to the U.S. Supreme Court along with *Kowalski v. Berkeley County School District*. The Supreme Court announced it was unwilling to accept the cases and allowed the lower courts' decisions to stand (Huffington Post, 2012), which was a huge blow to administrators across the country struggling with cyber-speech issues. Two of these cases are discussed here.

In "*J.S. v. Blue Mountain School District*, a Pennsylvania middle school student created a spoof MySpace profile page on her home computer for her principal calling him a hairy slut that hit on students along with other vulgar personal attacks. According to the Third Circuit Court of Appeals, the school district failed to demonstrate that it could reasonably forecast that the student's words would cause substantial disruption in school, and therefore, the suspension of the student was a violation of her First-Amendment right to free speech" (National School Board Association, 2011).

The companion case, *Layshock v. Hermitage School District*, also involved a Pennsylvania high school student who created a profile of his principal on MySpace that was disrespectful and lewd. The Third Circuit Court found the school district should not have punished the student "for expressive conduct which occurred outside of the school context" (National School Board Association, 2011, p. 1).

Public school administrators do not need to be in charge of ferreting out offensive student postings, but once they are brought to school officials' attention, they must determine if the speech is a substantial disruption to the learning environment and violates individual rights. Court rulings are not consistent, creating a difficult situation for school administrators to manage as to when they are able to discipline off-campus speech and when discipline will infringe on a student's freedom of speech. In the words of David Hudson, a First Amendment scholar at Vanderbilt University, "The court needs to explain when school officials have the power to regulate off-campus student speech. The phenomenon of cyber-bullying ratchets up the importance of the issue." (Savage, 2012)

ADMINISTRATORS INVOLVING SCHOOL COUNSELORS IN DISCIPLINE

Your administration continually involves you in discipline. In just the past month you have been asked to witness administrators' conversations with students, call parents and talk to them about their child's disruptive behavior and conduct conflict resolution, which was actually a bullying situation and not conflict. You are a team player, but discipline is not your role. What, if anything, can you do?

Points to Consider

Bullying is illegal by state statute in 49 states (all but Montana). Bullying is a discipline problem. School counselors are often asked to help with bullies or the bullied using their specialized skills and an April 2013 survey of ASCA members confirms this is often the case for school counselors. In this same survey, it was evident school counselors try to avoid treating bullying as conflict resolution.

	Strongly Agree or Agree	Neutral	Disagree or Strongly Disagree
My school administration asks me to do conflict resolution when the problem is actually a bullying situation and not a conflict.	26 percent	22 percent	52 percent
I am willing to work with students on conflict resolution, but when I discover it is a bullying situation and not conflict I immediately refer to the administration.	66 percent	19 percent	15 percent

School counselors struggle with the predicament of administrators involving them in discipline (Bryan, Day-Vines, Griffin & Moore-Thomas, 2012). Often this involvement is as a valued member of the school with specialized skills and abilities to participate in the overall effort to evaluate behavior and/or remediate behavior as part of the effort to stop bullying. However, a fair percentage of respondents (17 percent) to this survey said they are not just part of a larger plan or effort but that they are the plan, i.e., "school administration involves me in working with bullies instead of or in place of disciplining the bully" (Stone, 2013e).

	Every Time and Almost Every Time	Occasionally/ Sometimes	Almost Never or Never
My school administration involves me in working with bullies as part of the disciplining of bullying.	41 percent	35 percent	24 percent
My school administration involves me in working with bullies instead of or in place of disciplining the bully.	17 percent	46 percent	37 percent

School counselors are involved in helping teachers with disruptive students to support a student needing school counselor intervention before the teacher has to resort to discipline. School counselors are involved in helping to remedy disruption or unproductive behavior through membership on discipline committees, behavior modification programs, mediation, parent conferences, classroom guidance lessons, individual counseling and small-group counseling, just to name a few. Discipline is a role school counselors try to avoid as it can change the nature of the student/school counselor relationship from nonthreatening to threatening. Trust is an underlying factor in counseling, and it can be shaken with this role confusion. School counselors are not disciplinarians but facilitators of growth (American School Counselor Association, 2005).

In this same survey (Stone, 2013e), respondents indicated just how much their specialized skills are used in proactive methods to try to prevent bullying. Individual counseling (86 percent) was on par with school and classroom rules (87 percent) as a proactive means for administrators to rely on in addressing bullying.

Which of the following proactive methods does your school currently use to prevent bullying (Check all that apply):

	Percentage
School and classroom rules	87 percent
Individual counseling for students	86 percent
Classroom guidance lessons	66 percent
Schoolwide assemblies	52 percent
Group counseling	47 percent

Teacher in-services/professional development	45 percent
Classroom meetings	34 percent
Parent meetings	23 percent

THREATS OF BULLYING AND IMMEDIATE RESPONSES

You receive an e-mail from a student expressing fear of another student, describing incidents of being punched by this student, and asking you for ideas to help him cope with the bullying. You were in the middle of state testing and needed to proctor a test. You fully intended to get back to the student immediately but one interruption led to another, and it was two days later when it hit you that you had not responded to this student. Are there any legal and ethical issues here?

Points to Consider

Rosenstein was a middle school student at Eric Smith Middle School and was being continuously bullied by another student. The bullying was so incessant that Rosenstein e-mailed his school counselor asking for coping mechanisms to deal with it. Rosenstein also e-mailed the assistant principal stating he would like to have his bullying instances on file. Three months later Rosenstein was punched in the stomach by his bully. This injury resulted in a blood clot, 19 surgeries and paralysis from the waist down. Rosenstein filed a lawsuit against his attacker and school officials in 2009. Rosenstein stated that school officials knew about his attacker's violent tendencies and revealed other punching instances his attacker had with other students. The Ramsey Board of Education never agreed to any wrongdoing but settled with Rosenstein for $4.2 million (Leitsinger, 2012).

Shannon Sugg was a freshman in an Albuquerque Public School District when a fellow student, Alicia Andres, allegedly began tormenting her by pushing, shoving, kicking and making threats on her life. After approximately five of these incidents took place, Sugg sought the assistance of her school counselor, Vic Fantozzi, who allegedly told Sugg to try and work things out with Andres and inquired about Sugg's own conduct to see if her actions may have perpetuated the confrontation. He also spoke with Andres about the situation. Following Sugg's visit to the school counselor, Andres and a group of girls surrounded Sugg, and Andres threatened her with a knife. Sugg started missing her fourth-period English classes. Sugg's mother went to the school and spoke with Patricia Watts, a school administrator, about her daughter's absences. Sugg's father participated in the conference via the telephone. When Sugg was called into the meeting, she told her parents and Watts about Andres threatening to stab her or push her down the stairs. Watts was unable to locate Andres on the school computer and told Sugg and her parents she would need the exact spelling of the student's name to proceed. Watts told Sugg she should not get into a fight with Andres because she would be suspended from school. After the conversation, Sugg was instructed to go back to her classes. Later that same afternoon, after lunch, Andres stabbed Sugg in the left shoulder. Sugg's parents filed a claim against Albuquerque School Board members, a number of administrators and also the school counselor. The lower court refused to dismiss the case, but when the school district appealed the higher court dismissed the case saying under qualified immunity (making it difficult to sue government agencies) that the school district did not violate Sugg's right to due process (*Sugg v. Albuquerque Public School District* (1999)).

It can be difficult to drop everything and act when so many people depend on school counselors and pull at them in so many different directions. However, the risk of harm meant Rosenstein and Sugg's situations needed attention as soon as possible. If the school counselor in the Sugg case had brought the situation to the principal's attention, then this administrator would have at least had Andres' full name, as the school counselor knew it. Regardless, administration needed to dig deeper to find the perpetrator. This response may not have made any difference, but it would certainly have demonstrated a higher standard of care on the part of school officials.

Bullying incidents brought directly to the school counselor's attention should be reported to administration with few exceptions, and then the school counselor should consult and seek supervision. *In loco parentis* requires we act in place of the parents and can be considered negligent if a student is harmed.

The organization Bully Police USA (2013) provides a website with links to the specific laws and regulations against bullying for each state at *www.bullypolice.org*. The Education Commission of the States is also a good source for information about state anti-bullying statutes at *www.ecs.org*.

DIFFICULT-TO-STOP BULLYING

Last year a group of female students took harassment to a new level. They were caught on the school's security camera vandalizing the bathrooms and threatening other students, but the girls still pled innocent. At a meeting attended by the principal, school counselors, students and parents, the girls refused to acknowledge their guilt. They continued to threaten students outside their group. This school district has a policy in place defining harassment and the steps to take when dealing with it. The school followed the procedure, asking the parents and students to meet with school officials. However, the parents are themselves combative, and the negative behavior continues. Is there a role for the school counselor in this situation? What other considerations must be addressed in seeking a solution?

Points to Consider

This scenario of stubborn discipline problems is a reality. Student offenders and their parents are sometimes unwilling to acknowledge the existence of the harassing behaviors and tend to blame everyone else. A safe environment is a basic need for all children in schools, but educators are called on to make magic happen in some of these stubborn cases.

"Lawsuits against the parents of alleged bullies are rare, since school officials are usually the first to be accused of not doing enough to stop bullying. But *Shaposhnikov v. the Pacifica School District and John Roes 1-10* may be part of a new approach to finding legal fault, and somebody to pay financial damages, when bullying goes unchallenged, experts say" (Wykes, 2005, p. 1). In this case, a group of parents settled a lawsuit filed by Mark Shaposhnikov, whose son, a competitive dancer, was taunted with homosexual slurs for two years in middle school. Shaposhnikov says he met many times with school officials and that nothing changed until he filed the lawsuit. The suit used a legal principle called vicarious liability meaning the parents are responsible for the emotional distress their children are inflicting on others... Six of the parents of alleged bullies named in the suit settled, but terms of the deal are confidential (Wykes, 2005, p. 1).

In a recent 2012 lawsuit, the Culter family sued the families of two bullies after the Cutlers' home was vandalized, and their daughter was continuously bullied. The bullies tormented the minor through verbal abuse on social media networks, placing pictures of Dora the Explorer at the family's residence and ridiculing the minor at pool parties and at school. The Culters tried to ignore the bullying, but it started to take a toll on their daughter's emotional well-being. Therefore, the Culters decided to confront the bullies' parents, but the bullies' parents failed to take responsibility for their children's actions. Cecilia Culter, the victim's mother, stated that the police captain, the father of one of the bullies, even tried to intimidate Cutler into dropping the lawsuit by suggesting he could disregard police reports. The Culters maintained that the civil suit was not about the money but about giving their daughter peace of mind (Florendo & Bell, 2012).

Educators cannot always change behavior, but this is a good role for the school counselor to try to tackle in this situation. The school counselor can facilitate change through the use of leadership and advocacy skills. By engaging the administration, faculty and students in collaborative problem solving, school counselors can be instrumental in helping determine the underlying causes of harassment. School counselors who are knowledgeable about the various curricula resources can help facilitate change. One such resource, The Kinder & Braver World Project, hosts a series of papers with research-based strategies for schools to use as they develop bullying prevention and intervention practices and policies. This resource is located at *http://cyber.law.harvard.edu/node/7491.*

BULLYING BASED ON RACE, COLOR, SEX, NATIONAL ORIGIN, DISABILITY, HARASSMENT AND CIVIL RIGHTS

Aalia, a new student from Tunisia, is the first student in your memory who has come to this school wearing a hijab, a headdress often worn by Muslim women to meet religious requirements for modesty. You wonder if the fact that her dress is different will bring any kind of harassment or bullying but decide to take a wait-and-see approach. Several days after Aalia arrives at school you check in with her and, as feared, find she is experiencing verbal and physical harassment. Aalia had her hijab pulled off and thrown to the ground with taunts about her religion and nationality. Several students came to her aid and spoke up on Aalia's behalf, but some students pretended not to notice the harassment. What are your obligations in this situation? Are Aalia's civil rights being violated?

Points to Consider
The U.S. Department of Education's Office for Civil Rights (OCR) issued a Dear Colleague Letter explaining that some instances of bullying may fall

under federal civil rights statutes and regulations enforced by OCR (2010). School staff should be aware that when abusive behavior based on race, color, sex, national origin or disability creates a hostile environment, it violates students' civil rights. Statutes protecting these civil rights include (1) Title VI of the Civil Rights Act of 1964 (Title VI), which prohibits discrimination on the basis of race, color or national origin; (2) Title IX of the Education Amendments of 1972 (Title IX), which prohibits discrimination on the basis of sex; (3) Section 504 of the Rehabilitation Act of 1973 (Section 504); and (4) Title II of the Americans with Disabilities Act (Title II). Section 504 and Title II prohibit discrimination on the basis of disability (U.S. Department of Education Office for Civil Rights, 2010). These statutes require that schools respond directly to such discriminatory harassment to protect students' civil rights. The government has also put other policies in place like No Child Left Behind (2001), which ensures considerable attention is focused on creating and maintaining educational environments that are safe, drug-free and conducive to learning, an especially difficult task in some of America's schools.

PROTECTING POTENTIAL VICTIMS

Marsha tells you she heard Stevie plans to beat her up. You know Stevie well, and you are worried as she is a volatile student. You send for Stevie to meet with Marsha and review with them school board policies related to student fighting. Your impression is that Marsha is scared, and when you get her alone she says she doesn't even know why Stevie hates her. Is there anything more you must do as the school counselor?

Points to Consider

School counselors are often the first members of the school staff to become aware a student might be at risk for harm. As of Feb. 15, 2013, all states but Montana have anti-bullying legislation (Bully Police USA, 2013). Therefore, bullying is illegal in 49 states. This makes it a discipline issue, which requires administration to act. The potential for harm trumps confidentiality as the efforts of the school counselor shift to protecting the student from harm as well as to protect the student from being identified as the one who told. Students will endure great harm to avoid the worse fate of retaliation should it become known they told on their peers.

A school counselor was at the center of a court case that involved bringing the bully and the victim together for conflict resolution. The problem is the well-meaning intervention on the part of the school counselor was misguided and ended disastrously (*Gammon v. Edwardsville Community Unit School District* (1980)). An eighth-grade student was warned by her peers that another student who was making threats against her wished to see her in the restroom. The student went to her school counselor for help. The school counselor testified she had worked extensively with the offending student and had established a good rapport with her. The school counselor brought in the threatening student to give the two girls a chance to air their differences. The school counselor testified that the threatening student's considerable anger was apparent and did not diminish as a result of the joint counseling session or later when the school counselor met privately to warn her suspension would result if any fighting occurred. The school counselor subsequently conferred with the apprehensive student and recommended she avoid any encounter with the other girl. The student continued to express her fears and indicated clearly her difficulties with the aggressor were not over. The school counselor did not notify the administration or playground supervisors. Both girls were on the playground at the same time later in the day, and the aggressor struck the victim in the left eye with her fist, producing a skull fracture so serious it required corrective surgery (*Gammon v. Edwardsville Community Unit School District* (1980)).

The victim's mother contended that the school's response to a known threat of violence on school premises was inadequate under the circumstances. The school counselor was aware of the offending student's prior conduct, and there was evidence school officials knew of prior fighting on her part. The victim's mother argued immediate steps should have been taken following the morning counseling session to discipline the student who threatened her daughter (*Gammon v. Edwardsville Community Unit School District* (1980)).

The court cited the school counselor, as a school official, had *in loco parentis* status: "In all matters relating to the discipline in and conduct of the schools and the school children, they [educators] stand in the relation of parents and guardians of the pupils. This relationship shall extend to all activities connected with the school program and may be exercised at any time for the safety and supervision of the pupils in the absence of their parents or guardians" (Illinois Rev. Statute, 1977).

Professional school counselors must recognize the imbalance of power and unequal emotional responses associated with bullying and treat such cases differently from conflict-resolution cases. The minute this school counselor learned she was in the midst of a bullying situation and not conflict, she should have sought administration and made sure all parties knew of the potential for harm to the victim. School counselors would not bring a bullied student together with the bully unless a mature student would ask to face her tormenter in the safety of an adult who could facilitate. Bullying is illegal behavior, and a prudent school counselor would proceed carefully, assessing the developmental level of the victim before supporting a student's decision to face his or her attacker. This approach can quickly backfire and be dangerous.

PROTECTING THE VICTIM'S IDENTITY

Phillip confides in you he is being bullied by a group of boys. Phillip begs you not to do anything and says he just wants to be moved to another class far away from the boys. He tells you if you tell anyone and it gets back to the boys he is going to be mercilessly bullied. Phillip says, "They have everyone on their side, and even if they get in trouble it will not stop them. They will find ways to make me pay. I just want to be able to move to another class." Your instincts tell you to follow Phillip's instructions. You are looking into his eyes, and you see the fear and pain. You know that in your state bullying is illegal, and you have to notify administration. However, you are determined to work with the administration to develop a plan to protect Phillip's identity as the one who told because you know the administration will need to take steps to remedy the bullying.

Points to Consider

Shea Albers was bullied by three students while in seventh grade. He complained to his parents, who then contacted the school. The principal wanted to know the names of the students, but Shea and his mother would not disclose the information for fear of retaliation. A social worker, Breen, was then brought in to talk with Shea. Shea disclosed the names to Breen, who in turn told the principal. The principal told one of the bullies Shea had been complaining about being bullied by them. To avoid harm, Shea transferred to a new school and filed suit against the social worker and the principal. The circuit court and the appellate court dismissed the case (*Albers v. Breen*, 346 Ill.App.3d 799, 806 N.E.2d 667 (4th Dist.

2004)) on the basis of protections for school personnel under the state's Tort Immunity Act. The court understood the difficulty school principals have in trying to make discretionary decisions in dealing with bullying, stating that, "Certainly the way that a principal handles an instance of bullying in his school falls within the definition [of a discretionary act]; any student who has been sent to the principal's office could attest that he has broad discretion in how to handle such situations."

Even though the Albers case did not result in a ruling in the student's favor, revealing a student's name and complaint to the bullies should be avoided. To behave otherwise victimizes students like Shea twice and can inflame the situation, resulting in emotional distress for the bullied that could end up being worse than the bullying itself. Confidentiality presents a difficult dilemma for us. Supporting Phillip will be an ongoing process made more complicated by the fact that, whether his name is used or not, the bullies may well conclude Phillip told, and the reality is as educators we cannot protect Phillip at all times. The fear of retaliation is often the reason students do not confide in educators. Even if educators can protect students from further bullying at school, students know we cannot protect them from being bullied outside of school or, worse, the cruelty of social isolation that may follow when students tell on their peers. Even though bullying statutes and federal legislation prohibit retaliation, school officials need to reassure students their confidentiality will not be breached, especially to the perpetrator.

Phillip has an advocate in the school counselor, who will hopefully work with administration to minimize the additional trauma an investigation could have on Phillip. Our role is to encourage administration to act to provide a safe and nondiscriminatory environment for all students. School counselors should encourage administrators to allow Phillip to change his schedule so his school environment feels safe to him. Of course it is better to change the bully's schedule rather than the victim's schedule as the bully should be the one who is inconvenienced. Honoring Phillip's request, however, in this case is paramount. Sometimes educators just need to follow the student's lead; students know the players and the circumstances better than the school officials ever could. Administration has to weigh the request for confidentiality and schedule changes against the seriousness of the bullying. Optimally, it is better for an educator to catch the bullies in the act. If possible, remedy the bullying and prevent its reoccurrence without naming Phillip or giving him away as the one who told. The bullied and the bullies should never be brought together except in those rare incidences when the bullied wants to face his or her tormenter in a safe place, and the educator has assurance that the bullied is developmentally able to understand the risks of such a confrontation. Even then, the request to face one's bullies should be the rare approach.

BULLIED STUDENT WHO WANTS TO CHANGE SCHOOLS

Ryan, one of your students, struggles with feelings of inadequacy. Ryan's parents are asking the district to allow their son to go to a different high school to get away from bullies who have followed him for the last two years. Despite their efforts, school officials have not been able to stop the bullying. The principal will not agree to this special assignment, saying "to do so teaches children to run away from their problems." What, if any, might be your role in this situation?

Points to Consider

Shore Regional High School Board of Education v. P.S. (2004) ruled that a school district's failure to protect a student from bullying constituted a denial of a free appropriate public education required by the Individuals with Disabilities Education Act (1990). P.S., a New Jersey ninth-grader, had been teased and bullied throughout elementary school, to the point that he displayed suicidal tendencies and became eligible for special education on the basis of emotional disturbance. His parents wanted him to go to a different high school than the one to which he was assigned so he could avoid being with the same children who had previously emotionally and physically abused him.

Despite repeated complaints, the school administration failed to remedy the situation. After the district refused to place P.S. at the requested high school, the parents decided to take him to an out-of-district high school and requested a due process hearing to obtain reimbursement for the cost of having to go out of district. The new high school's plan was to mainstream P.S. for all his classes. The plan also included a program intended to combat bullying through discipline and diversity seminars. Court testimony described how P.S. thrived both academically and socially at the new high school. The plaintiffs presented testimony that the home high school could not provide P.S. with a free appropriate public education, as required by IDEA. The administrative law judge ordered the school district to reimburse the parents for the out-of-district placement. Perhaps the school counselor could have influenced the administration to relent and allow P.S. to attend the new high school. Special assignments for students are frequently made for far less critical reasons. This is an appropriate process to help principals and others make good decisions on behalf of students and to let students know that in the school counselor they will have support to try to protect them. The principal's comment, "to do so teaches children to run away from their problems" almost sounds like he believes being bullied is a rite of passage to adulthood.

ASCA states, "Professional school counselors collaborate with others in the school and community to promote safe schools and confront issues threatening school safety. Professional school counselors encourage the development of policies supporting a safe school environment, and they provide leadership to the school by assisting in the design and implementation of schoolwide prevention activities and programs. Additionally professional school counselors recognize differentiated interventions are needed for bullying and resolving a conflict. Comprehensive anti-bullying/harassment/violence-prevention and conflict-resolution programs require data-driven decision making, coordination, instruction and program evaluation (ASCA, 2005, p. 1).

CYBERBULLYING

Three girls come to you hysterical as they have become the target of what they guess is about 50 hate text messages that have been flying around today. They know the contents as they have been told and shown the messages by many of their peers. The girls do not want to go back to class, and they want you to help them. What can you do?

Points to Consider

The school counselor in this scenario will want to involve administration. The administrator has the unenviable job of struggling to balance a school's obligation to keep students safe from threats against students' rights to freedom of speech (Conn, 2011). Cyberbullying may be retaliatory, accidental (as in a joke that gets misunderstood) or intentional, with the perpetrator seeking power, belonging or fun. It may take the form of outing (making personal information public), exclusion, impersonation, stalking, baiting or blackmail (Sabella, 2012). Estimates of the pervasiveness of cyberbullying vary widely, depending on the definition of cyberbullying and the age group studied. The Cyberbullying Research Center defines cyberbullying as when someone "repeatedly makes fun of another person online or repeatedly picks on another person through e-mail or text message or when someone posts something online about another person they don't like." They report that about 20 percent of 4,400 randomly selected 11- to 18-year-old students identified as a victim of cyberbullying at some point in their life (Hinduja & Patchin, 2010).

The bullies in cyber situations often remain anonymous, making it difficult for administration to take down certain websites because it takes away the students' rights to free speech (Li, 2007). In New York, there was a student who sent a threatening e-mail to his teacher depicting an image of a gun being aimed at his English teacher's head. The student said the message was sent from a computer off campus and that the school was violating his free-speech rights. Administrators felt they reacted due to their concerns for safety and were right in suspending the student because the student's communication could potentially disrupt the school. Courts found in favor of the school district, saying the e-mail was a true threat to the teacher (Walsh, 2008).

ASCA reminds us that school counselors know children's developmental stages and can provide Internet guidelines to parents and school personnel (ASCA, 2006). School counselors can take a leadership role in implementing policies and practices encouraging students to respect each other online or offline. Research shows creating and promoting a positive school climate where students feel safe and cared about can be an effective means of curtailing cyberbullying (Hinduja & Patchin, 2012). Cyberbullying.us, the website of the Cyberbullying Research Center, and GuardingKids.com, a collection of resources and lesson plans curated by Russell Sabella, Ph.D., are websites for educators who are concerned about youth online safety.

CYBERBULLYING AND ZERO-TOLERANCE POLICIES

You are part of a committee charged by the administration to develop a zero-tolerance policy for cyberbullying on or off campus. What are the legal and ethical implications of such a policy?

Points to Consider

Revisit the case of Substantial Disruption and Cyber Speech at the beginning of this chapter. Students in Kentucky left school by the dozens to avoid what they perceived as a real threat to their safety. Two Bullitt

Central High School freshmen threatened a middle school student on MySpace, one with a picture of himself holding a gun. The school district decided to implement a new no-tolerance school board policy addressing both on school and off school cyber-speech that was bullying. The Kentucky Chapter of the American Civil Liberties Union (ACLU) reminded the school district that students have a right to free speech under the First Amendment and all policies have to carefully define how free speech will be regulated only if it forecasts a substantial disruption. Administrators and school districts are simply not able to write blanket zero-tolerance policies regarding cyberbullying. If taken to court by students and their parents, then the court will want to know how the speech substantially disrupted the school (National Association of Secondary School Principals, 2008).

SEXTING LEADING TO BULLYING

A student comes to you distraught because she sent her boyfriend a sex text, and he forwarded it to a friend who promised to keep it private. From there the picture spread widely. She is reaching out to you for help. What, if anything, can you do?

Points to Consider

Although people have been taking sexually explicit self-portraits for longer than most adults would care to admit, technology has advanced in such a way that these images now spread more quickly than ever. Pictures of girls "go viral," or spread rapidly, more frequently than those of boys because the sexual double standard leads to "slut-shaming" of girls by other girls and because homophobia prevents boys from forwarding pictures of other boys (Boyd, 2011).

Jessica Logan, an 18-year-old high school senior, faced relentless bullying and harassment in her Cincinnati, Ohio, high school after a series of nude cell phone photos of her circulated among students. She spoke out in a television interview, sharing how humiliated and hurt she was and warning other kids about the dangers of sexting. Although her voice was changed and her face was obscured, other kids at her school recognized her, and the situation worsened after the interview (Thomas, 2009).

Jessica had reached out to her school's resource officer for help, but he said there was little he could do since she was 18. After attending the funeral of an acquaintance of hers who had committed suicide, Jessica hung herself in her room the same day. Jessica's parents sued in state court the school, some students, their parents and the school resource officer. Eventually, her parents dropped the lawsuit to re-file in federal court against the school district with the goal of raising constitutional issues (Thomas, 2009). The case was settled in federal district court, with the school district paying her family $155,000 (United Press International, 2012).

Her story spurred the Ohio legislature to pass the Jessica Logan Act in 2012, which redefines bullying to include cyberbullying and dating violence and compels school districts to offer training for educators to address the problem (United Press International, 2012). The school counselor will want to support this student in a number of ways. Do her parents know about the bullying, and will she freely agree to allow the school counselor to involve them? If she is reluctant to allow the school counselor to involve her parents she has to be convinced it is in her best interest that her parents know because this is a crime against their child, and they should be involved from the onset (National Association of Secondary School Principals, 2008). Administration has to be contacted because this is illegal behavior. The administration is in the difficult position of having to protect this student while also protecting the bullies' free-speech rights. Since this is widespread and has even had national exposure, the administration is probably safe in labeling this bullying as creating a substantial disruption to the educational process, meaning the administration can punish and take action against the bullies. Conducting periodic surveys will help assess the environment and what is going on in cyberspace that is hurting students.

SEXTING AND PEDOPHILE CHARGES

You are on a committee to develop an assembly to help students understand the dangers of sexting. You are considering using the alleged information that sexting is illegal and those students who forward nude photos of themselves or others might be charged with distributing child porn. Would you be accurate in telling students that sexting is illegal?

Points to Consider

Margarite, an eighth-grader at Chinook Middle School in Lacey, Wash., was a victim of a sexting ordeal that escalated into child pornography. In fall 2009, Margarite had a crush on another eighth-grade student named Isaiah and sent him a nude picture of herself. Isaiah, after much persuasion, sent the picture to one of Margarite's ex-friends with whom Margarite had a bitter and volatile relationship. Margarite's ex-friend forwarded the text to a large population of the school urging them to forward it to all the people in their contacts. Within minutes parents started calling the school to complain, and Margarite and her mother got calls from concerned parents and friends. Ms. Rae, the principal, called in the police. Isaiah, Margarite's ex-boyfriend and another student were all to be charged with the dissemination of child pornography and spent the night at the county juvenile detention center. If they were charged they would face up to 36 weeks in the juvenile detention center and would have to be registered as sex offenders. Their state allowed young sex offenders to petition for removal from the registry with proof they no longer endangered the public. The district attorney (DA) struck a deal with the students, charging them with telephone harassment and requiring them to complete community service. The case was dismissed. In spring that year, the offending students completed a brochure, PowerPoint presentation and a poster about their experiences with sexting and research about dangers of sexting. The North Thurston Public Schools decided to follow suit and hold sessions to inform parents and students about the laws regarding child pornography and the emotional dangers of sexting. As a stipulation to their deal with the DA the reprimanded students had to attend a mediation session with Margarite. Students and parents were each given the opportunity to share their feelings about the ordeal. Based on disclosure, most participants viewed Isaiah as sincere and apologetic while Margarite's ex-friend was viewed as mechanical. Margarite's father took responsibility for being indulgent with his daughter and expressed how Margarite's decision will always be present in her life.

Miller, et. al. v. Skumanick (2010), a pivotal case in Pennsylvania, involved the threat of child pornography (felony) charges against three girls. The girls had taken provocative pictures of each other during a sleepover in 2008. Teachers later discovered the pictures on the cell phones of their male classmates. School officials confiscated the cell phones and turned them over to Skumanick, the county DA. Skumanick threatened the girls and other students who had stored the pictures on their phones with child pornography charges unless they participated in an educational and counseling re-education program, intended to teach them "what it means to be a girl in today's society." The girls' parents sought representation from the American Civil Liberties Union (ACLU) and sued the DA, arguing that the re-education program violated the 14th

Amendment, which guarantees parents' rights to raise their children as they see fit. They also argued that he violated the girls' First-Amendment right to freedom of expression. After two years of legal proceedings, the Third Court of Appeals ruled in March 2010 that the teens could not be prosecuted under child pornography laws solely for appearing in the images. One commentator summed up the decision, saying, "The court recognized that in pursuing this sexting case, a prosecutor had gone too far in trying to enforce adult moral standards" (McLaughlin, 2010, p.1).

Many states are rewriting their legislation in attempts to avoid an overlap between teen sexting and child pornography. The laws currently in place, some argue, were meant to protect children, but these laws incriminate children in some sexting cases to the detriment of their futures. New laws should protect voluntarily sexted images under the First Amendment, advocates say. Others argue that relaxing these laws could put more children at risk, by hindering prosecution of adults who possess and distribute child pornography. A circulated picture harms the child in it, and that harm can be serious, as it was for Jessica Logan (Sacco, Argudin, Maguire & Tallon, 2010).

Given the new and unique dangers associated with sexting, schools should create opportunities to educate teens about safe digital etiquette and about potential social, legal and professional consequences to risky behavior. As the school employee charged with the social, emotional and career aspects of students, school counselors can take the lead in developing digital safety curricula within a school. Most minors do not know about child pornography laws, but breaking them could land students in prison for five-15 years and place them on a sex offenders list for life (Sacco et. al., 2010). Students should learn about the laws surrounding sexting. They should also learn that, although the laws may change, social and professional consequences are always a risk.

School counselors and other educators can deliver curricula to empower students to make good decisions. In these worst-case scenarios, when a picture does circulate, adults in schools must discipline bullies. Additionally, school counselors must help students to avoid negative thought patterns, such as believing their self-worth depends on how many people have seen them naked (Schwyzer, 2012). As school counselors and educators, it is also important to listen to teens and understand sexting behavior from their perspective. Focus groups and case studies show that teens' perceptions of what is going on when they share sexually explicit content digitally does not necessarily match that of their parents, law enforcement officials or of adults in their schools (Boyd, 2011). Adolescents' brains are wired to reward novelty, excitement and peer approval over the short term. Potentially negative outcomes in the long-term are minimized (Dobbs, 2011). Although many teens recognize the potential negative outcomes associated with sexting, they may need some help from educators to urge them toward safe digital communication. Teens who recognize the risks of sexual activity (pregnancy, STDs) may see sexting as a safer alternative. In some places, having a naked picture of your boyfriend or girlfriend is considered a status symbol, like a "digital hickey" (*The New York Times*, 2011). Understanding your school's culture can be paramount to building trusting relationships with students and building an effective preventive education program. Small groups and classroom guidance lessons can be excellent forums for teaching resiliency skills and healthy relationship skills to girls and to bullying victims. In addition, school counselors should collaborate with administrators and teachers to crack down on name-calling and bullying behavior they see. Digital safety should be a part of every student's health or life skills coursework.

OFFENSIVE LANGUAGE IN CYBERSPACE

Serena, the school newspaper editor, has a blog she runs from home in which she writes freely about the principal's "heavy handiness in controlling what goes into the newspaper" and what a "narrow-minded bigot" he is and his "homophobic editing of anything to do with gays" as to "make me know he is a major douche bag." The principal removed Serena as editor of the school newspaper. Is the principal violating Serena's right to freedom of speech?

Points to Consider

Avery Doninger was junior class secretary, and in this capacity organized school events. She started a blog in which she vented after a less than perfect battle-of-the-bands event. Doninger created and ran her blog from home and wrote freely about the superintendent "g[etting] pissed off" and the school administrators being "douche bags." She also used other offensive language to further scrutinize the school employees. The administrators reacted by barring Doninger from applying for the class secretary as a senior. Doninger's mother sued school officials on behalf of her daughter. She brought her case to the U.S. District Court for the District of Connecticut and requested that a preliminary injunction be implemented allowing Doninger to rerun for senior secretary and enjoy the same privileges of students in that capacity. Her motion was denied by the District Court and 2nd Circuit. After graduating, Avery Doninger became a plaintiff in her case. She asked for damages from the court claiming her First- and 14th-Amendment rights were violated. In 2009, the District Court granted immunity for the school officials for disallowing Doninger from participating in the election, but they let the case against the school officials stand for refusing Avery's right to wear "Team Avery" T-shirts. In 2011 the 2nd Circuit Court sided with school officials and overturned the lower court's verdict regarding the T-shirt (Hader, 2009). Subsequently, the U.S. Supreme Court denied the student's motion declaring that her offensive language revoked her First-Amendment rights (*Doninger v. Niehoff*, 527 F.3d 41 (2d Cir. 2008); Hader, 2009).

SEARCH AND SEIZURE AND CYBERSPACE

The principal is technologically challenged and asks you to go through a student's phone and read the text messages to her. What should be your legal concerns in this situation?

Points to Consider

A reasonable search of a student's possession by school officials occurs when school officials are suspicious of a student's activities and have reason to infer the student has violated school regulations and when a conducted search is directly related to the initial suspicion. In this case however, the principal is drawing the school counselor into a disciplinary situation that might be a case of unreasonable search and seizure. This situation is politically fraught with landmines. To refuse is to appear uncooperative, but to oblige might mean you are now an unwitting party to an illegal search and seizure. As astutely as possible, school counselors will extract themselves from searching the phone's text messages. At the very least the school counselor will want to discuss with the principal the reasons for the search. Are the reasons connected to a strong suspicion the school's code of conduct has been violated, and when the text messages are searched, will school officials only attend to what is directly related to the initial suspicion? Unreasonable search and seizure has been the topic of many court cases involving school officials. One such case was *Klump v. Nazareth Area School District*. In this case, Klump's cell phone was confiscated by a teacher when he violated school rules and used it in class. The teacher and principal later accessed Klump's personal text messages, voicemails and phone calls to classmates to inquire about drug activity. A drug-related text message was received while the officials were in possession of the phone. Officials consequently used this information to determine that the student had violated the school's drug policy. Klump sued the district stating that his Fourth-Amendment rights, which protect against unlawful search and seizure, were violated. The court agreed and ruled in favor of the student, stating that the district "had no reason at the onset to suspect that such a search would reveal that [the student] was violating another school policy" (*Klump v. Nazareth Area School District*, 425 F. Supp.2d 622 (E.D. Pa., 2006).

In a Position to Know: A School Counselor Speaks

The case presented at the beginning of the chapter is revisited here and answered by a school counselor. Compare her answer with your own approach.

SCHOOL COUNSELORS AND BULLY PROOFING

The discipline referral rate for bullying in your school is high. You conduct an anonymous schoolwide survey and learn bullying is a problem for many students in fourth and fifth grades. What might you do to try and create a safer school climate for students?

Response from a School Counselor

Being an elementary school counselor for more than 1,000 students, I was outnumbered. To tackle the bullying problem at my school, I involved all the resources I could muster from inside and outside the school. I established a committee primarily of parent volunteers, and we set our sights on reducing the number of discipline referrals that involved fighting, name-calling, verbal harassment and other forms of bullying. Support and teamwork came from every part of the school: teachers, paraprofessionals, custodians, principal, physical education teacher, and music and art teachers.

Classroom teachers were especially active, and their buy-in for a bully-proofing program was strong because they could immediately see the program resulted in reduction of conflict among students. The teachers were consistent in implementing various conflict-resolution strategies, such as teaching the students to identify bullying behavior and charting it as a class, until they extinguished the behavior. Navy pilots helped mentor students with a history of discipline referrals for conflict. The art, music and physical education teachers and the media specialist coordinated with others and me in the bully-proofing program and made their lessons and activities coincide.

At the end of the year, the efforts reduced the number of discipline referrals from 183 to 98, almost a 50 percent reduction. I believe the ethical school counselor uses his or her time and talents to try to help create a safe, respectful school climate so all students can come to school and not feel molested or abused by others. Bullying is a form of child abuse, just at the hands of other children instead of adults. I believe by working with others who want to see bullying reduced we can make a difference.
– *Mary Ann Dyal, retired Jacksonville, Fla., elementary school counselor and a consultant for anti-bullying programs*

Making Connections

1. Bullying in your school has become so prevalent that your principal wants you to correspond with the neighboring schools to develop interventions or strategies that can lower bullying instances. List five interventions, and discuss how they relate to bullying statistics.

2. There is a group of students at your school who are chronic offenders with regard to bullying. Discipline referrals, pleading and behavior modification have worked only as long as someone is watching these students. You want to try to change their attitudes and beliefs about their right to bully those who are less able to defend themselves. What approach do you use?

3. Principals and teachers often send students with disruptive tendencies to the school counselor's office. As a school counselor, what is your role in working with these students?

4. Michael is an excellent student who excels in extracurricular activities. Recently, you've noticed Michael has started to remove himself from afterschool practices, and his grades have started to decline. Michael has been to your office many times to speak to you about an older student

who keeps bullying him. You have reported the occurrences to the principal, but she has failed to react. How can you advocate for Michael without losing your job?

5. You have recently noticed an increase in sexting at your school. Students often send nude pictures to each other as a form of flirting without realizing the possible implications of this behavior. What would you like to see happen to address this problem?

6. You have noticed an increase in student complaints about being bullied by their classmates on social media sites. What can you do to advocate for these students?

7. Discuss the First Amendment to the U.S. Constitution and how this affects your student's rights in cyberspace.

8. Write up a proposal to present to your school's administration advocating for anonymous reporting of bullying in your school. Include statistics and facts to support your proposal.

Key Terms

Amici curiae brief
Bullying
Bully-cide
Cyberbullying
Cyber-speech
Discriminatory harassment
Immunity

In loco parentis
Jessica Logan Act
Sexting
Slut-shaming
Social bullying
Viral

CHAPTER 13

Violence and Criminal Activity

IN THIS CHAPTER

Objectives

By the time you have completed this chapter, you should be able to:

- Discuss the prevalence of school violence.
- Identify forms of peer-on-peer aggression.
- Define and describe bystander behavior.
- Understand the *Tarasoff* ruling and duty to warn.
- Understand foreseeability and how it affects educators.
- Define risk factors, protective factors and threat assessments.
- Discuss the implications for educators to act and the federal mandates requiring action.
- Describe effective strategies to support a safe and respectful school climate.
- Describe the role of anonymous reporting in providing students with a safe environment.
- Define dating violence and the Office for Civil Rights Mandates to Educators.

Ethical Standards Addressed in This Chapter

Professionalism means knowing your professional associations' codes and adhering to them. The ASCA Ethical Standards for School Counselors most germane to this chapter are the following:

- Professional school counselors recognize the complicated nature of confidentiality in schools and consider each case in context. Keep information confidential unless legal requirements demand confidential information be revealed or a breach is required to prevent serious and foreseeable harm to the student. Serious and foreseeable harm is different for each minor in schools and is defined by students' developmental and chronological age, the setting, parental rights and the nature of the harm. School counselors consult with appropriate professionals when in doubt as to the validity of an exception. (A.2.c)
- Professional school counselors report risk assessments to parents/guardians when they underscore the need to act on behalf of a child at risk; never neglect a risk of harm as students sometimes deceive to avoid further scrutiny and/or parental notification. (A.7.b)
- Professional school counselors monitor the use of assessment results

and interpretations and take reasonable steps to prevent others from misusing the information. (A.9.e)

- Professional school counselors support and protect students' best interest against any infringement of their educational program. (D.1.a)
- Professional school counselors inform appropriate officials, in accordance with school policy, of conditions that may be potentially disruptive or damaging to the school's mission, personnel and property while honoring the confidentiality between the student and the school counselor. (D.1.b)

The full text of the ASCA Ethical Standards for School Counselors is available at *www.schoolcounselor.org*.

Introduction

Violent deaths in school are rare events, but each tragedy has far-reaching effects beyond the school community. The unfathomable events on Dec. 14, 2012, in Newtown, Conn., are a shocking example. Parents, students, educators and other stakeholders expect schools to be safe havens for children to learn, and any violence is unacceptable. Between 1992 and 2010, 826 deaths reportedly occurred as a result of school violence (Robers, Zhang & Truman, 2012). The number of incidents of targeted school shootings appears to have increased every decade since the 1960s (Vossekuil, Fein, Reddy, Borum & Modzeleski, 2002). From 1999–2006, 116 students were killed in 109 separate incidents, according to the Centers for Disease Control (CDC), averaging 16.5 student homicides yearly (2008). Eight of these events resulted in multiple deaths. Most of the homicides involved gunshot wounds (65 percent). Many involved stabbing or cutting (27 percent), and some included beatings (12 percent). In 2009, 9.6 percent of male students in grades 9–12 reported being threatened or injured with a weapon on school property within that year, compared with 5.5 percent of female students (CDC, 2010). During the 2009–10 school year, 85 percent of public schools reported one or more serious violent incidents such as students using a weapon on other students while at school, fighting in school and thefts of items valued at $10 or greater, which altogether amounted to 1.9 million crimes. To put it in a more simplified context, there were 40 crimes per 1,000 students who were enrolled in public schools for the 2009–10 school year (Robers et al., 2012).

School violence can encompass a wide range of activities, including physical fights, threats, robbery, harassment, dating violence, molestation, rape, bullying, hostile or threatening remarks between groups of students, assaults with or without weapons and gang violence (Espelage, 2004). Many attackers who perpetrate targeted school violence feel bullied or persecuted by others prior to the attack (Bernes & Bardick, 2007; Vossekuil et al., 2002). In 2009, 19.9 percent of students reported being bullied on school property during the previous year. Five percent of students had chosen not to go to school because they felt unsafe at school or on their way to or from school (CDC, 2010). In the 2008–2009 school year, 28 percent of students aged 12–18 (seven million students) reported being bullied at school (Robers et al., 2012).

The U.S. Secret Service and U.S. Department of Education (USDOE) studied targeted violence, which they characterized as a premeditated act an attacker commits when he/she chooses a target before the attack (Vossekuil, Fein, Reddy, Borum and, Modzeleski, 2004). The Secret Service and USDOE's study, the Safe School Initiative (SSI), was designed to assist in the prevention and knowledge of targeted violence in schools (Pollack, Modzeleski & Rooney, 2008). The SSI identified previous incidents of targeted school violence so pre-attack behaviors could be detected and future attacks prevented. Educators would find the results counterintuitive in one critically important area; there simply was not a clear profile of a school shooter. After comprehensively studying 37 instances with 41 perpetrators from 1974 to 2000 in the United States, some generalizations have emerged. Caution is needed as the generalizations allow for more preventive measures to be taken, but they cannot be used as the only markers of an attacker as each previous attack had its own particularities. Here are the key findings from the Vossekuil, Fein, Reddy, Borum and Modzeleski (2004) report:

- School attackers do not act on sudden impulse but methodically plan their attack.
- Schools are chosen in advance by the attacker for a reason such as a specific person(s) is targeted.
- The target is often someone in an authoritative position over the attacker such as an administrator, teacher or faculty member, and the attacker feels as though he or she has been wronged by this person. Many of the targets did not have any knowledge they were the targets or had caused any grievance from the attacker.
- Most of the attackers are successful in finding their targets as the planning and premeditation allows the attacker to know the victim's whereabouts.

- Generally speaking the attackers are Caucasian males between the ages of 13 to 18, come from two-parent households with at least one biological parent living with them, have grades of A's and B's, seem socialized with the mainstream of the student body, participate in organized social activities both in and out of school, are rarely in trouble and do not have evidence of violent or criminal behavior.
- Although they did not display violence, a majority of school attackers showed interest in violent books, movies and video games. The attackers showed signs of suicidal thoughts and suffered from depression. One-fourth of the attackers studied were alcohol and/or substance abusers. These attackers had access to weapons prior to the attacks, and most had used the actual weapons before the attacks. The weapon was in their personal household or that of a relative. The attackers used mainly handguns; they used one weapon during that attack but had many other weapons on their person.
- The attackers were victims of long-standing and severe bullying by others.
- Fully 98 percent of the attackers experienced a major loss or failure prior to the attack. Major losses or failures included job lay-off, terminal illness in the family and a relationship break up.
- Each of the attacks lasted no more than 15 minutes and were stopped by an educator or the attackers themselves. Only 27 percent of the attacks were stopped by law enforcement.
- Forty-four percent of the attackers were influenced by others who either dared or encouraged the attackers to carry out their plans (pp. 11-12).

Pollack, Modzeleski and Rooney (May 2008) found the bystander effect occurred in these school attacks and was documented by the SSI study. SSI found that 93 percent of attackers demonstrated disconcerting behavior prior to the attack. This statistic suggests observance can be essential in circumventing attacks. In a good number of cases, someone was told by the attacker what was going to occur. A majority of informants were told within days or weeks of the attack, and 82 percent of them were told directly from the attackers themselves. Most of these informants were friends of the attackers. The youth who did come forward immediately with information were in positive relationships with adults and felt as though they could trust adults to skillfully handle the information. Informants had parental influence to guide them to inform the administration of the plans.

Bystanders who knew but did not approach with the information felt as though it was an attention-seeking behavior, a mere joke or misjudged the immediacy and the seriousness of the attack. One bystander reported he had identified disconcerting behavior from the shooter that made him uneasy. He even chose to disclose his feelings to a trusted adult, who assured him there was no reason to tell anyone. He also had other reasons for not reporting his friend to the authorities. The bystander said it was "hard to believe" someone could carry out a school shooting. He and his friends had discussed the details of a school shooting that occurred in the area and had even given some pointers of how it could have been improved. But he never thought any of his friends would ever plan such an event. He assumed they were "kidding around" like he was. He thought the school officials were "too judgmental," which probably made it harder for him to disclose information to them (Pollack, Modzeleski & Rooney, 2008, p. 13). Another bystander stated he was certain school officials knew about the shooter's "violent temper and direct threats." The shooter shared his allure of bombs and killings with classmates and teachers through writing and was also penalized for taking a gun to school. Because of the shooter's outlandish behavior the bystander thought school officials "had everything under control" so he had no need to disclose additional information about threatening statements the shooter had made (Pollack, Modzeleski & Rooney, 2008, p. 13).

To protect a school from these attacks, schoolwide training can better prepare everyone. Teachers, administrators and other faculty, if trained, can act quickly to suspicions and know with whom to consult. Students need to be encouraged to report information if they know of a planned attack. Looking into bullying situations could provide insight into what is going on in the school and identify bullying victims who also might need a vigilant eye on them. School counselors need to be astute to students who come in claiming a teacher has it out for them. They need to look for signs since there are some generalities but no set profile of an attacker. It could be anyone at any time.

The recommendation from authors and researchers around keeping schools safe argues for an intentional approach to evaluating threat levels and the immediacy of the threat. In a January 2013 survey, roughly half of the ASCA members responding reported their school had an intentional and methodical approach to evaluating risk assessment and a protocol when a threat is posed.

Our school has an intentional and methodical risk assessment to evaluate threat level and the immediacy of the threat.

Strongly agree: ....26 percent
Agree: ....33 percent
Neutral: ....12 percent
Disagree: ....22 percent
Strongly disagree: ....6 percent

Our school has a practical, well-thought-out, research-based protocol when a threat is posed that protects educators and students alike.

Strongly agree: ....22 percent
Agree: ....36 percent
Neutral: ....18 percent
Disagree: ....18 percent
Strongly disagree: ....6 percent

Our school uses a very informal approach to evaluating threat levels and the immediacy of the threats.

Strongly agree: ....10 percent
Agree: ....33 percent
Neutral: ....12 percent
Disagree: ....31 percent
Strongly disagree: ....14 percent

(Stone, 2013b)

Another form of violence occurring frequently is dating violence. The Children's Safety Network (2012) has defined dating violence as a pattern of controlling behavior exhibited by one adolescent toward another in a dating relationship. Dating violence takes the form of physical, emotional or sexual abuse. Physical abuse includes hitting, punching, slapping, shoving or kicking. Emotional abuse can be threats, name calling, screaming, yelling, ridiculing, spreading rumors, isolation, intimidation, stalking and, more recently, using technology to harass or intimidate by texting, calling and/or bullying or monitoring via social networking sites. Sexual abuse is unwanted touching or kissing, forced or coerced engagement in sexual acts.

School attacks make headlines, but dating violence brings far less attention. However, it affects thousands of students every day. Dating violence affects 9 percent to 35 percent of adolescents (Davis, 2008). The large gap in the statistics is because of the differences in studies such as whether teens were asked about all of their dating relationships, only the current one or one occurring in the past year, and whether researchers measure exposure to dating violence without distinguishing between victimization and perpetration (O'Keefe 2005). Data from the CDC's 2009 Youth Risk Behavior Surveillance System, a national survey administered to high school students, shows 9.3 percent of female students and 10.3 percent of male students reported they were "hit, slapped or physically hurt on purpose by their boyfriend or girlfriend during the 12 months before the survey." The 2008 National Survey of Children's Exposure to Violence, a nationally representative sample of 4,549 children ages 0 to 17, indicates 5.6 percent of 14 to 17 year olds experienced dating violence in the past year, and 8.8 percent of them experienced dating violence in their lifetime (Finkelhor, Turner, Ormrod, Hamby & Kracke, 2009).

Dating violence has long-term effects. Teen victims are more likely to perform poorly in school, use drugs or alcohol, have eating disorders or be depressed or suicidal (Krug, Dahlberg, Mercy, Zwi & Lozano, 2002). They are also more likely to experience violence in future relationships. The Center for Disease Control Youth Risk Behavior Surveillance (2009) showed 9.8 percent of ninth- to 12th-grade students reported being hit, slapped or physically hurt on purpose by their boyfriend or girlfriend in the 12 months before the survey. More than 10 percent of ninth- to 12th-grade females reported they had been forced to have sexual intercourse, as did 4.5 percent of males.

Getting Started: What Would You Do?

The following case is discussed for you at the end of this chapter by a counselor educator. Before you read the response, formulate in your own mind how you would approach this ethical dilemma.

SUPPORTING A SAFE AND RESPECTFUL SCHOOL CLIMATE

Your student, Beth, came into your office with a letter from her best friend, Jane. In the letter Jane was very descriptive about the violence she wanted to inflict upon another girl, Samantha, who had "stolen her boyfriend." You know Jane fairly well and are sure she wouldn't do such a thing. However, since the threat was made in written form and given to

you, do you have to tell the administrator? This information was supposed
to be confidential, and you don't want to get Jane in trouble. She has
enough issues in her life without being suspended.

Working Through Case Studies

SCHOOL COUNSELORS AND THREAT ASSESSMENTS

The principal has assigned you to be in charge of risk assessment for
students who seem to have the penchant for and potential to harm others. You are uncomfortable with this assignment and expressed your
concerns that this responsibility should not fall on any one person to
try to predict if a student might be violent. You are trying to convince
the administration to make you part of an administrative-led team and
not the leader and sole assessor. Are you proceeding correctly?

Points to Consider

School counselors do believe they have a role to play in threat assessments.
In a March 2013 survey, 70 percent of ASCA member respondents said
they share this responsibility with the administration. Almost half the
respondents (49 percent) reported they conduct formal threat assessments
on individual students.

School counselors should not be involved in threat assessments in any
way.

Strongly agree: . . . . .3 percent
Agree: . . . . .2 percent
Neutral: . . . . .9 percent
Disagree: . . . . .41 percent
Strongly disagree: . . . . .45 percent

I share the responsibility for formal threat assessment for individual
students with others such as administrators, other educators, other
experts.

Yes: . . . . .70 percent
No: . . . . .30 percent

I conduct formal threat assessments to individual students who have exhibited behaviors indicating they may be a threat to another student or the school community.

A great deal: . . . . .10 percent
A moderate amount: . . . . .14 percent
Occasionally: . . . . .25 percent
Rarely: . . . . .25 percent
Never: . . . . .26 percent

(Stone, 2013b)

Threat assessments should not be the purview of the school counselor in isolation. If involved at all, school counselors might possibly be a member of an administrative-led team with other educators and experts sitting in the decision-making chair (Kanan, 2010). It is unwise to place the burden on a school counselor or any one person to determine the inexact science of predicting a person's potential to level harm on the school community. This responsibility falls on administration's shoulders with school counselors as contributors and consultants to the team approach. The school counselor is in a unique position to identify students who may be potential perpetrators or victims and to educate children, families and communities about violence prevention (Simmons, 2000). This school counselor is right to work diligently to convince administration it would be dangerous for only one person to be the sole determinant. Bring supportive research to the conversation if administration will not relent. The efforts to keep all students safe should not rest solely with the school counselor, but it is necessary to consult "with professionals trained in the field of violence assessment to improve the accuracy of risk estimation" (Bernes and Bardick, 2007, p. 12). In a January 2013 survey, school counselors agreed (78 percent) that risk assessments should not be the school counselor's responsibility in isolation but rather as a team member who is knowledgeable about violence and how to report any warning signs or activity.

> School counselors should be involved in risk assessments but only in collaboration with other trained professionals in the field of violence assessment.
>
> Strongly agree: ....30 percent
> Agree: ....48 percent
> Neutral: ....11 percent
> Disagree: ....8 percent
> Strongly disagree: ....3 percent
>
> (Stone, 2013b)

For school counselors, risk identification often originates in an individual counseling session in which a student's disclosures may necessitate the school counselor's breach of confidentiality. There are guides to help school counselors in their consultation role, and Bernes and Bardick (2007) suggest one such approach. A structured approach to risk assessment is important because "establishing liability for inaccurately assessing risk for violence without using structured methods and criteria will increasingly leave school counselors in a vulnerable position if asked how they determined the level of risk in a particular student" (p. 6).

Bernes and Bardick (2007) share risk factors: (a) history of violence, (b) history of nonviolent offending, (c) early initiation of violence, (d) past supervision/intervention failures, (e) history of self-harm or suicide attempts, (f) exposure to violence in the home, (g) childhood history of maltreatment, (h) parental/caregiver criminality, (i) early caregiver disruption and (j) poor school achievement.

Social/contextual risk factors include: (a) peer delinquency, (b) peer rejection, (c) stress and poor coping, (d) poor parental management, (e) lack of personal/social support and (f) community disorganization.

Individual risk factors include: (a) negative attitudes, (b) risk taking/impulsivity, (c) substance use difficulties, (d) anger management problems, (e) low empathy/remorse, (f) attention deficit/hyperactivity difficulties, (g) poor compliance and (h) low interest/commitment to school.

Protective factors include: (a) pro-social involvement, (b) strong social support, (c) strong attachments and bonds, (d) positive attitude toward intervention and authority, (e) strong commitment to school and (f) resilient personality traits (p. 423).

Since most acts of violence are planned, Borum and Reddy (2001) have identified six ACTION areas of inquiry to assess attack related behavior. ACTION stands for the six areas of inquiry: (a) Attitudes that support or facilitate violence, (b) Capacity, (c) Thresholds crossed, (d) Intent, (e) Others' reactions and responses and (f) Noncompliance with risk reduction interventions (p. 424).

ZERO-TOLERANCE POLICIES AND JUVENILE JUSTICE

Your school has a zero-tolerance policy for offenses such as skipping school, out of uniform and arguing with a teacher that would be better handled in other ways. You worry the school's approach is criminalizing offenses that should be handled by the school or parents/guardians. Whenever you bring up your concerns, administrators also point out the data indicating the school is being more successful academically and behaviorally since the inception of zero tolerance. What do you do?

Points to Consider

Zero-tolerance policies shift the focus of discipline away from the school setting and into the juvenile justice system, resulting in negative and mostly unintended consequences for the students, families and communities they are designed to protect (American Psychological Association Zero Tolerance Task Force, 2008). Educators are grappling with the daunting task of preventing school violence by adding security devices, searches and controversial zero-tolerance policies. The effort to prevent further violence will elude school officials unless they implement research-based policies addressing the power of confidentiality, methods for anonymous reporting and the impact of including students as vital links in violence prevention. Tran, a Texas honor student jailed for truancy, is one such example of zero tolerance gone awry. Tran's parents/guardians left her to care for her two siblings. Tran worked two jobs and kept up with a demanding academic load. Judge Lanny Moriarty was not sympathetic to Tran's situation. He focused on the overall prevalence of truancy cases and requested Tran suffer the consequences of her actions like other students would. After all, Judge Moriarty stated, "One night [in jail] is not a death sentence" (CBSAtlanta Staff, 2012, p.1). Although this is an extreme zero-tolerance case, it points to some of the controversy when educators have to shift discipline to the courts.

The educational system is starting to look more like the criminal justice system (Allen, 2004). Student transgressions, once handled by a principal or a parent, are now being handled by prosecutors and the police. The Civil Rights Project at Harvard University, Opportunities Suspended: The Devastating Consequence of Zero Tolerance and School Discipline, found zero-tolerance policies "are derailing students from an academic track in schools to a future in the juvenile justice system." Many of the arrests are for minor infractions such as arguing (not fighting), and some are absurd such as the two New Jersey elementary school students who were arrested and charged with terrorism for playing cops and robbers with paper guns. "Criminal behavior such as murder, serious violence or the sale or possession of illicit drugs, should be subjected to criminal charges, as they were even before zero tolerance became the watchword" (Allen, 2004, pp. 6-7).

The Anne Arundel, Md., School District's six-tier discipline system appeared to be much more reasonable than that of a zero-tolerance policy, but not after it was interpreted to mean that a 7-year-old boy who nibbled his toaster pastry into the shape of a gun had committed a tier-three offense and was punished by suspension. This disciplinary action was for Maryland's Sen. Jennings "the last straw," and he introduced legislation that would prohibit the suspensions of young children for imaginary guns, pictures of guns or objects resembling a gun but serving another purpose (St. George, 2013). Zero-tolerance policies still exist in many schools. In a January 2013 survey, 65 percent of the school counselors responding said their school has a formal zero-tolerance policy for violent behavior (Stone, 2013b).

Just as zero-tolerance policies do not work, putting students into the juvenile justice system as a result of the school's zero tolerance is questionable as the statistics regarding repeat offenders are grim. According to the Office of Juvenile Justice and Delinquency Prevention (OJJDP), "There is no data on the national recidivism rate for juveniles. Such a rate would not have much meaning since juvenile justice systems vary so much across states" (OJJDP, 2012, p.1). A search of the National Criminal Justice Reference Service (NCJRS) Abstracts Database reveals a number of state reports on recidivism. A look at five states recidivism rate within 24 months follows (Harris, Lockwood & Mengers, 2009):

State	Re-arrested within 24 months
New York (FY08 release cohort)	66 percent
California (FY04-05 release cohort)	76 percent
Maryland (FY08 release cohort)	72 percent
Texas (FY06 release cohort)	63 percent
Virginia (FY07 release cohort)	72 percent

The Southern Poverty Law Center (2013) estimates 100,000 students are in juvenile facilities and thousands more are in adult prisons. Southern Poverty Law Center (SPLC) points to some promising programs in Alabama, Florida, Louisiana and Mississippi, states with high rates of children entering the juvenile justice system or dropping out of school. These projects have sought to reduce the number of children in the juvenile justice system and provide adequate community-based alternatives. For instance, a positive behavior intervention program in Jefferson Parish, La., has been so successful that after two years out-of-school suspension for special education students has decreased by 50 percent, and out-of-school suspension for general education has fallen 24 percent. In Alabama, the juvenile justice code was rewritten, and children are not incarcerated for truancy and curfew violations.

STUDENTS CHANGING SCHOOL CULTURES

You believe students are a missing link in changing the climate and culture of your school. You have seen how student influence has helped create a college-going culture, and you believe the student voice is not only needed but essential in eliminating meanness, cruelty and bullying at your school. Your research, instincts and experience have taught you that if students are invested, change has a better chance of happening. You are so busy you fear if you push your point, the administration might over-involve you in discipline, and you cannot take on much more in your schedule. Should you just keep your head down and stay out of the discussions?

Points to Consider

Student's reactions, behavior and attitudes determine the quality of a school. Few cases exist where students' voices are heard in school-improvement planning (Zullig, Koopman & Huebner, 2009). When students believe they're in a safe school environment promoting growth and success, students improve in academic achievement, developing trusting relationships with school personnel, and display positive behavior (Zullig, Hucebuer & Patton, 2011). The Symposium on Youth Meanness and Cruelty took place at Harvard Law School in February 2012. Participants included experts, researchers, policymakers, foundation representatives, youth and others to discuss research and findings related to bullying, meanness and cruelty (Palfrey & Boyd, 2012). The symposium's purpose was to focus on the current research, curricula, school-based interventions, and the legal and policy landscape with emphasis on engaging a larger audience, especially a student-centered approach to interventions and solutions (Palfrey & Boyd, 2012). A student-centered approach to preventing bullying and violence against students was recognized by both adult and student participants as the most important method of resolving these issues. Student participants highlighted the importance of students and adults working together to allow students to educate adults in their lives on circumstances of which the adults are often not aware, such as social cruelty. Additionally, students stated these student-adult relationships would allow students to realize adults in their school cared about them. The discussion also noted bullying education and prevention must take place as early as possible and continue to be embedded in curricula throughout students' time in school. Participants agreed that continuing to increase credibility with young people was an important component of creating change (Palfrey & Boyd, 2012).

From all the research the results are clear; students need to be included in creating a safer, more respectful school climate for all. Engaging in conversations with other educators about alternative ways of disciplining, the zero-tolerance policy research, the abysmal statistics from the juvenile justice system and knowledge about best practices is a proactive, productive use of the school counselor's time. Myrick (2002) talks about the rule of parsimony, meaning school counselors must do their best to assist as many students as possible given time constraints and numbers of students. A safe, respectful school climate is a meaningful intervention that touches every student in the school. Helping to establish a better culture and climate for a healthy learning environment is not discipline but advocacy: a major component of school counseling.

CODE OF SILENCE

A student in your school was caught carrying a gun that discharged, injuring another student. A number of students gave convincing details indicating they had seen the gun but chose not to notify school officials. The principal has asked you to head a committee to recommend policies and practices to encourage students to report weapons, violence and bullying. What policies and procedures do you hope will emerge from this committee?

Points to Consider

In nearly every case of reported school violence, students saw warning signs in advance but did not report what they saw to adults because of peer pressure, fear of retaliation and absence of a sense of personal responsibility to help keep their school safe (Pollack et al., 2008). According to a survey by Stone & Isaacs (2002a), students are apprehensive about trusting adults to skillfully handle confidential information about potential violence. In many cases of school violence, there are other students who are peripherally involved. This chapter's introduction discussed research that clearly points to the fact attackers almost always share their plans for violence with peers, friends and classmates who chose not to report the information to authorities (Pollack et al., 2008). Worth reiterating is the point that bystanders are most likely to report threats of violence when they have positive relationships with adults in the school, believe the threats to be serious and feel school officials will take the information seriously and address the threats immediately (Pollack et al., 2008).

Anonymous reporting is a communication system whereby students can report concerns about violence through a mechanism that does not require them to reveal their identity. This manner of revealing potentially incriminating information enables students to report to a school counselor or other trusted adult crimes, harassment or violence without fear of being hurt by angry students or being labeled an outsider or one who discloses information to adults (Payne & Elliott, 2011). One such system implemented in Colorado, Safe2Tell, purports to have prevented an estimated 28 planned school attacks from 2004–2011 and has had a positive impact on other student concerns as well, such as self-mutilation, drug and alcohol abuse and potential suicide events (Payne & Elliott, 2011).

High school students enrolled in a three-week college seminar at Yale University persuasively argued that students, rather than adults, are key to curbing violence in school (Stone & Isaacs, 2002b). Dozens of high school students contended their peers are more aware than adults of the different elements of a school's potentially dangerous social landscape: the cliques, gangs, aggressive students, isolated brooders, victims, perpetrators, carriers of weapons and so on. Respondents reported they believed they should be allowed to anonymously alert, in a variety of ways, potential acts of violence or problems they had observed or heard about, including acts of bullying, weapons on campus, gang activity, pending fights and sexual harassment (Stone & Isaacs, 2002b). Respondents advocated for a democratic, intergenerational partnership to address school violence (Stone & Isaacs, 2002b). Schools nationwide are implementing policies and programs aimed at encouraging students to report potentially dangerous students (Payne & Elliott, 2011). The school counselor's role of being the recipient of critical information will be far less complicated with a policy or guideline to help protect minors while also respecting the inherent rights of parents/guardians and the larger society. A school culture whereby students know they can and should report threats and suspicious activity with the expectation that their identity will not be revealed and their confidences will be respected should be established. In a 2013 survey, ASCA members responded to questions about anonymous reporting. A large percentage of these respondents were in schools without anonymous reporting (46 percent).

My school has an anonymous reporting system, i.e., the reporters identity is kept confidential, so students can report their peers who have a weapon or are planning a violent act, crime or harassment.

Yes: . . . . .40 percent
No: . . . . .46 percent
Don't know: . . . . .14 percent

(Stone, 2013b)

CONFIDENTIALITY BALANCED AGAINST COMMUNITY PROTECTION

You are exchanging journal entries with a student who needs help with his impulse control and disruptive behavior. The student has problems with authority and wrote in the journal he would hurt a particular teacher, "but I know I cannot do that." Later in class this student shouted threats on this same teacher's life. The police were called, and they searched his belongings and found and read the journal, pausing and discussing the entry about the teacher. Even though the student qualified the threat as something he knew he could not do, the principal came to you concerned you had not reported this journal entry. You believe the journal, which clearly had your name and the student's name as owners of the journal, should not have been read as it was confidential. You retrieved the journal from the principal, and you refuse to return it as the police have indicated the journal entry might be used to further substantiate that the student represents a real danger to the threatened teacher. Are you proceeding ethically and legally?

Points to Consider

The protection of the school community supersedes confidentiality. The journal was needed to substantiate the potential for this student to be dangerous. Even though many school counselors would not find it necessary to alert administration to the journal entry, the fact that a particular teacher was named makes the threat all the more acute. If the threatening student had written in general, "Teachers can be horrible to kids and no wonder some students want to hurt teachers," this entry would have been vague enough that it might not have been reported. Once a teacher is named this increases the school counselor's responsibility to the larger school community. The journal was discovered in the course of investigating a very real and lethal-sounding threat, and it is the prudent school counselor who does not hinder the investigation.

The ASCA position statement on confidentiality reminds school counselors they have an ethical and professional responsibility to protect private information received through confidential relationships with students (ASCA, 2008). However, student confidentiality pales, and school counselors' responsibilities heighten, when a student confides in them or they learn through other means a student may be a danger to others. School counselors are charged with balancing students' rights and needs of their students with their obligations to the larger school community. School counselors must respond to teacher and administrator requests for information or mandates for sharing information among community or law enforcement agencies when safety is at issue. School counselors remember all educators share the responsibility for the well-being of the greater school community when there are competing interests for confidentiality.

A study by Moyer, Sullivan and Growcock (2012) showed school counselors reported they were more likely to breach confidentiality when their school or district had written policies to guide their actions. School counselors who get involved in teaming to create guidelines around reporting of bullying, school violence and criminal activity will have the opportunity to help shape the policies with which they will comply (Moyer et al., 2012).

WARNING POTENTIAL VICTIMS

Phillip, one of your students, has difficulty managing his frustration and is prone to violent outbursts. Phillip told you today that he hates Kimberly, that she annoys him; "Talk, talk, talk, is all she does. I am going to drive the heel of my hand upward under her chin and snap her neck." Additionally disturbing to you is that Phillip has spent years learning martial arts and describes the techniques he intends to use. What are your legal and ethical obligations in this situation? Do you inform the administration? Do you notify Kimberly, Kimberly's parents/guardians or Phillip's parents/guardians?

Points to Consider

Confidentiality is an important component of counseling. However, this situation demands a breach of confidentiality because of the possibility a student might be in harm's way. A counselor's duty to warn potential victims arises from the court case *Tarasoff v. Board of Regents of California* (1976). Posenjit Poddar killed Tatiana Tarasoff in 1969. Two months earlier, in a University of California hospital at Berkeley, Poddar had advised his psychologist, Dr. Moore, of his intention to kill Tarasoff. Tarasoff's parents/guardians filed a lawsuit charging negligence, with the claim that Moore had a duty to warn Tarasoff and her parents/guardians of the impending danger. The crux of the case was whether or not Moore had a duty to warn. The California Supreme Court ruled the psychologist-patient relationship is a special one and, as such, requires the duty to warn. The California court stated that the potential danger to Tarasoff outweighed the psychologist's obligation of confidentiality to his client.

A member of the general public who sees something dangerous has a moral duty, but not always a legal duty, to warn a potential victim. However, due to the special relationship school counselors have with their students, they are required by law to exercise the same skill, knowledge and care other members of their profession would demonstrate under similar circumstances (Hays, Craigen, Knights, Healey & Sikes, 2009). Since the *Tarasoff* ruling, a number of state courts have sought to limit or expand the scope of a duty to warn on the part of professionals. Some state legislatures have enacted laws granting greater privilege. Court cases that have followed *Tarasoff* have both broadened and narrowed the strength of the ruling. *McIntosh v. Milano* (1979), the first case decided after the *Tarasoff* decision, more broadly held the practitioner's obligations "to protect the welfare not only of the client as in Tarasoff but also of the community." In *Boynton v. Burglass* (1991), a court in Florida completely rejected the *Tarasoff* ruling. The court based its rejection of a duty to protect on its belief in the inexact science of psychiatry and the near-impossible task of predicting violence. The exact limits of the duty to warn from the *Tarasoff* case are uncertain because different state statutes address (1) who is subject to the duty to warn or take precaution, (2) the type of threats that will activate the duty, (3) the required identifiability of the victim and (4) the acceptable means of satisfying the duty (Fischer & Sorenson, 1996).

In some states, school counselors have a statutory obligation to breach confidentiality if they are aware of bullying. For example, a New Hampshire statute explains that if not met this duty may give rise to criminal liability on the part of the school counselor under N.H.R.S.A. 193-D:6. (New Hampshire Regulatory Statutes Act, 2004). Seventeen states have laws requiring school employees to report bullying incidents (Sacco, Silbaugh, Corredor, Casey & Doherty, 2012). Other states may have statutory obligations similar to those in New Hampshire mandating that educators alert supervisors to any acts of theft, destruction or violence in a safe school zone.

Foreseeability is a critical consideration in cases where school officials are accused of negligence. Foreseeability means "a reasonably prudent person could foresee injuries" (Terando, 2011). In a case involving a student who was shot by a classmate on an unsupervised sidewalk near school grounds, the court found the school liable. The court held that the school had a duty to "take reasonable steps to protect students from harm that may befall them," a duty stemming from "increasingly foreseeable risks to children at school as well as the special relationship between student and school that exists due to the compulsory nature of education" (*Durant v. Los Angeles Unified School District* (2003)).

In Phillip's case, a breach of confidentiality is necessary because Kimberly is vulnerable, and you have a "special legal relationship" to protect her. Also, you need to support Phillip by ensuring he receives additional help to manage his anger and by helping him understand the seriousness of threatening harm to another student. However, not all the steps that should be taken are within the realm of school counseling. An administrator or law enforcement official should be responsible for notifying Kimberly's parents/guardians of the threat, if such notification is deemed necessary.

DATE RAPE AND STATE LAWS

Whitney, a 17-year-old student in your school, comes to your office distraught. Between tears, she tells you she went to a party last weekend and ended up passed out in an upstairs bedroom. She vaguely remembers being in and out of consciousness with at least two boys forcing themselves on her. Whitney says her friends say there are pictures of her being hauled upstairs by Roger and Clyde, one who had her by her feet and one by her hands, and she was swinging between them. She is mortified that the whole school probably knows she got drunk and had sex with multiple boys. For the past three days, she has endured the snickering and sneering of Roger and his friends in the hallways "as they smugly march around with their worlds intact" while "I die a little more inside each day." She explains to you she may have been drugged since she only remembers sipping on a beer as she doesn't like the taste. She begs you not to tell anyone, especially her parents/guardians. What is the school counselor's advocacy and legal role?

Points to Consider

"Two high school football stars were found guilty on Sunday of raping a 16-year-old girl last summer in a case that drew national attention for the way social media spurred the initial prosecution and later helped galvanize national outrage. Because the victim did not remember what had happened, scores of text messages and cell phone pictures provided much of the evidence. They were proof as well, some said, that Steubenville High School's powerhouse football team held too much sway over other teenagers, who documented and traded pictures of the assault while doing little or nothing to protect the girl" (Oppell, 2013, p. 1). Trent Mays, 17, and Ma'lik Richmond, 16, were sentenced to two years and one year respectively in the state juvenile system with discretion by the system to extend this incarceration until they are 21. Mays' sentence was twice as long because he distributed a nude image of a minor.

Judge Thomas Lipps found both boys were guilty of rape under Ohio law for digital penetration, and Ohio law states it is rape if the victim is not able to give consent for sex. The trial also showed graphically the cruelty of cyberbullying as other teens widely spread the pictures of the naked, passed-out victim. The Ohio attorney general, Mike DeWine, believes the grand jury convened after the trial will mean more people could face charges such as obstruction of justice, failure to report a felony and failure to report child abuse. Other text messages from Mays were evidence of how he had tried to get friends to cover for him, tried to get the victim to drop her case against him as it would damage his football career and how he had gotten the coach to "take care of it." This case was so widely published the hope is that despite all the harm some good will come of this case and that students will understand the meaning of date rape; that there is no such thing as consensual sex when one party is unable to give consent. The school counselor's role might be one of advocacy to close the information gap. It would be proactive and would likely lessen the harm students inflict on each other if all schools had an assembly each year or use some other forum to raise students' awareness of cyberbullying, date rape, bullying, age of consent, sexting and minors' responsibilities and rights (Singer, 2013).

Rape is an unwanted sex act commonly referred to as sexual abuse or sexual assault. Date rape is not a legal term but a commonly used term to define forcible sexual contact during a voluntary social engagement in which a person does not intend to engage in sexual activities and resists the contact. Date rape is sexual assault, which is defined as any type of unwanted physical contact with a sexual organ and may include aggressive, sexually suggestive statements. Sexual assault may also occur between persons of the same gender.

Under many states' laws, the penalties for sexual assault are severe and may include incarceration, significant fines, psychiatric treatment and paying restitution to the victim. In addition, a person convicted of sexual assault may be required to register as a sex offender. In most states, you can be charged with first-degree sexual assault or rape if you forced sexual intercourse or had sexual intercourse with someone who was unable to give legal consent. It is not a legal defense if the victim and perpetrator knew each other or were on a date together or had previously had sexual contact. Laws vary by state, but in the majority of states a victim who is intoxicated is incapable of giving legal consent. Date rape drugs (rohypnol, gamma-hydroxybutyrate or GHB, ketamine) cause unconsciousness and in some cases death. Using these drugs on somebody is a federal crime with a possible 20-year sentence. In 2000, President Clinton signed a federal law banning the date rape drug GHB.

State statutes vary regarding date rape. Indiana specifically addresses drugging victims and raping and classifies it as a Class A felony carrying the most severe penalties for rape along with rape with deadly force. Here is an excerpt from the Indiana statute dealing with date rape. Rape. Sec. 1. (a) Except as provided in subsection (b), a person who knowingly or intentionally has sexual intercourse with a member of the opposite sex when: the other person is compelled by force or imminent threat of force; the other person is unaware that the sexual intercourse is occurring; or the other person is so mentally disabled or deficient that consent to sexual intercourse cannot be given; commits rape, a Class B felony. (b) An offense described in subsection (a) is a Class A felony if: it is committed by using or threatening the use of deadly force; it is committed while armed with a deadly weapon; it results in serious bodily injury to a person other than a defendant; or the commission of the offense is facilitated by furnishing the victim, without the victim's knowledge, with a drug (as defined in IC 16-42-19-2(1) or a controlled substance (as defined in IC 35-48-1-9) or knowing that the victim was furnished with the drug or controlled substance without the victim's knowledge.

Once charges are filed, the prosecutor will decide if the case goes forward. If convicted, the abuser may be jailed or placed on probation. Another approach victims can use is to obtain a protection order and in this civil (not criminal) case the abuser does not face criminal charges unless the protection order is violated. The judge can order no contact by the abuser at any time in any place and can also make the abuser attend substance abuse treatment and or counseling. Evidence may be needed and that can be pictures of injuries, threatening e-mails, text messages, voicemails and/or Facebook posts.

In the busy lives of school counselors there are those "drop-everything-and-attend" moments and this is one of those times. You are required by law to act quickly to prevent possible future victims, to protect the school from legal liability and to provide support for Whitney. Whitney needs guidance to come to terms with the fact that she was not responsible but was most likely a victim of a federal and a state crime that has to be reported.

DATING VIOLENCE AND CONFIDENTIALITY

Lynette's friends come to you for help because they believe Lynette is in trouble. Sixteen-year-old Lynette and 17-year-old Derrick are students in your school. Lynette has to report her whereabouts to Derrick, proof of her movements, and she is not allowed to speak or engage in any way with any other boys. When Derrick is not able to be around, he has one of his friends monitor Lynette's movements. If Derrick does not approve of one of Lynette's friends she has to drop that friend. Her friends tell you when they spontaneously change plans Lynette gets a terrified look on her face and says, "But this is not what I told Derrick I would be doing." From what her friends can deduct from the one-sided conversations they hear, Derrick dominates and terrorizes Lynette. Her friends tell you when they tried to get Lynette to drop Derrick, Lynette reported back to them that he slapped her in the face, told her he would decide when and if they broke up and he pushed her so hard into the lockers as to leave an imprint of the locker on her back. You reach out to Lynette, and she begs you to stay out of it or "things will get worse. You cannot protect me." As Lynette's school counselor what is your next step?

Points to Consider

You must report the dating violence to the school administration. School counselors are required by law to report dating violence to school officials who have to take immediate and appropriate steps to investigate, to try and determine facts and to take prompt and effective steps reasonably calculated to prevent further harm. If Lynette requests confidentiality or asks Derrick not be pursued, school officials cannot agree. The school must take action whether or not the student who was victimized explicitly requests school officials not investigate or take further action (U.S. Department of Education, Office for Civil Rights, 2011a). Once Lynette confides she is being harassed or abused, this constitutes "notice," triggering the school counselor's legal requirement to take corrective action. Confidentiality presents a difficult dilemma for school counselors when federal and ethical guidelines tell them they must act. Supporting and protecting Lynette will be an ongoing process made more complicated by the fact that Derrick will know or suspect she told, and retaliation is Lynette's biggest fear. The likelihood of retaliation is often the reason students do not confide in educators (American Association of University Women, 2011). Even if we can protect victims from taunts or physical abuse, students know we cannot protect them from social isolation and the other cruelties that follow when students make serious allegations against their peers. Despite the fact that the Office for Civil Rights (OCR) states school officials "should tell any complainants that Title IX prohibits retaliation and that school officials will not only take steps to prevent retaliation but also take strong responsive action if it occurs," school counselors know how important it is to many of their students that their confidentiality not be breached, especially to the perpetrator.

OCR understands that breaching a student's confidences will often discourage reporting dating violence. The school should take all reasonable steps to investigate while maintaining Lynette's confidentiality. If Lynette insists her name or other identifiable information not be disclosed, the school has the obligation to inform Lynette that its ability to respond may be limited. Reporting is critical; identifying the victim as the reporter is not critical, but it's difficult to maintain confidentiality as it stands to reason that the details of the dating violence came from the victim.

Maintaining confidentiality often interferes with the investigation and efforts to remedy the effects of the dating violence. School administrators and school counselors must struggle with the victim's confidentiality in terms of identity (U.S. Department of Education, Office for Civil Rights, 2011a). As an advocate, school counselors try to work with administration to minimize the additional trauma an investigation could have on student victims. The school counselor's role is to encourage administration to act as the federal law allows, evaluating Lynette's request "in the context of responsibility to provide her with a safe environment." Not only do school officials owe Lynette support but if Derrick remains in the school educators still owe him loyalty and support to teach him how to become a productive citizen and how to have healthy relationships.

DATING VIOLENCE AND THE OFFICE FOR CIVIL RIGHTS

You go to your principal with information about Derrick's violence toward Lynette. The principal responds that "Lynette has to figure out her own mess," that "this matter has nothing to do with the school or his responsibilities as an administrator." Is your principal correct? What is the school's obligation to Lynette? To Derrick?

Points to Consider

The principal is not correct. Dating violence is a form of sexual harassment and discrimination under Title IX of the Education Amendments of 1972. In April 2011, OCR, an arm of the U.S. Department of Education governing Title IX, wrote specific requirements related to sexual violence. Sexual violence is the term OCR uses to refer to "physical sexual acts perpetrated against a person's will or where a person is incapable of giving consent due to the victim's use of drugs or alcohol ... [or] due to an intellectual or other disability (U.S Department of Education, Office for Civil Rights, 2012, p 1.)" Sexual violence does not necessarily mean rape but can also be sexual assault, sexual battery and/or sexual coercion.

According to OCR, a hostile school environment is created when "conduct is sufficiently serious that it interferes with or limits a student's ability to participate in or benefit from the school's program" (U.S. Department of Education, Office for Civil Rights, 2012, p. 1). If the incident is severe as in the case of rape, the conduct does not have to be repeated or occur over time to label the environment hostile. Even when the assault occurs off campus the school should take the "sexual assault into account in determining whether there is a sexually hostile environment. The school also should take steps to protect a student who was assaulted off campus from further sexual harassment or retaliation."

OCR states, "a school that knows, or reasonably should know, about possible harassment must promptly investigate to determine what occurred and then take appropriate steps to resolve the situation." The school's Title IX investigation is different from any law enforcement investigation, and even if there is a law enforcement investigation this does not relieve school officials of their obligation to investigate. Even if Lynette had not come forward, if the school reasonably should know about possible harassment, e.g. the school counselor heard rumors, the school must take action. If Lynette had reported the incident to the police but not to the school, the fact that the police are investigating would not take the place of a school investigation necessary to comply with Title IX. The alleged victim's parents/guardians must give consent for a school to conduct an investigation if the student is under 18.

The school's inquiry must be prompt, thorough and impartial. "In states with mandatory reporting laws, schools may be required to report certain incidents to local law enforcement or child protection agencies." For example, in California, non-mutual violence against a minor typically constitutes reportable child abuse, regardless of whether the offender is a minor.

Most educators, and even the school system at large, feel there is little that can be done about sexual violence. OCR recently published a Dear Colleague Letter specifying the roles and duties schools have regarding sexual violence under Title IX of the Education Amendments of 1972 (Title IX). Title IX "prohibits discrimination on the basis of sex in any federally funded education program or activity" (U.S. Department of Education, Office for Civil Rights, 2012, p. 1). The Dear Colleague Letter provides guidance regarding the school's role in investigating sexual violence, publishing a sexual discrimination policy and determining protocol for grievance procedures, as well as information on enforcement strategies and prevention methods (U.S. Department of Education, Office for Civil Rights, 2011a). The school must protect the complainant before, during and after the investigation and must provide a grievance procedure allowing the alleged perpetrator an equal opportunity to present witnesses and evidences in cases involving sexual violence. Grievance procedures must be settled based on the preponderance of evidence, and both parties should be informed about the outcome of the complaint (U.S. Department of Education, Office for Civil Rights, 2011a).

PROACTIVE APPROACHES TO ADDRESSING DATING VIOLENCE

At a neighboring school, an incident of dating violence occurred on school campus, and the teacher who witnessed the violence did not report it. The parents/guardians of the victim are now suing the school. In response, all district principals have been given orders to put together a committee at their school to address dating violence. You are put in charge of the committee. What resources will you access? What do you want to recommend be put in place?

Points to Consider

First, try to astutely extract yourself from committee chair and participate as a member instead. This committee is best headed by someone in administration who is in charge of discipline. Here are some resources and information to help the committee in its work. OCR is your first line of defense in getting assistance to help with compliance. OCR's procedures to help schools prevent and address discrimination can be found at *http://wdcrobcolp01.ed.gov/CFAPPS/OCR/contactus.cfm*. OCR's customer service team is at (800) 421-3481. Other resources are the National Dating Abuse Helpline. The helpline operates around the clock to help teens in a violent relationship. This service has phone, text and chat capabilities. Alianza has a national directory of domestic violence prevention programs providing services in Spanish and is at *http://dvlianza.org*. The Centers for Disease Control and Prevention's Choose Respect initiative promotes healthy teen relationships to prevent dating violence, and materials are at: *www.cdc.gov/chooserespect/materials_and_resources/ playbook/index.html*. Break the Cycle, funded by the U.S. Department of Justice's Office for Victims of Crime, educates LGBTQ teens about healthy relationships and about the signs of abuse, provides safety planning guides and connects teen dating violence victims to help and legal services and can be found at *http://hearmyvoice.breakthecycle.org*.

A 2012 study of ASCA high school counselors revealed they aren't usually provided training in the area of dating violence. Khubchandani, Price, Thompson, Dake, Wiblishauser and Telljohann (2012) received a 58 percent return rate on their survey. More than 70 percent of respondents said they had never received formal training on dating violence, even though more than 60 percent of those surveyed reported they had assisted a victim of dating violence in the past two years (Khubchandani et al., 2012). School counselors who had received formal training on dating violence were at least twice as likely to have helped a victim in the past two years (Khubchandani et al., 2012, p. 209). Faculty and staff need to be knowledgeable so they can spot dating violence and will know to report it. "Research indicates that 30 percent to 60 percent of high school students tell no one about being victimized by their dating partner" (Khubchandani, et al., 2012, p. 9)." Responders reported their school did not have a committee that meets periodically to address health and safety issues including teen dating abuse (76 percent). Although many schools educated teens about healthy relationships (68 percent) and where to report an incident of dating violence (54 percent), only 42 percent said their schools dealt with dating abuse prevention or had resources clearly posted (25 percent). When faced with an incident of dating abuse, most of the school counselors (81.3 percent) had no protocol or procedure on how to respond (Khubchandani, et al., 2012).

Advocate for curriculum helping students form healthy relationships. States are beginning to take proactive/preventive measures around sexual violence. New Jersey and California are requiring educators teach healthy relationships as part of the curriculum. A proactive approach by school officials would encourage students to come forward and to prevent future occurrences. To better prevent dating violence in schools, school counselors need to advocate for educational trainings for the faculty and staff so they are knowledgeable about how to spot it and what to do to report it.

The Khubchandani, Price, Thompson, Dake, Wiblishauser, Telljohann, 2012 survey presented eight true/false questions indicating varying degrees of knowledge regarding dating violence. Here are four of the questions and the responses.

- Patterns of dating violence behavior often start in early adolescence and carry through into adult relationships. (True) (97 percent responded correctly.)
- Dating abuse can lead to risky sexual behaviors that can result in unintended pregnancy, sexually transmitted diseases and HIV infections. (True) (90 percent responded correctly.)
- Abuse in a dating relationship occurs more commonly in students from a lower socioeconomic background compared with students from higher socioeconomic backgrounds. (True) (25 percent responded correctly.)
- Adolescent dating violence occurs more frequently among racial and ethnic minorities as compared with whites. (True) (15 percent responded correctly.)

Another proactive approach is sometimes necessary. Helping the victim and the victim's parents/guardians work through plans to protect the student might mean they need to seek a protection order against the abuser. A protection order is a civil matter, and the victim and his or her parents/guardians are in charge of this effort. The school counselor's primary role is to strive to support and advocate for all students and help them learn to build healthy relationships.

In a Position to Know:
A Counselor Educator Speaks

The case presented at the beginning of the chapter is revisited here and answered by a counselor educator. Compare her answer with your own approach.

> Your student, Beth, came into your office with a letter from her best friend, Jane. In the letter Jane was very descriptive about the violence she wanted to inflict upon another girl, Samantha, who had "stolen her boyfriend." You know Jane fairly well and are sure she wouldn't do such a thing. However, since the threat was made in written form and given to you, do you have to tell the administrator? This information was supposed to be confidential, and you don't want to get Jane in trouble. She has enough issues in her life without being suspended.

Threats of violence by students against other students and/or educators have seemingly increased over the past few years. Many researchers agree violence in schools is a complex problem. Evaluating the level of intent and lethality is equally as complex, since many things factor into effectively conducting a threat assessment. It may seem that the ethical mandate of keeping the student population safe (ASCA Ethical Standards, A.7) while advocating for the individual student (ASCA Ethical Standards, A.1 and A.2) at the same time is an oxymoron. However, educated professional school counselors do indeed have an ethical commitment to both sides of this coin.

In the scenario above, defending Jane by saying she wouldn't do anything would not hold up in court if some violence were to occur. Applying ethics in this situation, consulting with another professional and following district policy and protocol, which would likely include disclosure to the administrator, would be a sound approach. In the school setting, one person in the system shouldn't shoulder the burden of threat assessment. Effective assessment includes many steps and involves a team approach for appropriate implementation.

Today's fast-paced culture requires district policy and an assessment protocol to responsibly evaluate the nature and danger of a student threat.

An intentional and methodical plan to evaluate threat level and immediacy of the threat should be a component of threat assessment implementation. In a threat assessment, utilizing a practical, well-thought-out, research-based protocol protects educators and students alike.

Because the prevalence of threat seems to be increasing in schools, involving school counselors seems to be a natural fit for threat assessment. This ethically requires school counselors to be educated in threat assessment evaluation and procedures. Therefore, the first ethical consideration for school counselors is the level of training they have regarding effective threat assessment. School counselors must be educated and up-to-date on current research and best practice. School counselors should recognize the high standard of care necessary to be part of a team assessing threats and suicidal behavior. Stay abreast of current research. Ethical practice encourages documentation of the training received by the school counselor and professional development updates so the school counselor can stay current on best practices and standard of care. However, the court case of *Wyke v. Polk County School Board* (1997) warns that without this type of training (threat assessment) there is a tendency for educators to underestimate the lethality of suicide and violent behavior. Underestimation exacts an even higher price than overestimation of violence in schools, but again, the ethical standard is the understanding and evaluation of violence potential.

If a legal situation were to occur from a threat assessment, it would be the "standard of care" against which educator's actions would be measured. Currently, the court system supports suspending students from school when they pose a threat to other students' safety as in *Davis v. Monroe County Board of Education* (1999). The rejoinder in this case warned school personnel they would be held responsible for failing to protect students from student-to-student violence. Although the courts encourage educators to take threats seriously, they also ask education personnel to act reasonably. Legal vulnerability is present when the school personnel cannot demonstrate reasonable care was taken in preventing school violence. Included in that caution are documented steps used to determine why the threat was classified as a "true threat," as in the court case of *Lovell v. Poway Unified School District* (1996). It is important in this assessment process to use guiding principles of threat assessment to evaluate for "true threat."

Whether it is an actual assessment, which requires a rigid protocol, or another type of assessment procedure, it's important to document the process. Identifying risk factors is a vital part of the process. Although risk factors don't always predict violence, research supports that as the volume of risk factors escalates, the level of violence potential also increases. Developing interventions for a student's risk factors demonstrate responsiveness on the part of school personnel. However, it is not the sole responsibility of the school counselor to develop and implement the interventions for each of the risk factors identified.

An ethical "fail safe" in the above-mentioned scenario would include documentation of all steps of the evaluation process, clarifying the details of where and how this information was attained. It is important to verify the information, along with documenting how interventions were developed and problem-solving planning occurred. Of course the tried-and-true ethical step is professional consultation and documentation of the consultation.

Hermann and Finn (2002) suggested school counselors be involved in policy-making for such situations. Following the established district policies and protocol will help guide the school counselor and the response team to effective problem-solving. These policies and procedures will allow the participants in the threat assessment to focus on the standard of care and responsible decision-making. In these difficult and emotional situations, it is important to follow established procedures and consider the needs of the at-risk individual, while keeping the needs and safety of those being threatened in balance. Both sides deserve your best and most ethical knowledge, decision-making and problem-solving skills in the ongoing effort to create a safe school.

Rhonda Williams Ed.D., LPC., NCC, associate professor, University of Colorado at Colorado Springs

Making Connections

1. Zero tolerance is a controversial topic in education, with some contending it is the only fair way to allocate discipline and curtail violence and others finding it does not work. Develop your position on zero tolerance by researching and writing a paper on the subject.

2. You have been told three students are planning to fight just off school grounds that afternoon. This is one of those dreaded days when all administrators are out of the building, and you are the principal designee for the day. What do you do?

3. Due to the recent increase in school violence your principal has decided threat assessments are needed for those students who are multiple offenders in victimizing others. As a school counselor what, if any, role would you serve in doing threat assessments?

4. Discuss duty to warn and the limits of duty to warn as you understand them. Do some additional research to find a case in your state that has ruled on a counselor's duty to warn. What does your state say about counselors' obligations regarding duty to warn?

5. Due to the increase of dating violence in your school what policies can you develop to tackle issues that may arise?

Key Terms

Anonymous reporting
Bystander
Code of silence
Date rape drugs
Dating violence
Dear Colleague Letter
Duty to warn
Gang violence
Historical risk factors
Identifiability of the victim
Mediation
Office for Civil Rights
Peer-on-peer aggression
Physical aggression
Protective risk factors

Rape
Recidivism rate
Risk factors
Safe school zone
School violence
Sexually hostile environment
Sexual violence
Social risk factors
Special relation
Statutory obligation
Threat assessments
True threat
Verbal aggression
Violent propensities
Zero tolerance

The Ethics of Advocacy

Objectives

By the time you have completed this chapter, you should be able to:

- Explain the ethical standards relating to advocacy for all students.
- Define the philosophy of social justice in a school counseling program.
- Understand the role of the school counselor as an advocate.
- Understand the role of the school counselor as a systems change agent.
- Describe how a school counselor's behavior promotes equity and opportunities for all students.
- Develop plans to responsibly challenge the institutional barriers denying equal access and prohibiting success for all students.

Ethical Standards Addressed in This Chapter

Professionalism means knowing your professional associations' codes and adhering to them. Those ethical standards from ASCA that are most relevant to this chapter include the following:

- Each person has the right to receive the information and support needed to move toward self-direction and self-development and affirmation within one's group identities, with special care being given to students who have historically not received adequate educational services, e.g., students of color, students living at low socio-economic status, students with disabilities and students from nondominant language backgrounds. (Preamble)
- Each person has the right to understand the full magnitude and meaning of his/her educational choices and how those choices will affect future opportunities. (Preamble)
- Professional school counselors provide and advocate for individual students' career awareness, exploration and postsecondary plans supporting the students' right to choose from the wide array of options when they leave secondary education. (A.3.c)
- Professional school counselors assess the effectiveness of their program in having an impact on students' academic, career and personal/social development through accountability measures especially examining efforts to close achievement, opportunity and attainment gaps. (A.9.g)

- Professional school counselors advocate for equal access to technology for all students, especially those historically underserved. (A.10.b)
- Professional school counselors provide professional personnel with accurate, objective, concise and meaningful data necessary to adequately evaluate, counsel and assist the student. (C.2.b)
- Professional school counselors extend their influence and opportunity to deliver a comprehensive school counseling program to all students by collaborating with community resources for student success. (D.2.b)
- Professional school counselors develop competencies in how prejudice, power and various forms of oppression, such as ableism, agism, classism, familyism, genderism, heterosexism, immigrationism, linguicism, racism, religionism and sexism, affect self, students and all stakeholders. (E.2.b)
- Professional school counselors affirm the multiple cultural and linguistic identities of every student and all stakeholders. Advocate for equitable school and school counseling program policies and practices for every student and all stakeholders including use of translators and bilingual/multilingual school counseling program materials representing all languages used by families in the school community and advocate for appropriate accommodations and accessibility for students with disabilities. (E.2.d)

The full text of the ASCA Ethical Standards for School Counselors is available at *www.schoolcounselor.org*.

Introduction

The ASCA National Model provides a roadmap to help school counselors implement ethical, data-driven programs with advocacy, leadership and accountability at their heart and center. School counselors solidify their position as important players in their school's mission through the accountability component of the ASCA National Model. The ASCA National Model promises to make a significant difference in closing the information, opportunity and achievement gaps that exist through the accountability component.

If all students are to realize brighter futures, the ethical and legal school counselor will need to take up the charge to promote a social justice agenda (Martin, 2002). Ethical school counselors act intentionally and strategically to increase each student's opportunity to participate fully in the economic and social rewards of our society (Stone & Martin, 2004). The ethical school counselor acts as an advocate, providing support and encouraging students to challenge their future by tackling the barriers hindering their success.

Problems individuals face can often be traced to the systems in which they live, work and play. This includes schools, families, social agencies, neighborhoods and many others (Stone & Dahir, 2004; Stone & Martin, 2004). Embracing a social justice agenda requires school counselors to "possess the awareness, knowledge and skill to intervene not only at the individual level but at the systemwide level" (Lee & Walz, 1998, p. 9). School counselors are in an influential position to challenge the status quo and to assist those who have been victims or may be victims of social and educational problems (Kiselica & Robinson, 2001; Capuzzi, 2002; Glosoff & Pate, 2002). The practice of counseling is more complete and effective when the school counselor helps students learn to negotiate through the systems in which they must move to advance in society. School counselors who act as a social change agent offer a more powerful position and increase their effectiveness in multiple ways (Stone & Martin, 2004; Froeschle & Nix, 2009). Ethical school counselors advocate for students by ensuring college and career readiness. They uncover equality gaps and areas of difficulty that may hinder students' success by using the results of analyzed data to eradicate problems (Hines, Lemons & Crews, 2011). Thus, school counselors become change agents who help bridge the gap between schools and students.

School counselors who couple the ethical imperative of social justice with an understanding of the issues affecting equity and opportunity can help change systems that continue to adversely stratify opportunities. They can influence attitudes and beliefs regarding equitable practices, provide attention to equity and access issues and provide resources designed to improve opportunities (Martin, 2004; Stone & Martin, 2004).

Getting Started: What Would You Do?

The following case is answered for you at the end of this chapter by a school counselor. Before you read his responses, decide how you would approach this ethical dilemmas.

PARENT VS. STUDENT ASPIRATIONS

Aarlyn has been a dedicated student throughout high school. She has built a transcript that will easily get her into any state university. You call

Aarlyn in for a college/career advising session, and she informs you her parents are not allowing her to pursue higher education. She explains she is needed to take over the family's business, which is conducted on the first floor of the building where they live. Aarlyn says she will not abandon her family's needs, and after graduation, she will obey her parents' wishes so her father and mother can work fewer hours. She says her place is to care for a family that has always cared for her. She admits it is hard to let go of her dreams for higher education, chokes back tears, mumbles an excuse and quickly leaves your office. What, if anything, could you do?

Working Through Case Studies

STATUS QUO AND ETHICAL BEHAVIOR

The school district has issued a policy that one indicator, such as a 3.5 grade-point average (GPA), cannot be used to deny students admissions into advanced, honors or advanced placement (AP) courses. The school counselors in your district have been vocal, along with others, that it is unwise to get rid of the GPA requirements. You disagree and believe GPA is often not a determinant of ability but simply a matter of who turned in homework. You are willing to give this new criterion an honest push and hope your colleagues will also. What might you say to your colleagues who are against this change?

Points to Consider

The ethical codes of the school counseling profession issue school counselors a directive, to envision a better world for students, and to seek ways to make that vision a reality. If the vision is ethical, it seeks to challenge the institutional and environmental barriers, such as criteria for admission into rigorous courses, and other system barriers impeding student success (Stone, 1998).

Challenging the status quo is not only an ethical imperative but also a legal one. The legal system is based on the premise that every citizen should be given the same considerations. Lady Justice is most often depicted with a set of scales typically suspended from her left hand, upon which she measures the strengths of a case's support and opposition. Also, she is often depicted wearing a blindfold, which means justice should be without fear or favor, regardless of the identity, power or weakness of the defendant.

Ethical school counselors make certain they create advantages for students by challenging the status quo and questioning the rules and regulations denying a level playing field for all students. Access to advanced coursework is a predictor of future economic opportunities and allows students to choose from the widest array of postsecondary opportunities (ASCA, 2010; Stone & Dahir, 2004).

Ethical codes change as the needs of students and schools change. School counselors cannot cling to the traditional roles of school counseling. They must, according to the changes of the 2004 ASCA Ethical Standards for School Counselors (2010), become social justice advocates, ferreting out things limiting certain students' opportunities. The language of the standards clearly defines the school counselor's role as a catalyst for change. The notion of social change, in whatever capacity necessary to help students reach their maximum development, lies at the heart of the school counselor's role (Stone, 1998; ASCA Ethical Standards, 2010).

Moreover, students have the right to be supported when choosing a program of study and to have the safety nets to be able to fulfill their dreams (Maddy-Bernstein, 2000). Providing educational and career planning from elementary school to graduation will present students with quality postsecondary opportunities and help close the information gap (Feller & Davies, 2003). Productive adults come to self-awareness and self-understanding not by walking smooth roads but by trial and error (Mitchell, Levin & Krumboltz, 1999).

There are so many unalterable factors in students' lives causing them hurt and harm. School counselors cannot change the parents/guardians of those students who do not have security and comfort, give them a loving home or establish optimal conditions for them during their time away from school. Although school counselors cannot give to every child what they would seek for their own children, they can offer every child optimum opportunities in school. School counselors can fervently influence the school environment so students have equitable access to rigorous course work.

STUDENT-DRIVEN OR DATA-DRIVEN: NO DIFFERENCE

In all the school counselor in-services this year, there is a new push called data-driven school counseling. This initiative has not been embraced by the majority of the school counselors. As one school counselor put it, "I did not come into the role of school counselor to look at pie charts or bar graphs." The school counselors who oppose this move have banded together in protest. These school counselors have a slogan, "Student-Driven not Data-Driven." You disagree with the naysayers. You believe disaggregated data can help you be more intentional in supporting all students. What do you say to the naysayers?

Points to Consider

Data are necessary to see whose opportunities are stratified. Achieving the best results for students requires school counselors to regularly examine data. Without disaggregated data, it is all just a guess as to whether the strategies and interventions school counselors have put into place are making a difference and advancing students.

Ethnic minority students and low-income students are less likely to be placed in college preparatory or high-ability courses (U.S. Department of Education & National Center for Educational Statistics, 2011). For instance, Caucasian students are 50 percent more likely to complete demanding course work than their African-American and Latin-American cohorts (U.S. Department of Education & National Center for Educational Statistics, 2011). School practices and procedures sometimes adversely limit students' opportunities, and using disaggregated data, the school counselor can determine who is being left out of the success equation.

In a 2013 survey by Kozlowski and Stone (2013), 72 percent of the ASCA members responding said it was their responsibility to build school counseling programs around critical data elements (Kozlowski & Stone, 2013). In this same survey ASCA members were asked about data collecting, disaggregating data, implementing strategies to have an impact on data, setting up an organizational framework to measure data changes and determining the impact of their data work. The results follow.

How confident are you in your ability to:	Confident or Very Confident	Somewhat Confident or Neutral	Not at all Confident
Complete a data-driven school counseling program from data collection to completion?	54 percent	52 percent	4 percent
Disaggregate data (break it down into small elements such as ethnicity, socio-economic status, gender, etc.)?	67 percent	29 percent	4 percent
Make a positive impact on the critical data element?	71 percent	27 percent	2 percent
Implement counseling strategies (such as group counseling, classroom-based counseling lessons, individual techniques, etc.) that will affect a change in the critical data element?	79 percent	17 percent	1 percent
Set up an accountability system and/or an organizational framework for your school counseling program to measure a change in the critical data element?	54 percent	29 percent	1 percent
Determine the overall impact of your strategies on the critical data element?	55 percent	41 percent	4 percent

(Kozlowski & Stone, 2013)

School counseling programs starting with and building around the school's data will be central to the unique challenges of that school. Starting with the data allows the program to be squarely in sync with the mission of the school. The ASCA National Model is a framework to be fleshed out based on the particular context and needs of a school. Starting with the data provides a roadmap from start to finish in the form of critical data elements that have improved as a result of implementing the ASCA National Model.

SCHOOL COUNSELOR EVALUATIONS AND ACCOUNTABILITY

Your school district has just initiated a new evaluation instrument for school counselors, which requires each school counselor to identify a critical data element on the school improvement plan and put a team of stakeholders together to deliver strategies to contribute toward moving the data in a positive direction. Many of your colleagues express their frustration, saying they know they make a difference and do not want to have to prove it. You believe the district is headed in the right direction. What might you say to your colleagues to convince them to give this accountability approach their best effort?

Points to Consider

An accountable school counseling program, now aligned with the educational enterprise, is data-driven, proactive and preventive in focus and assists students in acquiring and applying lifelong learning skills. Now, more than ever, school counselors, like all other educators, are expected to demonstrate the effectiveness of their work in measurable terms. Increasingly in school districts across the nation, school counselors' evaluations are being tied to impact data. How are students different as a result of the school counseling program? The evaluation of administrators and teachers is inextricably tied to student performance. School counselors have an opportunity to communicate with data how their work also positively affects student achievement.

One of the four pillars of the ASCA National Model is accountability. "To demonstrate the effectiveness of the school counseling program in measurable terms, school counselors analyze school and school counseling program data to determine how students are different as a result of the school counseling program. School counselors use data to show the impact of the school counseling program on student achievement, attendance and behavior and analyze school counseling program assessments to guide future action and improve future results for all students. The performance of the school counselor is evaluated on basic standards of practice expected of school counselors implementing a comprehensive school counseling program" (ASCA, 2012, p. xiv).

Results reports. These reports include process, perception and results data, ensure programs are carried out, analyzed for effectiveness and modified as needed. Sharing these reports with stakeholders serves to advocate for the students and the program. Immediate, intermediate and long-range results are collected and analyzed for program improvement.

School counselor performance standards. The school counselor's performance evaluation contains basic standards of practice expected of school counselors implementing a school counseling program. These performance standards should serve as both a basis for school counselor evaluation and as a means for school counselor self-evaluation.

Program audit. The primary purpose for collecting information is to guide future action within the program and to improve future results for students.

Stakeholders can help school counselors meet the challenges and changing demands of 21st-century schools. Stakeholders can be both within the school and outside of the school, supporting the comprehensive school counseling program by helping provide interventions. When ASCA members were asked about their confidence level regarding stakeholders, their response was strong (73 percent). Only 2 percent reported they lacked the confidence in their ability to identify stakeholders who assist in having an impact on critical data elements. Recruiting stakeholders proved to be more challenging, with only 44 percent responding they were "confident" or "very confident" in their ability to recruit stakeholders to support their data-driven efforts.

How confident are you in your ability to:	Confident or Very Confident	Somewhat Confident or Neutral	Not at all Confident
Recruit stakeholders and determine who will be responsible for the implementation of each strategy?	45 percent	49 percent	6 percent
Identify stakeholders (community, parents, staff, teachers, etc.) to work with to have an impact on the critical data element?	73 percent	25 percent	2 percent

(Kozlowski & Stone, 2013)

School counseling programs are data-driven. Data provide a quantifiable method whereby the school counselor will be able to graphically show the impact the school counseling program is having on student indicators of success. In this climate of accountability, connecting the work of school counselors to school improvement data is the most powerful indicator of the success of a school counseling program.

HAVING AN IMPACT ON THE INFORMATION, OPPORTUNITY AND ACHIEVEMENT GAPS

You have implemented a data-driven ASCA National Model program. You are looking at longitudinal data for your school and find the graduation rate by cohort is at 65 percent. You walk the halls with your ninth-graders, and the realization hits you that four out of every 10 faces will not make it to commencement. Your data reveal that college-going rates are at 60 percent. This means that of the six students out of every 10 who make it through their senior year, only 60 out of every 100 of those students will even apply to college. Another disturbing issue is the school's discipline referral rates. The disaggregated data tell you where your gaps are. What do you do?

Points to Consider

The ASCA Ethical Standards for School Counselors (2010) recognize that the origin of students' problems can often be traced to an impaired school environment (Stone, 1997). Attitudes and beliefs determine our behavior toward students, and the school counselor who believes in the dignity and worth of all students and their right to fully participate in society will behave in a way that assertively supports this belief (Stone, 1998; Stone & Turba, 1999). The school counselors of Lincoln Northeast High School in Lincoln, Neb., believe in the dignity and worth of each student in their school, and they work from a social justice mindset, attacking entrenched problems revealed by the data as a part of their ethical imperative to ensure brighter futures for the students in their school. They are getting results.

More than 50 percent of the Lincoln Northeast High School students are living in poverty. Twenty percent of the student body qualifies for special education services, and more than 70 percent of the student body will be first-generation college students should they make it that far. The likelihood of students making it to graduation was slim when the Lincoln Northeast High School counseling team members sat down four years ago to study their data. What the school counselors found was, in their words, "grim." Graduation rates were at 65 percent, college-going rates were around 60 percent, and discipline referrals were the highest in the city at double the average of the other five public high schools in town. Lincoln Northeast High School was labeled a persistently low-achieving school by the U.S. Department of Education.

The school counselors took action, and they have been recognized for their leadership and collaboration efforts toward systemic change. In 2012, the Lincoln Northeast High School counseling team received the Recognized ASCA Model Program (RAMP) award for the implementation of the ASCA National Model and being "data-informed." In spring 2009, the school counselors started a watch list of students failing two or more classes and shared it with all stakeholders: administrators, the school social worker, the school nurse, special education coordinators, the attendance coordinator and therapists. In weekly meetings, the school counselors and stakeholders established and strengthened interventions to ensure success for failing students. School counselors wrote additional graduation and "Hope Plans" for their at-risk students. Each year, from ninth-12th, students were told about their graduation status. If a student was not on track (NOT) to graduate with his or her class, documentation was added to the student's schedule to remind all stakeholders of this status and the interventions needed. The School Improvement Committee started looking at the data and followed through, with most teachers adopting one of the NOT students as their mentee. School counselors coordinated intensified summer school interventions and career planning classroom presentations. The school counselors collaborated to reposition therapists from a local agency to provide counseling to select students. These students' attendance and grades improved.

In 2008, the school counseling department received a College Access Grant from EducationQuest, a college and financial-aid planning nonprofit organization in Nebraska. With these monies, the school counseling department focused its efforts on the following: career fairs, college fairs, college club, field trips, afterschool workshops, college visits, college access week, KnowHow2Go assemblies and one-stop college admissions testing/application/financial aid workshops with area colleges.

Four years later, the graduation rate has risen by 8 percent for those graduating in four years and nearly 10 percent overall. The college-going rate has climbed by more than 15 percent. Ruth Lohmeyer, school counseling team leader, says the school counseling department is "smiling at the end of each day, knowing they have made a difference." Lohmeyer explains they are far from resting on their laurels. New data show improvement is needed in their students' college-readiness scores. Due to this, the team has set new goals and put interventions in place. Lincoln Northeast High School is no longer on the U.S. Department of Education's watch list for being a persistently low-achieving school. In fact, Lincoln Northeast High School's culture is now a "college-going culture, and we couldn't be more proud. Making a difference is the reason school counselors are in schools. School counselors are the only ones in a school who see a student in 3-D: academic achievement, career planning and personal/social development. Lincoln Northeast High School's counseling team is thankful for the students in northeast Lincoln we are privileged to serve" (personal communication, Ruth Lohmeyer, April 13, 2013).

School counselors are powerful allies in delivering strategies that affect the information, opportunity and achievement gaps. School counselors have the ability to open doors so every student has equitable access to a level playing field. On a daily basis, school counselors are confronted with issues of equity and access to opportunity. The data from the students of Lincoln Northeast High School tell the tale. Low socio-economic status and ethnicity are not predictors of rigorous coursework at Lincoln Northeast. Education and economic success are inextricably entwined, and 15 percent more of the Lincoln Northeast High School graduates are realizing this opportunity.

EQUITY OF SERVICES

You love being a school counselor, especially for a select group of students that you describe as very bright, engaging and accomplished. It is this group of students that receive most of your time and attention. You believe these students have tremendous potential and are destined to make a considerable contribution to society. You schedule this select group to have the best teachers and provide frequent academic advising sessions. Is your behavior ethical?

Points to Consider

This case is blatant unethical practice, but often the stratification of services is without malevolent or deliberate intent. School counselors are so outnumbered that there are certain students to whom they give more attention than others, and some students they rarely or never see. The struggle is to reach as many students as they can, not just the top 5 percent or the most at-risk 5 percent of the student population, but reaching all students is not easy. Ethical behavior requires school counselors to grapple with equitable service delivery. All students need support but especially those without strong advocates or savvy guardians. No Child Left Behind (2001) calls for school counselors to accept the responsibility of advocating for every student to be able to experience success. Reaching the total student body is the focus of the ASCA National Model (2012).

School counselors are critical players in student success and are ideally situated to identify policies and practices schoolwide and districtwide that stratify student opportunity (Stone & Dahir, 2004). The stratifier of opportunity cannot be the school counseling program and practice. Optimum learning is the gift school counselors can give students. As unwilling as school counselors are to engage in preferential treatment for just a few select students, as described above, let the school counseling profession also become intolerant of programs that fall short for some students (Stone & Martin, 2004).

EDUCATING VS. DIRECTING

You are a high school counselor in an urban school with a diverse student population. One of your seniors comes to you and requests your help with her application to Harvard. This senior has an 86.6 average, is on the yearbook staff, has spent two years on the track team and is enrolled in four Advanced Placement classes. Kimberly says, "I know Harvard may not be a sure thing, but I have to try." Your frustration rises as, once again, you are forced to look a student in the eye and explain that it is the practice and policy of the school's administration to only let the top five students in each graduating class apply to an Ivy League school. How do you advocate for a change of policy?

Points to Consider

The New York Times article, "Amid Policy Confusion, Senior Is Allowed to Apply to Harvard" (Herszenhorn, 2004) describes how a Brooklyn, N.Y., public high school senior was told she could not apply to Harvard. Kimberly Cummins was ranked 11 out of 400 seniors in her class with a solid academic and extracurricular activity record, but her school only allowed the top five students to apply to an Ivy League school. Shocked,

Kimberly's older sister rallied her fellow NYU law school students, and together they raised the issue with school and government officials and advocacy groups. Kimberly was allowed to apply. This case represents an extreme, but what about the numerous polices existing in schools today that defer dreams when there is no savvy advocate to question and challenge them?

This *New York Times* article came just a few months after the ASCA membership overwhelmingly declared at the June 2004 Delegate Assembly that it is a school counselor's ethical imperative to provide all students with equity of service. The delegates revised the ASCA Ethical Standards for School Counselors to add equity and emphasize that school counselors will survey the school landscape for practices and policies that adversely stratify students' opportunities and will responsibly work to eradicate those policies.

Self-awareness, autonomy and independence are watchwords for school counselors who value their role in helping students move toward becoming functioning, self-directed adults (Lapan, 2001). School counselors work with students to help them see the potential of their lives and gently push them toward being informed, solid decision makers. It is infinitely easier to mete out advice and to just "tell" students what they need to do in personal, social, career and academic issues. However, our professional ethics tell us to eschew the easy way and to help students make informed choices while being careful to promote their dreams (ASCA, 2010).

Dreams without preparation are hollow. Helping students realize their dreams is a critical and essential component of the work of school counselors (Dahir, 2001). School counselors at all levels, behaving as advocates, systemic change agents, and career and academic advisers, help students dream from the time they are in elementary school and assist them in understanding what they need to do in school to fulfill their dreams. When students discover their passion and see the connection between dreams and education, it serves to motivate them for higher grades, better attendance and a stronger commitment to their education (Schwallie-Giddis, Maat & Park, 2003).

Basic to self-direction and autonomy is a student's right to understand the full weight and meaning of his or her decisions, as well as the interrelatedness between what the student does in school and his or her future economic opportunities. "Each person has the right to receive the information and support needed to move toward self-direction and self-development and affirmation within one's group identities, with special care being given to students who have historically not received adequate educational services, e.g., students of color, students living at low socio-economic status, students with disabilities and students from nondominant language backgrounds" (ASCA, 2010). Kimberly had the right to try. It is unthinkable for school officials, whose mission it is to promote a student's self-direction and autonomy, to deny her the right to try.

In a Position to Know: A School Counselor Speaks

The case presented at the beginning of the chapter is revisited here and answered by a school counselor. Compare his answers with your own approach.

PARENTS/GUARDIANS' VS. STUDENT'S ASPIRATIONS

Aarlyn has been a dedicated student throughout high school. She has built a transcript that will easily get her into any state university. You call Aarlyn in for a college/career advising session, and she informs you her parents are not allowing her to pursue higher education. She explains she is needed to take over the family's business, which is conducted on the first floor of the building where they live. Aarlyn says she will not abandon her family's needs, and after graduation, she will obey her parents' wishes so her father and mother can work fewer hours. She says her place is to care for a family that has always cared for her. She admits it is hard to let go of her dreams for higher education, chokes back tears, mumbles an excuse and quickly leaves your office. What, if anything, could you do?

Response From a School Counselor

Within the atmosphere of the large urban high school with its diverse student population, school counselors meet many challenges. In addition to academic matters, there are cultural and social issues that one anticipates in school counseling work, and there are unexpected and surprising situations that arise as well. These less-than-ordinary cases can challenge our ready responses and demand thoughtful, original solutions. Here, too, outside the boundaries within which we usually work, we are confronted with perhaps more ethical concerns.

As school counselors we naturally ask, doesn't Aarlyn deserve the chance to make a better life for herself, and possibly her family, if she were to attend college? From our perspective, if we do nothing, we see her future as limited. Aren't we obligated to help her recognize her broader options within the expectations of her family? It is a delicate matter demanding that we balance cultural sensitivity and ethical responsibility.

The school counselor's ethical responsibility is to advocate for Aarlyn by allowing her to make an informed choice about her future. The ethical standards for school counselors state the student has the right to understand the full magnitude and meaning of educational choices and how those choices will affect future opportunities (Stone, 2001).

To permit Aarlyn simply to accept her fate would be wrong. That would amount to giving up on her without any concern for her development and self-direction. The school counselor's role is critical. An idea or suggestion, a plan or question can alter a young person's vision of the future. In the case of Aarlyn, the meetings the school counselor holds with her must accomplish several things. They must affirm her worth as a student who would be valued by a college. They must acknowledge her culture and duty to her parents, and they should encourage her to be open to other possibilities that maximize her potential. The meetings cannot push her away through lack of understanding or coercion on the school counselor's part.

An attempt should be made to invite Aarlyn's parents to join us for an informational meeting, but Aarlyn's insistence against that idea, perhaps because of language barriers, takes that step out of the process. Without the parents' participation, the school counselor must beware of exerting too much pressure on Aarlyn. The school counselor's responsibility is to constantly remind her that the values and beliefs of her parents are not in question, but that her own nascent college aspirations are also valuable and worth exploring.

My goal would be to assure Aarlyn that there might be practical solutions that satisfy her parents' expectations as well as her own desire for an education. These solutions might involve choosing a part-time university program close to home or perhaps weekend college classes or some online classes. Literally opening up college catalogues and reading about courses and designing an imaginary schedule of classes would be appropriate. I might emphasize the need to start off slowly, devoting time to the family business with the hope that more classes could be taken later. The important point to emphasize for her is that by taking some college classes, she would not be forsaking her parent's wishes, nor would she be sacrificing her own.

Aarlyn needs to see how the choices she makes in the present, to reject college or accept it in a limited way, will affect her in the near future. Should she go to college as I have counseled, her future may be more successful. Who knows? Perhaps her parents will recognize their daughter has profited from college, and they will be more supportive. Perhaps some other factor will change the equation altogether, and Aarlyn will be permitted to choose her path freely. The school counselor helps to point the student down the road or helps draw the map. The rest is up to her.

To advocate on Aarlyn's behalf means to defy knee-jerk responses. Helping her involves the school counselor's dedication to advocate for and affirm Aarlyn's right to an education, offered with compassion for her struggle and an application of ethical principles. All work toward one end: Aarlyn makes her decision in the most informed and respected manner.
– *Robert Weiss, retired high school counselor, John F. Kennedy High School, New York, N.Y.*

Making Connections

1. Your school only encourages students who are likely to score a three or above to take the AP exam. District administrators compare AP test results for schools, and it is widely understood that it is considered a black mark against you if you have too many students in your caseload scoring below a three. Many high schools in the district, including yours, consider it best to covertly select students to take the AP exam and gingerly dissuade others from it. Are there any legal or ethical obligations involving this practice by your school district? With fellow professionals, discuss or debate the following positions:

- Is it ethical to limit the students who can take the AP test so the school can enhance its standing and test scores?
- Regardless of AP exam results, students always benefit by taking the AP exam.
- Other test scores, such as the state test, are likely to be positively affected by students taking AP exams.

- If a student knows at the beginning of the school year he or she will be expected and supported to take the AP exam, these efforts will encourage the student to more actively prepare for the exam.
- School counselors do not narrow opportunities that might possibly lead to scholarship dollars or college credit for certain courses.

2. Discuss your beliefs about how an equitable and ethical school counseling program can serve all students. Describe the characteristics and behaviors of a systemic change agent. Discuss a time when you exhibited these characteristics.

3. Discuss ways a school counselor who is committed to equity for all students might avoid spending too much time with students who are among the top 5 percent of the class and those who are in the lowest 5 percent of the class.

4. Review the ASCA Ethical Standards for School Counselors (2010), and identify which ethical code dealing with equity is the most difficult to attain and maintain. Why?

5. Consider the student population in your building. Are some students underserved in achieving an equitable education? What first step can you take to begin to remedy the situation?

Key Terms

Advocacy
Challenging the status quo
Entrenched inequities
Equal access
Equity and opportunity for all
   students

Social justice
Social change agent
Unalterable factors

Conclusion

We are our ethical codes. We have professionalized ourselves by assigning core ethical characteristics that distinguish us from all other professions. Our special skills, competence and application of knowledge have guided the development of an ethical code, just as our code of ethics guides the acquisition of new knowledge. This symbiotic relationship requires continual vigilance if we are to stay informed and current.

We perform our school counseling role in an institution that both empowers and hinders our efforts to be legal and ethical. The personal, social and emotional aspects of education compound the legal complexities. I hope one of the primary objectives of this book was accomplished, namely to demystify some of these complexities that have an impact on school counselors' daily work. If you found this book to be user-friendly and if it helped you gain a better understanding of the law and the practical application of your ethical codes, then another primary objective of the book was met.

Unlike public education systems in most countries, the system in the United States is decentralized, so that there are very few one-size-fits-all laws prevailing in every state and affecting every school counselor. Laws and legal precedents that govern school counselors are dependent on 50 different states, each with their own approach to the educational process. Federal legislation and Supreme Court decisions can give the bottom-line directive regarding some educational issues but there are really few legal imperatives that can be uniformly applied to all school counselors; we have more exceptions than rules established by the variation in philosophies, perspectives, school law and community standards.

This book does not propose to do the impossible: to exhaustively review the law for each state. Instead, we set forth general guiding principles of law that have been established by federal legislation and courts. The court cases presented here do not apply to all situations and certainly not to all states. Each case in the book is intentionally followed not by answers, but by "Points to Consider." This book does not suggest hard-and-fast rules but a range of less-than-definitive responses for your contemplation and application to the context of your own particular school.

Thus, this book is not the last word. School counselors must always be consumers of their specific state statutes and school board rules. It cannot be overemphasized that you should always consult with local authorities and seek supervision from local professionals before drawing any conclusions based on what is stated here.

America is a litigious society. Almost every facet of schooling, from slogans written on a T-shirt to a student's right to access an appropriate education, has been the subject of judicial discourse. We have attempted here to help school counselors learn about some of the judicial debates that inform their practice. By raising our awareness, we can practice prevention and become legally literate.

More importantly, if we raise our awareness of the law we may also prevent the paralysis that can come from fear and anxiety about slipping up and becoming the subject of a lawsuit. This book was written to also dispel the myth that we should view the law with fear and trepidation. Yes, we are a litigious society, but a lawsuit is a rare occurrence for a school counselor, especially one who makes an honest attempt to act legally and ethically. The truth is that school counselors have a better chance of winning the lottery than of becoming the subject of a lawsuit if they practice as reasonably competent professionals. School counselors who are empowered to identify policies, practices or sources of potential legal and ethical conflict are better equipped to serve students and to reduce their own chances of becoming the center of a stressful lawsuit.

I hope that you will not put this book aside after reading it, but actively discuss and debate the cases and the issues presented with your colleagues or classmates. Remember, in the legal and ethical arena of our human services profession, there is rarely a single right answer to the dilemmas we face as school counselors.

Public schools have become increasingly important as the one institution in our country that is supposed to level the playing field for all Americans. Throughout this book the ethics of advocacy have been a primary focus. The extraordinary challenges, rewards and obligations of being an ethical educator require that we work to provide each student with an education that will allow him or her to participate in the global economy. Such a tremendous imperative carries additional legal and ethical obligations, and I hope this book has helped us to understand that even though we cannot do everything, we have to try to do everything we possibly can. It is my sincere hope that this book empowered you.

References

A Better Child. (n.d.). *How do online predators work?* Retrieved from http://www.a-better-child.org/page/784785

Adams, M., Bell, L. A., & Griffin, P. (2007). *Teaching for diversity and social justice* (2nd ed.). New York, NY: CRC Press.

Akos, P., Schuldt, H., & Walendin, M. (2009) School counselor assignment in secondary schools. *Professional School Counseling, 13*(1), 23-29.

Alexander, K., & Alexander, M. D. (2011). *American public school law* (8th ed.). Belmont, CA: Thomson West.

Albers v. Breen, 346 Ill. App. 3d 799, 806 N.E.2d 667 (4th Dist. 2004).

Alleman, J. R. (2002). Online counseling: The Internet and mental health treatment. *Psychotherapy: Theory/Research/Practice/Training, 39,* 199–209.

Allen, Z. (2004). Schools against kids: 'Zero tolerance' policies criminalize students, youth of color hardest hit. *The Indypendent, 44.* Retrieved from http://www.indypendent.org/2004/02/04/schools-against-kids-zero-tolerance-policies-criminalize-students-youth-color-hardest-hit

Ali, R. (2010, October 26). *Dear colleague letter: Harassment and bullying.* Washington, DC: U.S. Department of Education, Office of Civil Rights. Retrieved from http://www2.ed.gov/about/offices/list/ocr/letters/colleague-201010.pdf

American Academy of Child & Adolescent Psychiatry. (2006, January). *Gay, lesbian and bisexual adolescents.* Retrieved from http://www.aacap.org/cs/root/facts_for_families/gay_lesbian_and_bisexual_adolescents

American Academy of Pediatrics. (2000, July 21). *Parity, scope-of-practice issues in spotlight at AMA meeting.* Retrieved from http://psychnews.org/pnews/00-07-21/parity.html

American Association of University Women. (2001). *Hostile hallways: Bullying, teasing, and sexual harassment in school.* Washington, DC: Author. Retrieved from http://history.aauw.org/files/2013/01/hostilehallways.pdf

American Association of University Women. (2011). *Crossing the line: Sexual harassment at school,* executive summary. Washington, DC: Author. Retrieved from http://www.aauw.org/resource/crossing-the-line-sexual-harassment-at-school-executive-summary

American Bar Association. (2004). Rights and responsibilities of parents. In *American Bar Association family legal guide* (3rd ed.). Washington, DC: Author.

American Civil Liberties Union. (2003a, April 8). *ACLU sues Arkansas school district to guarantee gay student's right to be "out" at school.* Retrieved from http://www.aclu.org/lgbt-rights_hiv-aids/aclu-sues-arkansas-school-district-guarantee-gay-students-right-be-out-school

American Civil Liberties Union. (2003b, July 17). *ACLU secures sweeping changes in Arkansas school district.* Retrieved from http://www.aclu.org/lgbt-rights_hiv-aids/aclu-secures-sweeping-changes-arkansas-school-district

American Civil Liberties Union. (2005, December 1). *Federal judge rules that high schools cannot out lesbian and gay students.* Retrieved from http://www.aclu.org/content/federal-judge-rules-high-schools-cannot-out-lesbian-and-gay-students

American Civil Liberties Union. (2006, December 12). *Trial for Orange County teen 'outed' by principal concludes.* Retrieved from http://www.aclu.org/lgbt-rights_hiv-aids/trial-orange-county-teen-outed-principal-concludes

American Civil Liberties Union. (2007, September 25). *Nguon v. Wolf: Case profile.* Retrieved from http://www.aclu.org/lgbt-rights/nguon-v-wolf-case-profile

American Civil Liberties Union. (2008a, May 13). *Federal judge rules that students can't be barred from expressing support for gay people.* Retrieved from http://www.aclu.org/lgbt-rights_hiv-aids/federal-judge-rules-students-can%E2%80%99t-be-barred-expressing-support-gay-people

American Civil Liberties Union. (2008b, July 30). *Okeechobee, FL high school gay-straight alliance wins groundbreaking federal lawsuit.* Retrieved from http://www.aclu.org/lgbt-rights_hiv-aids/okeechobee-fl-high-school-gay-straight-alliance-wins-groundbreaking-federal-law

American Civil Liberties Union. (2009a, May 18) *High school student takes on anti-gay harassment—and wins.* Retrieved from http://www.aclu.org/lgbt-rights_hiv-aids/high-school-student-takes-anti-gay-harassment—and-wins

American Civil Liberties Union. (2009b, July 20). *Gillman v. Holmes County School District case profile.* Retrieved from http://www.aclu.org/lgbt-rights_hiv-aids/gillman-v-holmes-county-school-district-case-profile

American Civil Liberties Union. (2009c, July 20). *Morrison v. Boyd Co. Board of Education case profile.* Retrieved from http://www.aclu.org/lgbt-rights_hiv-aids/morrison-v-boyd-co-board-education-case-profile

American Civil Liberties Union. (2010a, March 5). *ACLU seeks order to protect right to form a gay-straight alliance at Yulee Middle School.* Retrieved from http://www.aclu.org/lgbt-rights/aclu-seeks-order-protect-right-form-gay-straight-alliance-yulee-middle-school

American Civil Liberties Union. (2010b, April 21.) *ACLU complaint takes on "decoy" prom for Mississippi lesbian student.* Retrieved from http://www.aclu.org/lgbt-rights/aclu-complaint-takes-decoy-prom-mississippi-lesbian-student

American Civil Liberties Union. (2010c, July 20). *Mississippi school agrees to revise policy and pay damages to lesbian teenager denied chance to attend prom.* Retrieved from http://www.aclu.org/lgbt-rights/mississippi-school-agrees-revise-policy-and-pay-damages-lesbian-teenager-denied-chance-a

American Civil Liberties Union. (2011a, July 1). *Sweeping anti-bullying settlement announced following federal investigation into teen suicide.* Retrieved from http://www.aclu.org/lgbt-rights/sweeping-anti-bullying-settlement-announced-following-federal-investigation-teen-suicide

American Civil Liberties Union. (2011b, December 8). *Sturgis v. Copiah County School District.* Retrieved from http://www.aclu.org/lgbt-rights/sturgis-v-copiah-county-school-district

American Civil Liberties Union of Virginia. (2012, March 5). *Under pressure, Suffolk School Board back off discriminatory gender-based dress code policy.* Retrieved from https://acluva.org/9783/under-pressure-suffolk-school-board-backs-off-discriminatory-gender-based-dress-code-policy/

American Counseling Association. (2005). *Code of ethics and standards of practice.* Alexandria, VA: Author.

American Counseling Association (2012). *Ethics.* Retrieved from http://www.counseling.org/Resources/aca-code-of-ethics.pdf

American Lawyer Newspapers Group, Inc. (2000, March 6). Justices divided on interpretation of parental notification law. *Texas Lawyer*, p. 15.

American Medical Association. (2006). H-160.991 *Health care needs of the homosexual population*. Retrieved from http://www.ama-assn.org/ama/pub/about-ama/our-people/member-groups-sections/glbt-advisory-committee/ama-policy-regarding-sexual-orientation.page

American Psychiatric Association. (2000). *Position statement on therapies focused on attempts to change sexual orientation (reparative or conversion therapies)*. Retrieved from http://www.psychiatry.org/File%20Library/Advocacy%20and%20Newsroom/Position%20Statements/ps2000_ReparativeTherapy.pdf

American Psychological Association. (2008). *Sexual orientation and homosexuality*. Retrieved from http://www.apa.org/helpcenter/sexual-orientation.aspx

American Psychological Association Zero Tolerance Task Force. (2008). Are zero tolerance policies effective in the schools? An evidentiary review and recommendations. *American Psychologist, 63*(9), 852-862. doi:10.1037/0003-066X.63.9.852

American School Counselor Association. (n.d.). *ASCA position statements*. Retrieved from http://www.schoolcounselor.org/files/PositionStatements.pdf

American School Counselor Association. (2003). *ASCA position statement: The professional school counselor and child abuse and neglect prevention*. Retrieved from http://www.schoolcounselor.org/files/PS_Child%20Abuse.pdf

American School Counselor Association. (2005). *The ASCA National Model: A framework for school counseling programs* (2nd ed.). Alexandria, VA: Author

American School Counselor Association. (2012). *ASCA position statement: The professional school counselor and student safety and the use of technology*. Retrieved from http://www.schoolcounselor.org/files/PS_Technology.pdf

American School Counselor Association. (2007a). *ASCA position statement: The professional school counselor and corporal punishment*. Retrieved from http://www.schoolcounselor.org/files/PS_CorporalPunishment.pdf

American School Counselor Association. (2007b). *ASCA position statement: The professional school counselor and discipline*. Retrieved from http://www.schoolcounselor.org/files/PS_Discipline.pdf

American School Counselor Association. (2007c). *ASCA position statement: The professional school counselor and LGBTQ youth.* Retrieved from http://www.schoolcounselor.org/files/PS_LGBTQ.pdf

American School Counselor Association. (2008). *ASCA position statement: The professional school counselor and confidentiality.* Retrieved from http://www.schoolcounselor.org/files/ PS_Confidentiality.pdf

American School Counselor Association. (2009a). *ASCA governing policies.* Alexandria, VA: Author.

American School Counselor Association. (2009b). *ASCA position statement: The professional school counselor and student mental health.* Retrieved from http://www.schoolcounselor.org/files/ PS_StudentMentalHealth.pdf

American School Counselor Association. (2009c). *The role of the professional school counselor.* Retrieved from http://www.schoolcounselor.org/content.asp?contentid=240

American School Counselor Association (2010). *Ethical standards for school counselors.* Alexandria, VA: Author.

American School Counselor Association. (2011). *ASCA position statement: The promotion of safe schools through conflict resolution and bullying/harassment prevention.* Retrieved from http://www.schoolcounselor.org/files/PS_Bullying.pdf

American School Counselor Association. (2012). *The ASCA National Model: A framework for school counseling programs* (3rd ed.). Alexandria, VA: Author.

Amy Hestir Student Protection Act. Senate Bill 54 (2011).

Andrews and Beard Education Law Report. (2008). Teacher terminated for religious conduct has no title VII claim. *Andrews and Beard Education Law Report, 3*(2), 5.

Applebome, P. (2009, March 7). Grades fixed: An allegation shocks no one. *The New York Times.* Retrieved from http://www.nytimes.com/ 2009/03/08/nyregion/08towns.html?_r=0

Arnold v. Board of Education of Escambia County, 880 F. 2d 305 (Ala. 1989).

Aronson, B. (2002, March). *Why statutes of limitations for child abuse should be extended, as Pennsylvania legislators have proposed.* Retrieved from http://writ.news.findlaw.com/aronson/20020321.html

Association for Specialists in Group Work. (2008). *Best practice guidelines.* Retrieved from http://www.asgw.org/pdf/Best_Practices.pdf

Association of American Educators. (n.d.) *AAE code of ethics for educators.* Retrieved from: http://aaeteachers.org/images/pdfs/ aaecodeofethicsforeducators.pdf

Associated Press. (1980, May 31). Six police protect homosexual, date at school's prom. *Eugene Register-Guard*. Retrieved from http://news.google.com/newspapers?nid=1310&dat=19800531&id=-a5hAAAAIBAJ&sjid=3OEDAAAAIBAJ&pg=4621,9325617

Associated Press. (2012, May 24). Ohio school shooter to be tried as an adult. *CBSNews*. Retrieved from http://www.cbsnews.com/8301-201_162-57441009/ohio-school-shooter-to-be-tried-as-adult/

Associated Press. (2012, June 5). Antigay-shirt ban illegal, group says. *The New York Times*. Retrieved from http://www.nytimes.com/2012/06/06/nyregion/aclu-says-antigay-shirt-ban-at-connecticut-school-was-illegal.html?_r=0

Associated Press. (2012, September 24). Morning-after pills available at 13 NYC public schools. *USA Today*. Retrieved from http://www.usatoday.com/news/nation/story/2012/09/24/morning-after-pills-available-at-13-nyc-public-schools/57836354/1?csp=34news

Associated Press. (2013a, February 26). Seth Groody, Connecticut teen, has anti-gay t-shirt approved by high school. *Huffington Post*. Retrieved from http://www.huffingtonpost.com/2013/02/26/seth-groody-connecticut-teen-anti-gay-shirt_n_2767945.html?utm_hp_ref=anti-bullying

Associated Press. (2013b, March 27). Tenn. bill to prohibit discussion of gay issues dies. *TriCities.com*. Retrieved from http://www.tricities.com/news/local/article_1700a86e-967a-11e2-82e8-001a4bcf6878.html

Austin, S. M., Reynolds, G. P., & Barnes, S. L. (2012). School leadership and counselors working together to address bullying. *Education, 133*(2), 283-290.

Avert. (2008). *Coming out*. Retrieved from http://www.avert.org/hsexu4.htm

Baca, M. E. (2012, March 6). Anoka-Hennepin School District settles bullying lawsuit. *StarTribune: Newspaper of the Twin Cities (Minneapolis, MN)*. Retrieved from http://www.startribune.com/local/north/141427303.html?page=1&c=y

Baker, S. B., & Gerler, E. R. (2007). *School counseling for the twenty-first century* (5th ed.). Upper Saddle River, NJ: Merrill Prentice Hall.

Baldwin, D. & Kaufman, M. (2002, March 9). *The Laramie project* [Motion picture]. United States: Home Box Office (HBO).

Barboza, G. E., Schiamberg, L. B., Ochmke, J., Korzeniewski, S. J., Post, L. A., & Heraux, C. G. (2009). Individual characteristics and the multiple contexts of adolescent bullying: Anecological perspective. *Journal of Youth and Adolescence, 38*, 101-121. doi:10.1007/S10964-0089271-1

Bardick, A., Bernes, K., McCulloch, A., Witko, K., Spriddle, J., & Roest, A. (2004). Eating disorder intervention, prevention, and treatment. *Professional School Counseling, 8*(2), 168-175.

Beckham, J., & Klaymeier Wills, B. (2009). School boards: Duties, responsibilities, decision-making, and legal basis for local school board powers. *Education Encyclopedia*. Retrieved from http://education.stateuniversity.com/pages/2391/School-Boards.html

Belanger v. Nashua, New Hampshire, School District, 856 F. Supp. 40 (1994).

Belch, H. E. (2012). Teachers beware! The dark side of social networking. *Learning & Leading with Technology, 39*(4), 15-19.

Bellotti v. Baird, 443 U.S. 622 (1979).

Bell, V., & De la Rue, D. (1995). *Gender harassment on the Internet.* Atlanta, GA: Georgia State University College of Law.

Bernes, K. B., & Bardick, A. D. (2007). Conducting adolescent violence risk assessments: A framework for school counselors. *Professional School Counseling, 10*(4), 419-427.

Bethel School District No. 403 v. Fraser, 478 U.S. 675, 106 S. Ct. 3159 (1986).

Bhatt, S., Vinh, T., & Shaw, L. (2003, September 20). Accusations bring wave of support for Franklin trio. *The Seattle Times*. Retrieved from http://community.seattletimes.nwsource.com/archive/?date=20030920&slug=grades20m0

Bidell, M. P. (2011). School counselors and social justice advocacy for lesbian, gay, bisexual, transgender, and questioning students. *Journal of School Counseling, 9*(10).

Blum, R., Resnick, M., & Stark, T. (1990). Factors associated with the use of court bypass by minors to obtain abortions. *Family Planning Perspectives, 22*(4), 158.

Board of Education of Tonica Community High School District v. Adelbert E. Sickley, 479 N.E.2d 1142 (Ill. 1985).

Bobek, B. L., Robbins, S. B., Gore, P. A., Harris-Bowlsbey, J., Lapan, R. T., Dahir, C. A., & Jepsen, D. A. (2005). Training counselors to use computer-assisted career guidance systems more effectively: A model curriculum. *Career Development Quarterly, 53*, 363–371.

Bodenhorn, N. (2006). Exploratory study of common and challenging ethical dilemmas experienced by professional school counselors. *Professional School Counseling 10*, 195-202.

Bogust v. Iverson, 102 N.W.2d 228 (Wis. 1960).

Bonvento v. Board of Public Instruction of Palm Beach County, 194 So. 2d 605 (Fla. 1967).

Borum, R., & Reddy, M. (2001). Assessing violence risk in Tarasoff situations: A fact-based model of inquiry. *Behavioral Sciences and the Law, 19*, 375-385.

Bowers, J. (2005, June 3). Hand in hand. *ASCA School Counselor.* Retrieved from http://www.ascaschoolcounselor.org/article_content.asp?article=778

Boyd, D. (2011, June 13). *Teen sexting and its impact on the tech industry.* Presentation at the Read Write Web 2WAY Conference, New York, NY. Retrieved from http://www.danah.org/papers/talks/2011/RWW2011.html

Boyd, D. (2011, December 12). Four difficult questions regarding bullying and youth suicide. *Digital media and learning research hub.* Retrieved from http://dmlcentral.net/blog/danah-boyd/four-difficult-questions-regarding-bullying-and-youth-suicide

Boynton v. Burglass, 590 So. 2d 446, 448-49 (Florida Dist. Ct. App. 1991).

Brady, S. S., & Halpern-Felsher, B.L. (2007). Adolescents reported consequences of having oral sex versus vaginal sex. *Pediatrics, 119*(2), 229-236.

Brown v. Compton Unified School District, 68 Cal. App. 4th 114; 80 Cal. Rptr. 2d 171 (Cal. App. 1998).

Bryan, J., Day-Vines, N., Griffin, D., & Moore-Thomas, C. (2012). The disproportionality dilemma: Patterns of teacher referrals to school counselors for disruptive behavior. *Journal of Counseling & Development, 90*(2), 177-190. doi:10.1111/j.1556-6676.2012.00023.x

Bryan, J. A., & Griffin, D. (2010). A multidimensional study of school-family-community partnership involvement: School, school counselor, and training factors. *Professional School Counseling, 14*(1), 75-86.

Bully Police USA (2013). *A watch-dog organization – advocating for bullied children & reporting on state anti bullying laws.* Retrieved from http://www.bullypolice.org/

Bureau of Labor Statistics. (2012). *Current population survey.* Retrieved from http://data.bls.gov/cgi-bin/srgate Data were accessed using codes LNU04027675 (men) and LNU04027679 (women).

Burpee v. Burton, 45 Wis. 150, 30 Am. Rep. 706 (1878).

Burrow-Sanchez, J., Call, M. E., Zheng, R., & Drew, C. J. (2011). How school counselors can help prevent online victimization. *Journal of Counseling & Development, 89*(1), 3-10.

Buz, E. (2012, February, 29). Sexual harassment roundup. *Title IX Blog.* Retrieved from http://title-ix.blogspot.com/2012_02_01_archive.html

C.A. v. William Hart Union High Sch. Dist., No. S188982 (Cal. Mar. 8, 2012).

California Education Code § 49602 (2004).

Camlin v. Beecher Community School District, App. 3d 1013; 791 N.E.2d 127 (2003).

Capital-Gazette Communications, Inc. (2004, October 19). *Annapolis, MD*. Retrieved from http://www.capitalgazette.com/

Capuzzi, D. (2002). Legal and ethical challenges in counseling suicidal students. *Professional School Counseling, 6*(1), 36-46.

Cardi, J., & Green, M. (2008). Duty wars. *Southern California Law Review, 81*, 672-733.

Carney, J. M., & Scott, H. L. (2012). Eating issues in schools: Detection, management, and consultation with allied professionals. *Journal of Counseling & Development, 90*(3), 290-297. doi:10.1002/j.1556-6676.2012.00037.x

Carroll v. Rondout Valley Central School District, Ulster County, New York (1999).

Carr, T. (2003, October 24). School forming death talk protocol. Traverse City (Mich.) *Record-Eagle*, pp. 1-2.

CBSAtlanta.com Staff. (2012, May 25). Texas honor student jailed for missing too much school. *CBSAtlanta.com*. Retrieved from http://www.cbsatlanta.com/story/18626605/texas-honors-student-jailed-for-excessive-truancy

Centre for Suicide Prevention. (2002). No-suicide contracts: A review of the findings from the research. *SEIC Alert #49*. Retrieved from http://suicideinfo.ca/Library/Resources/SIECAlertArchive.aspx

Centers for Disease Control and Prevention. (2009) *Youth risk behavior surveillance–United States, 2009*. Surveillance Summaries. MMWR 59(SS–5). Retrieved from http://www.cdc.gov/mmwr/PDF/ss/ss5905.pdf

Centers for Disease Control and Prevention. (2010, June 4). *Youth risk behavior surveillance – United States, 2009*. Retrieved from http://www.cdc.gov/healthyyouth/yrbs/cdcreports.htm

Centers for Disease Control and Prevention. (2013, March 18). *Sexual Risk Behavior: HIV, STD, & Teen Pregnancy Prevention*. Retrieved from http://www.cdc.gov/HealthyYouth/sexualbehaviors/

Chaney, M. P, Filmore, J. M., & Goodrich, K M. (2011, May 1). *No more sitting on the sidelines*. Retrieved from http://ct.counseling.org/2011/05/no-more-sitting-on-the-sidelines/

Chen, E. C., Budianto, L., & Wong, K. (2010). Professional school counselors as social justice advocates for undocumented immigrant students in group work. *Journal for Specialists in Group Work, 35*(2), 255-261.

Chesir-Teran, D., & Hughes, D. (2009). Heterosexism in high school and victimization among lesbian, gay, bisexual, and questioning students. *Journal of Youth Adolescence, 38*, 963-975. doi:10.1007/s10964-008-9364-x

Chester, A., & Glass, C. A. (2006). Online counseling: A descriptive analysis of therapy services on the Internet. *British Journal of Guidance and Counseling, 34*, 145–160.

Child Protective Services Act, Wyoming Code. § 14-3-2(1999).

Children's Safety Network. (2012, February). *Teen dating violence as public health issue*. Retrieved from http://www.childrenssafetynetwork.org/sites/childrenssafetynetwork.org/files/TeenDatingViolenceasaPublicHealthIssue.pdf

Child Welfare Information Gateway (n.d.) *Child Prevention and Treatment Act (CAPTA) of 1974 P.L. 93-247*. Retrieved from https://www.childwelfare.gov/systemwide/laws_policies/federal/index.cfm?event=federalLegislation.viewLegis&id=2

Child Welfare Information Gateway. (2005). *Statutes of limitations for offenses against children: Summary of state laws*. Retrieved from http://www.childwelfare.gov/systemwide/laws_policies/state/can/reporting.cfm

Child Welfare Information Gateway. (2007a). *Definitions of child abuse and neglect* [State statutes series]. Retrieved from http://www.childwelfare.gov/systemwide/laws_policies/statutes/define.cfm

Child Welfare Information Gateway. (2007b). *Recognizing child abuse and neglect: Signs and symptoms*. Retrieved from http://www.childwelfare.gov/pubs/factsheets/signs.cfm

Child Welfare Information Gateway, (2008a). *Long-term consequences of child abuse and neglect*. Retrieved from http://www.childwelfare.gov/pubs/factsheets/long_term_consequences.cfm

Child Welfare Information Gateway. (2008b). *What is child abuse and neglect?* Retrieved from https://www.childwelfare.gov/pubs/factsheets/whatiscan.cfm

Child Welfare Information Gateway. (2009). *Child witnesses to domestic violence: Summary of state laws*. Retrieved from https://www.childwelfare.gov/systemwide/laws_policies/statutes/witnessdv.cfm

Child Welfare Information Gateway. (2010). *Infant safe haven laws: Summary of state laws*. Retrieved from http://www.childwelfare.gov/systemwide/laws_policies/statutes/safehaven.cfm

Child Welfare Information Gateway. (2012). *Immunity for reporters of child abuse and neglect.* Retrieved from https://www.childwelfare.gov/systemwide/laws_policies/statutes/immunity.pdf

Christensen, H., Griffiths, K. M., & Jorm, A. F. (2004). Delivering interventions for depression by using the Internet: Randomized controlled trial. *British Medical Journal, 328,* 265-269.

Clark, M. A., & Horton-Parker, R. (2002). Professional development schools: New opportunities for training school counselors. *Counselor Education and Supervision, 1,* 58-75.

CNN Wire Staff. (2010, July 20). *Mississippi school pays damages to lesbian teen over prom dispute.* Retrieved from http://www.webcitation.org/5woNLWDDr

Colín v. Orange Unified School District, 83 F. Supp. 2d 1135 (C.D.Cal. 2000).

College Board. (2004). *National Office for School Counselor Advocacy.* Retrieved from http://nosca.collegeboard.org/

College Entrance Examination Board. (1986). *Keeping the options open. Recommendations: Final report of the commission on precollege guidance and counseling.* New York, NY: College Entrance Examination Board. (ERIC Document Reproduction Service No. ED275948).

Collins v. Scottsboro City Bd. of Educ., CV-2008-90 (38th Judicial District March 28, 2008).

Commonwealth v. Allen, 980 S.W.2d 278 (Ky. 1998).

Connick v. Myers, 461 U.S. 138, 146 (1983).

Conn, K. (2011). Allegations of school district liability for bullying, cyberbullying, and teen suicide after sexting: Are new legal standards emerging in the courts? *New England Journal on Criminal and Civil Confinement, 37*(2), 227-246.

Conyne, R. K., & Bemak, F. (2004). Teaching group work from an ecological perspective. *Journal for Specialists in Group Work, 29,* 7-18.

Cook, J. E. (2001) *Working alliance and Internet therapy: Comparison across modalities* (Unpublished doctoral dissertation). Lewis & Clark College, Portland, OR.

Cook, J. E., & Doyle, C. (2002). Working alliance in online therapy as compared to face-to-face therapy: Preliminary results. *CyberPsychology & Behavior, 5,* 95-105.

Corey, G. (2011). *Theory and practice of group counseling* (7th ed.). Pacific Grove, CA: Brooks/Cole.

Corey, G., Corey, M. S., & Callanan, R. (2010). *Issues and ethics in the helping professions* (8th ed.). Pacific Grove, CA: Brooks/Cole.

Couch v. Wayne Local School District; 2012 U.S. Dist. LEXIS 123046 (May 21, 2012).

Courson, J., & Farris, A. C. (2012). Title IX liability for anti-gay bullying. *Children's Rights Litigation, 14*(3), 20-24.

Craig v. Rich Township High Sch. Dist., No. 12-7581 (N.D. Ill. Feb. 19, 2013).

Crehan, A. (n.d.). *Professional distance: Defining it, maintaining it managing it.* Centre for Applied Philosophy and Public Ethics (Working Paper No. 2002/6). Retrieved from http://www.cappe.edu.au/docs/working-papers/CorboCrehan1.pdf

Cromarty, K., & Richards, K. (2009). How do secondary school counselors work with other professionals? *Counselling &Psychotherapy Research, 9*(3), 182-186. doi:10.1080/14733140903083821

Cullitan, C. M. (2011). Please don't tell my mom! A minor's right to informational privacy. *Journal of Law & Education, 40*(3), 417-460.

Curry, J. R., & Hayes, B. (2009). Bolstering school based support by comprehensively addressing the needs of an invisible minority: Implications for professional school counselors. *Journal of School Counseling, 7*(7).

Dahir, C. A. (2001). The national standards for school counseling programs: Development and implementation. *Professional School Counseling, 4*, 320-327.

Dahir, C. A., Burnham, J. J., Stone, C. B., & Cobb, N. (2010). Principals as partners: Counselors as collaborators. *NASSP Bulletin, 94*(4), 286-305.

Dahir, C., & Stone, C. (2004). Leaving no school counselor behind. *VISTAS - Perspectives on counseling 2004*, 177-182. Retrieved from http://www.counselingoutfitters.com/vistas/vistas04/18.pdf

Davis, A. (2008, September). Interpersonal and physical dating violence among teens. FOCUS views from *National Council on Crime and Delinquency.* Retrieved from http://www.nccdglobal.org/sites/default/files/publication_pdf/focus-dating-violence.pdf

Davis v. Monroe County Board of Education et al., 120 F.3d 1390. (Supreme Court, May 24, 1999).

Day of Silence. (2011). *Frequently asked questions.* Retrieved from http://www.dayofsilence.org/content/getinformation_faq.html

Decker, A. (2007). More teens victimized by cyber-bullies. *The New York Times.* Retrieved from http://www.NYTimes.com

Dell'Antonia, K. (2012, September, 25). New York City schools provide morning-after pills. *The New York Times*. Retrieved from http://parenting.blogs.nytimes.com/2012/09/25/new-york-city-schools-provide-morning-after-pills/

Demitchell, T., & Demitchell, T. (2007). A crack in the educational malpractice wall. *School Administrator, 64*(9), 34-60. Retrieved from WilsonWeb.

Dezen, K. A., Gurl, A., & Ping, J. (2010). School psychologists working with children affected by abuse and neglect. *Communique, 38*(7), 1, 18.

Di Marzo, G. M. (2012). Why can't we be friends? The banning of teacher-student communication via social media and the freedom of speech. *American University Law Review, 62*(1), 123-166.

Dinsmore, J. (2009). Who am I? *Scholastic Choices, 24*(4), 18-21. Retrieved from ProQuest database.

Dobbs, D. (2011). Beautiful brains. *National Geographic*. Retrieved from http://ngm.nationalgeographic.com/2011/10/teenage-brains/dobbs-text

Doe v. Anoka-Hennepin School District No. 11, No. 11-cv-01999 (D. Minn. March 6, 2012).

Doe v. Blandford, 402 Mass. 831, 835, 525 N.E.2d 403 (2000).

Doe v. Coleville Sch. Dist, 2012 WL 554430 (E.D. Wash. Feb. 21, 2012).

Doe v. Fournier, 2012 WL 591669 (D. Mass. Feb. 22, 2012).

Doe v. Rains Independent School District, 865 F. Supp. 375 (E.D. Tex 1994).

Doe v. Yunits, 15 Mass. L. Rep. 278; 2001 Mass. Super. LEXIS 327.

Doe and Doe v. Greendale Baptist Church and Academy, 327 F.3d 492 (Wisconsin 2003).

Doll, B. (2011). Youth privacy, school records, and the ethical practice of psychology in schools. *Professional Psychology: Research and Practice, 42*(3), 259-263.

Doninger v. Niehoff, 527 F.3d 41 (2d Cir. 2008).

Duhaime's Online Legal Dictionary (n.d.). Retrieved from http://www.duhaime.org/dictionary/dict-c.aspx

Durant v. Los Angeles Unified School District, Court of Appeal of California, 2nd Appellate District, Div. 8, B155739 (2003).

Durso, L.E., & Gates, G.J. (2012). *Serving our youth: Findings from a national survey of service providers working with lesbian, gay, bisexual, and transgender youth who are homeless or at risk of becoming homeless.* Los Angeles, CA: The Williams Institute with True Colors Fund and The Palette Fund.

Duval County Public Schools. (2011). *Student code of conduct 2011.* Jacksonville, FL: Author.

Eckholm, E. (2011, September 13). Eight suicides in two years at Anoka-Hennepin School District. *The New York Times.* Retrieved from http://www.nytimes.com/2011/09/13/us/13bullysidebar.html?_r=0

Eckholm, E. (2012, November 28). Gay 'conversion therapy' faces test in courts. *The New York Times.* Retrieved from http://www.nytimes.com/2012/11/28/us/gay-conversion-therapy-faces-tests-in-courts.html

Edelman, S. (2012, October, 9). Manhattan HS guidance counselor stripped of job over steamy-photo past. *New York Post.* Retrieved from http://www.nypost.com/p/news/local/manhattan/educator_stripped_of_job_XD3Njj11p6sVTwS8IO3JZI

Eisel v. Board of Education of Montgomery County, 324 Md. 376, 597 A. 2d 447 (Md Ct. App. 1991).

Electronic Code of Federal Regulations. (2012). *Title 34, part 99—family educational rights and privacy.* Retrieved from: http://www2.ed.gov/policy/gen/reg/ferpa/index.html

Elder, G. (n.d.). *Texas law tough on sexual relationships between teachers and students.* Retrieved from http://www.totalcriminaldefense.com/news/articles/sex-crimes/teacher-student-sex.aspx

Elias, M. (2007, February 11). Gay teens coming out earlier to peers and family. *USA Today.* Retrieved from http://usatoday30.usatoday.com/news/nation/2007-02-07-gay-teens-cover_x.htm

Equal Access Act, 20 U.S.C. § 4071-74 (1984). *Title 20-Education, Chapter 52-Education for economic security, Subchapter VIII–Equal access.* Retrieved from www.justice.gov/crt/about/cor/byagency/ed4071.php

Equal Rights Advocates. (2012). *Know your rights: Sexual harassment at school.* Retrieved from http://www.equalrights.org/legal-help/know-your-rights/sexual-harassment-at-school/

Eng, J. (2011, December 8). No tuxes or dresses for senior portraits after school settles lawsuit with lesbian. *NBC News.* Retrieved from: http://usnews.nbcnews.com/_news/2011/12/08/9304669-no-tuxes-or-dresses-for-senior-portrait-after-school-settles-lawsuit-with-lesbian

Espelage, D. L. (2004). An ecological perspective to school-based bullying prevention. *The Prevention Researcher, 11*(3), 3-6.

Facebook Education Notes. (2012). *Facebook for school counselors.* Retrieved from http://www.facebook.com/notes/facebook-in-education/facebook-for-school-counselors/10151499151175570

Fallon, K. (2013, January 13). 'Don't say gay' is back: 5 things to know about the Tennessee bill. *The Daily Beast.* Retrieved from http://www.thedailybeast.com/articles/2013/01/31/don-t-say-gay-is-back-5-things-to-know-about-the-tennessee-bill.html

Family Educational Rights and Privacy Act, 20 U.S.C.§1232g (1974).

Federal Register (2000). *Rules and regulations department of education 34 CFR part 99. 65*(130).

Feller, B. (2006, March 10). Christian, gay groups unite on school conflicts. *The Boston Globe.* Retrieved from http://www.boston.com/news/nation/washington/articles/2006/03/10/christian_gay_groups_unite_on_school_conflicts/

Feller, R. W., & Davies, T. G. (2003). Contemporary issues changing the career planning context. In T. Harrington (Ed.), *Handbook of career planning for students with special needs* (pp. 345-374). Austin, TX: ProEd.

Finkelhor, D., Turner, H., Ormrod, R., Hamby, S., & Kracke, K. (2009, October) Children's exposure to violence: A comprehensive national survey. *Juvenile Justice Bulletin.* Retrieved from http://www.unh.edu/ccrc/pdf/DOJ-NatSCEV-bulletin.pdf

First Amendment Center. (2006). *1st consensus guidelines offered for schools on sexual orientation news release: First Amendment framework suggested to help educators, parents, students find 'common ground.'* Retrieved from http://www.glsen.org/cgi-bin/iowa/all/news/record/1912.html

Fischer, L., & Sorenson, G. P. (1996). *School law for counselors, psychologists, and social workers* (3rd ed.). White Plains, NY: Longman.

Florendo, T., & Bell, M. (2012, August 19). Teens, parents target of bullying lawsuit. *8newsnow.com.* Retrieved from http://www.8newsnow.com/story/19308427/teens-parents-target-bullying-lawsuit

Focus on the Family. (2010, November 6). *New focus on day of truth: Now "day of dialogue".* Retrieved from http://www.focusonthefamily.com/about_us/news_room/news-releases/20101111-new-focus-on-day-of-truth-now-day-of-dialogue.aspx

Fortenberry, J., Schick, V., Herbenick, D., Sanders, S., Dodge, B., & Reece, M. (2010). Sexual behaviors and condom use at last vaginal intercourse: A national sample of adolescents ages 14 to 17 years. *Journal of Sexual Medicine, 7,* 305-314.

Forester-Miller, H., & Davis, T. (1996) *A practitioner's guide to ethical decision making.* Retrieved from http://www.counseling.org/docs/ethics/practitioners_guide.pdf?sfvrsn=2

Forester-Miller, H., & Rubenstein, R. L. (1992). Group counseling: Ethics and professional issues. In D. Capuzzi & D. R. Gross (Eds.), *Introduction to group counseling* (pp. 307-323). Denver, CO: Love Publishing Co.

Fossey, R. & Zirkel, P. (2004). Liability for student suicide in the wake of Eisel. *Texas Wesleyan Law Review, 10*(2), 1.

Fowler v. Szostek, 905 S.W.2d 336, 342 (Tex. App. 1995).

Frank, D., & Cannon, E. P. (2009). Creative approaches to serving LGBTQ youth in schools. *Journal of School Counseling, 7*(35), 1-25.

Franklin v. Gwinnett County Public Schools, Supreme Court of the United States, 1992. 503 U.S. 60, 112 S. Ct. 1028.

Free Application for Federal Student Aid. (2012). *Will I need my parents' information?* Retrieved from http://www.fafsa.ed.gov/help/fftoc02k.htm

Fricke v. Lynch, 491 F. Supp. 381; 1980 U.S. Dist. LEXIS 11770

Froeschle, J. G., & Crews, C. (2010). An ethics challenge for school counselors. *Journal of School Counseling, 8*, 1-25.

Froeschle, J. G., & Nix, S. (2009). Solution focused leadership. *Journal of School Counseling, 7*(5). Retrieved from http://www.jsc.montana.edu/articles/v7n5.pdf

Galassi, J., & Akos, P. (2004). Developmental advocacy: Twenty-first century school counseling. *Journal of Counseling & Development, 82*(2), 146.

Gammon v. Edwardsville Community Unit School District, 82 Ill. App. 3d 586 (1980).

Garcetti v. Ceballos, 547 U.S. 410 (2006).

Gavin, I., & Zirkel, P. (2008). An outcome analysis of school employee-initiated litigation: A comparison of 1977-81 and 1997-2001 decisions. *West's Education Law Reporter, 232*, 19-36.

Gay & Lesbian Advocates & Defenders. (n.d.a). Not in my school: Doe v. Yunits. *GLAD thirty years: Equal justice under law.* Retrieved from http://www.glad.org/30years/case_aug.html

Gay & Lesbian Advocates & Defenders. (n.d.b). Tuxedoes for two: Fricke v. Lynch. *GLAD thirty years: Equal justice under law.* Retrieved from http://www.glad.org/30years/case_jun.html

Gay & Lesbian Advocates & Defenders. (2000, January 1). Doe v. Yunits. Retrieved from http://www.glad.org/work/cases/pat-doe-v-yunits

Gay, Lesbian & Straight Education Network. (2004, December 8). *The 2003 national school climate survey.* Retrieved from http://www.glsen.org/cgi-bin/iowa/all/news/record/1609.html

Gay, Lesbian & Straight Education Network. (2005a). *State of the states report.* Retrieved from http://www.glsen.org

Gay, Lesbian & Straight Education Network. (2005b). *The 2005 national school climate survey.* Retrieved from http://www.glsen.org/binary-data/GLSEN_ATTACHMENTS/file/585-1.pdf

Gay, Lesbian & Straight Education Network. (2007). *Gay-straight alliances: Creating safer schools for LGBT students and their allies* (GLSEN research brief). Retrieved from http://www.glsen.org/binary-data/GLSEN_ATTACHMENTS/file/000/000/930-1.pdf

Gay, Lesbian & Straight Education Network. (2009). *Safe space kit.* Retrieved from http://safespace.glsen.org/

Gay, Lesbian & Straight Education Network. (2010) *The 2009 national school climate survey.* Retrieved from http://www.glsen.org/cgi-bin/iowa/all/news/record/2624.html

Gay, Lesbian & Straight Education Network. (2012) *The 2011 national school climate survey.* Retrieved from http://www.glsen.org/cgi-bin/iowa/all/news/record/2897.html

Gibson, R. L., & Mitchell, M. H. (2007). *Introduction to counseling and guidance* (7th ed.). Upper Saddle River, NJ: Merrill Prentice Hall.

Gillman v. Holmes County School District, 567 F. Supp. 2d 1359, 1362 (N.D. Fla. 2008).

Givhan v. Western Line Consolidated School District, 439 U.S. 410 (1979).

Glosoff, H., & Pate, R. (2002). Privacy and confidentiality in school counseling. *Professional School Counseling, 6*(1), 20-27.

Goin, M. (2003). The suicide-prevention contract: A dangerous myth. *Psychiatric News, 38*(14), 3.

Gonzalez, T. (2012, February 12). 'Don't say gay' bill troubles Tennessee school counselors. *USA Today.* Retrieved from http://usatoday30.usatoday.com/news/education/story/2012-02-21/tennessee-bill-homosexuality/53189982/1

Gonzaga Univ. v. Doe, 536 U.S. 273 (2002) 143 Wash. 2d 687, 24 P.3d 390.

Gonzalez v. Sch. Bd. of Okeechobee County, 571 F. Supp. 2d 1257, 1267 (S.D. Fla. 2008).

Granello, D. H. (2010). The process of suicide risk assessment: Twelve core principals. *Journal of Counseling & Development, 88*, 363-372.

Grant v. Board of Trustees of Valley View School District, No 365-U, 676 N.E.2d 705 (Ill. App. Ct. 1997).

Gray, L., Thomas, N., & Lewis, L. (2010). *Teachers' use of educational technology in U.S. public schools: 2009* (NCES 2010-040). Washington, DC: National Center for Education Statistics, Institute of Education Sciences, U.S. Department of Education.

Greenberg, K. R. (2003). *Group counseling in K-12 schools: A handbook for school counselors.* Boston, MA: Allyn & Bacon.

Griffin-Carlson, M. S. & Mackin, K. J. (1993). Parental consent: Factors influencing adolescent disclosure regarding abortion. *Adolescence, 28*(109), 1–11.

Grossman v. South Short Public School District, 507 F.3d 1097 (7th Cir. 2007).

Gruenke v. Seip, 225 F.3d 290 (3rd Cir. 2000).

Guttmacher Institute. (2012, March). *State policies in brief as of March 1, 2012: Parental involvement in minors' abortions.* Retrieved on from www.guttmacher.org/pubs/spib_PIMA.pdf

Guttmacher Institute. (2013, February). *State policies in brief: Minors access to contraceptive information.* Retrieved from http://www.guttmacher.org/statecenter/spibs/spib_MACS.pdf.

H. L. v. Matheson, 450 U.S. 398 (1981).

Haas, L. J., & Malouf, J. L. (1989). *Keeping up the good work: A practitioner's guide to mental health ethics.* Sarasota, FL: Professional Resource Exchange, Inc.

Hader, H. A. (2009). Supervising cyberspace: A simple threshold for public school jurisdiction over students' online activity. *Boston College Law Review, 50,* 1563.

Hansen, A. (2007). School-based support for GLBT students: A review of the three levels of research. *Psychology in the Schools, 44*(8), 839-849. doi:10.1002/pits.20269

Hansen, S. (2012). *Confidentiality guidelines.* Retrieved from http://www.school-counseling-zone.com/confidentiality.html

Harris, J. (2010, July 7). *Parents sue school officials for defamation, alleging guidance counselor falsely completed recommendation form.* Alexandria, VA: National School Boards Association. Retrieved from http://legalclips.nsba.org/?p=989

Harris, K. (2011). *Opinion of Kamala D. Harris, attorney general, no. 08-509.* Retrieved from http://oag.ca.gov/system/files/opinions/pdfs/08-509.pdf

Harris, P., Lockwood, B., & Mengers, L. (2009). *Defining and measuring recidivism.* Braintree, MA: Council of Juvenile Correctional Administrators.

Harris, R. & Tichenor, D. (2010). *A history of the U.S. political system: Ideas, interest, and institutions.* Santa Barbara, CA: ABC-CLIO, LLC.

Harrison, T. (2003). Adolescent homosexuality and concerns regarding disclosure. *The Journal of School Health, 73*(3), 107-12. doi:10.1111/j.1746-1561.2003.tb03584.x

Harris-Williams, D. (2012, September 25). High school counselor sues after being fired over book. *Chicago Tribune*. Retrieved from http://articles.chicagotribune.com/2012-09-25/news/ct-met-rich-central-counselor-lawsuit-20120925_1_high-school-counselor-graphic-book-guidance-counselor

Hayden, L., Poynton, T., & Sabella, R. (2010). School counselor's use of technology. *Journal of Technology and Counseling*, Retrieved from http://jtc.colstate.edu/Vol5_1/Hayden.htm

Haynes, C. (2006, March 19). A moral battleground, a civil discourse. *USA Today*. Retrieved from http://www.usatoday.com/news/opinion/editorials/2006-03-19-faith-edit_x.htm

Hays, D. G., Arredondo, P., Gladding, S., & Toporek, R. L. (2010). Integrating social justice in group work: The next decade. *Journal for Specialists in Group Work, 35*(2), 177-206.

Hays, D. G., Craigen, L. M., Knight, J., Healey, A., & Sikes, A. (2009). Duty to warn and protect against self-destructive behaviors and interpersonal violence. *Journal of School Counseling, 7*(11).

Health Insurance Portability and Accountability Act of 1996, 45 C.F.R. 164.530. Retrieved from http://www.hhs.gov/ocr/hipaa

Heatherington, L., & Lavner, J. (2008). Coming to terms with coming out: Review and recommendations for family systems-focused research. *Journal of Family Psychology, 22*(3), 329-343. doi:10.1037/0893-2300.22.3.329

Hein, L., & Matthews, A. (2010). Reparative therapy: the adolescent, the psych nurse, and the issues. *Journal of Child & Adolescent Psychiatric Nursing, 23*(1), 29-35. doi:10.1111/j.1744-6171.2009.00214.x

Henshaw, S., & Kost, K. (1992). Parental involvement in minors' abortion decisions. *Family Planning Perspectives, 24*(5), 196.

Hermann, M., & Finn, A. (2002). An ethical and legal perspective on the role of school counselors in preventing violence in schools. *Professional School Counseling, 6*(1), 46-54.

Hermann, M. A., Legett, D. G., & Remley, T. P. (2008). A study of counselors' legal challenges and their perceptions of their ability to response. *International Journal of Education Policy and Leadership, 3*(5), 1-11.

Hernández, T. J., & Seem, S. R. (2004). A safe school climate: A systemic approach and the school counselor. *Professional School Counseling, 4*, 256-262.

Herszenhorn, D. (2004, October 18). Amid policy confusion, senior is allowed to apply to Harvard. *The New York Times*. Retrieved from http://query.nytimes.com/gst/abstract.html?res=FA0A11FB3F5E0C758DDDA90994DC404482&incamp=archive:search

Hill, C., & Kearl, H. (2011). *Crossing the line: Sexual harassment at school*. Washington, DC: American Association of University Women. Retrieved from: http://www.aauw.org/research/crossing-the-line/

Hinduja, S., & Patchin, J. W. (2010). *Cyberbullying: Identification, prevention and response*. Retrieved from http://www.cyberbullying.us/Cyberbullying_Identification_Prevention_Response_Fact_Sheet.pdf

Hinduja, S., & Patchin, J. W. (2012). *School climate 2.0: Preventing cyberbullying and sexting one classroom at a time*. Thousand Oaks, CA: Corwin Press.

Hines. P., Lemons, W. R., & Crews, D. K. (2011). Poised to lead: How school counselors can drive college and career readiness. *The Education Trust*. Retrieved from http://www.edtrust.org/dc/publication/poised-to-lead

Hobbs v. County of Moore, 267 N.C. 665, 149 S.E.2d 1 (1966).

Hoffman, J. (2009, November 6). Can a boy wear a skirt to school? *The New York Times*. Retrieved from http://www.nytimes.com/2009/11/08/fashion/08cross.html?pagewanted=all

Hoffman, J. (2011, September, 23). When your therapist is only a click away. *The New York Times*. Retrieved from http://www.nytimes.com/2011/09/25/fashion/therapists-are-seeing-patients-online.html?pagewanted=all&_r=1&

Hoffman, S. D. (2006). *By the numbers: The public costs of adolescent childbearing*. Washington, DC: The National Campaign to Prevent Teen Pregnancy. Retrieved from http://www.thenationalcampaign.org/resources/pdf/pubs/btn_full.pdf

Holt v. Bellflower Unified School District, Court of Appeal of California, Second Appellate District, Division Eight 2002 Cal. App. Unpub. LexisNexis 6135, June 28, 2002.

Houston-Vega, M. K., Nuehring, E. M., & Daguio, E. R. (1997). *Prudent practice: A guide for managing malpractice risk*. Washington, DC: National Association of Social Workers Press.

Huffington Post. (2012, January, 17). *Online student speech appeals rejected by supreme court*. Retrieved from http://www.huffingtonpost.com/2012/01/17/court-rejects-appeals-in-_0_n_1210399.html

Hughes, T. (2001). Releasing student information: What's public and what's not. *School Law Bulletin*. Retrieved from http://sogpubs.unc.edu//electronicversions/slb/slbwin01/article2.pdf?

Hughes v. Stanley County School Board, 594 N.W.2d 346 (S.D. 1999).

Humphreys, C. & Stanley, N. (2006). *Domestic violence and child protection: Directions for good practices*. London, U.K.; Philadelphia, PA: Jessica Kingsley Publishers, 2006.

Huss, S., Bryant, A., & Mulet, S. (2008). Managing the quagmire of counseling in a school: Bringing the parents onboard. *Professional School Counseling, 11*(6), 362-367.

Hyde, W. B., & Soronen, L. (2004). Reducing liability for sexual harassment. *Principal Leadership (Middle School Ed.), 5,* 57-61.

Idaho Code § 9-203 (2001).

Illinois Rev. Statute. 1977, ch. 122, par. 24 – 24.) n1.

Imber, M., & Van Geel, T. (2004). *Education law* (3rd ed.). Mahwah, NJ: Erlbaum.

Imber, M., & Van Geel, T. (2009). *Education law* (4th ed.). Mahwah, NJ: Erlbaum.

Ind. Code Ann. § 20-6.1-6-15 (2004a).

Ind. Code Ann. § 31-33 (2004b).

Independent College Counselors & Educational Consultants. (2007). *Statement of principles of good practice.* Retrieved from http://www.admissionsacademy.com/about/PGP.pdf

Individuals with Disabilities Education Act. (1990). 20 U.S.C. 1400-1485.

Individuals with Disabilities Education Improvement Act of 2004, 20 U.S.C. §1400 (2004).

International Society for Mental Health Online. (2000). *Suggested principles for the online provision of mental health services.* Retrieved from http://www.ismho.org/suggestions.html

Internet Keep Safe Coalition & American School Counselor Association. (2012) *Facebook for counselors.* Retrieved from http://www.ikeepsafe.org/wp-content/uploads/2012/04/Facebook-For-School-Counselors-Final-Revision1.pdf

Isaacs, M., & Stone, C. (1999). School counselors and confidentiality: Factors affecting professional choices. *Professional School Counseling, 2,* 258-266.

Isaacs, M., & Stone, C. (2001). Confidentiality with minors: Mental health counselor's attitudes toward breaching or preserving confidentiality. *Journal of Mental Health Counseling, 23*(4), 342-356.

Iyer, N. N., & Baxter-MacGregor, J. (2010). Ethical dilemmas for the school counselor: balancing student confidentiality and parent's right to know. *NERA Conference Proceedings 2010.* Paper 15. Retrieved from http://digitalcommons.uconn.edu/cgi/viewcontent.cgi?article=1017&context=nera_2010

Jacob, S., Decker, D. M., & Hartshorne, T. S. (2010). *Ethics and law for school psychologists* (6th ed.). Hoboken, NJ: John Wiley & Sons, Inc.

James Madison University. (2008). *Sexual Harassment.* Retrieved from http://www.jmu.edu/assaultprev/Harassment.shtml

James, S. (2008, July 16). Young teens openly express sexuality; LGBT pre-teens proud, not safe. *ABC News Online*. Retrieved from http://abcnews.go.com/Health/Sex/story?id=5381271&page=1#.T5W3 UBwg1DQ

Jane Doe v. Unified School District, School Counselor, and Elementary School Principal, 255 F. Supp. 2d 1251 (D. Kan. 2003).

Johnson, L. (2013, February 3). New version of 'Don't Say Gay' bill filed in Tennessee. *The Commercial Appeal*. Retrieved from http://www.commercialappeal.com/news/2013/feb/03/new-version-of-dont-say-gay-bill-filed-in/?CID=happeningnow

Johnson, M. (2010, July 7). Southern belle: Constance McMillen's suit over the prom is winning over the South. *Slate*. Retrieved from http://www.slate.com/articles/double_x/doublex/2010/07/southern_belle.html

Jones, D. (2012). *Statement on the role of the Appalachian State University Counseling and Psychological Services Center managing potentially dangerous students*. Retrieved from http://counseling.appstate.edu/pagesmith/263

Jones, R. K., Finer, L. B. & Singh, S. (2010, May). *Characteristics of U.S. abortion patients, 2008*. New York, NY: Guttmacher Institute.

Jonsson, P. (2010, March 11). Constance McMillen takes fight over same-sex prom date to court. *The Christian Science Monitor*. Retrieved from http://www.csmonitor.com/USA/Society/2010/0311/Constance-McMillen-takes-fight-over-same-sex-prom-date-to-court

J.S. v. Blue Mountain Sch. Dist., No. 08-4138 (3d Cir. Jun. 13, 2011).

Joyner, C. (2010, March 11). Miss. prom canceled after lesbian's date request. *USA Today*. Retrieved from http://www.webcitation.org/5okMbDs7o

Just the Facts Coalition. (2008). *Just the facts about sexual orientation and youth: A primer for principals, educators, and school personnel*. Washington, DC: American Psychological Association. Retrieved from www.apa.org/pi/lgbc/publications/justthefacts.html

Kaffenberger, C. J., & Seligman, L. (2003). Helping students with mental and emotional disorders. In B. T. Erford (Ed.), *Transforming the school counseling profession* (pp. 249-283). Upper Saddle River, NJ: Merrill Prentice Hall.

Karnowski, S. (2012, March 6). Anoka-Hennepin School District settles lawsuits over gay bullying, gender neutral policy. *The Huffington Post*. Retrieved from http://www.huffingtonpost.com/2012/03/06/minn-school-district-sett_n_1323791.html

Kampf, A. (2009) *Confidentiality for mental health professionals: A guide to ethical and legal principles.* Toowong, Australia: Australian Academic Press.

Kanan, L. M. (2010). When students make threats. *Education Digest, 76*(3), 24-29.

Kaplan, L. (1996). Outrageous or legitimate concerns: What some parents are saying about school counseling. *The School Counselor, 43,* 165-170.

Kaplan, P. (2004). *Adolescence.* Boston, MA: Houghton Mifflin.

Keeping Children and Families Safe Act of 2003. Pub. L. No. 108-36. [Reauthorization of the Child Abuse Prevention and Treatment Act, PL 93-247, 42 USCS [sections] 5101 (1974)].

Keith, S., & Martin, M. (2005). Cyberbullying: Creating a culture of respect in a cyber world. *Reclaiming Children and Youth, 13*(4), 224-228.

Kennedy, A. (2008). Proactive protection pointers. *Counseling Today, 50*(9), 1-26.

Kentucky Revised Statutes § 506 (2004).

Khubchandani, J., Price, J. H., Thompson, A., Dake, J. A., Wiblishauser, M., & Telljohann, S. K. (2012). Adolescent dating violence: A national assessment of school counselors' perceptions and practices. *Pediatrics, 130*(2) 202-210.

Killen v. Independent School Dist. No. 706, 547 N.W.2d 113, 117 (Minn. App. 1996).

King, K. A., & Smith, J. (2000). Project SOAR: A training program to increase school counselors' knowledge and confidence regarding suicide prevention and intervention. *Journal of School Health, 70,* 402-407.

King, R., Bambling, M., Lloyd, C., Gomurra, R., Smith, S., Reid, W., & Wegner, K. (2006). Online counselling: The motives and experiences of young people who chose the Internet instead of face-to-face or telephone counselling. *Counselling and Psychotherapy Research, 6*(3), 169174.

Kiracofe, N., & Wells, L. (2007). Mandated disciplinary counseling on campus: Problems and possibilities. *Journal of Counseling & Development, 85*(3), 259-269.

Kiselica, M., & Robinson, M. (2001). Bringing advocacy counseling to life: The history, issues, and human dramas of social justice work in counseling. *Journal of Counseling & Development, 79,* 387-397.

Kitchener, K. S. (1984). Intuition, critical evaluation and ethical principles: The foundation for ethical decisions in counseling psychology. *Counseling Psychologist, 12*(3), 43-55.

Kitchener, K. S., & Anderson, S. K. (2010). *Foundations of ethical practice, research, and teaching in psychology and counseling* (2nd ed.). New York, NY: Routledge.

Klump v. Nazareth Area Sch. Dist., 425 F. Supp.2d 622 (E.D. Pa., 2006).

Koebler, J. (2011, November). Survey: Nearly half of students sexually harassed in school. *US News & World Report*. Retrieved from http://www.usnews.com/education/blogs/high-school-notes/2011/11/09/survey-nearly-half-of-students-sexually-harassed-in-school

Kolmes, K. (2009a). *Managing Twitter as a mental health professional*. Retrieved from http://drkkolmes.com/for-clinicians/articles/

Kolmes, K. (2009b). *Managing Facebook as a mental health professional*. Retrieved from http://drkkolmes.com/for-clinicians/articles/

Komo Staff & News Services. (2003, November 25). Grade tampering investigation at Franklin High ends. *Komo News*. Retrieved from http://www.komonews.com/news/archive/4111136.html

Koocher, G. P. (2008). Ethical challenges in mental health services to children and families. *Journal of Clinical Psychology, 64*(5), 601-612.

Koschoreck, J. W., & Tooms, A. K. (2009). *Sexuality matters: Paradigms and policies for educational leaders*. Lanham, MD: Rowman & Littlefield Publishers.

Kost, K. & Henshaw, S. (2012). *U.S. teenage pregnancies, births and abortions, 2008: National trends by age, race and ethnicity*. New York, NY: Guttmacher Institute.

Kowalski v. Berkeley County Sch., No. 1098 (4th Cir. Jul. 27, 2011).

Kozlowski, K., & Stone, C. (2013, January). [School Counselors and the Ethics of Advocacy survey]. Unpublished raw data.

Kraft, W. (2012, December 10). *Resolution of Julea Ward case leaves program, policies intact at Eastern Michigan University*. Retrieved from http://www.emich.edu/univcomm/releases/release.php?id=1355161741

Kramer, S. (2011, May 20). 'Coming out': Gay teenagers, in their own words. *The New York Times*. Retrieved from http://www.nytimes.com/2011/05/23/us/23out.html

Krug, E., Dahlberg, L., Mercy, J., Zwi, A., & Lozano, R. (2002). *World report on violence and health*. Geneva, Switzerland: World Health Organization. Retrieved from http://whqlibdoc.who.int/publications/2002/9241545615_eng.pdf

Lambie, G., Ieva, K., Mullen, P., & Hayes, B. B. (2011). Ego development, ethical decision-making and legal and ethical knowledge in school counselors. *Journal of Adult Development, 18*(1). 50-59. doi:10.1007/s10804-010-9105-8

Lambda Legal. (1998). *Complaint by gay student triggers historic civil rights agreement*. Retrieved from http://www.lambdalegal.org/news/ny_19980622_complaint-by-gay-student-triggers-historic-agreement

Lambda Legal. (2012). *Amicus brief of Parents, Families and Friends of Lesbians and Gays ("PFLAG"), Gay, Lesbian and Straight Education Network ("GLSEN"), affirmations, and Ruth Ellis Center in support of defendant-appellee for affirmance, Ward v. Wilbanks, 667 F.3d 727 (2012)*. Retrieved from http://www.lambdalegal.org/in-court/legal-docs/ward_mi_20110211_amicus-pflag-et-al

LaMorte, M. W. (2001). *School law*. Boston, MA: Allyn & Bacon.

Landstrom v. Illinois Department of Children and Family Services, 892 F.2d 670 (7th Cir. 1990).

Lapan, R. T. (2001). Results-based comprehensive guidance and counseling programs: A framework for planning and evaluation. *Professional School Counseling, 4*, 289-299.

Larson, J. (2007). RLUIPA, distress, and damages. *The University of Chicago Law Review, 74*(4), 1443-1473.

Lawson, B. (2012). Hammad Memon trial could be several months away due to mental evaluations, schedule conflict. *The Hunstville Times*. Retrieved from http://blog.al.com/breaking/2012/05/hammad_memon_trial_could_be_se.html

Layshock v. Hermitage Sch. Dist., No. 07-4465 (3d Cir. Jun. 13, 2011).

Lazovsky, R. (2008). Maintaining confidentiality with minors: Dilemmas of school counselors. *Professional School Counseling, 11*(5) 335-346.

Lee, C. (1998). Counseling and the challenges of cyberspace. *CT Online*. Retrieved from http://ct.counseling.org/category/counseling-today/

Lee, C. C., & Walz, G. R. (Eds.). (1998). *Social action: A mandate for counselors*. Alexandria, VA: American Counseling Association.

Leenaars, A. A., & Wenckstern, S. (1995). Suicide prevention in schools: The art, the issues, and the pitfalls. *Crisis, 20*(3), 132-142.

Lehrer, A. (2011). Keep the poking to yourself, Mrs. Robinson: The Missouri Facebook statute and its implications for teacher free speech under the First Amendment. *Student Scholarship*, Paper 2. Retrieved from http://erepository.law.shu.edu/student_scholarship/2

Leibert, T., Archer, A., Munson, M., & York, Y. (2006). An exploratory study of client perceptions of Internet counseling and the therapeutic alliance. *Journal of Mental Health Counseling, 28*, 69-83.

Leitsinger, M. (2012, April 19). $4.2 million settlement for student paralyzed by bully. *NBCnews.com*. Retrieved from http://usnews.nbcnews.com/_news/2012/04/19/11289813-42-million-settlement-for-student-paralyzed-by-bully?lite

Lewin, T. (2007). Laws limit options when a student is mentally ill. *The New York Times.* Retrieved from http://www.nytimes.com/2007/04/19/us/19protocol.html

Lewis, K. (2013, March 3). Student at center of same-sex prom date policy change says he wanted to help people. *Southeast Missourian.* Retrieved from http://www.semissourian.com/story/1946462.html

Lezner v. Shaw and Gresham School District, 156 Wis. 2d 466; 458 N.W.2d 388; 1990 Wisc. App. LEXIS 357 (April 17, 1990).

Li, Q. (2007). New bottle but old wine: A research of cyberbullying in schools. *Computers in Human Behavior, 23,* 1777-1791. doi:10.1016/j.chb.2005.10.005

Lindberg, L. D., & Maddow-Zimmet, I. (2011). *Consequences of sex education on teen and young adult sexual behaviors and outcomes.* Retrieved from http://www.guttmacher.org/pubs/journals/j.jadohealth.2011.12.028.pdf

Littlefield, J. (n.d). State-by-state list of free online public schools, K-12. *About.com.* Retrieved from http://distancelearn.about.com/od/onlinepublicschools/a/OnlinePS.htm

Lobron, A. (2007). Easy out. *The Boston Globe.* Retrieved from http://www.boston.com/bostonglobe/magazine/articles/2007/11/11/easy_out/?page=full

Lovell v. Poway Unified School District, 90 F.3d 367 (9th Cir. 1996).

Ludeke, M. (2009). Transgender youth. *Principal Leadership, 10*(3), 12-16.

Ludington, S. (n.d.). *The Supreme Court further limits First Amendment protection for public employees.* Retrieved from http://web.law.duke.edu/publiclaw/supremecourtonline/commentary/garvceb.html

Maddy-Bernstein, C. (2000). *Career development issues affecting secondary schools.* Columbus, OH: National Dissemination Center for Career and Technical Education.

Mallen, M. J., & Vogel, D. L. (2005). Counseling psychology and online counseling. *The Counseling Psychologist, 33,* 761–775.

Mallen, M. J., Vogel, D. L., & Rochlen, A. B. (2005). The practical aspects of online counseling: Ethics, training, technology, and competency. *The Counseling Psychologist, 33,* 776–818.

Mandrusiak, M., Joiner, T. E., & Rudd, M. D. (2006). The case against no-suicide contracts: The commitment to treatment statement as a practice alternative. *Journal of Clinical Psychology, 62,* 243-251.

Manning, A. (2010) Educators advised to be cautious on Facebook profile. *Education Week, 30*(5), 8.

Marsh, J. (2013, January 22). Hildebran Elementary School child pornography teacher sex abuse: Additional federal civil rights lawsuit filed. *ChildLaw Blog*. Retrieved from http://www.childlaw.us/2013/01/hildebran-elementary-school-ch.html

Martin, P. (2004, July). *Our little red wagon* [Unpublished speech]. Rhode Island School Counselor Conference.

Martin, P. J. (2002). Transforming school counseling: A national perspective. *Theory Into Practice, 41*, 148-153.

Martinez, G., Abma, J., & Copen, C. (2010). *Educating teenagers about sex in the United States*. NCHS data brief, no 44. Hyattsville, MD: National Center for Health Statistics.

Martinez, G., Copen, C. E., & Abma, J. C. (2011). Teenagers in the United States: Sexual activity, contraceptive use, and childbearing, 2006–2010. National Survey of Family Growth, *Vital and Health Statistics, 23*(31).

Massachusetts State Ethics Commission. (1997, June 24). Sansone, Casper Charles Docket No. 566 G.L. c. 268B, s.4(a). Retrieved from http://www.mass.gov/ethics/opinions-and-rulings/enforcement-matters/enf-section-23/section-23-s-z/casper-sansone-da.html

Mattingly, J. B. (2007). *Child safety alert: New guidelines for mandated reporters*. Retrieved from http://www.nyc.gov/html/acs/downloads/pdf/childsafty_alert_oct2007.pdf

McIntosh v. Milano, 403 A.2d 500 (NJ, 1979).

McLaughlin, J. (2010). Crime and punishment: Teen sexting in context. *Penn State Law Review, 115*(1), 135-181.

McMillen v. Itawamba County School District, et al., 702 F.Supp.2d 699 (2010); 2010 U.S. Dist. LEXIS 27589.

Meyer v. Nebraska, 262 U.S. 390, 399-401 (1923).

Michels, S. (2008). Teachers' virtual lives conflict with classroom. *ABC News*. Retrieved from http://abcnews.go.com/TheLaw/story?id=4791295&page=1#.UWLTcKLU-So

Mikell v. School Admin. Unit No. 33, 972 A.2d 1050 (N.H. 2009).

Miller et al. v. Skumanick, Court of Appeals 3d Cir. 3:09cv540 (PA 2010).

Miller, R. A. (2011). Teacher facebook speech: Protected or not? *Brigham Young University Education & Law Journal, 2*, 637-665.

Miller v. Mitchell, 598 F.3d 139 (2010).

Mitchell, C., & Rogers, R. (2003). Rape, statutory rape, and child abuse: Legal distinctions and counselor duties. *Professional School Counselor: Special Issue on Legal and Ethical Issues in School Counseling, 6*(1).

Mitchell, C. W., Disque, J. G., & Robertson, P. (2002). When parents want to know: Responding to parental demands for confidential information. *Professional School Counseling, 6*(2), 156-162.

Mitchell, K., Levin, A., & Krumboltz, J. (1999). Planned happenstance: Constructing unexpected career opportunities. *Journal of Counseling & Development, 77,* 115-124.

Moore v. Vanderloo, 386 N.W.2d 108 (Iowa 1986).

Montana Code, Ann., § 26-1-809 (2003).

Montana Code, Ann., Ch. 9, § 305 (2007).

Morrison v. Board of Education, 2006 U.S. Dist. LEXIS 6373 (E.D. Ky. Feb. 17, 2006).

Movement Advancement Project. (2013, January 15). *Safe schools laws.* Retrieved from http://www.lgbtmap.org/equality-maps/safe_school_laws

Moyer, S. M., Sullivan, R. J., & Growcock, D. (2012). When is it ethical to inform administrators about student risk-taking behaviors? Perceptions of school counselors. *Professional School Counseling, 15*(3), 98-109.

Mullins, S. (2008). *Teenagers and the struggle for identity.* Retrieved from http://articles.familylobby.com/355-teenagers-and-the-struggle-for-identity.htm

Myrick, R. (2002). *Developmental guidance and counseling: A practical approach* (4th ed.). Minneapolis, MN: Educational Media.

Nabozny v. Podlesny, 92 F. 3d 446 (7th Cir. 1996).

Najmabadi, S. (2012, May, 7). Berkeley High counselor suspended following sexual misconduct. *The Daily Californian News.* Retrieved from http://www.dailycal.org/2012/05/07/berkeley-high-counselor-suspended-following-alleged-sexual-misconduct/

National Association for College Admission Counseling. (2012). *How to write effective letters of recommendation.* Retrieved from http://www.nacacnet.org/research/PublicationsResources/Marketplace/research/Pages/StateofCollegeAdmission.aspx

National Center for Education Statistics. (2011). *Student reports of bullying and cyber-bullying: Results from the 2009 School Crime Supplement to the National Crime Victimization Survey.* Retrieved from http://nces.ed.gov/pubs2011/2011336.pdf

National Forum on Education Statistics. (2006). *Forum guide to the privacy of student information: A resource for schools* (NFES 2006-805). Washington, DC: U.S. Department of Education, National Center for Education Statistics.

National Association of School Psychologists. (n.d.). *Preventing youth suicide: Tips for parents and educators.* Retrieved from http://www.nasponline.org/resources/crisis_safety/suicideprevention.aspx

National Association of School Psychologists. (2006). *Corporal punishment* [Position statement]. Bethesda, MD: Author.

National Association of Secondary School Principals (2008). Expression rights of public school employees and students. *A Legal Memoradum*, *8*(4). Retrieved from http://www.nassp.org/portals/0/content/58255.pdf

National Association of Social Workers (2008). *Code of ethics*. Retrieved from http://www.socialworkers.org/pubs/code/code.asp

National Board for Certified Counselors. (2012a). *Code of ethics*. Retrieved from http://www.nbcc.org/assets/ethics/nbcc-codeofethics.pdf

National Board for Certified Counselors. (2012b). *Policy regarding the provision of distance professional services*. Greensboro, NC: Author. Retrieved from http://www.nbcc.org/Assets/Ethics/NBCC%20Policy%20Regarding%20the%20Practice%20of%20Distance%20Counseling%20-Board%20-%20Adopted%20Version%20-%20July%202012-%20PDF.pdf

National Center for Lesbian Rights and Gay Lesbian Straight Educators Network. (n.d.) *Expensive reasons why safe schools laws and policies are in your district's best interest*. Retrieved from http://www.nclrights.org/site/DocServer/15reasons.pdf?docID=1621

National Education Association. (2006). *Strengthening the learning environment: A school employee's guide to lesbian, gay, bisexual, and transgender issues* (2nd ed.). Retrieved from http://www.nea.org/assets/docs/glbtstrengthenlearningenvirong2006.pdf

National School Boards Association. (n.d.). *Dealing with legal matters surrounding students' sexual orientation and gender identity*. Retrieved from http://www.nsba.org/cosa/sexualorientation

National School Boards Association. (2011, November 10). *Sua Sponte: NSBA files amicus brief urging Supreme Court to provide guidance on off-campus online speech*. Retrieved from http://legalclips.nsba.org/?p=10079

National School Boards Association. (2012, January 19). *Supreme Court declines to hear student Internet speech cases*. Retrieved from http://legalclips.nsba.org/?p=11474

National School Boards Association. (2013, February, 28) *Federal District Court upholds dismissal of guidance counselor for writing a sexually explicit "self-help" book*. Retrieved from http://legalclips.nsba.org/?p=18402

National Women's Law Center. (2007). *How to protect students from sexual harassment: A primer for schools*. Retrieved from http://www.nwlc.org/sites/default/files/pdfs/Final%20SH%20Fact%20Sheet-Schools.pdf

National Women's Law Center. (2010). *Cyberbullying and sexual harassment: FAQs about cyberbullying and Title IX.* Retrieved from http://www.nwlc.org/resource/cyberbullying-and-sexual-harassment-faqs-about-cyberbullying-and-title-ix

National Women's Law Center. (2012a, June 19). *Title IX fact sheet. Pregnant and parenting students: A guide for schools.* Retrieved from http://www.nwlc.org/resource/title-ix-protections-pregnant-and-parenting-students-guide-schools

National Women's Law Center. (2012b, June). *The next generation of Title IX: Pregnant and parenting students.* Retrieved from http://www.nwlc.org/resource/next-generation-title-ix-pregnant-and-parenting-students

N.C. ex rel M.C. v. Bedford Cent. Sch. Dist., 348 F. Supp. 2d 32, 35 (S.D.N.Y. 2004).

Neiman, S. (2011). *Crime, violence, discipline, and safety in U.S. public schools: Findings from the School Survey on Crime and Safety: 2009–10* (NCES 2011-320). Washington, DC: U.S. Department of Education, National Center for Education Statistics.

New Hampshire Regulatory Statutes (2004). H.R.S.A. 193-F:3(II).

Newman, B. M. & Newman, P. R. (2012). *Development through life: A psychological approach* (11th ed). United States: Wadsworth CENGAGE Learning.

New York State Office for the Prevention of Domestic Violence. (1998, January). *Model domestic violence policy for counties.* Retrieved from http://www.opdv.ny.gov/professionals/coordination/model_policy/index.html

New York Times. (2003, July 18). National briefing | South: Arkansas: Gay student settles suit. *The New York Times.* Retrieved from http://www.nytimes.com/2003/07/18/us/national-briefing-south-arkansas-gay-student-settles-suit.html

Nicholson v. Williams, 205 F.R.D. 92 (E.D. NY 2001).

Nguon v. Wolf, 517 F. Supp. 2d 1177 (C.D. Cal. 2007).

No Child Left Behind Act of 2001, 20 U.S.C. § 6301 (2002).

North Carolina Gen. Stat. § 8-53.4 (2004).

North Dakota Century Code § 31-01-06.1 (2003).

Office of Juvenile Justice and Delinquency Prevention. (2012). *Aftercare.* Retrieved from http://www.ojjdp.gov/mpg/progTypesAftercare.aspx

O'Keefe, M. (2005). Teen dating violence: A review of risk factors and prevention efforts. *VAWnet.org.* Retrieved from http://new.vawnet.org/assoc_files_vawnet/ar_teendatingviolence.pdf

Oppel, R. (2013, March 17). Ohio teenagers guilty in rape that social media brought to light. *The New York Times*. Retrieved from http://www.nytimes.com/2013/03/18/us/teenagers-found-guilty-in-rape-in-steubenville-ohio.html?ref=ohio&_r=0

Oregon Rev. Stat. § 40.245, Rule 504-3 (2003).

Osborn, C. (2010). *Ethical issues with distance and online counseling* [PowerPoint slides]. Retrieved from http://www.slideshare.net/plisasm/ethics-presentation-5672614

Owasso Independent School Dist. v. Falvo, 534 U.S. 426 (2002) 233 F.3d 1203.

Pacer v. White, 2006 U.S. Dist. LEXIS 47955.

Pachankis, E. (2007). The psychological implications of concealing a stigma: A cognitive-affective-behavioral model. *Psychological Bulletin, 133*(2), 328-345. doi:10.1037/0033-2909.133.2.328

Paisley, P., & Milsom, A. (2007). Group work as an essential contribution to transforming school counseling. *Journal for Specialists in Group Work, 32*(1), 9-17.

Page, Petitioner v. Rotterdam-Mohonasen Central School District et al., Respondents, Supreme Court of New York, 109 Misc. 2d 1049; 441 N.Y.S. 2d 323 (June 3, 1981).

Palfrey, J., & Boyd, d. (2012). *Final report: Symposium on youth meanness and cruelty*. Retrieved from: http://cyber.law.harvard.edu/publications/2012/kbw_final_report_symposium_on_youth_meanness_+and_cruelty

Parents against child abuse in school v. Williamsport Area School District, 594 A.2d 796 (Pa. Commw. Ct. 1991).

Parents, Family and Friends of Lesbians and Gays. (2005). *From our house to the schoolhouse*. Retrieved from http://community.pflag.org/page.aspx?pid=358

Parents, Family and Friends of Lesbians and Gays. (2012). *Advocacy and issues: Reparative therapy*. Retrieved from http://community.pflag.org/Page.aspx?pid=503

Parker-Pope, T. (2008, May 1). Sexual harassment at school. *The New York Times*. Retrieved from well.blogs.nytimes.com/2008/05/01/sexual-harassment-at-school

Parker v. Hurley, 474 F. Supp. 2d 261; 2007 U.S. Dist. LEXIS 12751.

Parker v. Hurley, 514 F.3d 87; 2008 U.S. App. LEXIS 2070.

Parrott, J. (2001, July 9). Are advisors risking lawsuits for misadvising students? *The Mentor: An Academic Advising Journal*. Retrieved from http://dus.psu.edu/mentor/old/articles/010709jp.htm

Parry, S. (2007). *Helping mothers and children in the aftermath of domestic violence.* Albany, NY: New York State Office for the Prevention of Domestic Violence. Retrieved from http://opdv.ny.gov/professionals/mental_health/helpmoms.html

Payne, S. T., & Elliott, D. S. (2011). Safe2Tell®: An anonymous, 24/7 reporting system for preventing school violence. *New Directions for Youth Development,* (129), 103-111.

Penna, L., Clark, A., & Mohay, G. (2005). Challenges of automating the detection of pedophile activity on the Internet. *Proceedings of the First International Workshop on Systematic Approaches to Digital Forensic Engineering,* 206-222.

Perper, K., Peterson, K., & Manlove, J. (2010). *Diploma attainment among teen mothers* [Fact sheet]. Retrieved from http://www.childtrends.org/Files/Child_Trends-2010_01_22_FS_DiplomaAttainment.pdf

Perry, S. J., & Marcum, T. M. (2008). Liability for school sexual harassment under title IX: How the courts are failing our children. *University of La Verne Law Review, 30*(1), 3-38.

Peter W. v. San Francisco Unified School District, 60 Cal. App. 3d 814, 825 [131 Cal. Rptr. 854] (California 1976).

Phelan, J., Whitehead, N., & Sutton, P. (2009). What research shows: NARTH's response to the APA claims on homosexuality. *Journal of Human Sexuality, 1,* 1-82. Retrieved from http://www.scribd.com/doc/92277808/NARTH-2009-What-Research-Shows-NARTH's-Response-to-the-APA-Claims-on-Homosexuality-literature-review

Picarella v. Terrizzi, 893 F. Supp. 1292 (Pa. 1995).

Policarpio, R. (2007). *A brief summary on trial procedures.* Retrieved from http://ezinearticles.com/?A-Brief-Summary-on-Trial-Procedures&id=844676

Pollack, W. S., Modzelesky, W., & Rooney, G. (2008). *Prior knowledge of potential school-based violence: Information students learn may prevent a targeted attack.* Washington, DC: U.S. Secret Service and U.S. Department of Education. Retrieved from http://www.secretservice.gov/ntac/bystander_study.pdf

Portner, J. (2000) Suicide: Many schools fall short on prevention. *Education Week.* Retrieved from http://www.edweek.org/ew/articles/2000/04/19/32solution.h19.html?qs=suicide+prevention

Port Washington Teachers' Association v. Board of Education of the Port Washington Union Free School District, 361 F. Supp. 2d 69, 81 (E.D.N.Y. 2005).

Potoczniak, D., Crosbie-Burnett, M., & Saltzburg, N. (2009). Experiences regarding coming out to parents among African American, Hispanic, and White gay, lesbian, bisexual, transgender, and questioning adolescents. *Journal of Gay & Lesbian Social Services, 21*(2-3), 189-205. doi:10.1080/10538720902772063

Prado, O. Z., & Meyer, S. B. (2006). Evaluation of therapeutic relations in asynchronous therapy via Internet through working alliance inventory. *Psicologia em Estudo, 11,* 247–257.

Price, S. (2005, July 25). *Reporting child abuse and neglect.* Report to Connecticut General Assembly (OLR Report No. 2005-R-0591). Retrieved from http://www.cga.ct.gov/2005/rpt/2005-R-0591.htm

Primary & Secondary Education. (2012). *Journal of Law and Education, 41*(1), 223-235.

Prober, M. (2005). Please don't tell my parents. *Brooklyn Law Review, 71*(1), 557-587.

Prosser, W. (1971). *The law of torts.* St. Paul, MN: West.

Puzio, E. R. (2013). Why can't we be friends?: How far can the state go in restricting social networking communications between secondary school teachers and their students? *Cardozo Law Review, 34,* 1099.

Quilloin v. Walcott, 434 U.S. 246 (1978).

Rankin v. McPherson, 483 U.S. 378 (1987).

Raquel R. S. v. Necedah Area Sch. Dist., 2003 WI App 22 (2002).

Ratts, M., DeKruyf, L., & Chen-Hayes, S. (2007). The ACA advocacy competencies: A social justice advocacy framework for professional school counselors. *Professional School Counseling, 11*(2), 90-97.

Reed, A. (2012). Adult student-teacher sex ban struck down by Arkansas supreme court. *Huffington Post.* Retrieved from www.huffingtonpost.com/2012/03/29/arkansas-strikes-teacher-student-sex-ban_n_1389860.html

Reid, K. (2001, May 2). Iowa's high court holds counselors liable. *Education Week.* Retrieved from http://www.edweek.org/ew/articles/2001/05/02/33guide.h20.html?qs=Iowa+counselor+liable

Remley, T. P., Jr., & Herlihy, B. (2001). *Ethical, legal, and professional issues in counseling.* Upper Saddle River, NJ: Merrill Prentice Hall.

Remley, T. P., Jr., & Herlihy, B. (2007). *Ethical, legal, and professional issues in counseling* (2nd ed). Upper Saddle River, NJ: Merrill Prentice Hall.

Remley, T. P., Jr., & Herlihy, B. (2009). *Ethical, legal, and professional issues in counseling* (3rd ed.). Upper Saddle River, NJ: Merrill Prentice Hall.

Remley, T. P., Jr., & Huey, W. C. (2002). An ethical quiz for school counselors. *Professional School Counseling, 6*(1), 3-11.

Repa, B. K. (2012, Febuary). Bullycide prompts new law. *California Lawyer.* Retrieved from http://www.callawyer.com/Clstory.cfm?eid=920434

Richardson v. Braham, 125 Neb. 142, 249 N.W. 557 (1933).

Ricker v. Board of Education of Millard County School District, 16 Utah 2d 106, 396 P.2d 416 (1964).

Roberts, G. (2003, December 4). Franklin counselors play down district reprimand. *Seattle Post-Intelligencer.* Retrieved from http://www.seattlepi.com/local/article/Franklin-counselors-play-down-district-reprimand-1131370.php#ixzz289R5bZZp

Rivers, I., Poteat, V. P., Noret, N., & Ashurst, N. (2009). Observing bullying at school: The mental health implications of witness status. *School Psychology Quarterly, 24,* 211-223. doi:10.1037/a0018164

Roberts, A. L., Rosario, M., Corliss, H. L., Koenen, K. C., & Austin, S. B. (2012). Childhood gender nonconformity: A risk indicator for childhood abuse and posttraumatic stress in youth. *Pediatrics, 129*(3), 410-417. Retrieved from http://pediatrics.aappublications.org/content/early/2012/02/15/peds.2011-1804.abstract

Robers, S., Zhang, J., & Truman, J. (2012). *Indicators of school crime and safety: 2011* (NCES 2012-002/NCJ 236021). Washington, DC: National Center for Education Statistics, U.S. Department of Education, and Bureau of Justice Statistics, Office of Justice Programs, U.S. Department of Justice. Retrieved from http://nces.ed.gov/pubsearch/pubsinfo.asp?pubid=2012002

Rochlen, A. B., Land, L. N., & Wong, Y. J. (2004). Male restrictive emotionality and evaluations of online versus face-to-face counseling. *Psychology of Men and Masculinity, 5,* 190–200.

Rollini, G. (2003). Davis v. Monroe County Board of Education: A hollow victory for student victims of peer sexual harassment. *The FSU Law Review, 30*(4), 987-1016. Retrieved from http://www.law.fsu.edu/journals/lawreview/downloads/304/rollini.pdf

Rummell, C. M., & Joyce, N. R. (2010). 'So wat do u want to work on 2day?' The ethical implications of online counseling. *Ethics & Behaviors, 20*(6), 482-496. Doi:10.1080/10508422.2010.521450.

Russo v. Diocese of Greensburg, 2010 WL 3656579 (W.D. Pa. Sept. 15, 2010).

Russo, C. J. (2010) *Encyclopedia of law and higher education.* Thousand Oaks, CA: Sage Publications.

Ryan, C., Huebner, D., Diaz, R. M., & Sanchez, J. (2009). Family rejection as a predictor of negative health outcomes in white and Latino lesbian, gay and bisexual young adults. *Pediatrics, 123*(1), 346–352. Retrieved from http://pediatrics.aappublications.org/content/123/1/346.full

S. 3472—112th Congress: Uninterrupted Scholars Act (USA). (2012). Retrieved from http://www.govtrack.us/congress/bills/112/s3472

Sabella, R. A. (2012). *Confronting cyberbullying in schools: A five point plan.* Presentation at Florida School Counselor Association Convention 2012, St. Petersburg, Florida.

Sacco, D., Argudin, R., Maguire, J., & Tallon, K. (2010). Sexting: Youth practices and legal implications. *Berkman Center Research Publication No. 2010-8.* doi:10.2139/ssrn.1661343

Sacco, D., Silbaugh, K., Corredor, F., Casey, J., & Doherty, D. (2012). An overview of state anti-bullying legislation and other relevant laws. *Kinder & Braver World Project: Research Series.* Retrieved from http://cyber.law.harvard.edu/publications/2012/state_anti_bullying_legislation_overview

Sain v. Cedar Rapids Community School District, 626 N.W. 2nd 115 (Iowa 2001).

Sampson, D. (2013). Get on the blogging bandwagon. *ASCA School Counselor, 50*(3), 12-13.

Sanchez, R. (2000). District, parents settle over abortion. *Philly.com.* Retrieved from http://articles.philly.com/2000-03-16/news/25607294_1_second-trimester-abortion-guidance-counselor-stephanie-carter

Sanders, T. (2010, April, 14). Clay school counselor's employer not told about student-sex probe before hiring. *Jacksonville News.* Retrieved from http://jacksonville.com/news/schools/2010-04-16/story/clay-counselor%E2%80%99s-employer-not-told-about-student-sex-probe-hiring

Savage, D. (2012, January 14). Supreme Court to consider educators' response to cyber-bullying. *Los Angeles Times.* Retrieved from http://articles.latimes.com/2012/jan/14/nation/la-na-adv-student-speech-20120114

Savage, T. A., & Harley, D. A. (2009). A place at the blackboard: Including lesbian, gay, bisexual, transgender, intersex, & queer/questioning issues in the education process. *Multicultural Education, 16*(4), 2-9.

Schaefer, R., & Bambrick, K. (2005). Proposing an answer: A community problem meets a community approach. *ASCA School Counselor, 42*(5). Retrieved from http://www.schoolcounselor.org/article.asp?article=775&paper= 91&cat=137

Scharffs, B., & Welch, J. (2005). An analytic framework for understanding and evaluating the fiduciary duties of educators. *Brigham Young University Education and Law Journal, 2005*(1).

Scheidegger, K. (2008, May 5). *"Exonerated," not necessarily innocent.* Retrieved from http://www.crimeandconsequences.com/crimblog/2008/05/exonerated-not-necessarily-inn.html

Schnitzer, P. G., Covington, T. M., & Wirtz, S. J. (2008). Public health surveillance of fatal child maltreatment: Analysis of 3 state programs. *American Journal of Public Health, 98*(2), 296-303.

Schulman, M. (2013, January 9). Generation LGBTQIA. *The New York Times.* Retrieved from http://www.nytimes.com/2013/01/10/fashion/generation-lgbtqia.html

Schultze, N. (2006). Success factors in Internet-based psychological counseling. *CyberPsychology & Behavior, 9*, 623–626.

Schwallie-Giddis, P., Maat, M., & Park, M. (2003). Initiating leadership by introducing and implementing the ASCA National Model. *Professional School Counseling, 6*(3),170-173.

Schwyzer, H. (2012, October 26). One mistake won't ruin your life. Remember that. *Jezebel.com.* Retrieved from http://jezebel.com/5955277/one-mistake-wont-ruin-your-life-remember-that

Scott, Elizabeth. (2001). The legal construction of adolescence. *Hofstra Law Review, 29*(547), 547598. Retrieved from http://www.hofstra.edu/PDF/law_lawrev_esscott.pdf

Scott v. Stevens Point Area Public School District, 650 N.W.2d 560 (Wisconsin 2003).

Severson, K. (2012, October 14). Christian group finds gay agenda in an anti-bullying day. *The New York Times.* Retrieved from http://www.nytimes.com/2012/10/15/us/seeing-a-homosexual-agenda-christian-group-protests-an-anti-bullying-program.html

Shah, N. (2012, October 18). Conservative group pressures schools to nix 'Mix-It-Up' Day. *Education Week's blogs: Rules for Engagement.* Retrieved from http://blogs.edweek.org/edweek/rulesforengagement/2012/10/conservative_group_pressures_schools_to_nix_mix-it-up_day.html

Shapira, I. (2005, October 10). A differing definition of justice: Acquitted of abuse, Va. teacher fired. *The Washington Post.* Retrieved from http://www.washingtonpost.com/wp-dyn/content/article/2005/10/09/AR2005100901506.html

Shapira, I. (2008, April 27). When young teachers go wild on the Web: Public profiles raise questions of propriety and privacy. *The Washington Post.* Retrieved from http://www.washingtonpost.com/wp-dyn/content/article/2008/04/27/AR2008042702213.html

Shaw, H. E., & Shaw, S. F. (2006). Critical ethical issues in online counseling: Assessing current practices with an ethical intent checklist. *Journal of Counseling & Development, 84,* 41–53.

Shore Regional High School Board of Education v. P.S., No. 03-3438 (3d Cir. August 20, 2004).

Sikes, A., Remley, T. P., Jr., & Hays, D. G. (2010). Experiences of school counselors during and after making suspected child abuse reports. *Journal of School Counseling, 8,* 1-30.

Sileo, F., & Kopala, M. (1993). An A-B-C-D-E worksheet for promoting beneficence when considering ethical issues. *Counseling and Values, 37,* 89-95.

Simmons, J. (2000, October). Kids' mental health tackled. *Counseling Today,* 1 & 22.

Simpson, M. (1999). Student suicide: Who's liable? *NEA Today, 17*(5), 25.

Sink, C. A. (Ed.). (2005). *Contemporary school counseling: Theory, Research, and Practice.* Boston, MA: Lahaska Press, Houghton Mifflin.

Singer, D. (2013, January 30). Rape trial of teenaged football players to be open to public: Ohio judge. *Reuters.com.* Retrieved from http://www.reuters.com/article/2013/01/30/us-usa-crime-ohio-idUSBRE90T1AL20130130

Singh, A. A., Urbano, A., Haston, M., & McMahon, E. (2010). School counselors' strategies for social justice change: A grounded theory of what works in the real world. *Professional School Counseling, 13*(3), 135-145.

Sohaili, T. (2011). Securing safe schools: Using Title IX liability to address peer harassment of transgender students. *Law & Sexuality: A Review of Lesbian, Gay, Bisexual & Transgender Legal Issues, 20,* 79-95.

Solomon, J. (2012, August 30). Counselor at Jovon Robinson's high school wouldn't say why she changed a player's grade. *The Birmingham News.* Retrieved from http://www.al.com/sports/index.ssf/2012/08/counselor_at_jovon_robinsons_h.html

Smead, R. (1995). *Skills and techniques for group work with children and adolescents.* Champaign, IL: Research Press.

Smith, C. (2013, March, 23). How many people use the top social media, apps & services? *Digital Marketing Ramblings.* Retrieved from http://expandedramblings.com/index.php/resource-how-many-people-use-the-top-social-media/

Smith, M., Robinson, L. & Sega, J. (2012). Helping someone with an eating disorder. *Helpguide.org.* Retrieved from http://www.helpguide.org/mental/eating_disorder_self_help.htm

Smith v. The School Board of Orange County, Court of Appeals of Florida, 5th District, 642 So. 2d 577; 1994 Fla. August 12, 1994.

Snyder v. Millersville, WL 5093140 (ED Pa 2008).

Sostek, A. (2010, October 11). ACLU puts faces on violations of civil liberties. *Pittsburgh Post-Gazette*. Retrieved from http://www.post-gazette.com/stories/local/neighborhoods-city/aclu-puts-faces-on-violations-of-civil-liberties-267763/

South Dakota Code § 19-13-21.1, Rule 508.1 (2003).

Southern Poverty Law Center. (2013). *Children at risk*. Retrieved from http://www.splcenter.org/what-we-do/children-at-risk

Spanierman v. Hughes, 576 F.Supp.2d 292 (2008).

Stadler, H. A. (1986). Making hard choices: Clarifying controversial ethical issues. *Counseling & Human Development, 19*, 1-10.

Stadler, H. A. (1990). Confidentiality. In B. Herlihy & I. B. Golden (Eds.), *AACD ethical standards-casebook* (4th ed., pp.102-110). Alexandria, VA: American Association for Counseling and Development.

Steele, T., Ferranti, D., & Stone, C. (2013, March). [School counselors and cyberspace survey]. Unpublished raw data.

Stevenson, C. (2002). *Teaching ten to fourteen year olds* (3rd ed.). White Plains, NY: Longman.

Stillman, S. (2011). Working the system: School counselors aligning to advantage. *Grounded Theory Review, 10*(2), 113-132.

St. George, D. (2013). Appeal for Maryland 7-year-old suspended for nibbling pastry into shape of a gun. *The Washington Post*. Retrieved from http://articles.washingtonpost.com/2013-03-14/local/37711264_1_anne-arundel-schools-spokesman-pastry-gun

Stone, C. (1997). Extending the reach of academic counseling in middle schools. *Principal Journal, 76*, 48-51.

Stone, C. (1998). Leveling the playing field: An urban school system examines access to mathematics curriculum. *Urban Review, 30*(4), 295-307.

Stone, C. (Speaker). (2001). *Legal and ethical issues in working with minors in schools* [Film]. Alexandria, VA: American Counseling Association.

Stone, C. (2002). Negligence in academic advising and abortion counseling: Courts rulings and implications. *Professional School Counselor: Special Issue on Legal and Ethical Issues in School Counselor, 6*(1).

Stone, C. (2003a). Counselors as advocates for lesbian, gay, and bisexual youth: A call for equity and action. *Journal of Multicultural Counseling and Development, 31*(2), 143-155.

Stone, C. (2003b). Leadership and advocacy in personal/social development: Sexual harassment. In R. Perusse & G. Goodnough (Eds.), *Leadership and advocacy in school counseling* (1st ed., pp. 353-377). Belmont, CA: Brooks/Cole.

Stone, C. (2004a). Legal and ethical dilemmas in abortion counseling. *ASCA School Counselor, 41*(3), 8-9.

Stone, C. (2004b). [Survey of school counselors attending legal and ethical workshops: September 2000 to January 2005]. Unpublished raw data.

Stone, C. (2005a). Students' self-direction and autonomy: Educating versus directing. *ASCA School Counselor, 42*(3), 6-7.

Stone, C. (2005b). The art and ethics of collaboration. *ASCA School Counselor.* Retrieved from http://www.ascaschoolcounselor.org/article_content.asp?edition=91&section=140&article=779

Stone, C. (2006). Subpoenas, court orders and the trusting relationship. *ASCA School Counselor.* Retrieved from http://www.schoolcounselor.org/article.asp?article=851&paper=91&cat=140

Stone, C. (2008). Corporal punishment and community standards. In L. Tyson, J. Culbreth, & J. Harrington (Eds.), *Critical incident in supervision: Addictions, community, and school counseling.* Alexandria, VA: American Counseling Association.

Stone, C. (2012a). Confidentiality, privileged communication and your legal muscle. *ASCA School Counselor, 49*(4), 6-9.

Stone, C. (2012b). District policy and student pregnancy. *ASCA School Counselor, 50*(1), 6-9.

Stone, C. (2012c, September). [School counselors and child abuse survey]. Unpublished raw data.

Stone, C. (2012d, October). [School counselors and sexually active students survey]. Unpublished raw data.

Stone, C. (2012e, December). [School counselors and individual and group counseling survey]. Unpublished raw data.

Stone, C. (2013a, January). [School counselors and professionalism survey]. Unpublished raw data.

Stone, C. (2013b, January). [School counselors and student violence survey]. Unpublished raw data.

Stone, C. (2013c, February). [School counselors and Family Educational Rights and Privacy Act survey]. Unpublished raw data.

Stone, C. (2013d, February). [School counselors and negligence and obligations to the courts survey]. Unpublished raw data.

Stone, C. (2013e, April). [Bullying and cyberbullying]. Unpublished raw data.

Stone, C., & Dahir, C. (2004). *School counselors and accountability: A measure of student success*. Upper Saddle River, NJ: Merrill Prentice-Hall.

Stone, C., & Glicksteen, S. B. (2012a). *The implications of the Julea Ward court case*. Unpublished manuscript.

Stone, C., & Glicksteen, S. B. (2012b, December). [American School Counselor Association members weigh in on Ward v. Wilbanks]. Unpublished raw data.

Stone, C., & Isaacs, M. (2002a). Confidentiality with minors: The effects of Columbine on counselor attitudes regarding breaching confidentiality. *The Journal of Educational Research, 96*(2), 140-150

Stone, C., & Isaacs, M. (2002b). Involving students in violence prevention: Anonymous reporting and the need to promote and protect confidences. *National Association of Secondary School Principals Bulletin, 86*(633), 54-65. doi:10.1177/019263650208663305

Stone, C., & Martin, P. (2004). School counselors using data driven decision making. *ASCA School Counselor, 41*(3), 10-17.

Stone, C., & Turba, R. (1999). School counselors using technology for advocacy. *The Journal of Technology in Counseling, 1*,1.

Stone, C., & Zirkel, P. A. (2010). School counselor advocacy: When law and ethics may collide. *Professional School Counseling, 13*(4), 244-247.

Sturgis, C. (2011, December 8). My name is Ceara Sturgis, and I am not a troublemaker. *ACLU Blog of Rights*. Retrieved from http://www.aclu.org/blog/lgbt-rights/my-name-ceara-sturgis-and-i-am-not-troublemaker

Substance Abuse and Mental Health Services Administration & U.S. Department of Health and Human Services. (2010) *Applying the substance abuse confidentiality regulations 42 CFR part 2 (REVISED)*. Retrieved from http://www.samhsa.gov/about/laws/SAMHSA_42 CFRPART2FAQII_Revised.pdf

Sugg v. Albuquerque Public School District, 988 P.2d 311 (NMCA; 1999).

Suler, J. (2004). The online disinhibition effect. *CyberPsychology & Behavior, 7*, 321–326.

Sullivan, K., & Zirkel, P. (1999). Student to student sexual harassment: Which tack will the Supreme Court take in a sea of analyses? *West Education Law Reporter, 132*, 609-628.

Swinton, D.C. (2005). Criminal liability, failure to report child abuse, and school personnel: An examination of history, policy and caselaw. *Education Law & Policy Forum, 1*, 1-28. Retrieved from http://www.educationlawconsortium.org/forum/2005/papers/swinton.pdf

Tarasoff v. Board of Regents of California, 551 P.2d 334 (Cal.1976).

Terando, J.J. (2011, March). Defining the scope of a school's duty to supervise students. *Los Angeles Lawyer*. Retrieved from http://www.lacba.org/files/lal/vol34no1/2791.pdf

Title IX of the Education Amendments of 1972, 20 U.S.C. §§ 1681-1688 (1994).

Thomas, R. V., & Pender, D. A. (2008). Association for specialists in group work: Best practice guidelines 2007 revisions. *Journal for Specialists in Group Work, 33*(2), 111-117.

Thompson, C. L., & Henderson, D. (2010). *Counseling children* (8th ed.). Pacific Grove, CA: Brooks/Cole.

Thomas, M. (2009). Teen hangs herself after harassment for a 'sexting' message, parents say. *Courthouse News Service*. Retrieved from http://www.courthousenews.com/2009/12/07/Teen_Hangs_Herself_After_Harassment_For_a_Sexting_Message_Parents_Say.htm

Tinker v. Des Moines Independent Community School District (393 U.S. 503, 1969).

Turning Point. (n.d.) Children of domestic violence statistics. Retrieved from http://www.turningpointservices.org/Domestic%20Violence%20-%20Children%20and%20Domestic%20Violence%20Statistics.htm

U.S. Const., amend. XIV. (20 U.S.C. §§ 1681 et seq. (2006); 34 C.F.R. § 106.40).

Uniform Law Commission. (2012). *Marriage and divorce act, model summary*. Retrieved from http://uniformlaws.org/ActSummary.aspx?title=Marriage%20and%20Divorce%20Act,%20Model

United Press International. (2012, October 10). Family settles bullying lawsuit. *UPI.com*. Retrieved from http://www.upi.com/Top_News/US/2012/10/10/Family-settles-bullying-lawsuit/UPI-65211349893663/?spt=hs&or=tn

U.S. Department of Education. (2002) *Recent changes affecting Protection of Pupil Rights Amendment* (PPRA). Retrieved from http://www.fldoe.org/safeschools/pdf/ppra_recent_changes.pdf

U.S. Department of Education. (2007). *Secretary Spellings announces new guidance to improve emergency preparedness in schools, joins secretaries Chertoff and Gutierrez to praise Fairfax County for its emergency preparedness efforts*. Retrieved from http://www.aasa.org/uploadedFiles/Policy_and_Advocacy/files/FERPA_GuidanceRelease.pdf

U.S. Department of Education. (2011a). *Addressing emergencies on campus*. Retrieved from http://www2.ed.gov/policy/gen/guid/fpco/pdf/emergency-guidance.pdf

U.S. Department of Education. (2011b). *December 2011—Revised FERPA Regulations: An Overview for SEAs and LEAs*. Washington, D.C.; Author.

U.S. Department of Education, Family Policy Compliance Office. (2004). *Letter to parent re: Amendment of special education records.* Retrieved from http://www.ed.gov/policy/gen/guid/fpco/ferpa/library/parent.html

U.S. Department of Education, Family Policy Compliance Office. (2005). *Protection of Pupil Rights Amendment.* Retrieved from http://www2.ed.gov/policy/gen/guid/fpco/ppra/index.html

U.S. Department of Education, Family Policy Compliance Office. (2007). *Balancing student privacy and school safety: A guide to the Family Educational Rights and Privacy Act for elementary and secondary schools.* Retrieved from http://www2.ed.gov/policy/gen/guid/fpco/brochures/elsec.html

U.S. Department of Education, Family Policy Compliance Office. (2008). *Family Educational Rights and Privacy Act (FERPA) final rule 34 CFR part 99: Section-by-section analysis.* Retrieved from http://www.ed.gov/policy/gen/guid/fpco/pdf/ht12-17-08-att.pdf

U.S. Department of Education, Family Policy Compliance Office. (2011a). *Family Educational Rights and Privacy Act.* Retrieved from http://www2.ed.gov/policy/gen/guid/fpco/ferpa/index.html.

U.S. Department of Education, Family Policy Compliance Office. (2011b). *FERPA general guidance for parents.* Retrieved from http://www2.ed.gov/policy/gen/guid/fpco/ferpa/parents.html.

U.S. Department of Education, Family Policy Compliance Office. (2011c). *FERPA general guidance for students.* Retrieved from: http://www2.ed.gov/policy/gen/guid/fpco/ferpa/students.html

U.S. Department of Education, Family Policy Compliance Office. (2011d). *Model notice for directory information.* Retrieved from http://www2.ed.gov/policy/gen/guid/fpco/ferpa/mndirectoryinfo.html

U.S .Department of Education, Family Policy Compliance Office. (2012). *The Family Educational Rights and Privacy Act guidance for reasonable methods and written agreements.* Retrieved from http://www2.ed.gov/policy/gen/guid/fpco/pdf/reasonablemtd_agreement.pdf

U.S. Department of Education, National Center for Educational Statistics. (2011). *America's high school graduates: Results of the 2009 NAEP High School Transcript Study* (NCES 2011-462). Washington, DC: U.S. Government Printing Office.

U.S. Department of Education, Office for Civil Rights. (2001, January 19). *Revised sexual harassment guidance: Harassment of students by school employees, other students, or third parties.* Retrieved from http://www2.ed.gov/offices/OCR/archives/pdf/shguide.pdf

U.S. Department of Education, Office for Civil Rights. (2005). *Joint "dear colleague" letter to chief state school officers.* Retrieved from http://www2.ed.gov/about/offices/list/ocr/letters/chief-state-school-ofcrs-2005.pdf

U.S. Department of Education, Office for Civil Rights. (2006). *Dear colleague letter.* Retrieved from http://www2.ed.gov/about/offices/list/ocr/letters/sexhar-2006.html

U.S. Department of Education, Office for Civil Rights. (2008). *Sexual harassment: It's not academic.* Retrieved from www2.ed.gov/about/offices/list/ocr/docs/ocrshpam.pdf

U.S. Department of Education, Office for Civil Rights. (2010, October 26). *Dear colleague letter: Harassment and bullying.* Retrieved from http://www2.ed.gov/about/offices/list/ocr/letters/colleague-201010.pdf

U.S. Department of Education, Office for Civil Rights. (2011a) *Dear colleague letter: Sexual violence.* Retrieved from http://www2.ed.gov/about/offices/list/ocr/letters/colleague-201104.pdf

U.S. Department of Education, Office for Civil Rights. (2011b, April 3). *Frequently asked questions about sexual harassment.* Retrieved from http://www.ed.gov/about/offices/list/ocr/qa-sexharass.html

U.S. Department of Education, Office for Civil Rights. (2011c). *Protecting students with disabilities.* Retrieved from http://www2.ed.gov/about/offices/list/ocr/504faq.html#introduction

U.S. Department of Education, Office for Civil Rights. (2012). *Title IX enforcement highlights.* Retrieved from http://www2.ed.gov/documents/press-releases/title-ix-enforcement.pdf

U.S. Department of Education, Office of Safe and Healthy Students. (n.d.). *Programs/ initiatives.* Retrieved from http://www2.ed.gov/about/offices/list/oese/oshs/tacenters.html

U.S. Department of Health and Human Services. (1996, December, 31). *Child Abuse Prevention and Treatment Act, as amended, 1996.* Retrieved from http://www.acf.hhs.gov/sites/default/files/cb/capta_manual.pdf

U.S. Department of Health and Human Services. (2011, December, 31). *The Child Abuse Protection and Treatment Act (CAPTA) 2010.* Retrieved from http://www.acf.hhs.gov/programs/cb/resource/capta2010

U.S. Department of Health and Human Services, Administration for Children and Families, Children's Bureau. (2011). *Child maltreatment 2010.* Washington, DC: U.S. Government Printing Office. Retrieved from http://www.acf.hhs.gov/programs/cb/resource/child-maltreatment-2010

U.S. Government Accountability Office. (2011). *Child maltreatment: Strengthening national data on child fatalities could aid in prevention.* Retrieved from http://www.gao.gov/products/GAO-11-599

U.S. Legal. (2008). *Sexual harassment.* Retrieved from http://employment.uslegal.com/sexual-harassment/

Van Hoose, W. H., & Paradise, L. V. (1979). *Ethics in counseling and psychotherapy: Perspectives in issues and decision-making.* Cranston, RI: Carroll Press.

Veazy Morris, K. D., Parra, G. R., & Stender, S. R. S. (2011). Eating attitudes and behaviors among female college students. *Journal of College Counseling, 14*(1), 21-33.

Veazey, K. (2012, August 30). Counselor wouldn't tell Memphis City Schools why she changed player's grade. *The Commercial Appeal.* Retrieved from http://www.commercialappeal.com/news/2012/aug/30/counselor-wouldnt-tell-memphis-city-schools-why/

Venkatesh, S. (2006). *Group counseling.* Retrieved from http://changingminds.org/articles/articles/group_counseling.htm

Vernon, A. (2004). *Counseling children & adolescents* (3rd ed.). Denver, CO: Love Publisher.

Volokh, E. (2008, July 28). *Suppressions of homosexuality-related speech.* Retrieved from http://www.volokh.com/posts/1217288105.shtml

Vossekuil, B., Fein, R., Reddy, M., Borum, R., & Modzeleski, W. (2002). *The final report and findings of the safe school initiative: Implications for the prevention of school attacks in the United States.* Washington, DC: U.S. Secret Service and U.S. Department of Education. Retrieved from www.secretservice.gov/ntac/ssi_final_report.pdf

Vossekuil, B., Fein, R., Reddy, M., Borum, R., & Modzeleski, W. (2004, July). *The final report and findings of the safe school initiative: Implications for the prevention of school attacks in the United States.* Washington, DC: U.S. Secret Service and U.S. Department of Education.Retrieved from http://www2.ed.gov/admins/lead/safety/preventingattacksreport.pdf

Walsh, M. (2008). *Justices decline appeal over student's online threat.* Retrieved from http://www.edweek.org/ew/articles/2008/04/09/32scotusside.g27.html

Walsh v. Tehachapi Unified School District, 827 F. Supp. 2d 1107; 2011 U.S. Dist. LEXIS 125175.

Ward v. Wilbanks, 667 F.3d 727 (2012).

Warner v. St. Bernard Parish School Board, 99 F.Supp.2d 748 (2000).

Watts, J. (2005). Educational malpractice: If our children aren't learning who should be held responsible? *Journal of Law & Education, 34*(1), 167-171. Retrieved from Criminal Justice Periodicals database (Document ID: 788943801).

Wehrman, J. D., Williams, R., Field, J., & Schroeder, S. (2010). Accountability through documentation: What are best practices for school counselors?. *Journal of School Counseling, 8*(38).

Wei, H., & Williams, J. H. (2009). Instrumental or emotional aggression: Testing models of bullying, victimization, and psychological maladjustment among Taiwanese seventh graders. *Social Work Research, 33*, 231-242.

Welfel, E. R. (2012). *Ethics in counseling and psychotherapy* (5th ed.). Pacific Grove, CA: Brooks/Cole.

Widdice, L. E. & Halpern-Felsher, B. L. (2006). Do teens care more about pregnancy or STD/HIV? *Journal of Adolescent Health, 38*(2), 125-126. doi:10.1016/j.jadohealth.2005.11.103

Wilczenski, F. L., & Cook, A. L. (2011). Virtue ethics in school counseling: A framework for decision making. *Journal of School Counseling, 9*(7).

Willis, S. P. (2004). Iowa school counselors had better get it right! *Iowa Law Review, 89*, 1093.

Winter, G. (2004, July 8). Wooing of guidance counselors is raising profiles and eyebrows. *The New York Times*. Retrieved from http://www.nytimes.com/2004/07/08/us/wooing-of-guidance-counselors-is-raising-profiles-and-eyebrows.html?pagewanted=all&src=pm

Wisconsin v. Yoder, 406 U.S. 205, 231-233 [**1172] (1972).

What they're saying about sexting. (2011, May 16). *The New York Times*. Retrieved from http://www.nytimes.com/2011/03/27/us/27sextingqanda.html?_r=1&ref=us

Wolke, D., Woods, S., & Samara, M. (2009). Who escapes or remains a victim of bullying in primary school? *British Journal of Developmental Psychology, 27*, 835-851. doi:10.143/026151008X383003

Wolak, J., Mitchell, K., & Finkelhor, D. (2006). *Online victimization: 5 years later* (NCMEC 07–06–025). Alexandria, VA: National Center for Missing & Exploited Children.

Woodlock v. Orange Ulster B.O.C.E.S., 2006 WL 1738014 (S.D.N.Y. 2006).

Woodlock v. Orange Ulster B.O.C.E.S., 281 F. App'x. 66 (2d Cir. 2008).

Wooledge, S. (2012, March 11). Major victory in Anoka-Hennepin school district bullying lawsuit. *Daily Kos*. Retrieved from http://www.dailykos.com/story/2012/03/11/1072927/-Major-victory-in-Anoka-Hennepin-school-district-bullying-lawsuit

Worden, L. (2012, March 8). State Supreme Court: Hart District can be held liable in molestation case. *SCVNews.com*. Retrieved from http://scvnews.com/2012/03/08/state-supreme-court-hart-district-liable-in-2007-molestation/

Wykes, S.L. (2005). Parents settle suit for alleged bullying by their children: Father faults them and school district for the two years of taunts his son endured. *San Jose Mercury News*. Retrieved from http://www.chron.com/disp/story.mpl/nation/3397491.html

Wyke v. Polk County School Board, 137 F.3d 1292 (11th Cir. 1997).

Wyoming Mental Health Professions Practice Act, Wyoming Code § 33-38-113 (2004).

Yell, M. L., & Katsiyannis, A. (2000, Spring). Student-on-student sexual harassment: What are schools' responsibilities? *Preventing School Failure, 44*, 130-132.

Young, E. L., Allen, M., & Ashbaker, B. Y. (n.d.). *Sexual harassment. National Association of School Psychologists*. Retrieved from http://www.nasponline.org/educators/Sexual%20Harassment.pdf

Zamstein v. Marvasti, 240 Conn. 549, 692 A.2d 781 (1997).

Zirkel, P. (2001). Ill advised. *Phi Delta Kappan, 83*, 98-99.

Zirkel, P. (2001/2002, December/January). Decisions that have shaped U.S. education. *Principal Leadership, 59*, 6-12.

Zirkel, P. A. (2001). A pregnant pause? *Phi Delta Kappan, 82*(7), 557-558.

Zullig, K. J., Huebner, E. S., & Patton, J. M. (2011). Relationships among school climate domains and school satisfaction. *Psychology in the Schools, 48*(2), 133-145.

Zullig, K. J., Koopman, T. M., & Huebner, E. S. (2009). Beyond GPA: Toward more comprehensive assessments of students' school experiences. *Child Indicators Research, 2*, 95–108.

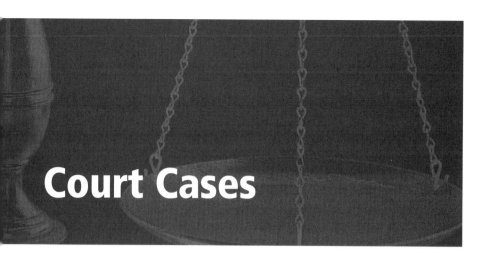

Court Cases

CHAPTER 4: FAMILY EDUCATIONAL RIGHTS AND PRIVACY ACT

CHAPTER 5: NEGLIGENCE

CHAPTER 6: OBLIGATIONS TO THE COURT

CHAPTER 7: CHILD ABUSE

Subject Index

A

M

N

O

Z

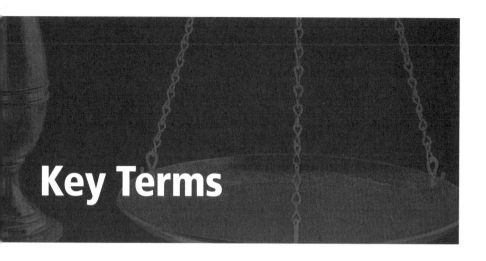

Key Terms

Abortion: termination of a pregnancy and expulsion of an embryo or fetus.

Addressing a known danger: a situation that is obviously harmful or has the potential for harm and, therefore, requires school officials to respond in a particular way.

Adversely stratified education opportunities: education opportunities unfavorably arranged in a school, especially unequal opportunities for historically disadvantaged students such as minority and low-income students.

Advocacy: intervening on behalf of a particular student or group of students.

Age of consent: the age minors can legally engage in sexual activity; age of consent varies from state to state.

***Amici curiae* brief:** a legal opinion, testimony or learned treatise filed by a friend of the court who is neither defendant not plaintiff as a way to introduce concerns about the broader legal effects of a court decision that is not dependent solely on the parties directly involved in the case. For example, the American School Counselor Association has been *amicus curiae* (friend of the court) in *amici curiae* briefs involving cyberbullying.

Anonymous reporting: reporting of a situation without revealing the identity of the reporter; it is an effort to protect the identity of informants to encourage student reporting of dangerous situations in schools.

Anorexia: a disorder characterized by fear of becoming fat and refusal of food, leading to debility and even death.

"ASCA Aspects": monthly publication by the American School Counselor Association. Each issue includes information about new projects, events, resources and more from ASCA.

ASCA SCENE: a networking site that is a professional meeting place for school counseling professionals to share and learn from each other.

Autonomy: promoting students' ability to choose their own direction.

Beneficence: promoting good for others. Ideally, counseling contributes to the growth and development of the student.

Biological sex: The condition or character of being female or male; the physiological, functional and psychological differences distinguishing the female and the male.

Bisexuality: relating to or characterized by a tendency to direct sexual desire toward both sexes.

Blogs: a website containing an online personal journal with reflections, comments and often hyperlinks provided by the writer.

Breach: violation of the duty owed, such as confidentiality. Whether or not a breach occurred is based on reasonableness and the standard of care.

Breach of trust: a betrayal of a person's trust; breach of a student's confidence.

Bulimia: a serious eating disorder characterized by compulsive overeating usually followed by self-induced vomiting or laxative or diuretic abuse, often accompanied by guilt and depression.

Bully-cide: term used to describe children/teens who were victims of bullying and became so emotionally distressed they committed suicide.

Bullying: verbal or physical aggression demonstrated in words, actions or social exclusion intended to specifically hurt or harm another; the most common form of school violence.

Bystander: a person who observes a conflict, bullying or other unacceptable behavior either minor or serious, but the bystander knows the behavior is destructive or likely to make a bad situation worse but does not react positively.

Case law: laws pronounced by the courts.

Case notes: sole-possession records that act as memory aids or professional opinion or observation for the creator. They are to be kept separate from education records but may become education records when they are 1) shared with others in verbal or written form, 2) include information other than professional opinion or personal observations and/or 3) made accessible to others.

Causal connection: connection between the school counselor's breach of duty and the injury the student suffered.

Challenging the status quo: stimulating change in conditions already established or currently in existence.

Child abuse: physical or psychological mistreatment of a child by his or her parents, guardians or other adults.

Child maltreatment: general term used to describe all forms of child abuse and neglect.

Child neglect: lack of care that risks or causes harm to a child, including lack of food, clothing, supervision or medical attention.

Child Protective Services: a constituted authority and agency in the state providing protection from harm to children and providing services to meet the needs of the child and family.

Chronological level: the level at which a student has reached based on actual age.

Cisgender: an individual whose gender self-perception matches the sex they were assigned at birth.

Civil law: the set of rules governing relations between persons.

Civil wrong: a wrong against another person causing physical, emotional or monetary damage and for which the plaintiffs can seek compensation.

Classroom guidance: leading, advising and informing students on appropriate topics in a classroom setting.

Clear and imminent danger: now known as serious and foreseeable harm, a known or perceived harm to a student or others that has a risk of danger resulting in damage, injury and/or death if an action is not taken. School counselors consider in context their obligation to breach confidentiality and inform parents and administrators if a student indicates a serious and foreseeable harm to himself/herself or others.

Code of silence: a condition in effect when a person opts to withhold what is believed to be vital or important information voluntarily or involuntarily.

Common law: judge-made law based on legal precedents developed over hundreds of years; also referred to as the "body of general rules prescribing social conduct" and "unwritten" law.

Community standards: written and unwritten standards of behavior for a community; school counselors adhere to the written and unwritten prescribed behavioral norms of the community while working responsibly to change standards detrimental to students.

Confidentiality in group counseling: confidentiality cannot be guaranteed in a group; school counselors use extraordinary care when putting young people together in groups where highly sensitive and personal materials may be disclosed.

Constitutional law: consists of two major categories: criminal law and civil law.

Corporal punishment: deliberate infliction of pain intended as a disciplinary action or punishment; used in judicial, domestic and/or education settings.

Court of Appeals: a court having jurisdiction to review the actions of an inferior court (such as trial court) but not having the power to hear a legal action initially.

Court order: an order requiring a person to do a specified act, such as producing material or appearing in court. The government has the right to obtain a person's information by court order.

Criminal law: a crime against society; criminal law can be categorized as either a felony or a misdemeanor.

Cross-tabulate data: displays the joint distribution of two or more variables.

Custodial parent: a term used for the parent having primary physical custody of a child.

Cyberbullying: the use of cell phones, instant messaging, e-mail, chat rooms or social networking sites such as Facebook and Twitter to harass, threaten or intimidate someone.

Cyberspace: the online world of computer networks and the Internet.

Cyber-speech: speech on the Internet or in cyberspace (especially in discussions of free speech).

Dangerous school climate: atmosphere of a school that is unsafe or unwelcoming for one or more students; atmosphere of harassment, violence, crime and/or bullying.

Data warehousing: a database used for reporting and data analysis.

Date rape drugs: controlled substances administered surreptitiously (as in a drink) to induce an unconscious or sedated state in a potential date rape victim.

Dating violence: the perpetration or threat of an act of violence by at least one member of an unmarried couple on the other member within the context of dating or courtship.

Dear Colleague Letter: April 2011 discussion by the Office for Civil Rights regarding Title IX's requirements related to student-on-student sexual harassment, including sexual violence; explains schools' responsibility to take immediate and effective steps to end sexual harassment and sexual violence.

Defamation: injuring a person's character or reputation by false or malicious statements.

Defendant: the person against whom a legal action is brought. School counselors become defendants in cases such as academic advising and/or failure to report child abuse.

Deliberate indifference: intentional, unresponsiveness or lack of concern.

Deposition: testimony under oath, especially a statement by a witness that is written down or recorded for use in court at a later date.

Developmental level: a student's maturity level based on problem-solving ability, competence and maturity; does not necessarily correlate to chronological age.

Developmentally delayed: maturity, behavior and competency level that is below that person's chronological level.

Digital footprint: the trail, traces or "footprints" people leave online such as forum registration, e-mails and attachments, uploading videos or digital images.

Directory information: basic public information about a student such as name, address, telephone number, date and place of birth, etc.

Discriminatory harassment: verbal or physical conduct that demeans or shows hostility or aversion toward an individual because of his/her race, color, religion, gender, national origin, age, disability or because of retaliation for engaging in protected activity.

Disinhibition effect: pertains to cyberspace interactions and is a loosening (or complete abandonment) of social restrictions and inhibitions that would otherwise be present in normal face-to-face interactions.

Dogmatic solution: a black-and-white answer to a problem, without examining multiple perspectives in the context of a situation.

Domestic violence: assaultive and/or coercive behaviors, including physical, sexual and psychological as well as economic coercion adults or adolescents use against their intimate partners.

Dual relationship: a relationship where professional distance is violated and impairs a school counselor's objectivity and increases the risk of harm to the student (e.g., counseling one's family members, close friends or associates).

Duces tecum: a Latin term meaning "you shall bring with you"; a court order issued by a clerk of court, justice of the peace, notary public or lawyer, usually signed by a lawyer; a lawyer-signed subpoena.

Due-process hearing: procedures or steps the school district and parents must take to settle disagreement.

Duty of care: a legal requirement that a person act toward others and the public with watchfulness, attention, caution and prudence.

Duty to warn: obligation to notify members involved in a potential harmful or dangerous situation; school counselors have a duty to warn parents if serious and foreseeable harm is perceived from a student.

Educational malpractice: a comparison between the acceptable standard of care for the school counseling profession and the specific act or conduct claimed to be malpractice.

Emotional harm: intentional infliction to a person's ability to think, reason or have feelings, such as cruel acts or statements, intimidation, rejection and indifference.

Entrenched inequities: established injustice or unfairness.

Equal access: providing opportunities, rights and privileges by all people or groups, especially those who have historically been disadvantaged such as minority and low-income individuals.

Equal Access Act: a U.S. federal law passed in 1984 to compel federally funded secondary schools to provide equal access to extracurricular clubs. Lobbied for by religious groups who wanted to ensure students the right to conduct Bible study programs during lunch and after school, it has become an essential right in students' efforts to form gay-straight alliance (GSA) clubs.

Equity and opportunity for all students: access to rights, privileges, opportunities and social institutions by all students or groups, especially those who have historically been disadvantaged such as minority and low-income students.

Ethical Standards for School Counselors: guidelines developed by ASCA, used to clarify the standard of behavior and responsibility of all school counselors regardless of ASCA membership to students, parents, colleagues, the profession, the community and to themselves.

Ethics: agreed-upon values, norms, customs and mores that have withstood the test of time; provide a general framework for professional conduct.

Ex-gay ministry: Christian ministries specializing in helping homosexually oriented persons change their sexual orientation or live as a heterosexual.

Expert witness: a person called to testify because he or she has a recognized competence in an area.

Facebook: a social networking website launched in 2004 with more than one billion active users.

Falsifying student records: fraudulently altering a student's education record with or without a reasonable cause or authorization.

Family Educational Rights and Privacy Act (FERPA): federal legislation governing education records and dictating how all maintained information regarding a student will be handled and disseminated for the protection of students and their families.

Family Policy Compliance Office: an arm of the U.S. Department of Education, which administers the Family Education Rights and Privacy Act.

Federal court: litigation court for cases involving citizens of several states and cases involving federal statutes.

Federal law: a bill that makes it through both the House and the Senate and goes to the president, who takes action by signing it into law, letting it become law without a signature or vetoing it.

Foreseeable harm: a reasonable person would be able to predict or expect the ultimately harmful result of their actions.

Gang violence: criminal and nonpolitical acts of violence committed by a group of people who regularly engage in criminal activity against innocent people.

Gay, Lesbian & Straight Education Network: a national group of parents, students, teachers and others working to put an end to discrimination based on sexual orientation and gender identity/expression in K-12 schools.

Gay-Straight Alliance Club: a student club in schools for the support of gay, lesbian, bisexual and transgender youth and their straight friends.

Gender expression: all of the external characteristics and behaviors that are socially defined as either masculine or feminine, such as dress, grooming, mannerisms, speech patterns and social interactions; a range of physical, mental and behavioral characteristics distinguishing between masculinity and femininity.

Gender identity: a person's innate, deeply felt psychological identification as male or female, which may or may not correspond to the person's body or designated sex at birth (meaning what sex was originally listed on a person's birth certificate).

Gender nonconforming: behavior or gender expression that does not conform to dominant gender norms.

Governmental immunity: protection from civil or tort liability while engaged in school functions of a governmental nature.

Group counseling sessions: counseling multiple members at the same time based on mutual needs and goals of the members; school counselors avoid putting young people together in groups where highly sensitive and personal materials may be disclosed.

Guardian *ad litem*: a guardian appointed by a court to represent a minor unable to represent himself or herself.

Heterosexism: a belief that male-female sexuality is the only natural or moral mode of sexual behavior.

Historical risk factors: issues in a student's family that are dysfunctional behaviors or medical, social or psychological problems that may contribute to an individual's risk of having those same problems.

Homophobia: fear of or prejudice against homosexuality or homosexual individuals.

Homosexuality: refers to an individual's sense of personal and social identity based on attractions primarily or exclusively to people of the same sex or gender identity.

Hostile environment: involves student-on-student sexual harassment, in which a student feels school is not a safe place.

Identifiability of the victim: the ability or inability to recognize the victim and/or perpetrator in a sexual harassment case.

Immune from liability: incapable of being held legally responsible.

Immunity: exemption from performing duties the law generally requires other citizens to perform or from a penalty or burden the law generally places upon other citizens.

In loco parentis: Latin term for "in place of parent" in which the person or entity acts as a parent with respect to the care, supervision and discipline of a child. School counselors act *in loco parentis* with minors in a school setting.

Individual with Disabilities Education Act: federal legislation for exceptional student education (ESE) administered by the Office of Special Education, which spells out parents' and students' rights regarding ESE records.

Informed consent: counselee chooses to enter a counseling relationship after being given direct information about the purposes, goals, techniques, rules of procedure and limits of confidentiality in which he or she may receive counseling.

Injury suffered: harm an individual suffered such as injury, lost scholarship or death.

Institutional standards: written and unwritten standards in which members of that institution must behave consistently and ethically within its parameters, while working to change those standards that are detrimental to its members.

Intersex: an individual displaying sexual characteristics of both male and female.

Intervening, superseding cause: breaks the line of causation from the wrongful act to the injury suffered and does not render liability.

Isms: an oppressive and especially discriminatory attitude or belief.

Jessica Logan Act: Ohio cyberbullying law in honor of a student who committed suicide after being severely cyberbullied over a sex-text she sent to her boyfriend.

Judicial bypass: a process by which minors can get state approval to have an abortion without parental consent or notification in states requiring parental involvement.

Justice: providing equal treatment to all people regardless of age, sex, race, ethnicity, disability, socioeconomic status, cultural background, religion or sexual orientation.

Lambda Legal: a nongovernmental organization devoted to promoting the legal rights of gays, lesbians, bisexuals, transgender and people with HIV or AIDS, through impact litigation, education and public policy work.

Laws: the minimum standard society will tolerate; used to codify a value or set of values. Laws and their interpretations differ from one geographic location to another.

Legal status of minors: generally under the age of 18 children are legally unable to make decisions on their own behalf.

Legitimate educational interest: FERPA allows educators to access education records for the purpose of performing appropriate tasks within their job description to provide a service or benefit to the student or to the student's family.

Liability: accountability to another party or to the state, which can be enforced through damages or criminal punishment.

List-servers: a special usage of e-mail allowing for widespread distribution of information to many Internet users.

Loyalty: staying connected with students and being available to them to the extent possible.

Maintaining student records: keeping, organizing and updating student education records in compliance with FERPA.

Malicious, willful and intentional torts: occurs when one acts in a determined way and harms another; not an error but deliberate.

Malpractice: improper or unethical conduct by a professional resulting in injury, damage or loss.

Mandated reporter: a person who is required by law to report suspected child abuse to proper authorities under penalty of criminal charges.

Mediation: an attempt to bring about a peaceful settlement or compromise between disputants through the objective intervention of a neutral party.

Ministerial: a duty plainly laid out and requiring no discretion.

Missouri's Facebook Statute: addresses teacher's use of electronic communications with students.

Monitoring your competence: ASCA's Ethical Standards for School Counselors outline seven major practices school counselors should engage in to ensure they are adhering to the standard of care expected of school counselors (see E.1).

Multiculturalism: the preservation of different cultures or cultural identities within a unified society, as a state or nation.

MySpace: a social networking site allowing users to create blogs, upload videos and photos and design profiles to showcase their interests and talents.

Negligence: civil liability if a school counselor is found to owe a duty to another person, breaches that duty and causes damages to another person.

No-harm contract: an agreement that the individual signing the contract will not commit suicide.

Noncustodial parent: term used for the parent who has physical custody of a child for a lesser amount of time than the custodial parent. Typically the child does not reside with the noncustodial parent except when that parent exercises visitation rights.

Nonmaleficence: avoiding doing harm to students and families.

Office for Civil Rights: the arm of the federal government requiring compliance with anti-discrimination policies and practices for school districts.

Opacity of law: sometimes it takes a court to interpret the meaning of a statute that on face value could be interpreted in different ways.

Over-discipline: nonaccidental injury usually at the hands of a child's parents that goes beyond the boundaries of reasonable punishment into maltreatment (abuse or neglect).

Parental permission: written or unwritten consent from a parent or guardian for a student to participate in services such as small-group counseling.

Parents, Family and Friends of Lesbians and Gays (PFLAG): an organization whose mission it is to promote the health and well-being of gay, lesbian, bisexual and transgendered persons and their families and friends.

Peer-on-peer aggression: hostility between peers; includes teasing, harassment, verbal aggression and bullying.

Personal bias: a subjective preference or behavior based on personal values and beliefs.

Physical aggression: hostile or abusive behavior toward another person or group.

Physical and emotional safety: an atmosphere or condition free from physical or emotional harm.

Plaintiff: a person or party who initiates a lawsuit.

Planned Parenthood: health service organization providing reproductive health care and sexual health information to men, women and teens.

Potential courses of action: possible strategies or procedures.

Precedent: a court decision serving as a guide or direction on how to decide future cases with similar facts or legal questions.

Prevailing community standards: written and unwritten standards in which the community and those who work in it must behave consistently and ethically within its parameters, while working to change those standards detrimental to its members.

Privacy rights of minors: privileges given to the parents of a minor student to make critical decisions regarding disclosure of personal information.

Privileged communication: a creature of statute pertaining to court testimony. Students in some states can render school counselors incapable of breaching their confidential conversations in court, or the breach can only happen under certain conditions such as the student is in danger.

Privity: having an interest in a transaction, contract or legal action to which one is not a party but where the interest arises out of a relationship to one of the parties of the legal action.

Process of discovery: practice in which the attorneys may require an oral or written deposition, written interrogatories requiring written responses to questions, certain documents or materials, a request to submit a listing of facts not in dispute and/or physical or mental examination of one of the parties of the lawsuit.

Professional communication: choosing words judiciously and in an effort to maintain optimal communication with those who have the "need to know."

Professional distance: the appropriate familiarity and closeness a school counselor engages in with students and their family members.

Professionalism: internal motivation to perform at the level of practice representing the ideals of the profession. For school counselors, professionalism is used to maintain a school counselor's standing with peers, teachers, staff members, administrators, parents and students and involves adhering to local, state and federal laws; school board policy; ethical standards; and community standards.

Protection of Pupil Rights Amendment: provides protective rights to parents regarding their students taking surveys. It requires written parental consent prior to administering Department of Education-funded surveys.

Protective risk factors: research on supportive conditions, internal traits, resources that make youth more resistant to victimization and perpetration and decreases the likelihood a young person will become violent or engage in criminal activity.

Qualified privilege: permits persons in positions of authority or trust to make statements or relay or report statements that would be considered slander and libel if made by anyone else.

Queer: an umbrella identity term encompassing lesbian, questioning people, gay men, bisexuals, non-labeling people, transgender folks and anyone else who does not strictly identify as heterosexual.

Questioning: someone who is exploring his or her sexual identity.

Quid pro quo harassment: involves providing a student with a need or want, such as a better grade, contingent on the provision of sexual acts.

Rape: sexual intercourse/contact without the lawful consent of the victim. In a forcible rape, the victim is prevented from resisting the sexual act because of the offender's use of force or threats of physical violence.

Real threat: a danger that can be validated with evidence of a written threat, the presence of a weapon or other indicators pointing to serious intent to harm.

Reasonableness: a person acting within the standard of care and taking necessary precautions.

Reasonable suspicion: the standard requiring school counselors to report child abuse. The certainty that a child is being abused or neglected is not required.

Recidivism rate: the rate at which repeated relapse into criminal or delinquent behavior occurs.

Relational aggression: bullying or other forms of harm caused through damage to one's social status.

Reparative therapy: psychotherapy aimed at eliminating homosexual desires, also known as conversion therapy.

Risk factors: characteristics, conditions or behaviors increasing the possibility of disease or injury.

Safe-haven law: a law allowing birth mothers to leave their newborns at hospitals, fire stations or police stations anonymously, with no legal repercussions. Each state sets the outside age limit to which this law applies.

Safe Schools Coalition: partnership of organizations seeking to promote tolerance in schools by providing resources for students, parents and schools.

Safe school zone: established parameters around schools and school activities, e.g, 1,000 feet from a school or 100 feet from a school bus stop. If a crime is committed within those parameters, state law may impose increased penalties.

School board policy: guidelines or procedure developed by the school board relating to issues that may hinder the education process that all schools in the district must follow.

School climate: the quality and character of school life based on patterns of students', parents' and school personnel's experience of school life, teaching and learning practices and organizational structures.

School counselors' values: the ethical, moral, doctrinal, ideological and social intrinsic beliefs and actions influencing all aspects of the school counselor's role.

School culture: patterns of meaning or activity (norms, values, beliefs, relationships, rituals, traditions, myths, etc.) shared in varying degrees by members of a school community.

School violence: encompasses a wide range of violent activities including physical fights, threats, destruction, robbery, harassment, dating violence, molestation, rape, bullying, hostile or threatening remarks, assault with or without weapons and gang violence.

Screening member: assessing, usually through interviews, the suitability of students for their appropriateness and commitment to participate in small groups.

Self-direction: a course guided by oneself; autonomous action.

Separation of power: each division of government functions freely within the area of its responsibility.

Sexting: the act of sending sexually explicit messages and/or photographs, primarily between mobile phones.

Sexual harassment: conduct that is sexual in nature or related to the gender of the person. The behavior occurs in an unequal relationship where one person has more power over another and the behavior is unsolicited or unwelcome.

Sexual harassment policy: a procedure protecting all students from sexual harassment.

Sexual minority: a group whose sexual identity, orientation or practices differ from the majority of the surrounding society.

Sexual orientation: the focus of a person's desires, fantasies and feelings; the gender(s) one is primarily oriented toward.

Sexual violence: any sexual act perpetrated against someone's will.

Sexually active students: students who are intimate in a sexual way, such as touching someone's genitals, oral sex or intercourse.

Sexually hostile environment: created when conduct is sufficiently serious that it interferes with or limits a student's ability to participate in or benefit from the school's program.

Slander: oral defamation; the speaking of false and malicious words that injure another person's reputation, business or property rights.

Slut-shaming: the deliberate act of impugning a woman's character in sexual terms to embarrass, humiliate, intimidate, degrade or shame her for actions or behaviors that are a normal part of female sexuality.

Social change agent: a representative in a position to affect and bring about change in schools regarding unequal procedures, policies and regulations.

Social justice: promotion of equity for all people and groups in schools to give special care to those who historically have not received adequate educational opportunities.

Social bullying: deliberate, repetitive and aggressive social behavior intended to hurt others. Sometimes referred to as relational bullying, involves hurting someone's reputation or relationships.

Social risk factors: the absence of support from family, friends, community that offers youth both emotional and physical resources that may protect them to achieve better outcomes. Research shows the presence of one or more positive and significant individuals in a child's life may act as a buffer against negative outcomes.

Special relation: a legal existing connection such as *in loco parentis*.

Standard of care: what the reasonably competent professional would do; following laws, ethical standards and school board policies.

State court: a system including the court of last resort such as state supreme courts, intermediate appellate courts, courts of general jurisdiction and courts of limited jurisdiction or small-claims courts.

State legislature: provides the basis for public school law, interprets the laws and gives school boards authority to create their own rules and regulations.

State statutes: laws issued by the state.

Statute of limitations: a law setting the maximum period one can wait before filing a lawsuit.

Statutory obligation: a responsibility passed into law by a unit of federal, state or local governments.

Statutory rape: adults, usually 18 years or older, who have a sexual relationship with a minor of a certain age; the age of both the victim and the perpetrator are variable depending on the state.

Solutions to Ethical Problems in Schools (STEPS): a nine-step model adapted from the seven-step American Counseling Association ethical decision-making model addressing the emotional influence of a problem and considering chronological and developmental appropriateness as well as parental rights.

Student-on-student sexual harassment: one student is harassed by another student and doesn't feel safe in that environment, also known as hostile environment.

Subpoena: a Latin term meaning "under penalty"; a court order requiring the recipient to perform a specified act such as appearing in court to answer questions about something he or she has witnessed or heard or producing records as evidence. There are penalties if a person fails to respond to a subpoena.

Suicide assessment: an assessment used to evaluate a student's risk of attempting suicide.

Teacher-on-student sexual harassment: a student is harassed by a teacher; typically a teacher gives a better grade or favor in exchange for a sexual act, also known as quid pro quo.

Technologically literate: the ability of an individual, working independently and with others, to responsibly, appropriately and effectively use technology tools to access, manage, integrate, evaluate, create and communicate information.

Testimony: declarations, spoken or written, offered in a legal case or deliberative hearing.

Threat assessments: set of investigative and operational techniques used to identify, assess and manage the risks of targeted violence and its potential perpetrators.

Threat of harm: activities, conditions or persons placing a child at risk of harm.

Title IX of Educational Amendment of 1972: federal law requiring educational institutions to maintain policies, practices and programs that do not discriminate against anyone based on sex.

Tolerance for ambiguity: acceptance and open-mindedness of situations without clear-cut solutions.

Transgender: applies to a variety of individuals, behaviors and groups involving tendencies to vary from culturally conventional gender roles. It is the state of one's self-identification as woman, man, neither or both not matching one's assigned sex. Transgender does not imply any specific form of sexual orientation.

True threat: a threatening communication that can be prosecuted under the law.

Twitter: a messaging system that lets a person send brief text messages of up to 140 characters to a list of followers.

Unalterable factors: aspects of a student's life that are stable and difficult to change that may cause harm.

Unconditional positive regard: a term coined by the humanist Carl Rogers promoting basic acceptance and support of a person regardless of what the person says or does.

Uniform Child Custody Jurisdiction Act: designed to deter interstate parental kidnapping and promote uniform jurisdiction and enforcement provisions in interstate child-custody and visitation cases.

Uniform Marriage Act: procedure followed by many states when deciding custody, which encourages custodial decisions in part to favor the parent who is most likely to keep the other parent involved in the child's life.

Uninterrupted Scholars Act: a provision of FERPA allowing child care agencies working on foster care cases to have access to education records without written parental consent.

USA Patriot Act: a response to the terrorist attacks of Sept. 11, it significantly reduces restrictions in law enforcement agencies' gathering of intelligence and immigration authorities in detaining and deporting immigrants suspected of terrorism-related acts.

Value-laden counseling: a caution for school counselors to be objective and not to impose their beliefs or infringe on a parent's right to be the guiding voice in their child's life in issues rooted in religion or ethnicity such as abortion.

Verbal aggression: hostile or abusive language used toward another person or group.

Vested with rights: having the legal rights of ownership.

Video conferencing: the holding of a conference among people at remote locations by means of transmitted audio and video signals.

Violent propensities: tendencies to act in a violent manner.

Viral: an image, video, advertisement, etc. that is circulated rapidly on the Internet.

Webinar: short for web-based seminar, a presentation, lecture, workshop or seminar transmitted over the web.

Willful and wanton disregard: used in negligence law to describe extreme carelessness or indifference to safety.

Witnesses: school counselors act as witnesses for the court usually in cases of child custody, child abuse or disciplinary action.

Written interrogatories: written responses to questions required under the process of discovery.

Zero tolerance: a strict approach to rule enforcement stating absolutely no deviation will be allowed.

ABOUT THE AUTHOR

Carolyn Stone, Ed.D., has been a counselor educator
at the University of North Florida since 1995, where
she teaches and researches in the area of school counselors and legal and ethical issues. Prior to becoming
a counselor educator, Stone spent 22 years with
Duval County Public Schools in Jacksonville, Fla.,
where she served as a middle school teacher, elementary and high school counselor and school counseling
supervisor for 225 school counselors.

Stone is a past president of the American School
Counselor Association and ASCA Ethics Committee
chair. She is a past president of the Florida
Counseling Association and the Florida Association
of Counselor Educators and Supervisors.

Stone has delivered over 400 workshops in 48 states
and 15 countries. Her professional path as an elementary and high school counselor, middle school
teacher, school counseling supervisor for the nation's
17th largest school district and counselor educator
has prepared her with first-hand experience and
understanding of the legal and ethical world of
school counselors.